FRANZ SCHUBERT

$30.40

FRANZ SCHUBERT

A BIOGRAPHY

Elizabeth Norman McKay

CLARENDON PRESS · OXFORD

1996

Oxford University Press, Great Clarendon Street, Oxford OX2 6DP

Oxford New York

Athens Auckland Bangkok Bogota Bombay
Buenos Aires Calcutta Cape Town Dar es Salaam
Delhi Florence Hong Kong Istanbul Karachi
Kuala Lumpur Madras Madrid Melbourne
Mexico City Nairobi Paris Singapore
Taipei Tokyo Toronto
and associated companies in
Berlin Ibadan

Oxford is a trade mark of Oxford University Press

Published in the United States
by Oxford University Press Inc., New York

British Library Cataloguing in Publication Data
Data available

Library of Congress Cataloging in Publication Data
McKay, Elizabeth Norman.
Franz Schubert: a biography / Elizabeth Norman McKay.
p. cm.
Includes bibliographical references and index.
1. Schubert, Franz, 1797–1828. 2. Composers—Austria—Biography.
I. Title.
ML410.S3M34 1966 780'.92—dc20 [B] 95-51812
ISBN 0-19-816523-4

3 5 7 9 10 8 6 4 2

Set by Hope Services (Abingdon) Ltd.
Printed in Great Britain
on acid-free paper by
Biddles Ltd.,
Guildford & King's Lynn

PREFACE AND
ACKNOWLEDGEMENTS

UNTIL the early autumn of 1992 the idea of writing a biography of Schubert had crossed my mind only fleetingly, and always in an entirely negative way. However, the invitation at this time to consider such a project made me reconsider. In the last twenty or so years there have been many new developments and advances in research into Schubert and his music, particularly in Germany, Austria, and the United States. Much of this has failed to become general knowledge in Britain. With this in mind, I began writing the biography at the beginning of 1993.

I began the book, as I had been requested, as a 'straight biography', to be read through without interruptions by too much detail or too many references to sources in footnotes. I also agreed to limit information about the music to a minimum, and concentrate on the man. In 1994 Oxford University Press took over publication of the book and, at the request of my new editor Bruce Phillips and according to my own inclination, the requirements changed. The result is a book of greater length, with more emphasis on Schubert's life as a composer and the importance of his music in his life. While these changes have involved a more scholarly presentation than originally intended, I have endeavoured to present the material in a form acceptable to the interested general reader. I hope, however, that it will also prove acceptable to more informed and specialist readers.

In the writing of any biography there are built-in difficulties and hazards, on account of both the source material available and the biographer's personal reaction to this material and to the subject of the biography. In Schubert's case, surviving examples of his own writings are somewhat sparse. There are just eleven—mostly short—entries in a diary and a notebook, written over very brief periods in the years 1816 and 1824, four short poems reflecting his personal thoughts or philosophies written between 1813 and 1824, several other occasional poems or verses, an allegorical tale in prose ('Mein Traum'), a fair number of letters to publishers between spring 1822 and the month before his death in 1828, other professional communications, and a few applications for professional positions. Of his private letters to family and friends, excluding a few brief notes with practical information, some two dozen have survived. There are of course dangers in attempting to evaluate the contents of all these written communications. Some are youthful responses, even extravagances. None was written for posterity. The apparently spontaneous letters written to family and close friends were surely couched in language, and express modes of thought, that were acceptable to or suitable for the addressee. For this reason it is important to know as much as possible about the recipients, and of Schubert's relationships with them at the time of writing. In this context, as also in any attempt to appreciate the composer's attitudes, both conforming and unconforming, to the society in which he moved, and the influence of his friends on his life, some knowledge of Schubert's close associates and the kind of people they were helps us to gain some understanding of the composer.

Otto Erich Deutsch's *Schubert: A Documentary Biography* and *Schubert: Memoirs by his Friends*, also in their later revised German editions, the first volume of *Franz Schubert: Neue Dokumente, 1817–1830* (1994), and the twice-yearly journal *Schubert durch die Brille*, both published by the Internationales Franz Schubert Institut, are invaluable sources of information, as are the two smaller *Neue Dokumente zum Schubert-Kreis* (New Documents from Schubert's Circle of Friends), edited by Walburga Litschauer. These volumes together contain not only all except one of Schubert's surviving writings, but a large collection of entries in diaries and letters containing contemporary comments, some not previously published, descriptions, and accounts from those with whom Schubert was in close contact, and printed notices of performances, publications, and reviews. While I have used the material written by his friends and quoted freely from it, the reader will be aware that there is often no way of ascertaining the accuracy of the matters discussed and reactions of the commentator. This presents another difficulty in the process of creating a fair picture of the composer. A further hazard lies in the fact that accounts, though contemporaneous with the occasion they describe, were generally written as personal responses to events which took place often without the writer being fully aware of Schubert's situation in that context.

The material contained in memoirs and recollections written with hindsight long after the occasion, and frequently several decades later, was generally given to the first biographers of Schubert, such as Kreissle von Hellborn, and therefore very much with an eye to posterity. Here there are fresh hazards in accepting everything at its face value: the memoirs may be ill remembered or inaccurate in detail, if not in basic substance. They also sometimes show signs of prejudice, and occasionally even of attempts at self-glorification through their writers' proximity, real or imagined, to the great composer. For this reason, I have tended to maximize quotations from accounts written by those contributors I judge to be more reliable, and have tended to omit or ignore most, if not all, accounts by those I deem less reliable.

Problems in using the sources of knowledge are also exacerbated by the biographer's own response to available material—even in deciding on the most reliable. Although I have endeavoured to make it clear where the lines of apparent fact, probability, possibility, and surmise are drawn, I have found it necessary, and indeed have been advised by some of the readers of my manuscript, to make certain considered decisions about Schubert, his life, his health, and his personality. This has presented one of the greatest problems for me in writing the biography. On the other hand, the process of searching into the composer's life and attempting to understand something of his mind and his soul through a myriad pieces of evidence, many of them at first apparently of minor importance, has proved absorbing and exciting.

In attempting to portray the composer in the different scenes of his life, the background sometimes emerges in sharper focus than the foreground. It has been my conscious decision not to suppress such scenes simply because of inadequate information on the part Schubert played in them, but rather to leave a shadowy sketch of the composer in them while painting in the background in a fair amount of detail. To omit the scene, or the detail, as known, would seem to obscure important influences which were acting on Schubert. This is why I have included matter which at first might appear to be irrelevant: for example, the attitude to marriage of his older friend Josef von Spaun, some details of the early careers of Bauernfeld and Schwind, social occasions at which Schubert may or may not have been present, and the probably only partly authentic descriptions of Schubert's travels in 1825 through Salzburg and Gastein and the surrounding countryside. A similar approach has influenced my choice of illustrations for the book. These include land- and townscapes which informed Schubert's reactions to his surroundings. They also include some pictorial material which may already be familiar to some readers, and these appear here again either because there is no choice, or else because the alternatives are of inferior quality.

Several chapters contain at least one extended section in which I have considered in some detail an aspect of Schubert's life or experience which is relevant to the period in question. These include the kind of education he received at school; the influence and ethos of the 'Bildung Circle', the group of friends who met to discuss literature, art, aesthetics, and morality, and who had a great influence on him in his teens; his negotiations and relationships with publishers; the importance to him of his membership of the Gesellschaft der Musikfreunde; his travels outside Vienna, and so on.

It is improbable that anyone will pick up this biography, or begin to read it, unless he or she is already interested in the composer as a result of prior experience of some of his music. The purpose of this book is to enhance the reader's pleasure in, and understanding of, Schubert's music. If it also excites interest in the composer as a human being, with new concern for the many facets of his background and his genius, then the reader has captured some of my own excitement in researching for this book.

There are many people who have helped me in various ways in the preparation and writing of the book, with advice, information, encouragement, and in practical ways, and to all, named and unnamed, I am grateful. To Gitta Holroyd-Reece Deutsch, daughter of Otto Erich Deutsch, I am especially grateful for giving generous permission for me to use the English translations of her father's books freely, both without and, where it seemed preferable, with amendments. I am also indebted to a number of distinguished members of the medical profession who have helped and advised me in the study of Schubert's physical and mental health, the symptoms and, as far as is possible, the diagnoses of his various conditions. Of these, the psychiatrist Dr Anthony Storr has both warmly encouraged me and given invaluable assistance while I was writing the book. He read my completed manuscript and made further helpful suggestions. He also put me in touch with Professor Kay Redfield Jamison of Johns Hopkins University School of Medicine, an expert on manic-depressive disorders and the creative artist, who also gave me valuable advice. Dr Irvine Loudon, a medical historian, contributed interesting information on medical knowledge in the early nineteenth century, particularly in connection with typhoid fever. Dr Stephen Lock, of the Wellcome Institute in London, a former editor of the *British Medical Journal*, read all the medical sections, corrected errors and misunderstandings, and made suggestions. Medical consultant, friend, piano pupil, and duet partner, Dr Daphne Clark advised me in the earlier stages, and read the final version of the completed manuscript for a final check of my presentation of medical matters. At the same time she recommended other improvements. I am enormously grateful to all these medical doctors, every one of whom has generously and very promptly responded to my request for assistance. In doing so, they have encouraged me where necessary to reach my own final conclusions on Schubert's health and on the nature of his last illness and death. Any errors, misunderstandings, and misjudgements in the medical discussion are my own.

Dr Ernst Hilmar has supported me throughout the writing of the book, and has continued, as always, to respond to calls for assistance. His own publications on the composer I have also used continually for reference. To

Dr Walburga Litschauer (Austrian editor of the *Neue Schubert-Ausgabe*—explained below) and Till Gerrit Waidelich (Berlin) I am grateful for passing on to me results of their own researches, sometimes before publication. To the music librarians of the Bodleian Library (Peter Ward-Jones) and University Faculty of Music (John Wagstaff) in Oxford, who have helped in many ways in my researches for material, I am deeply indebted. To Dr Walter Wieser of the Österreichische National Bibliothek in Vienna, Dr Adelbert Schusser and Ferdinand Fellinger of the Historisches Museum der Stadt Wien, and Dr Otto Biba, director of the archive of the Gesellschaft der Musikfreunde in Vienna (who in addition assisted me in the selection of a representative page of the 'Great' C major Symphony) I am indebted for various illustrations and permission to publish, as also Gerhard Lechner of the Akademische Druck- u. Verlagsanstalt (Adeva) in Graz. Both Rosl Schwab (Atzenbrugg) and Dr Zuzana Vitálová (Zseliz) supplied me with copies of photographs. A descendant of Schubert's brother Ferdinand, Martha Böhm-Schubert (Vienna) provided me with information about the home and family of Schubert's father.

Professors Peter Branscombe, Brian Newbould, and Dr Ewan West have read the manuscript and given valuable advice. They have also been ever ready to respond to requests for help. I offer them my warm thanks and, where I have failed them, my apologies. To Andras Schiff I am indebted for his generous help in my search for understanding of Hungarian influences on Schubert's music. I am also grateful to Helen Foster of Oxford University Press for her constant editorial assistance. Finally, to my husband Gilbert, I have turned very frequently for help of many kinds; and he has responded with remarkable patience. He has checked, and where necessary rewritten, all translations from German into English. His expertise in the field of German literature, especially poetry, has been a source of invaluable help when I was studying the literary background and influences on Schubert. And he kept a sharp eye on my English. Without his help, and the brilliant scholarship of the late Otto Erich Deutsch and Maurice J. E. Brown, two giants in Schubert research who were known to me personally and gave me great encouragement and help in my early work on the composer and his music, it is unlikely that this book could have been written. If it had been, without their assistance, and that of all those mentioned above, the book would have been totally inadequate.

E.N.M.

Long Hanborough, Oxfordshire
February 1996

CONTENTS

LIST OF TEXT ILLUSTRATIONS

LIST OF PLATES

(between pp. 176 and 177)

NOTE ON AUSTRIAN CURRENCY

Austrian currency was complicated for many years by the coexistence of two different currencies. The old currency, Konventions-Münze, or KM (distinguished by O. E. Deutsch in his *Documents*, p. 19, as assimilated coinage, or AC), had been established by treaty with Bavaria in 1753 with a 20-florin standard (coined from a pure silver Cologne Mark, approximately half a German pound in weight). After the wars with France and the resulting bankruptcy of the Austrian state, on 15 March 1811 a new emergency currency, the Wiener Währung, or WW (distinguished by Deutsch as Viennese currency, or VC), was introduced, also in florins. In both currencies there were 60 kreuzer to the florin. (The florin was also referred to as the gulden.)

By the 1811 decree, paper money in the old currency was devaluated to one-fifth of its normal value, so that 100 fl. KM was now worth only 20 fl. At the same time, the exchange value from old to new currency was 20 fl. KM to 50 fl. WW. Thus, goods costing 100 fl. KM before devaluation and the introduction of the new currency would now cost 500 fl. (new KM) or 1,250 fl. WW. It is therefore little wonder that the Wiener Währung was derisively called 'Weh! Weh!' (Woe! Woe!).

ABBREVIATIONS

Brille	*Schubert durch die Brille*, journal of the Internationales Franz Schubert Institut
Catalogus	E. Hilmar, *Verzeichnis der Schubert-Handschriften in der Musiksammlung der Wiener Stadt- und Landesbibliothek (Catalogus Musicus VIII)* (Kassel, 1978)
Doc.	O. E. Deutsch, *Schubert: A Documentary Biography* (London, 1946)
Dok.	O. E. Deutsch, *Schubert: Die Dokumente seines Lebens* (Kassel, 1964)
Erin.	O. E. Deutsch, *Schubert: Die Erinnerungen seiner Freunde* (1st pub. Leipzig, 1957; reissued Wiesbaden, 1983)
GdM	Gesellschaft der Musikfreunde
Mem.	O. E. Deutsch, *Schubert: Memoirs by his Friends*, trans. R. Ley and J. Nowell (London, 1958)
MGG	*Die Musik in Geschichte und Gegenwart* (Kassel, 1965)
ML	*Music and Letters*
MMR	*Monthly Musical Record*
MQ	*Musical Quarterly*
MR	*Music Review*
MT	*Musical Times*
NCM	*Nineteenth Century Music*
ND	*Franz Schubert: Dokumente 1817–1830*, i: *Texte*, ed. T. G. Waidelich (Tutzing, 1993): all references are to the entry number, not the page number
NGA	*Franz Schubert: Neue Ausgabe sämtlicher Werke*, ed. W. Dürr, A. Feil, C. Landon, *et al.* (Kassel, 1964–); also known as *Neue Schubert-Ausgabe*
ÖMZ	*Österreichische Musikzeitschrift*
Th.V.	O. E. Deutsch, *Franz Schubert: Thematisches Verzeichnis seiner Werke in chronologischer Folge* (Kassel, 1978)
WL	W. Litschauer (ed.), *Neue Dokumente zum Schubert-Kreis*, 2 vols. (Vienna, 1986 and 1993)
n	the addition of the suffix 'n' after a page number of *Doc.*, *Dok.*, *Erin.*, or *Mem.* refers to O. E. Deutsch's comments on the documents, in small print

1

SON OF IMMIGRANTS
(1797–1808)

FRANZ PETER SCHUBERT was born on Sunday, 31 January 1797 at 1.30 in the afternoon in the Himmelpfortgrund suburb of Vienna. He was the twelfth child born to the then 40-year-old Maria Elisabeth Katharina, known as Elisabeth (1756–1812), and Franz Theodor Florian Schubert (1763–1830), the local elementary schoolteacher. The boy was baptized on the following day by Father Johann Wanzka, parish priest of the nearby Lichtental church dedicated to 'the fourteen friends in need' (*Zu den vierzehn Nothelfern*); Johann Karl Alois Schubert (1755–1804), his father's elder brother, was the child's godfather. In this time of high infant mortality, when children frequently died within a few days of birth, prompt baptisms were the order of the day. Of the Schuberts' eleven children so far, although all had survived the first two weeks, seven had subsequently died. The survivors were Ignaz (almost 12), Josef (3), Ferdinand (2), and Karl (14 months). Of these, Josef was to die at the end of the following year, probably of smallpox.[1]

Franz Peter, like the three youngest of the four surviving older children, was born in one of the sixteen one-roomed family apartments of the Red Crayfish, a two-storey building with two wings and central courtyard, now still standing as 54 Nussdorferstrasse, in the ninth district of Vienna. The January cold encouraged Elisabeth to prepare for the birth in the tiny kitchen alcove which led off the family room, with a small window onto the open walkway by which the upper-storey apartments, of which theirs was one, were approached. Here she and the new baby would be warmed by the open fire, generally used to cook their food but now no doubt heating the pans of hot water needed at the birth of a child.

Whether a local midwife was in attendance at the birth or not, it is likely that Elisabeth's sister, Maria Magdalena, nine years younger than herself,

---

[1] *Dok.* 5.

FIG. 1. Courtyard of the Red Crayfish, where Schubert was born, still standing as Nussdorferstrasse 54. *Anonymous drawing, after an old original; taken from Ernst Hilmar, Schubert, © Akademische Druck- u. Verlagsanstalt, Graz, 1989, reproduced by permission.*

was with her. The Vietz sisters, already devoted, had been brought even closer by their marriages to the Schubert brothers. For five years earlier Magdalena, as she was known, had married Karl Schubert shortly after the death of his first wife. By 1797 she had probably given birth to four of their nine children, only one of whom was to survive to adulthood. Elisabeth and Magdalena, like many women of their time, were further bonded by continuous childbearing, sharing the same hardships and domestic drudgery, trying to do their best for their families in cramped conditions, with meagre resources, and in a routine only too frequently punctuated by the births and deaths of their children.

The family in which Franz Schubert grew up was a close one. There existed both affection and a strong sense of mutual responsibility between his parents and his uncle and aunt. Although Franz Theodor Schubert and Elisabeth Vietz had met in Vienna, they were not Austrians, but had come as migrants from distant rural areas in the extreme northern region of the central area of the Austro-Hungarian empire. German was their native tongue, and yet their alien German accents and differences in vocabulary, as well as their country customs, quickly distinguished them from the home-grown Viennese, who had their own broad dialect and accompanying culture. The Schubert brothers, Karl and Franz Theodor, came from northern Moravia, some sixty miles north of Brünn (Brno), the capital of Moravia. They were born in Neudorf (Vysoká), a village in the neighbourhood of Moravian-Schönberg (Sumperk), in the administrative district of Altstadt (Staré Mĕsto) bordered in the west by Bohemia, in the north by Prussia (now Poland) and in the north-east by Austrian Silesia. After the Seven Years War, which was fought ostensibly over the sovereignty of Silesia, most of Silesia was annexed by Prussia. Only the most southerly part, known as Austrian Silesia, remained in the Austro-Hungarian empire. Here, in the western area of the country not far from the Moravian boundary, in the mountain village or small town, of Zuckmantel (Zlaté Hory), the Vietz family had lived. Neudorf and Zuckmantel, each on the outskirts of the empire, were little more than thirty miles apart but linked only by rough mountain roads across the provincial boundary and Sudetic mountains.

The father of Karl and Franz Theodor, Karl Josef Schubert (1723–87), was a rather prosperous peasant farmer and 'senior jurist' (magistrate) of his community in Neudorf. He was an important and influential man of some enterprise who had the well-being of the small community in which he lived at heart. In 1780 a sizeable monument, 'Christ on the Mount of Olives', was erected in Neudorf at his expense. More importantly, it was his inspiration and initiative that later led to his building of a small chapel of ease in Neudorf, which previously had no church of its own. All costs for this building were met by himself and another member of the family, Johann Schubert. Until this time the locals had to walk across country a distance of some two miles to the neighbouring village of Hohen-Seibersdorf to attend mass, for weddings, and for funerals. The new chapel, still standing today, was intended specifically for the celebration of mass on 'high festival' days.

Karl Josef's two surviving sons (only four of his thirteen children survived infancy or childhood) were intelligent, and they were accepted as students (boarders) at the Gymnasium (grammar-school) of the Jesuit monastery in Brünn. Here much of their lives centred on the beautiful monastery church and its fine musical tradition. After their schooldays, at the customary age of 16 or so, each in turn underwent a year's college training in order to qualify as an assistant schoolteacher; this was followed by a year or two's probationary teaching. However, the Seven Years War had brought great misery to the area, and first Karl and then Franz Theodor determined to leave their home and travel to Vienna to follow their chosen career. Their father, who was to die on Christmas Eve 1787, a 'dearly loved and venerated father',[2] as he was described at the time by his second son, does not appear to have stood in the way of his sons, nor expected them to inherit and work the family farm. Their younger sister, Anna Maria Thekla (1770–1830), was 12 years old and still living at home with her parents when, in 1782 or 1783, Franz Theodor followed Karl to Vienna. (The older surviving sister, Maria Theresia, 1765–1830, had already married and left the village.) In 1789, two years after their father's death and some seven years after Franz Theodor's departure, Anna Maria married (at the age of 19), in the Seibersdorf church, Florian Harbich, a master tailor from Woitzdorf. Together the Harbichs inherited the Schubert family home and farm. A small legacy which Franz Theodor received after his father's death he spent on rent and equipment for the new school in the Himmel-pfortgrund, to which he had recently been appointed.

Karl Schubert may have been encouraged by another migrant from the same area, Andreas Becker, some twenty years older than Karl, to join him in Vienna, where he had been since 1765. Becker had done well for himself. He had found work as an assistant schoolteacher in the Carmelite elementary school in the Leopoldstadt suburb of Vienna; he married the daughter of the school's headmaster, on whose death Becker succeeded to the headship. When Karl arrived in Vienna, Becker employed him as his assistant. After Becker died a few years later in 1778, Karl married his widow Anna, who was almost twice his age; and in turn, he succeeded to the headship of the Carmelite school.

Like his brother Karl, Franz Theodor had gained two or three years' teaching experience before he left Moravia and joined his brother as his assistant at the Carmelite school, probably in 1783, at the age of 20. Here he remained as a teacher for around three years until the summer of 1786, when he was appointed to his own school. This was a small and depressed establishment with few pupils in the deprived Himmelpfortgrund, a suburb of some 3,000 residents occupying eighty-six buildings and served by a single school, in the parish of Lichtental. Before this, Franz Theodor had lived for some while in the Lichtental suburb, where he met and fell in love with his future wife, Elisabeth Vietz. In the autumn of 1784, with Elisabeth already expecting their first child, she and Franz Theodor moved into lodgings in the house of a shoemaker, Ignaz Wagner, at the house named 'In the Golden Ring', Lichtental no. 152 (now Badgasse 20, two streets behind the Lichtental church). Their landlord, in accordance with the statutes of the

---

[2] *Doc. 2, Dok. 4.*

day, registered them both as new residents in the parish, him in August and her in September of 1784.[3] On this occasion Franz Theodor's age was given as 25, whereas it was in truth no more than 21, and his occupation as instructor rather than assistant schoolteacher. Elisabeth's age was given as 30 (but only 28 in the marriage register five months later) and her occupation that of a maidservant then living on her savings but in search of local employment. Strangely, on this occasion her place of birth was entered not as Zuckmantel, as in the marriage register, but as Engelsberg (Andělská Hora), also in Silesia but some twelve miles further south.

In Zuckmantel, Franz Johann Vietz, the father of Elisabeth, Magdalena, and their brother Felix, had been a successful locksmith and gunmaker by profession, a well-respected member of the community who had risen to be master of the local guild of locksmiths and blacksmiths. The Seven Years War had had particularly devastating effects on the people of Silesia, and early in 1772 Franz Vietz, in serious financial difficulties, was found to have appropriated for his own use some of the guild's money placed in his care. He was arrested, imprisoned, and charged, but not convicted, of what was then a capital offence. However, he was disgraced. Shattered by his shame, he hurriedly left his home and any effects remaining to him, and taking his wife and three children, he set out to walk with them the 200 or so miles to Vienna in search of anonymity and to attempt to rebuild his life and fortunes. At some stage on the journey his wife, weakened by the strain of events and exhausted by the journey, was taken ill and died. After he had buried her, Franz Vietz, himself far from well, resumed the weary trek with his three children, intent on finding work in Vienna and securing somewhere for himself and his family to live. He reached the city gravely sick, only to die a few hours after entering the inner city and finding temporary accommodation in the Golden Lamb inn in the Naglergasse. The children were now alone, penniless, and probably friendless, left to make their own way in a strange city. Even if they had friends or acquaintances in the capital, the shame of their father's offence might have deterred them from making contact or seeking help. Thus the most likely explanation for the false entry of Elisabeth's birthplace in the Lichtental church register of new arrivals in 1784 is the desire of the young Vietzes to establish themselves in Vienna in anonymity. Felix now adopted the role of head of the family, found work as a weaver, and settled with Elisabeth (aged 16) and Magdalena (aged 7) in the Lichtental suburb of Vienna, where the weaving trade flourished. Here Elisabeth kept the home and looked after her younger sister until both were able to find domestic work.

[3] E. Benedikt, 'Die "Meldezettel" von Schuberts Eltern', *Brille*, 10 (1993), 42–4.

When Elisabeth fell in love with Franz Theodor Florian Schubert and their first child was conceived, she knew that her future husband's meagre salary as an assistant teacher would not go far towards supporting her and their child. He was a responsible young man and, in preparation for his marriage and the birth of the child, he took on any extra work as a private tutor that he could find in order to augment his salary. The marriage took place in the Lichtental church on 17 January 1785, witnessed by the couple's landlord, Ignaz Wagner, and the groom's elder brother, Karl.[4] Ignaz was born on 8 March following, and a sister for him one week before his first birthday. When three months later, on 13 June 1786, Schubert's young father was given full charge of his own school, the joy of the parents must have been great. The school was a humble establishment situated only a short walk from their lodgings with Wagner; but with the appointment came an apartment of their own in the same building as the school. From this time on, whatever her own talents may have been, for Elisabeth Schubert life was concerned almost entirely with supporting her husband in his work and nurturing their children. Her husband was a dedicated teacher, and he also had some musical talent. He played the cello and violin; but there was at first little time to spare for music after his new appointment, as he concentrated on building up the number of pupils in his school and improving its reputation.

Franz Theodor was a hard-working, conscientious, and able schoolteacher who, starting from very humble beginnings in the Himmelpfortgrund with a handful of pupils, continued to expand his numbers and to provide for his pupils a sound basic education, in so far as he was allowed by the restrictive education laws of the day. In time he earned considerable esteem with the city authorities, and before 1812 was awarded the title of Imperial Almoner for his work with needy children. In 1826 he was honoured with citizen's rights of the City of Vienna in recognition of his forty-five years of school service and seventeen years of charitable work for children's welfare, an honour which was petitioned by the parish and community of the Rossau district where he was then teaching and living.[5]

By 1796 Franz Theodor already had 174 scholars in the one-and-a-half-room school, which occupied one of the ground-floor apartments of the Red Crayfish. Unfortunately, many of the parents of his pupils, indeed far more than the statutory number required of him by law, were too poor to pay the weekly dues for tuition, low though these were. As his own salary came directly from these tuition fees, he still found it necessary to continue

---

[4] *Doc.* 1, *Dok.* 4.

[5] Biba, 'Franz Schubert und die Gesellschaft der Musikfreunde', in O. Brusatti (ed.), *Schubert-Kongress Wien 1978* (Vienna, 1979), 30.

to supplement his income by giving private coaching in order to support his growing family. By the next year, when Franz Peter was born, the school facilities were no longer adequate for the continually increasing number of pupils. Franz Theodor got round this by instituting a two-session day, with morning and afternoon sessions for two separate groups of children. Already from January of the previous year he had been applying for jobs at various other schools where facilities were better, but he had been unsuccessful each time. By 1801, having worked an eight-hour day for four years and supplemented his income with private tuition, he was eventually in a financial position to buy, with the help of a mortgage, a small house for himself and his school. The Black Horse was a short distance from the Red Crayfish and it is still standing, as 3 Säulengasse.[6] In the autumn of that year, shortly after the birth of Elisabeth Schubert's last child Maria Theresia, the family moved into their own house to enjoy more rooms, more space, and greater comforts. Franz Theodor was now able to expand his school even further, and by 1804 he had 300 pupils. Meanwhile, in 1803 his youngest son, Franz Peter, at the age of 6, had entered his father's school and soon proved his intellectual abilities by coming, and remaining, top of his class. In 1815, soon after Franz Peter returned to the school for the first time as a teacher, he became his father's sixth assistant.

Schubert's father's applications for new school appointments were to continue until 1818, when at last he was successful. There followed a move to a smart new school, only a year old, in the wealthier Rossau district a mile or two away, and here the family settled contentedly until the death of Franz Theodor at the age of 67 in 1830.

The required standard of education and accomplishment for an elementary schoolteacher at this time was low, and his status in society a humble one. An education act in force from 1805 to 1869 required that schoolteachers must stick to the prescribed textbooks, since they could not be expected to compile texts of their own; they should see to it that their students learned their lessons by heart; and the officially prescribed task of teachers was to inculcate, along with basic skills, religious orthodoxy and obedience to authority.[7] Franz Theodor's own education, like that of his brother Karl, was undoubtedly superior to the norm. He was proud of his six years at the Brünn Gymnasium, where Greek and Latin would have featured in a Classics-orientated education. Throughout his career, from the time of his marriage to Elisabeth in 1785, he supplemented his basic salary with earnings from private tuition in Latin, which he gave to pupils hoping

---

[6] *Doc.* 5, *Dok.* 7.
[7] D. Gramit, 'Schuberts "bildender Umgang": Denken und Ästhetik bei Schuberts Jugendfreunden', *Brille*, 8 (1992), 5.

FIG. 2. The schoolhouse 'Zum schwarzen Rössel' (the Black Horse), the Schubert family home and schoolhouse from 1801 until the end of 1817. Still standing as Säulengasse 3. *Anonymous sketch; taken from Ernst Hilmar, Schubert,* © *Akademische Druck- u. Verlagsanstalt, Graz, 1989, reproduced by permission.*

to transfer from elementary (or 'trivial') schools to a Gymnasium. Apart from this, he took responsibility for the education of his own children, supplementing the instruction they received in school and preparing those of them who wished to move on to more advanced studies. Franz Peter was prepared by his father for his entrance examination in 1808 for a place as a chorister at the Court chapel. The boy had to show that he was 'sufficiently able to enter the first grammar class',[8] or Latin class, as it was sometimes called.

However sound his own education may or may not have been, Franz Theodor's time and opportunity for serious reading or further cultural development must have been very limited. There are few clues as to the way he spent any free time that he may have had outside family concerns. However, as his children recorded, he played the cello in the family string quartet; and he took part in early days with family and friends in the chamber music sessions which were held in the Säulengasse schoolroom.

Elisabeth Schubert was a gentle and good woman, who had been well prepared for the deprivations of her early married life by the hardships she

---

[8] *Doc. 6, Dok. 8.*

experienced after the tragic deaths of both parents and her arrival in Vienna. The impression she has left is of a warm-hearted mother, generous in her love for her husband and her children, and for her brother and sister and their families, whom she, along with her husband, welcomed into their own home when they were in trouble. Indeed, her brother Felix and his small family occasionally moved in with the Schuberts; and, after Karl died in December 1804, her sister Magdalena and her two daughters, one of whom died shortly after her father, lived with the family in the Säulengasse. Magdalena's only surviving child, also Magdalena, was born in the same year as Franz Peter and they grew up good companions.

Franz Theodor was a fortunate man to be lovingly supported first by Elisabeth and then, after her death in 1812, by his more well-to-do second wife, Anna Kleyenböck. He seems to have been a physically strong man, determined and ambitious for both himself and his children, but also compassionate towards members of his family and the poorest of his pupils. As a Moravian immigrant he had to work hard for all he achieved; and coming from a comparatively comfortable peasant family, he would have wished to improve his situation in Vienna, the city of opportunities as he saw it. For this reason, he conformed to the expected norms and respected the laws of the land and the church, in the process giving the impression of being a stern father of strict, conventional Catholic morality. However, in the cramped conditions in which the family lived for much of Franz Peter's youth, discipline and obedience were necessary.

But was Franz Theodor really morally above reproach? On some evidence, it would appear that he was more of an opportunist than has been supposed. When he married in January 1785, his future wife already heavily pregnant, he gave his age as 25, just three years younger than Elisabeth.[9] If he was born in 1763, as he entered on the family registration form, completed, as he was legally obliged to do, on the family's removal to the Rossau in January 1818,[10] then he was only 21, or perhaps 22 at the time of his first marriage. His reason for overstating his age by four years or so could have been fear that the church would consider him too young to marry. Another explanation could be that the appointment and promotion to a new school that he was seeking was dependent on his age and experience. Again, in the 1818 registration form, he gave the date of birth of his eldest son, Ignaz, as 1786, possibly an adjustment he had contrived in order to conceal the fact that the child was conceived outside wedlock. On the same form he went on to misdate the births of both Ferdinand and Karl, his next two surviving sons, making them a year younger than they were.

---

[9] *Doc.* 1, *Dok.* 4. [10] *Doc.* 83, *Dok.* 55–6.

Although these may have been inadvertent inaccuracies, the same is less likely in the case of Ignaz, the first child. There does appear to have been a streak of deceit in Schubert's father, not very serious, and even well motivated: certainly of a kind to be compared with that of his otherwise laudably upright and successful son Ferdinand. Indeed Ferdinand, who in 1824 became a professor and in 1851 director of the teachers' training college in the Annagasse in Vienna where both he and Franz Peter had been students, was not above acts of plagiarism in later life, taking and using music or ideas of his composer brother and passing them off as his own.

Schubert's parents recognized that their sons were gifted, and they gave them the best opportunities they could afford. They took pride in their successes and were concerned if they seemed to be falling short of their expectations. Between members of the family there was considerable affection as is apparent from family celebrations, music-making, conversation, and, in the case of the young men, in their taking country walks and visiting local inns together. But of higher culture and intellectual stimulation there may have been less to satisfy the young composer–musician, Franz Peter, when he returned home on vacation from his school in the city, his work as a chorister in the Imperial chapel, and the company of his friends and colleagues from more sophisticated backgrounds.

Such was Franz Peter Schubert's background, nothing very unusual for that period in one of the less favoured suburbs of Vienna, but likely to have a strong influence on any child. Nor was there anything unusual in his birth. As his parents already had four sons, it is likely that they had hoped for a girl. There had been four daughters, but, like three of their sons, they had all died in infancy. Their strongest prayer would be that the child might be healthy and survive to adulthood, perhaps to become a good schoolteacher, like his father and uncle.

Of the boy's earliest years, little or nothing is known. One strange fact stands out, however: after his birth, Elisabeth bore no other child for almost three years. Until then, children were born at intervals averaging thirteen months. Not until 17 December 1799, only seven weeks before Franz Peter's third birthday, did Aloisia enter the world, only to be snatched away on the following day. But the parents were blessed with one more child, a daughter Maria Theresia, who, born twenty-one months after Aloisia when her mother was already 44 years old, lived until 1878.

Before Maria Theresia was born, for almost four years except for Aloisia's one day of life, Franz Peter was the youngest of the four surviving children of the Schubert family. On account of her age, his mother may well have thought that he could be her last child. Surely it is likely that Elisabeth had a special affection for the sturdy, clever, sensitive boy as, anxious for his health and survival, she nurtured and sheltered him with particular care. She observed him developing fast as he watched, copied, and tried to keep up with his older brothers. Maybe she longed for the open spaces, natural beauties, and mountain air of her own childhood for her sons, cooped up as they were in one overcrowded room, in insanitary conditions and a climate which was too cold in winter and too hot in summer. Doubtless she told them stories of the countryside she had known and of her own early life, thus unconsciously sowing in the mind of her youngest son the seeds of passion for mountains, rivers, streams, and lakes which were to germinate and blossom through the Romantic climate of his youth, and then inspire some of his most beautiful songs.

Franz Peter's uncommon musical gifts as a small child could not have escaped the notice of his parents: his sensitivity to and love of musical sounds wherever he heard them, whether of the organ and choir in the Lichtental church, of street musicians, or of his family singing and playing instruments. They surely remarked on his ability to remember melodies that he heard, as, later, did his friends at the Stadtkonvikt.[11] It is not known when he received his first musical instruction, but to his brother Ignaz fell the task of giving the boy his first piano lessons. These lasted for a very short time, as Ignaz himself explained: 'after barely a few months, he [Schubert] announced to me that he now had no further use for my teaching and would henceforth continue on his own. In fact, within a very short time he progressed so far that I myself had to recognize in him a master who far excelled me and whose standard I would never reach.'[12] If Ignaz' account is correct, here is the first evidence of Schubert's self-possession and quiet confidence in his own musical abilities, and of his independent musical spirit, attributes of his character which were to remain vital and influential throughout his life.

Schubert's father gave his son his first violin lessons when he was 8 years old: 'I taught him the basic rudiments of violin playing and trained him to the point of being able to play easy duets quite well.'[13] He must also have realized that his own musical accomplishment was soon to be outstripped by that of his precociously gifted son, and he took him to the local professional musician, Michael Holzer, choirmaster of the Lichtental church. Holzer (1772–1826) was not outstandingly gifted, and suggestions that he may have had a weakness for drink could explain why he, a pupil of the renowned Albrechtsberger (with whom Beethoven had studied

---

[11] *Mem.* 18, *Erin.* 25.　　[12] *Mem.* 212–13, *Erin.* 244.　　[13] *Mem.* 212, *Erin.* 244.

counterpoint and a skilled contrapuntist), seems to have had little personal ambition. But he was a kindly man, and his affection and admiration for his exceptionally talented pupil were both genuine and generous throughout his life. According to Schubert's brother Ferdinand, writing in 1839 long after the composer's death, Holzer used to speak of the boy 'with tears in his eyes': 'Whenever I tried to tell him something which I thought would be new to him, he always knew it already. I was often left gaping at him in silence.'[14] Ferdinand also claimed that Holzer gave his brother tuition not only in music theory but also in piano, violin, and, of course, singing. Gifted with a beautiful treble voice and intuitive musicianship, the boy was soon a member of the church choir, and no doubt singing solos whenever required. On at least one occasion during a service he had to leave his place with the choir in the organ loft and stand beside Holzer (on the organ) to play a violin solo. For some while, and most likely from the time he had learned to read music, he had been composing for himself, including (again according to Ferdinand) songs, string quartets, and piano pieces.[15] None of these first compositions of his childhood has survived.

Such a talent was surely remarkable, and it may have been Holzer who recommended to Schubert's father that the boy should be taken to the great Anton Salieri, composer, conductor, and teacher, and Court Kapellmeister (musical director) to the Emperor Franz, for advice concerning his musical future. The meeting took place in 1807. Schubert took with him examples of his latest compositions. He also went prepared to sing to Salieri and to play both the violin and piano. Salieri was impressed by what he saw and heard and, making a note of the boy's gifts for future reference, he advised that as soon as Schubert reached the age of 11 he should enter for one of the examinations for selection of new choristers for the Court chapel. On 28 May of the following year an announcement appeared in the official daily newspaper, the *Wiener Zeitung*, that two boy choristers were required; those who wished to compete for the places were 'to present themselves on 30 September at 3 pm, at the I. & R. [Imperial and Royal] Seminary [Stadtkonvikt], 796 Universitätsplatz, to be tested for their progress so far in general subjects and for the musical knowledge they have already acquired'.[16] They were also requested to bring school reports with them. On this occasion, there were vacancies for a treble and alto voice. The advertisement which appeared in the same paper on 3 August was for one soprano only:

Anyone applying for this place for his son or ward must prove to the Directorate of the Stadtkonvikt, where an examination is to be held on 1 October at 9 a.m., that

---

[14] *Mem.* 34, *Erin.* 44.   [15] Ibid.   [16] *Doc.* 6, *Dok.* 8.

the candidate is fit to enter the first Latin class, possesses a good voice and has been well instructed in singing. In the meantime, certificates should be submitted to the said Directorate concerning the candidate's progress during the last two terms, his state of bodily health, and also proof that he is past the danger of small-pox.[17]

For the successful candidate, a place in the Court chapel choir was accompanied by a foundation scholarship at the Academic Grammar-School (Akademisches Gymnasium) which was associated with the University of Vienna, and free boarding at the Stadtkonvikt nearby. They were also informed that their free education at the Gymnasium would continue until the end of the school year in which their voices broke. Thereafter, provided that they 'excelled' in their moral behaviour and studies, they could remain at the school and complete their studies. When Schubert's father entered his son for the examination, he knew that, if successful, Franz Peter would have the chance of a good general education, of the kind that he himself had enjoyed in Brünn. And his son knew that a great and wonderful new musical world was beckoning.

---

[17] Ibid.

2

SCHOOLDAYS
(1808–1813)

ON September 1808 Schubert attended the Stadtkonvikt to compete in the audition and entrance examination for a place in the Court chapel choir and for the academic privileges which would accompany it. Among his examiners were Anton Salieri and Dr Franz Innocenz Lang, the director of the Stadtkonvikt. According to his brother Ferdinand (1794–1859), jokes were made by other candidates about the pale, whitish-blue coat that Franz Peter was wearing.[1] No doubt dressed for the occasion as smartly as his hard-pressed parents could afford and in a style they thought appropriate, Schubert overheard the comments, and noticed the mirth of the other boys at his expense: 'He must be a miller's son. He'll get in, for sure!'[2]—a jest maybe, but reflecting the hard and hungry times in which they were living. Thus, even before his acceptance at the school the boy could have been made to feel awkward, shy, socially inferior or different from his peers, many if not most of whom would have come from more comfortable and privileged backgrounds than his own.

In the examination, however, Schubert, along with young Franz Müllner and in that order, was found to be far ahead of all the other candidates, both in musical attainment and promise and in their academic achievement and potential. One other boy, Maximilian Weisse, was accepted at the same time but with some hesitation; his standards did not match up to those of the two Franzes, but it was hoped that they would prove adequate. (In later life, Weisse became a distinguished professor of astronomy at the University of Krakow and director of the observatory there.) Schubert and Müllner were selected to join the trebles, and Weisse the altos, in the Court chapel choir: the habit, as in most European church choirs, was to use boy altos rather than the adult male altos customary in British churches. A few weeks after the examination, early in November, Schubert bade farewell to his family,

---

[1] *Mem.* 35, *Erin.* 44. [2] Ibid.

including his three brothers Ignaz, Ferdinand, and Karl, who were all still living at home, to enter a world completely new to him: that of the emperor's private chapel with its music and musicians, the Academic Grammar-School of some considerable repute, and the boarding establishment, the Stadtkonvikt.

On this, possibly his first return to the Stadtkonvikt since his appearance for the entrance examination, Schubert may have gained confidence from, and felt some pride in, his new school uniform. The uniform of the emperor's choristers was strikingly distinctive, if outmoded, with its 'low, three-cornered hat, white neckerchief, a cut-away coat of dark, blackish-brown colour, with a small gold epaulette on the left shoulder, shiny, polished buttons, an old-fashioned waistcoat which reached below the stomach, short breeches with buckles, shoes with buckles and no sword'.[3] So attired, Franz Peter, a small and rather timid lad some three months off his twelfth birthday, from an unsophisticated background and probably speaking a rather broad version of the local Viennese dialect, entered the unfamiliar surroundings where he had as yet neither friends nor acquaintances.

The Stadtkonvikt had been founded in 1803 by Emperor Franz as a boarding establishment and educational institution to house students, both those attending the nearby Academic Grammar-School, many of them on foundation scholarships, and university undergraduates (other than medical students). Originally part of the old Jesuit University of Vienna, the Stadtkonvikt building occupied (as it still does) the best part of one side of a small square situated behind the cathedral. The handsome university church (formerly a Jesuit church) occupied an adjoining side of the square, the fine old university hall (now the Akademie der Wissenschaften) the side opposite the Stadtkonvikt. Amongst the boarders at the Stadtkonvikt were the boy choristers, all with scholarships at the Academic Grammar-School, ten from the Court chapel and eight from the Kirche am Hof (also known as the Church of the Nine Choirs of Angels).[4] A few adult members of the choirs, as well as some instrumental musicians of the Court chapel, also boarded in the Stadtkonvikt. There were in all some 130 student boarders, boys and young men, many of them the sons of army officers and state officials, some ennobled, but none belonging to the older Austrian aristocracy, who were catered for by the Löwenberg seminary in the suburb of Josefstadt. The boarders were divided into seven *Kameraten*, or houses, each containing a private room for the 'prefect' (teacher) in charge of that house, a study or assembly-room with a modest supply of books, and a

---

[3] *Mem.* 98, *Erin.* 114.   [4] *Mem.* 351, 368n, *Erin.* 405, 424n.

dormitory with some twenty beds.[5] Both this establishment and the Löwenberg seminary were run by Piarist monks, who belonged to a charitable Roman Catholic holy order founded in the sixteenth century, originally for the purpose of assisting in the education of poor children; and from their number were drawn both the prefects at the Stadtkonvikt and the teachers at the school.

Life at the Stadtkonvikt in Schubert's time was in many ways spartan— the buildings often cold, only partially heated in winter; the food insufficient and of poor quality. For this was Vienna during and immediately after the Napoleonic Wars, when conditions generally were very hard and there was little money for basic comforts, let alone for luxuries. Indeed, the Austrian economy collapsed entirely early in 1811, and the state was declared bankrupt. Discipline for the students was strict, at times rigorously enforced by the Piarist brothers, though with no obvious cruelty. The director, Dr Lang, a theologian of some standing in the city, was also rector of the university church and later rector of the university. He appeared to the students as 'very severe and gloomy',[6] but he was a fair man, of strong character, and he won the respect, if not the love, of many of his students. (Schubert, soon after he left the Stadtkonvikt, dedicated his Second Symphony to him.) Most importantly for the students with musical interests Lang, although himself without musical training or accomplishment, genuinely loved music and gave great encouragement to the musical activities of the Stadtkonvikt. In 1869 the renowned music critic Eduard Hanslick (1825–1904) described the Stadtkonvikt in Schubert's day as, in his opinion, 'a music conservatoire in miniature'.[7] For here, under Lang's directorship, every evening the establishment's own orchestra met to rehearse one or two overtures and a symphony, under the professional direction of Wenzel Ruzicka (1785–1823), who was in charge of the music tuition. A Czech by birth, Ruzicka was also Court organist and a violinist in the Burg-Theater (Court Theatre) orchestra.[8] Although he was officially engaged as a visiting tutor only for piano and organ, when needed he seems willingly to have added instruction in viola, cello, and music theory to his commitment, as well as conducting the rehearsal orchestra. When other evening commitments prevented him from attending Stadtkonvikt rehearsals, one of the older students, who was designated student musical director, had to organize the sessions. In this task the student had the practical assistance of a younger boy, usually one of the chapel choristers. For each of the choristers, tuition in piano, violin, and music theory was obligatory. For other students it was not; but Lang himself provided

---

[5] *Doc.* 7n, *Dok.* 8n.   [6] Spaun: *Mem.* 350, *Erin.* 404.
[7] *Mem.* 271, *Erin.* 310–11.   [8] *Doc.* 14n, *Dok.* 12n.

and paid for the instruments and instruction of many who wished to learn orchestral instruments, including wind, brass, and percussion.[9] As a result, the orchestra was soon able to attempt a wide range of the available symphonic repertory.

Before his arrival at the Stadtkonvikt Schubert may never have heard a symphony orchestra. The thrill and joy that he experienced on first hearing these school rehearsals, and his excitement when very soon afterwards he was invited to bring his violin and join the second violin section, are not hard to imagine. The student musical director at this time was a law student, Josef von Spaun, some nine years older than the small bespectacled boy who stood behind him to play from the same second violin part. Spaun, who was soon to become Schubert's friend and benefactor, was quick to recognize his exceptional musical talent. It was not long before he invited Schubert to be his orchestral assistant at the rehearsals, a somewhat 'irksome job which involved looking after the stringing of the instruments, lighting the tallow candles, putting out the parts, and keeping the instruments and music in good care and condition' as Anton Holzapfel (1792–1868), also a student at the Stadtkonvikt, described it.[10] However, for a shy new boy, passionate about music but finding it difficult to settle in to his new surroundings, this was a position of responsibility which gave him some status and purpose, and also brought him into close contact with musical scores and instruments which might otherwise have been unavailable to him. Perhaps even more importantly, this job brought him to an affectionate understanding with Spaun, an admirable and high-minded young man, with whom a relationship was to develop which was to last throughout Schubert's life.

As Schubert had already been singing for a year or two in the choir of the Lichtental church, the move to the Court chapel choir may not have been difficult for him. In the chapel, he was now in a small choir of talented singers, including a maximum of only ten boy sopranos and altos. Perhaps because this was a private chapel, and the choir gave no concerts outside, the daily routine became a burden for some of the singers. For Schubert, however, it was always a delight;[11] he took pleasure in performing to a high standard and relished the opportunity to get to know a wider repertory of church music. For the first few years, influenced by his father's strict and conservative attitudes to the Catholic Church and its teachings, he probably accepted unquestioningly the religious conventions as presented by the Court's clerics, in the same way that he accepted the firm discipline of the Stadtkonvikt. Later he was to become disillusioned with some of the church's teaching and practices.

[9] *Mem.* 57, *Erin.* 67.   [10] *Mem.* 58, *Erin.* 67.   [11] Spaun: *Mem.* 18, *Erin.* 24.

Apart from the choristers' daily walks to and from the Imperial Palace and occasional school walks for exercise, there were few chances to escape the rigid pattern of life in the Stadtkonvikt and at the Academic Grammar-School, which the boys attended each morning. Here the tuition in the first three years, much of it conducted in Latin[12] (to which Schubert had been introduced by his father in preparation for the entrance examination), was limited to religious instruction and the study of Latin language and style, some German grammar, and a smattering of literature, mathematics, natural history, physics, geography, and history. School reports were issued (without mention of German studies) twice in each academic year and included assessment gradings for each subject, and also for 'morals' (conduct) and 'application'. In addition, at the end of each of the two terms in April and September, the progress of chapel choristers was recorded and passed on to Court officials in a separate report. The gradings were 1 (eminent), 1, 1–2, 2. A '2' grading was considered inadequate—a failure. The Academic Grammar-School was associated with, and over an eight-year course prepared its pupils for, entry to the University of Vienna. Classes for the first four years were labelled 'grammar' or 'Latin' classes, with Greek entering the syllabus in the fourth year. After this there were two years of humanities ('humaniora' or 'studia inferiora') followed by the final two years of philosophy ('studia superiora') which specifically prepared students for entry to university courses.[13] Many of Schubert's peers followed the school course through to university. He left after his first year in the humanities class, three months before his seventeenth birthday. (His father, at school in Brünn, had completed six years, leaving after two years in the humanities class.)

Away from home for the first time, Schubert may have needed all the help and encouragement he could find to survive without too much distress his first few weeks or even months of loneliness and isolation. For him, new musical experiences and opportunities may have been his only lifeline—until, that is, Spaun took him under his protective wing. Spaun was quick to mark his talent, his total absorption and quiet excitement when making or discovering music. 'I noticed how the normally quiet and indifferent-looking boy surrendered himself in the most lively way to the impressions of the beautiful symphonies we played', Spaun remembered, in 1858;[14] 'His delight in the music and zeal with which he took part made me notice him.'[15] Spaun was also aware that Schubert was already composing avidly:

---

[12] Elementary schools, such as that of Schubert's father, where classes were conducted in German, were known as German schools; the Gymnasiums, where many classes were in Latin, were known as Latin schools.

[13] *Doc.* 35–6n, *Dok.* 28n.   [14] *Mem.* 126, *Erin.* 147.   [15] *Mem.* 353, *Erin.* 407.

'He was timid and blushed, but my approval delighted him.'[16] Helped by enjoyable musical experiences and the kindly attention of Spaun, Schubert began to adjust to his new life. But the advances he was making in this direction were all too soon interrupted. In the spring of 1809, a few months after Schubert joined the Court chapel choir, news reached Vienna of the threatening advance on the city of the French army, under the command of Napoleon. The Austrian Emperor Franz fled, and the Court chapel doors closed.

For students at the Stadtkonvikt this period was not without excitements, as well as consternation and fears. Many years later, in 1864, Spaun described what it was like:

As the French approached Vienna, a students' corps was formed. We Stadtkonvikt pupils were forbidden to volunteer: but after we had heard the rallying cry of *Feldmarschall-Leutnant* Koller, in the large hall of the University [opposite the Stadtkonvikt], and had seen the enthusiasm with which [other] students pressed forward to volunteer, we could not resist enrolling ourselves; and we returned jubilant to the Stadtkonvikt, bearing the white and red arm-bands, the emblem of the volunteers.[17]

Director Lang was angry at their unpremeditated action, but powerless to act until three days later, when 'there came a supreme command' from the emperor's representative in Vienna ordering the Stadtkonvikt recruits to resign from the army immediately.[18] In the mean time, of course, the patriotic fervour of the older student-recruits could not fail to arouse the interest and admiration of the younger boys.

On 9 May the French army took up positions outside the city walls. Vienna was under siege. Three days later, on 12 May, at nine o'clock in the evening the bombardment began. Spaun (again retrospectively, in 1864) described the vivid impression of this attack: 'glowing cannon balls curving across the night sky', and 'many fires reddened the sky'.[19] The young men watched as a howitzer shell fell in the university square in front of them, bursting and shattering one of the fountains of the old university hall opposite. While they contemplated this, there was an even louder crash, this time inside the Stadtkonvikt itself. Another shell had entered the Stadtkonvikt, passing directly through the roof and rooms of the prefects on the upper two floors, to burst on the first floor in the room of a third prefect, Josef Walch, a very unpopular mathematics teacher at the Academic Grammar-School, just as he was unlocking the door to enter. Although, not surprisingly, there were unkind schoolboy jokes made about the narrow escapes of the 'tormentors', many of the students, and especially the

---

[16] *Mem.* 127, *Erin.* 148.   [17] *Mem.* 353, *Erin.* 407.   [18] Ibid.   [19] Ibid.

younger boys, must have been frightened during the bombardment, as were those parents, like Schubert's, living in the suburbs outside the walls, who could see and hear the attack and were anxious for the safety of their children.

For the Stadtkonvikt students the French occupation of Vienna resulted in a tightening of the already resented restrictions. For Schubert in particular the cessation of the daily orchestral rehearsals, coming on top of the closure of the Court chapel, was a painful deprivation. His days no longer brightened by musical performances and the ready encouragement of the kindly Spaun, he withdrew into himself again, lonely and unhappy. Spaun, who recorded that he saw little of the boy at this time, referred to one chance meeting at which Schubert whispered to him: 'You are my favourite in the whole Seminary, the only friend I have there.'[20] Later in the year and shortly before Spaun, having completed his university studies in early September, left the Stadtkonvikt for good, Schubert told him: 'You lucky thing! you are about to escape from this prison. I am so sorry you are leaving.'[21] These remarks, however ill remembered in detail by Spaun fifty years after the event, imply that Schubert was a sad and homesick child during this first year. In practical terms, his social inferiority and superior musical talents may have set him apart and made it difficult for him at first to make contact with his peers. On the other hand, his school reports suggest that he was earnest and hard-working, his scholastic achievements well up to standard; and he was picked out for special mention in official letters and records concerning the Court chapel choristers as deserving particular commendation for his 'exemplary application to the art of music'.[22] It is also worthy of note that official records observed with appreciation the exceptional zeal of Ruzicka, the music tutor, 'even in the last disturbed six months' continuing to give choristers 'extra lessons in the various branches of music, for their better advancement',[23] and, no doubt, for any pupils with enthusiasms in any way comparable with Schubert's, for their delectation. Judging from Schubert's 'exemplary application' and progress, it is not possible that he should have suffered unmitigated unhappiness during the first year away from home, or that his unhappiness in any way amounted to pathological distress. More likely, he was at this time something of a loner, not making friends easily but finding sufficient satisfaction for his emotional needs in music.

After the departure of Napoleon and slow return to normality in Vienna, Schubert's life in music rather than in social communication was remembered by another of his fellow students at the Stadtkonvikt, Georg Franz

---

[20] *Mem.* 127, *Erin.* 148.   [21] Ibid.   [22] *Doc.* 15, *Dok.* 12.   [23] *Doc.* 14, *Dok.* 12.

Eckel. He wrote in 1858: Even on the walks which the pupils took together, he mostly walked apart, pacing along pensively with eyes down and with his hands behind his back, playing with his fingers (as though on keys), completely lost in his own thoughts.'[24] It is possible that during the next year or two Schubert's total commitment to music—that of a creative genius in the making, if not of a child prodigy—isolated him from boys of his own age. On the other hand, his father wrote in 1829, shortly after his son's death, that Schubert as a small schoolboy at his own Himmel-pfortgrund school 'loved society' and 'was never happier than when he could spend his leisure hours in the company of lively friends'.[25] Certainly the two pictures of the young Schubert, by Eckel and by his father, are contradictory; and yet, while written several years apart, they suggest a dichotomy in Schubert's nature, which became increasingly apparent as he grew older.

At the same time as Schubert received his special commendation for his musical application at the end of his first year at the Stadtkonvikt, another chorister, Johann Baptist Wisgrill (b. 1795) was commended for 'good progress in his studies'.[26] (Did Wisgrill, a chorister from 1808 to 1811, remember this linking of his name with that of Schubert when, in November 1828, now an eminent doctor, he was called to attend the composer on his deathbed?)[27] In contrast, Franz Müllner and Maximilian (Max) Weisse, who joined the choir at the same time as Schubert and Wisgrill, were 'to be seriously enjoined to earn our satisfaction by greater industry'.[28]

When Schubert returned to school for his second academic year in November 1809, he knew that Spaun would no longer be there. However, the French had left Vienna, Emperor Franz had returned to the Imperial Palace, the chapel choir was again needed, and the daily orchestral rehearsals at the Stadtkonvikt were soon to be revived. Schubert was now a year older, and he was better able to cope with the daily routine of choir, school, and the Stadtkonvikt. Over the next two years his academic work more than satisfied his teachers, while in the choir and in his private musical studies he was excelling. Thus in September 1810 a note was sent to the Imperial Court Music Count (k.k. Hofmusikgraf) Kuefstein, suggesting that 'especial care should be given to the musical education of Franz Schubert, since he shows so excellent a talent for the art of music'.[29] When Josef von Spaun returned to Vienna from his home town of Linz at the end of March 1811 to take up a government appointment in the capital, he found Schubert, now just 14 years old, well settled: 'grown up and in good

---

[24] *Mem.* 50, *Erin.* 59. [25] *Mem.* 212, *Erin.* 244. [26] *Doc.* 15, *Dok.* 12.
[27] *Doc.* 821, *Dok.* 547. [28] *Doc.* 15, *Dok.* 12–13. [29] *Doc.* 18, *Dok.* 15.

spirits'.[30] His school work in this his third year was still well up to standard, his conduct 'very good', and his musical progress remained excellent. In September 1811, for the third successive year, Schubert received official commendations for his musical attainments, in addition, that is, to the comment in his September musical report: 'Fiddles, and plays difficult pieces at sight'.[31] He was already an impressive leading solo treble in the chapel choir, and he frequently directed the Stadtkonvikt orchestra from his position as leading first violin when Ruzicka was absent.[32] He was also beginning to acquire some reputation in the Stadtkonvikt for his compositions. Only one completed work from 1810 has survived: his Fantasia in G for piano duet D1, written between 8 April and 1 May. This is a long, rambling piece owing much to the orchestral music, and in structure to the ballads of Zumsteeg, with which he was then familiar. The duet was described by his brother Ferdinand in a notice for the Leipzig *Neue Zeitschrift für Musik*: '[there are] more than twelve different movements, and indeed each with a character of its own: it consists of 32 very closely written pages'.[33] Schubert's first surviving song, 'Hagars Klage' (Hagar's lament) D5, a dramatic piece 370 bars long, closely modelled on Zumsteeg's setting of the same text (by Schücking), dates from March 1811. An Overture for String Quartet D8A, dedicated to his brother Ferdinand, and another piano duet Fantasia in G minor D9, both completed in 1811, have also survived. Interestingly, none of these early compositions, written when he was 13 or 14 years old, indicate the prodigious talent for composition of a Mozart, Rossini, Mendelssohn, or of the many other composers who wrote music of appreciably superior quality to that of Schubert at the same age, even if they had far more rigorous and distinguished instruction than the so far almost self-taught Schubert had received.

Through Stadtkonvikt orchestral rehearsals, Schubert was now becoming intimately acquainted with orchestral music of Haydn, Mozart, and Beethoven, which he particularly admired. Mozart's Symphony No. 40 in G minor, and Beethoven's overtures and Symphony No. 2 in D were his especial favourites at this time. He also experienced the music of many lesser composers such as Cherubini, Kozeluch, Méhul, and Weigl, and the compositions of the Abbé Vogler and Krommer (for the latter's music he was far from enthusiastic[34]). At other times, groups of the students met to sing through part-songs, ballads (of Zumsteeg, for example), and *Lieder*, or to play duets or chamber music. For Schubert, accustomed during vacations and on his fortnightly visits home to playing viola in the family quartet (with his father playing cello, and brothers Ferdinand and Ignaz the

---

[30] *Mem.* 127, *Erin.* 148.   [31] *Doc.* 21, *Dok.* 17.   [32] *Doc.* 853.
[33] *Mem.* 36, *Erin.* 46.   [34] *Mem.* 126, *Erin.* 147–8.

violins), and performing part-songs with his brothers, this was already a familiar musical environment.

In 1811 Schubert's contact with Spaun was largely confined to the latter's visits to the Stadtkonvikt outside his professional working hours. Spaun now renewed his support and encouragement for his young friend. His return to Vienna had coincided with the announcement of the bankruptcy of the Austrian state—the result of the cripplingly expensive wars against France—and the introduction of a new emergency currency, the Wiener Währung (WW).[35] Although as a junior civil servant his pay was low, he was willing to share what little he had with the 14-year-old Schubert, both by supplying him with manuscript paper for his compositions and by paying for occasional visits to the theatre for performances of operas. At the Court Opera House, the Kärntnertor-Theater, they sat together 'in the fifth gallery'[36] in cheap seats, which were all that Spaun could afford. Because boys at the Stadtkonvikt were not permitted to leave the educational premises during term-time except for fortnightly day visits home and in special circumstances, each of these visits to the theatre had to be fitted into school (and choir) holiday periods.

The first operas that Schubert saw were probably *Das Waisenhaus* (The Orphanage) and *Die Schweizerfamilie* (The Swiss Family).[37] Both were idyllic pastoral singspiels (with spoken dialogue) with music by Josef Weigl (1766–1846), who had been musical director at the Court Opera House since 1805. Weigl, as a young *répétiteur* and assistant conductor, had worked under Mozart during the preparation of the Viennese premières of both *Le nozze di Figaro* and *Don Giovanni*, and his own music, at its best, shows the influence of Mozart, especially in the extended finales and ensembles. From this period of theatre visits in the company of Spaun sprang Schubert's first enthusiasm for opera and his high regard for, and interest in, certain singers whose performances had particularly impressed him.

In his fourth year at the Stadtkonvikt, from November 1811, Schubert's attitudes began to change, and there were indications of the direction in which he was soon to move. The effects of the collapse of the Austrian economy early in 1811 were many and diverse. One by-product may have been the emperor's permission for his boy choristers of the Court chapel to take part in two charity performances outside the Imperial Palace precincts, totally contrary to former policy and practice. The first concert, on Sunday, 15 December 1811, was held in the university hall, directly opposite the Stadtkonvikt building, and was intended to raise money for a memorial

---

[35] See Note on Austrian Currency, p. xv above.   [36] *Mem.* 129, *Erin.* 150.
[37] Spaun: *Mem.* 21, *Erin.* 28.

monument to the Austrian poet and dramatist Heinrich von Collin (1772–1811).[38] Collin was author of the tragedy *Coriolan*, for a revival of which, in 1807, Beethoven had composed his overture of that name. The first concert was instigated by the recently appointed 'curator' of both the Stadtkonvikt and the Löwenbergkonvikt, Count Josef Karl Dietrichstein, not to be confused with the Count Moritz Dietrichstein. The programme of this special event, known as the 'Collin-Feier' (Collin celebration), included four choruses from the poet's tragedy *Polyxena*, set to music by the Abbé Stadler. The first concert may have had some special personal significance for Schubert, as von Collin was a cousin of his friend Spaun. The same choral works were repeated in the second charity concert on 24 December, in the Burg-Theater, on this occasion in aid of a new hospital in Baden, the spa town south of the city. The conductor at each performance was the choristers' singing-master, Philipp Korner, who was also a tenor in the Court chapel choir, but certainly no favourite with his pupils. Anton Holzapfel, a good friend of Schubert's, described Korner as 'a lean, desiccated figure with a long thin pigtail, who often kept the children in order during singing classes and rehearsals by hitting us and pulling our ears'.[39]

Probably during the same final month of 1811, shortly before his fifteenth birthday and some weeks or months after he had been introduced to live opera by Spaun, Schubert began to compose his own first opera, of which he never got beyond the first act. For a libretto he chose a three-act magic play *Der Spiegelritter* (The Looking-Glass Knight) by the controversial German dramatist August von Kotzebue (1761–1819), some of whose 200 or so works for the theatre were extremely popular in Vienna during the first decades of the nineteenth century. Schubert was to select another of Kotzebue's magic plays, *Des Teufels Lustschloss* (The Devil's Pleasure Castle) for his second operatic effort in the autumn of 1813. Spaun may have supplied Schubert with the texts of these plays, for the limited nature of the Stadtkonvikt library makes it unlikely that these comedies were included in its collection. Kotzebue's irony and parody of Romantic ideas in both plays were completely lost on the teenage composer, whose narrow education in German literature at the Academic Grammar-School had ill prepared him for an understanding of contemporary literature.[40]

In this, Schubert's last year of the four grammar, or Latin, classes, Greek replaced natural history and physics in the school curriculum. There is still no mention at all in his school reports of any German studies. However, in recent years, research into school curricula of the day has shown that some

[38] *Doc.* 21n, *Dok.* 18n.   [39] *Mem.* 63, *Erin.* 73–4.

[40] D. Gramit, *The Intellectual and Aesthetic Tenets of Franz Schubert's Circle* (UMI, Mich., 1989), 26.

German studies, under various guises, were included, although the system of rules governing instruction was inflexible, and far outmoded even by the standards of that time.[41] The state-authorized instruction books used between 1779 and 1848 as the basis for teaching rhetoric and poetics (*Institutio ad eloquentiam*—a school reader) incorporated strict and unchanging precepts for language and grammar. This standard selection of German texts included excerpts, fables, and poetry. In the 1812 edition the selection was still weighted towards the literature of the Enlightenment, especially the works of Lessing and Klopstock, and of the now largely forgotten fable-writer Pfeffel,[42] while examples of *Sturm und Drang* and the Romantic movement were not included. Kotzebue's popular plays certainly did not fit into this educational scene.

The intermittent attention which Schubert gave to *Der Spiegelritter* (D11) in short bursts of activity over a period of fourteen or fifteen months in 1811–12 may well be explained by three factors which surely affected his life in 1812: the death of his mother; starting his studies with Salieri; and his voice breaking. On 28 May his mother, much beloved by himself and the family, died rather suddenly at the age of 55.[43] The *Nervenfieber* (nervous fever) given as the cause of death in the Lichtental church register of deaths (and later also as the cause of the death of Schubert himself) was a diagnosis common for any illness with deliriousness and fever, and was probably typhoid fever. Schubert may not have visited her on her deathbed, but it can probably be assumed that he attended her funeral two days later and mourned her passing, along with his father, brothers, and sisters, his mother's sister Maria Magdalena (widow of Schubert's uncle, Karl) and her daughter Magdalena, who had remained in the family home in the Säulengasse. Of the composer's brothers, Ignaz was still his father's assistant in the Himmelpfortgrund school; Ferdinand was in his third year as an assistant elementary schoolteacher at the city orphanage, while Karl was an art student at the Academy of Fine Arts in Vienna and presumably still living at home. There is no evidence to support a theory occasionally voiced, and based on an allegorical tale that Schubert wrote down in July 1822, that he had quarrelled with his father before his mother's death and that they were reconciled at the funeral. There is every reason to believe that up to this point relationships with his father were good, and that he was confident and secure at school, behaving and conforming well. This situation was to continue for yet a little while longer. The distress and shock caused by his mother's death, however, left scars; and he may have suffered the regrets or bad conscience common to many an adolescent who loses a parent, wishing

[41] Ibid. 27. [42] I. Dürhammer, 'Zu Schuberts Literaturästhetik', *Brille*, 14 (1995), 16.
[43] *Doc.* 23, *Dok.* 19.

that their last communication, or indeed their relationship, had been happier or other than it was.

A week or two after his mother's death, Schubert was informed that he was to start private studies in music theory and composition with the illustrious Court Kapellmeister, Anton Salieri.[44] The timing was opportune. Not only was he grieving for his mother, but he was also only too aware that his voice was on the point of breaking; and for this reason he was now singing alto in the chapel choir. Salieri's attentions and the excitement they occasioned must have concentrated the boy's mind, if that was necessary, on his musical studies. In order to attend Salieri's lessons at his home in the Seilerstätte, Schubert was granted special permission from the directorate of the Stadtkonvikt to leave the establishment twice a week: a 'special favour . . . an exception to the strict school rules', in the words of Eckel.[45] Under the guidance and instruction of Salieri, Schubert's talents were quick to ripen, and over an interval of only a few months there was considerable change and progress in his compositional technique. At first Salieri insisted on his young pupil completing didactic exercises in counterpoint and fugue and the setting of Italian texts to music. Some of these exercises, complete with Salieri's corrections, have survived. For a short while, during which time Schubert followed his teacher's directions with great thoroughness, Schubert seems to have found little opportunity to compose freely for his own satisfaction. Maybe Salieri forbade him even to try. But by early autumn and before the new school year began in November, he was composing probably more than ever before. Works from this period include renewed attempts at his ambitious *Spiegelritter* opera, 12 Minuets and Trios for Piano (D22), which were especially admired by his friends but are now sadly lost,[46] the String Quartet D32, the orchestral Overture D26, the Salve Regina D27, the one-movement Piano Trio in B flat D28, the Kyrie D31, and some songs.

One reason for this remarkable productivity during the late summer and early autumn was the end of his career as a boy chorister in the Court chapel. On 26 July Schubert wrote into the third of the chapel's alto scores of Peter Winter's Mass No. 1 in C: 'Schubert, Franz, crowed for the last time, 26 July 1812.'[47] From now on he attended neither rehearsals nor performances (services) in the chapel; and as a result, he found himself with considerably more free time for composing. Whether he was still eligible, after the end of the school year in October, for further free tuition in piano and violin is doubtful; and reports of his musical progress ceased after September 1812.

---

[44] *Doc.* 24, *Dok.* 20.   [45] *Mem.* 50–1, *Erin.* 59.
[46] *Mem.* 128, *Erin.* 149–50.   [47] *Doc.* 26, *Dok.* 21.

Schubert's academic work at this time was still well up to standard. His 'moral conduct', however, had declined to a mere 'good' rather than the until now customary 'very good' or even '1 em[inent]', which suggests that he was becoming less amenable to school discipline, and showing signs of adolescent questioning of authority. He had arrived at the Stadtkonvikt a strictly brought up, shy boy who was ready and content to conform to the patterns of behaviour expected of him. After four years at the school, he was now developing a mind and will of his own, ready to oppose restrictions he considered to be obstructing his musical development, whether these were applied by his school or by the Stadtkonvikt, by his father or the church. His next, and final year at the Stadtkonvikt was to see further growth and change, with self-assurance and independence of spirit. The considerable impression he had made as a leading treble in the chapel choir, and the authority with which he both led and directed the Stadtkonvikt orchestra, sometimes in trial performances of his own music, helped to increase his confidence in his abilities. With this confidence came a social self-assurance which contributed to an improvement in his relationships with his peers, some of whom remembered him in later years in a markedly more relaxed and jovial light than those who knew him only in his early years at the school. In this context it is worth looking at a humorous letter he wrote only a few weeks after the start of his fifth and final year at the Stadtkonvikt. This was sent to one of his working brothers, either Ignaz or Ferdinand, but probably the latter. In it he begged for a little extra pocket-money:

I have long been thinking about my situation and have concluded that, although it is satisfactory on the whole, it is not beyond some improvement here and there. You know from experience that we all like to eat a roll or a few apples sometimes, the more so if after a middling lunch we have eight-and-a-half hours to wait for a mediocre evening meal. This wish, which has often become insistent, is now becoming more and more frequent, and I had willy-nilly to make a change. The few Groschen [pennies] I get from Father go to the deuce the very first days, and what am I to do for the rest of the time? 'Whosoever believeth on Him shall not be put to shame.' Matthew, iii.4. I thought so too.—How if you were to let me have a few Kreuzer [shillings] a month? You would never miss it, while I in my cell should think myself lucky, and be content. I repeat, I take my stand upon the words of the Apostle Matthew: 'He that hath two coats, let him give one to the poor,' etc. Meanwhile I hope that you will give ear to the voice which calls unceasingly to you, the voice of—

> Your
> loving, poor, hopeful
> and again poor brother
> Franz[48]

[48] *Doc.* 28, *Dok.* 22–3.

The irony and obviously intentional biblical misquotations are typical of a bright 15-year-old schoolboy with a healthy appetite, trying to keep body and soul together on somewhat poor-quality and infrequent food at a time of severe and widespread economic deprivation in Vienna. He was suffering adolescent hunger pangs that no amount of musical excitement could cause him to forget.

Having earned one further year's study and residence at the Stadt-konvikt through his satisfactory work over four years as a chorister, Schubert had entered his fifth year at the Gymnasium, moving from the junior grammar classes into the first of the more senior humanities classes. From this time onwards the only musical instruction he was receiving may have been his twice-weekly sessions with Salieri, who now put him to the study of scores of the great operas, notably the classical operas of Gluck, but also his own *Azur, ré d' Ormus* and *Les Danaïdes*, and probably those of Mozart. All the scores were lent to Schubert by his teacher. Also during this period his visits to the opera with Spaun continued, and by the end of 1812 he had experienced some six operas, including the two Weigl singspiels already mentioned, Mozart's *Zauberflöte*, Cherubini's *Medea*, Boïeldieu's *Jean de Paris*, and Isouard's *Cendrillon*.

A highlight of this academic year was undoubtedly a performance of Gluck's *Iphigenia in Tauris* at the Kärntnertor-Theater in January 1813,[49] which he saw with Spaun, and which made an enormous impression on him. Spaun recorded his own memories of the occasion (in 1858): 'He [Schubert] was totally beside himself over the effect of this magnificent music and asserted that there could be nothing more beautiful in the world.'[50] He praised the performances of Anna Milder (later Milder-Hauptmann) as Iphigenia and of Johann Michael Vogl as Orestes, both of whom he was to meet and, in the case of Vogl, work with some years later. The memorableness of the evening both for Spaun and Schubert was further heightened by their being able to share their enthusiasm with the young poet Theodor Körner, a friend of Spaun's whom they met by chance as they left the theatre. Körner invited them to join him for supper at a nearby inn, and here their praise for the opera and its performance continued unabated until an older man, supposedly a university professor, sitting at the next table began cynically to mock their ardour. At this Schubert and Körner leapt to their feet in a rage, Schubert knocking over a full glass

---

[49] *Iphigenia in Tauris* was performed at this theatre on 5 and 23 Jan. 1813: P. Branscombe, 'Schubert and the Melodrama', in E. Badura-Skoda and P. Branscombe (eds.), *Schubert Studies: Problems of Style and Chronology* (Cambridge, 1982), 110.

[50] *Mem.* 129, *Erin.* 150–1.

of beer in the process. After a violent exchange of words, and with Schubert ablaze with anger, the event would have come to blows had it not been for 'some calming voices, which came in on our side'.[51] Schubert had found a soulmate in Körner.

In a quieter period of the same evening Körner, himself a convinced idealist, clearly impressed by Schubert's talents and commitment to music, gave him the advice he most wanted to hear: he must 'live only for Art'; only in music would he find true happiness and fulfilment.[52] At a time when the voices of authority were opposing this view, Schubert was waiting to hear just such words of encouragement for the life of a composer on which he had already decided. Sadly, this was his only meeting with Körner: the poet was killed a few months later (in August) at the age of 22 on the battlefield of Gadesbusch in north Germany, while fighting with the Lützow volunteers. After his death he became a cult hero in German-speaking nations, inspiring patriotism with his posthumously published (1814) collection of poems *Leyer und Schwert* (Lyre and Sword). In 1815 Schubert, who never forgot his friend of that January evening two years before, was to compose his one-act singspiel *Der vierjährige Posten* (The Four-year Sentry Duty) and thirteen of his fourteen songs to Körner's texts. Schubert now 'felt keenly that he was destined to live for art and that through this alone could he achieve happiness';[53] as a result of this, his attitude to academic studies and school authority underwent a decisive turn for the worse. Spaun described how Schubert lost all interest in school work: he stopped listening to the lectures on Latin and Greek[54] and he was sometimes caught composing when he should have been working on school preparation. In the light of his new determination to dedicate his life to music, it can be no coincidence that the early months of 1813 (especially March and April) saw a considerable outpouring of Schubert's compositions. These included the two string quartets, D36 and D46 (the first begun on 19 November of the previous year), two solo and six part-songs (all except one settings of texts from Schiller's *Elysium* or *Der Triumph der Liebe*), two kyries, D45 and D49, and the beginning of the piano duet, Fantasia in C minor D48, a long piece which he completed in mid-June.

Schubert's father was almost certainly informed of his son's neglect of his academic studies and 'time-wasting' on composition. Not for the first time, he found it necessary to speak firmly to his son. On this occasion, however, Schubert may have escaped lightly, as his father had other

[51] Spaun: *Mem.* 129, *Erin.* 151.
[52] *Doc.* 32–3, *Dok.* 26; *Mem.* 129, *Erin.* 151.
[53] Spaun: *Mem.* 19, *Erin.* 25–6.
[54] *Mem.* 19, *Erin.* 26.

matters on his mind. He was contemplating remarriage. On 25 April, eleven months after the death of his first wife, Franz Theodor married Anna Kleyenböck.[55] This was, for him, a good marriage. His bride was 30 years old, twenty years his junior, and the daughter of a silk manufacturer from the Gumpendorf suburb south-west of Vienna. The marriage service was conducted by one of her cousins, a priest who remained in contact with the family even after his move a few years later to Hungary. Tradition has it that Anna was good to her stepchildren, as well as to the four children she herself bore. (A fifth, a son, died in his first year.) Schubert's references to his stepmother in letters home are always couched in affectionate and appreciative terms.

In May, as in the previous month, Schubert was mainly occupied with setting words to music, and in particular with writing trios for two tenors and bass to words by Schiller. A four-verse poem of his own, 'Die Zeit' (Time), the first of his several surviving 'literary' efforts, also dates from this month. Here, in a style which owes much to the poet Klopstock, Schubert expressed views on the transience of time and its importance to man and music. At this period of his life the 16-year-old composer was attracting the attention of some of the older students at the Stadtkonvikt, on account not only of his rare musical talents but also of some of his literary perceptions. Amongst these students was Anton Holzapfel, who kept a copy of 'Die Zeit'. In his reminiscences of the composer, written in 1858, Holzapfel referred to another longer poem of Schubert's written during his last year at school, which seems to have made a considerable impression on the older students who recognized his abilities as

far in advance of his years; this was proved by a long poem of his, dating from that time, which I kept but which has since been lost, written in the enthusiastic style of Klopstock's odes, a style hardly understood by us [older] pupils, and on something like the theme of God's omnipotence in the creation . . . it made all the more impression on me . . . [as in the junior classes they barely heard of poetry.[56]

Whether Holzapfel's memory more than fifty years after the event was accurate in detail or no, his comments underline three things that were surely true about Schubert during his last year or so at the Konvikt. First, he showed uncommon interest in and love for poetry and, considering his age, surprising sensitivity to it. (Salieri's negative attitude towards the German *Lied* was presumably the reason why Schubert left only a half-

---

[55] *Doc. 30, Dok. 24.*   [56] *Mem. 57, Erin. 67.*

dozen or so completed settings of texts by German poets for solo voice and piano dating from 1813.) Secondly, his intellectual concerns and abilities, which did not necessarily have much in common with the arid academic training he was receiving at the Academic Grammar-School, were greatly in advance of his age-group. Thirdly, older Stadtkonvikt students were becoming interested in Schubert for his intellectual companionship. The social and cultural backgrounds of most of these young men, many of whom had been educated at the Kremsmünster seminary where they had also known Spaun and his brothers, were very different from Schubert's own. Although their influence on him was to increase appreciably in the years after Schubert had left the Stadtkonvikt, already in his schooldays they fired his intellect, not least in lively discussions about poetry; and from thenceforth they were always on the look-out for texts, either by known poets or written by themselves, suitable for him to set to music.

During the summer months of 1813 Schubert was again busy composing. The string quartets in B flat and in D, D68 and D74, a further bunch of vocal trios for male voices, and the early Octet in F for wind instruments (D72) all date from this period. At the same time, he was composing exercises for Salieri. Although prospects for his future at the school and Stadtkonvikt were promising, and negotiations were well in hand for his being offered a further scholarship (an endowment) to continue his studies, his own thoughts were working in a different direction, along the lines earlier encouraged by Theodor Körner. A disturbing occurrence of a political nature in the Stadtkonvikt during this summer is likely to have intensified his longing to be free of the establishment's restrictions. One of the older students at the Academic Grammar-School, Johann Bacher, who was in his final year (the second 'Philosophie' class) is thought to have been secretly imprisoned for unspecified trouble-making of a political nature. Angry at this, some of his comrades at the school sought his release and staged a revolt over the injustice meted out to their friend. Amongst them were two of Schubert's older friends who lived at the Stadtkonvikt, Michael von Rueskäfer (1794–1872) and Johann Christoph Senn (1785–1857). Another student, Josef Kenner, wrote (in 1858) that Rueskäfer left the Stadtkonvikt voluntarily at this time while Senn, who was dependent on a scholarship for his studies in Vienna, lost his foundation award because he refused on principle to accept that the punishment was just.[57] After this, Senn became a prime suspect in any student unrest. Indeed, in 1820 Schubert was with him when he was arrested for subversive activities by Chancellor Metternich's

---

[57] *Mem.* 88–9, *Erin.* 103.

police officers. Senn was then imprisoned for more than a year before he was permanently exiled from Vienna, with disastrous results for any career prospects he may have had.

The affair over Bacher may well have provoked Schubert to anger, intensified his sensitivity to injustice, and increased his frustration with the restrictions of the Stadtkonvikt. At only 16, he did not play an active role in the revolt of the older students. This is borne out by the fact that in the following October he was offered another scholarship: had he recently been guilty of disruptive behaviour or had there been suggestions that he presented any threat to the smooth running of the school, this would have surely occasioned the removal of his name from the list of prospective candidates. Such awards were dependent on the exemplary moral behaviour of the recipients.

The school year ended without any confirmation of endowment awards to the ex-choristers. Schubert's school report for the year shows that in the first term his Latin was below standard (2–1); but this he succeeded in bringing back to the necessary first grade by the end of the second term. On the other hand, his mathematics grade fell to a failure level, grade 2, in the second term. The offer of an award would therefore come with the proviso that he must work at mathematics during the coming vacation, and then retake and pass another examination in the subject on his return to the school at the beginning of the next term. Thereafter he should maintain a first-grade standard. Johann Nestroy, the future dramatist, was another student among several in Schubert's class whose mathematics was sub-standard in the same term. For their failure, the students blamed their teacher, the ever unpopular Prefect Walch, who had so nearly fallen victim to Napoleon's howitzer shell. Schubert must have returned home in the autumn of 1813 with some foreboding at the prospect of presenting his father with his decision. He was determined to quit the Stadtkonvikt, to abandon further school education, and thus to avoid the waste of valuable time, as he saw it, in working at mathematics and other subjects with no relevance to his musical development. There is also a possibility that he was losing patience with the standard of musical activities at the Stadtkonvikt. He was now by far the most accomplished musician there, and needed new musical challenges and stimuli, perhaps in the circle of Salieri's pupils.

On 4 October the Schubert family celebrated the name-day of both Schubert and his father, an occasion for which young Schubert supplied both words and music of a 'Cantata for my Father's Name Day' D80. Schubert performed the cantata, a musical eulogy to a 'beloved Father' wishing him a long and happy life, written for two tenors and one bass and guitar accompaniment, with his brothers.[58] Before this family celebration, Schubert may not have dared to broach with his father the subject of his withdrawal from his school. Certainly members of the Imperial Court Education Commission (k.k. Studien-Hofkommission) were unaware of his intention to leave. On 22 October it was announced that he was to be awarded a Meerfeld Endowment. The other three former choristers eligible for awards were now academically better qualified than Schubert, and they received rather more generous Windhag Endowments. Schubert's award, as expected, was subject to the specific condition that he work harder and behave well: he must 'raise himself above the second grade'. The comment was also made that 'singing and music are but a subsidiary matter . . . good morals and diligence in study are of prime importance and an indispensable duty for all those who wish to enjoy the advantages of an Endowment'.[59] Schubert's concept of 'duty' and matters 'of prime importance' did not concur with that of the educational establishment. Towards the end of the school vacation, and probably in early November, it was finally agreed with his father that he should leave school.[60] But there was a condition on which his father insisted and which his brother Ferdinand, perhaps mediating in the heated arguments about Schubert's future, supported. For reasons of financial security in difficult times, and as a possible insurance against military conscription, Schubert must train as an assistant elementary schoolteacher, as had his uncle Karl, his father, and his older brothers, Ignaz and Ferdinand, before him. With this agreed, letters went to the school authorities and to the college which Schubert was to enter within the next week or two: the Imperial Normalhauptschule (teachers' training college), from where Ferdinand had graduated two or three years earlier.

On 28 October 1813 Schubert completed his Symphony No. 1 in D D82, originally intended for performance by the Stadtkonvikt orchestra. Two days later, on 30 October, he began work on his second opera (with text by Kotzebue) *Des Teufels Lustschloss*, on which he was to work under the guidance of Salieri over a period of some twelve months, producing two complete versions of the full three-act singspiel. He also worked on several string quartets.

Schubert had entered the Stadtkonvikt towards the end of 1808 a small, reserved 11-year-old with exceptional musical talents, according to Spaun, a remarkable memory, and passionate involvement with music. At first he did not make friends easily with his peers. Later he joined in with their

[58] *Doc.* 38, *Dok.* 30.   [59] *Doc.* 37, *Dok.* 29.
[60] Kreissle gives the date as between 26 Oct. and 6 Nov.: H. Kreissle von Hellborn, *Franz Schubert*, trans. A. D. Coleridge, 2 vols. (London, 1869), i. 34.

activities and conversations, even though none became a long-term friend. As far as is known, after leaving the Stadtkonvikt he remained in touch, though not closely, with only a few of those in his own age-group, such as the former alto Max Weisse[61] and Josef Streinsberg.[62] (Both Weisse and Streinsberg remained at school after Schubert moved to the teachers' training college.) His time and his mind were so deeply engrossed with music that he may have felt little need, and found few opportunities to cultivate, their friendship. He was already showing both enormous powers of concentration and a propensity for the aloneness which mark the lives of many creative artists, the need sometimes for isolation which is frequently an important element in the creative personality.

At first Schubert's closer relationships with older (mostly university) students with mature musical talents were of a different kind, the result of shared musical experiences. Only later did they grow on an intellectual and emotional plane. His considerable musical attainments and responsibilities, first as leading treble in the Court chapel choir, later as student musical director of the Stadtkonvikt orchestra and composer of some of the music it played, enhanced his self-confidence and his status amongst them. As he became more confident, he began to enjoy their company rather than just their musical talents, and he was stimulated intellectually to embrace their wider interests outside music: poetry, art, politics, and philosophy. As he enjoyed the young men's company so a new sociable dimension to his personality was awakened: the affable, convivial Schubert. This sociability, combined with innate sensitivity and a burgeoning sensuality at first restrained, but often sublimated in his music, appealed to the older companions. Several of these were to have an enormous influence on Schubert's life, both professional and private.

[61] *Doc.* 100–1, *Dok.* 67; *Mem.* 171, *Erin.* 199–200.
[62] *Doc.* 36, 128–9, *Dok.* 28, 88–9; *Mem.* 167, *Erin.* 195.

3

STUDENT AND SCHOOLTEACHER
(1814–1816)

'Today I composed for money for the very first time.'

FOR a full three years from the autumn of 1813, Schubert lived at home with his parents and aunt Magdalena in the Säulengasse schoolhouse. He entered the Imperial teachers' training college as a 'secular' (*weltlicher*) student in November, almost three months before his seventeenth birthday. Here, and in a model school incorporated into the college, the students were trained over a ten-month period to be assistant elementary schoolteachers. They studied basic educational subjects and teaching methods. Schubert tolerated the course and worked sufficiently hard to pass his final examination on 19 August 1814 with comparative ease, and to be described as 'industrious' (*fleissig*) in his practical work.[1] His best subjects, or those that came most easily to him, were German language, grammar, and spelling, and also handwriting. In the light of his future rather well written descriptive letters to family and friends, his literary attempts at prose and poetry, and his neat manuscripts, his marked facility for these subjects might be expected. His worst report was for 'religion', for which he received his only 'bad' (*schlecht*); but as he was a secular candidate this did not affect his overall success in the examination. While studying at the college, Schubert travelled in from the Himmelpfortgrund to the Annagasse in the inner city six days a week, often walking with his brother Karl, who was then studying at the Academy of Fine Arts housed in the same building as the training college, which was a former Jesuit monastery associated with the church of St Anna.[2]

If Schubert made new friends at the college, not one name of any particular companion amongst his fellow students there has been recorded as such. In his student life it is likely that he was enjoying new freedoms, both with his own friends and with his brother Karl and Karl's fellow art

---

[1] *Doc. 43, Dok. 34.*   [2] *Doc. 62, Dok. 44.*

students. Karl had entered the academy to study landscape painting two
years previously, in November 1811, just after his sixteenth birthday. Over
several years of full- and latterly part-time study there, he followed a broad
course covering various disciplines of the fine arts.[3] From 1813 to 1814,
while his brother was at the training college, these included copper-engrav-
ing as well as drawing and painting; and at the end of that year he was
awarded, according to his father (who was not averse to a little exaggera-
tion if it suited his interests), the first prize for figure-drawing.[4] Among
Karl's friends and associates was the very talented art student Leopold
Kupelwieser (1796–1862), who had been accepted as a student at the academy at the age of 13 in 1809. Early in 1813, Leopold's father having died, he
moved in with his brother Josef, who was four years his senior and was
employed in a low-paid position in the theatre. (Josef was to provide
Schubert in 1823 with the text for his last completed opera, *Fierrabras*.) As
Josef was unable to support his younger brother financially, Leopold had to
learn quickly how to earn money, both by painting the then very popular
lacquered beakers (*Blechtassen*) and, increasingly, portraits. Leopold, a
good-looking young man with a kindly disposition who made friends easily, was soon introduced by Karl to his younger brother Franz. An unsigned
crayon portrait, supposedly the work of Kupelwieser, of an attractive-look-
ing boyish student of some 16 years, now in the Liechtenstein Gallery in
Vaduz, and from 1891 in the possession of the family of Prince
Liechtenstein, may well be of Schubert. It is likely that the portrait was
acquired by Prince Liechtenstein, who owned a large baroque palace and
park not far from the Lichtental church, from the Schubert family, members of which authenticated the portrait on the reverse side as being of the
composer and by Kupelwieser. The authentication was by Schubert's two
half-brothers. As they were mere toddlers when the composer died, it may
perhaps be assumed that information concerning the portrait was passed on
to them by older members of the family. The signatures themselves, however, are authentic.[5] If this sympathetic portrait is of Schubert, it would
suggest that a friendship between Schubert and Kupelwieser began during

----

[3] I am grateful to Frau Dr Draxler of the archive dept. of the Academy of Fine Arts in Vienna for
information relating to Karl's studies there.

[4] *Doc.* 48–9, *Dok.* 36–7.

[5] I have come to this conclusion after comparing them with autograph correspondence and
diaries (unpublished) of the half-brothers in the Krasser collection of Schubert manuscripts in the
manuscript collection of the Vienna Stadt- und Landesbibliothek. The younger of the two, Anton
Edward (b. 1826), was known as Father Hermann Schubert. He signed his name in this form on the
back of the portrait in the same roman script which he used in some of his diary entries and letters,
rather than the more usual gothic script. His brother Andreas (b. 1823) signed his name, clearly
identifiable as such from letters (e.g. of 1878) in gothic script.

this period. Within a few years they had certainly become close friends, and were spending much of their free time in each other's company.

During the ten months while Schubert was studying to be a school-teacher, his life outside the college was full and to varying degrees stimulating. He continued with his twice-weekly tuition from Salieri, an important part of which was Salieri's correction of his latest compositions. Notable among these was the three-act opera *Des Teufels Lustchloss*, on two versions of which Schubert worked between 30 October 1813 and 22 October 1814. Salieri also set his students tasks such as contrapuntal exercises and composing to Italian texts, and he supervised their study of musical scores of the old masters, especially Gluck. He regularly gathered his pupils around him in his own home to sing through mostly Italian operas and oratorios; and at these gatherings of his pupils, Schubert made valuable contacts and friends. As he was now living at home, Schubert for a while returned with some enthusiasm to the musical life of the Lichtental church, where Michael Holzer still directed the choir and Schubert's brother Ferdinand was now unpaid organist. According to Ferdinand, Schubert 'was again active in the choir . . . each Sunday and holiday [church festival]'.[6] Recent examination of the archives of the Lichtental church has thrown light on both the music that was performed there at the time Schubert was involved, and the resources available (for example, in festival performances, some thirty singers and a complement of full orchestra). Michael Haydn, Mozart, and Josef Haydn, in that order, seem to have exceeded all others in terms of the number of their works played. Other composers represented were Albrechtsberger (Holzer's teacher), Dittersdorf, Vanhal, and Peter Winter.[7] Schubert himself was to compose a fair number of sacred works over the next three years to add to the existing library of the church.

Schubert's musical activities were not restricted to the home of Salieri and the local church. He also played chamber music with his family and friends. What had begun several years earlier as string quartet evenings with his father and his brothers Ignaz and Ferdinand were expanding steadily into occasions of chamber music for larger ensembles. Friends and acquaintances now swelled the numbers at these rehearsals which took place in one of the larger schoolrooms in the Säulengasse until, that is, there were too many of them for the space available and they were forced to look for larger premises. In addition, Schubert did not lose contact with his old friends at the Stadtkonvikt. Frequently on a Sunday afternoon, having first

[6] *Mem.* 36, *Erin.* 46.
[7] E. Benedikt, 'Schubert und das Kirchenmusik-Repertoire in Lichtental', *Brille*, 12 (1994), 107–11.

taken a musical part in the morning services in the Lichtental church, he would return to his old boarding-school to try out some of his latest compositions on his friends, and to make music with, in particular, Albert Stadler and Anton Holzapfel who, as law students at the university, were still living there.

The first important event of 1814 for the Schubert family was the birth, on 22 January, of her first child to Schubert's stepmother, Maria Barbara Anna, bringing a new baby into the household after an interval of more than twelve years.[8] Three months later there was cause for much general celebration in Vienna and its surroundings, indeed in much of Europe, after allied armies opposing Napoleon's advances across the continent entered Paris on 15 April. Napoleon was forced to surrender, and to abdicate (for the first time), and he was banished to the island of Elba. The people of Vienna, which had been twice occupied by the French, were very ready to celebrate enthusiastically the outbreak of peace. During this time of celebration, an eight-verse poem of lush patriotic fervour celebrating the allies' victory appeared anonymously in the Vienna newspaper *Der Sammler*, entitled 'Die Befreyer Europas in Paris' (The Liberators of Europe in Paris). Schubert set the first verse of the poem to music, completing it on 16 May, and implied by the addition of a *da capo* marking at the end of the composition that this was a strophic setting of the poem (D104). The song was completed (in three different versions on the same sheet), but the poor state of the manuscript suggests Schubert's considerable dissatisfaction with what he had written. He never returned to improve on it because in the mean time he had received an invitation to compose a major work for an important local occasion: a festival mass, which was to be the centrepiece in the centenary jubilee celebrations in the following autumn of the parish church of Lichtental. The very next day, 17 May, he began composing his Mass in F. A few days later, Schubert attended a performance of Beethoven's final version of *Fidelio* at the Kärntnertor-Theater either on 23 May (the première) or soon afterwards. This was musically and politically a great event, arousing intense passions in Viennese members of the audience; for it combined memories of the disastrous first production of the opera's first version in 1805, given before an audience largely made up of French soldiers who were newly occupying the city, with their own current mood of celebration at the recent defeat of Napoleon and the end of French oppression.

On 16 June the Emperor Franz was welcomed back to Vienna with exuberant ceremony, a public holiday, and joyful festivities. Schubert's father

---

[8] *Doc.* 42, *Dok.* 33.

was one of those who openly showed his patriotic fervour with a prominent banner, written in German and proudly displayed outside his house for all to see:

> House of Herr Schubert, Schoolteacher:
>
> O could I, as I would,
> I'd honour, as all should
> The best of emperors, Franz!
> Only candles are burning here
> But sprouting from my heart
> Are sprigs of laurel.[9]

Beneath this verse was a chronogram in Latin, again extolling the virtues of the emperor on his victorious return:

franCIsCO Magno, VICtorI
reDeVntI![10]

The total sum of the large roman numerals appearing in the chronogram is 1814, the current year. Thus Schubert's father, the local schoolmaster, was confirming his unwavering loyalty to the emperor, and expressing his personal joy in an unreserved attempt at noble language and sentiment. At the same time, he was demonstrating his educational prowess to his neighbours with both a Latin inscription and its mathematical connotation. The placard was indicative of his tendency to pomposity and unbridled pride in his own achievements as well as an over-respectful, indeed obsequious, attitude to authority, an aspect of his character which his sons found increasingly difficult to live with.

In September, when Schubert had finished his studies at the training college, he had several weeks free before he began work in his father's school. In the previous month, while taking his final examinations, he did not complete any compositions—at least none have survived with an August date. In September his output was rather small: a couple of songs and also the remarkable String Quartet in B flat D112, completed in little over a week, between 5 and 13 September. (The first movement he completed in four and a half hours.) However, throughout August and September, while still engaged in the final revisions of the opera *Des Teufels Lustschloss*, he was also making the final amendments and preparing the score and parts, orchestral and vocal, of his grand Mass in F D105, on which he lavished enormous care. Finally, after soloists and orchestral players had been appointed, rehearsals for the important event began. Some of the players

---

[9] Ibid.   [10] Ibid.

came from the orchestra which was developing from the original nucleus of the Schubert family quartet, and had now transferred to larger premises in the home of the merchant Franz Frischling, who lived within the city walls in the Dorotheergasse.[11] Schubert's former teacher, Michael Holzer, choral director at the Lichtental church, who was at least partly responsible for the commissioning of this mass, stood down as director on the occasion of its performance in deference to the talents of his former pupil. Schubert directed the rehearsals and then the performance itself—the first public hearing of any of his compositions. The most likely date for this performance of the mass is Friday, 25 September, just a week after the consecration of a new high altar,[12] and the day set apart by the church for its jubilee celebrations, of which the mass was the musical highlight.[13]

The commission to write the mass, although unpaid, was a prestigious one for the 17-year-old composer. That he was not paid can be deduced from an entry in his diary of 17 June 1816, some twenty-one months later: 'Today I composed for money for the first time . . .'.[14] There were thirty-five singers (chorus and six soloists, probably drawn from the choir), strings and wind (including brass) sections of fourteen and thirteen players respectively, drums, and organ. Among the performers was Josef Mayseder (1789–1863), a violinist and composer already renowned in Vienna, and since 1810 leader of the Kärntnertor-Theater orchestra. One of the two soprano soloists was the 16- or 17-year-old Therese Grob, a member of the church choir and a family friend of the Schuberts, with whom the composer may now have been falling in love. The composer's brother Ferdinand was the organist, and it is to him that we owe the information that 'the remaining musicians consisted of none but friends of his [Schubert's] youth or people among whom he had grown up'.[15] From this it may be assumed that Josef von Spaun (violin) and Anton Holzapfel (cello), along with other former students at the Stadtkonvikt, were probably among the orchestral players.

Even today the music of this mass can take the listener by surprise. It is a fine, festive choral work in the classical tradition, in turn both exhilarating and lyrical. Schubert directed with calm authority and efficiency, inspiring a performance which occasioned great enthusiasm amongst both performers and audience. His proud, though certainly not unbiased

---

[11] *Mem.* 339, *Erin.* 391.   [12] *Doc.* 44, *Dok.* 34.

[13] For arguments against Deutsch's date of 16 Oct., see *NGA* editorial by T. B. Berio (*NGA*, ser. 1, vol. i, 1989) and R. Steblin, *Ein unbekanntes frühes Schubert-Porträt?* (Tutzing, 1992), 24–5. A further argument against the later date is the unlikelihood that Schubert would have composed his setting of Schiller's 'Das Mädchen aus der Fremde' (The Maid from afar) D117, dated 16 Oct., on the same day as he directed the mass.

[14] *Doc.* 65, *Dok.* 45.   [15] *Mem.* 36, *Erin.* 46.

brother Ferdinand claimed: 'Even if he'd been Court Musical Director for the last 30 years, he could not have done better.'[16] The Court musical director himself, Antonio Salieri, was indeed in the audience, and deeply moved by the occasion. According to a friend of the family, Josef Doppler, who played in the orchestra, after the performance Salieri embraced Schubert, with the words: 'Franz, you are my pupil, and you are going to bring me much further honour.'[17] Schubert's father glowed with pride at his son's achievement and the attention it attracted, especially amongst the more important dignitaries of church and state attending the celebration, and in his joy, again according to Ferdinand, promised to buy him a piano of his own.

Until this occasion, Schubert's only experience of directing comparatively large-scale works was with the Stadtkonvikt orchestra. In order to take full control and to direct an inspiring performance of this mass to a packed church, including in the audience a number of influential people and aristocrats, Schubert must have possessed considerable musical authority and charisma, despite his personal modesty and reticence. (The mass was probably performed again ten days later in the Court church of St Augustine, but if it was, not by Schubert and his friends.[18])

Schubert began his short career as a schoolteacher during the autumn of 1814, probably early in November. His father put him, as the sixth assistant, in charge of the youngest children in the so-called ABC class.[19] His sister Theresia told Schubert's first biographer, Kreissle, that Franz was strict with the children, ill-tempered and sometimes rather quick to raise his hand and use it on the side of the head of any particularly difficult child.[20] Otherwise he was conscientious in his teaching, while yet strongly resenting the time he had to spend employed in this manner. He was not happy living at home, although this did not mean that he was not fond of his family. His frustration was rather on account of the restrictive conditions that prevailed and the stern attitude of his father, with whom he frequently disagreed. For this reason he had to escape to the houses of friends like the Grobs who lived near the church, or to the city, to make music with friends there, and to retreat into his own world of composition. His occasional harshness with the small children in his charge was not associated with a dislike of children in general; he was held in considerable affection by his own family, and was especially popular with his little half-sisters with whom he used to play. In the autumn of 1818 they were missing Schubert who was then in Zseliz, and according to Ferdinand they asked 'day after

---

[16] Ibid. [17] Kreissle, *Schubert*, i. 36. [18] *Mem.* 36, *Erin.* 46.
[19] 'ABC-Schützen' or 'Taferl'-Klass, *Dok.*, p. xix. [20] Kreissle, *Schubert*, i. 34.

day' when Franz was coming back, as they were bored without him.[21] The children were then aged nearly 5 and 3½.

In the last three months of 1814, though inhibited by the time he was now spending in the schoolroom, Schubert started composing, on 10 December, his Symphony No. 2 in B flat D125, which he was to dedicate to the director of the Stadtkonvikt, Dr Innocenz Lang. In the same period he wrote some eleven songs, including his first six Goethe settings, the first of them, 'Gretchen am Spinnrade' (Gretchen at the Spinning-wheel) D118, written on 19 October, arguably his first truly great song.

From this time on, Schubert's visits to the Grob family became more frequent. The widowed Frau Grob, who was on good terms with the Schubert family, ran a small silk-weaving business which her husband had established, and looked after her children. Therese (1798–1875) was a year younger than Schubert; her younger brother Heinrich (1800–55), who later took over the silk business, was also very musical, played the violin, and was already an accomplished pianist. Schubert was charmed by Therese's sweet, easy, natural, high soprano voice and her fresh, musical manner of singing. These qualities, combined with her agreeable and kindly nature and her reassuring enthusiasm for his music, resulted in a deepening of his feelings for her. The increasing amount of time they spent together suggests that these feelings were reciprocated. In later life Therese, who remained childless after her marriage in 1820 to a master baker, was less than forthcoming about her relationship with Schubert. Her reserve could have been in deference to her husband's feelings, or on account of her own disturbing memories of her love for Schubert whether reciprocated to the same degree or not, or even the result of embarrassment at some intimate knowledge of Schubert's later life. This she could have learned from her aunt Wilhelmine, her mother's younger sister, who in 1825 married Schubert's brother Ignaz.[22] (Wilhelmine was the widow of a Berlin medal-engraver, Leopold Hollpein, and they lived next door to the Grob family.[23])

Schubert was in love with Therese; but he spoke little about it. Throughout his life he was reticent in personal matters, sharing only occasionally, and with intimate friends, his innermost thoughts and feelings. One of those he confided in, early in 1815, about his love for Therese was his close friend Anton Holzapfel, a former chorister in the Court chapel choir, and now a willing singer of Schubert's songs in private at the Stadtkonvikt. Many years later, in 1858, Holzapfel remembered the letter he had received from Schubert concerning his passion for Therese:

---

[21] *Doc.* 106, *Dok.* 72.   [22] *Doc.* 438n, *Dok.* 301n.   [23] *Doc.* 47n, *Dok.* 35n.

I do not know if a note [in my possession] about Schubert's first youthful passion, which probably remained unrequited, for a girl from a good middle-class family, named Therese Grob, may be of use . . . [I] confine myself to the admittedly obvious remark that Schubert's feelings were intense and kept locked within himself and were certainly not without influence on his first works, as the Grob household was given to serious music-making.

. . . Schubert was usually sparing of words and not very communicative . . . and in this connection, it may have been characteristic that F.S. did not tell me about his affection for Therese Grob by word of mouth, which he could have done very easily in private, but in a lengthy enthusiastic letter, unfortunately since lost; and I absurdly tried to dissuade him from this passion in a long and, as I thought in those days, immensely wise, bombastic epistle. The latter, the draft of which I have come across, is dated at the beginning of 1815 . . .

About Therese Grob I can give you the following reliable information . . . The Schuberts were all well known in the [Grob] household whether as teachers in the German [elementary] schools or as friends and fellow music-lovers of the son; and in this way, on the occasion of a musical celebration for Therese's name-day . . . I spent an evening with this family . . . Therese was by no means a beauty but she was well built, rather plump and with a fresh, child-like round face; she had a lovely soprano voice . . . Schubert wrote several things for her . . .[24]

Anselm Hüttenbrenner (1794–1868), who came to know Schubert in 1815, is not always entirely reliable in his reminiscences of the composer, which he wrote in the 1850s, but from him came the following description of Schubert's confession of his love for Therese:

I loved someone very dearly and she loved me too . . . in a Mass, which I composed, she sang the soprano solos most beautifully and with deep feeling. She was not exactly pretty and her face was pock-marked; but she had a heart, a heart of gold. For three years she hoped that I would marry her; but I could not find a position which would have provided for us both . . . She then bowed to her parents' [sic] wishes and married someone else, which hurts me very much. I still love her and there has been no-one who appealed to me as much as, or more than she. She was just not meant for me.[25]

Hüttenbrenner was for a while very close to Schubert, and remained on good terms with him throughout his life. He joined the Law Faculty in Vienna in the autumn of 1815 to study there during the winter months, transferring to the University of Graz, his home town, for the summer months. As a fine pianist and keen if only moderately talented amateur composer, he took the opportunity while in Vienna to study composition with Salieri, and it was in the house of their teacher that he and Schubert

---

[24] *Mem.* 59–62, *Erin.* 69–72.   [25] *Mem.* 182, *Erin.* 209.

met. He was a personable, cheerful, companionable young man, the elder son of a landowner and not short of a penny or two, and became one of Schubert's few close friends in early years who was also a professionally trained musician, perhaps the only one.

When Schubert wrote of his love for Therese to Holzapfel early in 1815, he had probably just passed his eighteenth birthday, and was in no state to heed his friend's attempts to persuade him of the folly of his passion. His song inspired by a young girl's love, 'Gretchen am Spinnrade', was sung for him first by Therese, as were many more songs written with her particular voice in mind, if not actually for her, over the next year or two, and several sacred works for solo soprano. These included the beautiful Salve Regina D223 in July 1815 (revised in 1823), and soprano roles in the Mass in G D167 (March 1815) and in the Mass in B flat D324 (begun in November 1815). By early 1816 the young couple may have been seriously contemplating marriage; but by this time, indeed already early in 1815, a law had been introduced that for a while required that the majority of men in Austria must seek state approval before they could marry (the Ehe-Consens Gesetz).[26] Members of the aristocracy, property-owners, higher officials, and professional people were exempt from the ban. For others, permission was granted only to those who could give proof of an adequate income to support themselves and any children who might be born to them. The humble and low-paid profession of assistant schoolteacher was one of the many categories of people for whom official approval was obligatory. Unless Schubert could gain a position with higher status and salary, marriage was out of the question for him. His application in early 1816 for an appointment as music master at the teachers' training college in Laibach (now Ljubljana), formerly in the Austrian empire, fits well with his determination to find such a position, one that would enable him to offer marriage to Therese. To this we shall return later.

On 7 December 1814 Schubert wrote his song 'Am See' (By the Lake) D124 to a text by Johann Baptist Mayrhofer (1787–1836), which was probably given to him by Josef von Spaun, who described the poet, also a native of Upper Austria, as his oldest friend. A day or two after composing the song Schubert, with the manuscript in hand, was taken to meet the poet in his apartment in the city. Mayrhofer, ten years older than Schubert, had served as a clerk (without taking holy orders) in the St Florian monastery for four years before moving to Vienna to study law. He is best remembered as the poet of many (almost fifty) of Schubert's songs. Spaun's pur-

---

[26] R. Steblin, 'Franz Schubert und das Ehe-Consens Gesetz von 1815', *Brille*, 9 (1992), 32–42.

pose in introducing Schubert to Mayrhofer was not just a social one, but part of an overall plan he had for advancing the composer's education and development. In 1814, up to and including the month of October, thirteen of some seventeen *Lieder* that Schubert composed were to texts by the contemporary German poet Friedrich von Matthisson (1761–1831). Just two were by Schiller. The six Goethe settings came at the end of the year. It is probable that Spaun was responsible for directing Schubert's attention to some of this poetry, and almost certainly, we can deduce from later events, to Mayrhofer's 'Am See'.

The four or five years from early 1815 were marked by considerable advances in Schubert's intellectual and aesthetic thinking. These were brought about through the influence of a number of older friends he had made at the Stadtkonvikt, including Spaun and Josef Kenner, and other like-minded companions, such as Mayrhofer. This circle of friends, founded in Linz in 1811, was centred on a group of former students at the Kremsmünster seminary (a grammar-school associated with the monastery), including Anton von Spaun (younger brother of Josef) and Anton Ottenwalt. Other friends of Schubert who were connected with the circle included Franz von Bruchmann, Johann Senn, and, later, Leopold Kupelwieser and Franz von Schober. The bonding of groups of young men into brotherhoods founded on intense personal friendships, affection, and openness, and cultivating idealistic theories such as the 'love of all that is good' (*Liebe zum Guten*) and the means of attaining this in practice, were not uncommon in German-speaking areas at the turn of the century. Such were the tenets of the Linz circle, and some of the members worked with missionary zeal to convert others, especially younger men, to accept their ideals. When loyalty to the cause wavered, as it sometimes did, especially in the case of Schober whose destructive passions, even from early days, were felt to need tempering,[27] then the younger friends were duly encouraged back into the fold by their seniors. An informative collection of letters which passed between members of the circle has survived, and much can be gleaned from this about the thinking and practice of its members.[28] Self-improvement through learning and artistic activity was zealously sought by the protagonists, whose attitudes showed considerable knowledge of, and sympathy for, the late eighteenth-century ideals of *Bildung* (self-improvement and education). In 1817, the circle started a short-lived yearbook, high-mindedly entitled *Beyträge zur Bildung für Jünglinge* ('Contributions towards the Education of Young Men'). The foreword of

---

[27] Gramit, *Intellectual and Aesthetic Tenets*, 142.

[28] Ibid.; Gramit, 'Schuberts "Bildender Umgang" '; id., 'Schubert and the Biedermeier: The Aesthetics of Johann Mayrhofer's "Heliopolis" ', *ML* 74/3 (1993), 355–82.

the first volume explained the reasons for the emphasis on youth: through diligent study of the good, the true, and the beautiful, young men would mature into men who were manly, noble, and beneficial to society as a whole. But much of the educational process was conducted through discussion and by acts of friendship. Self-improvement and avoidance of inactivity were synonymous. The study of literature was very important in the educational programme: Herder, Goethe (but with notable reservations), Schiller, Greek and Roman texts of classical antiquity, Friedrich Jacobi, and, for light relief, Jean Paul.

The programme for the circle's aesthetics was no more systematic than that for its education. The consideration of works of art was integral to its ideals; and the attitudes of some of the members to art and the artist are recorded. For them, the ideal world could exist only in art (Kenner), and therefore appreciation of the arts must further the development of an individual into a productive and active member of society (A. von Spaun). Poetry could be dangerous, but at its best could stir 'feelings to noble ends' (Kenner). A painting could also inspire noble thoughts by its original theme, but only if the painter had poetic imagination (Spaun). And music was a force with power greater and more direct than any other art (Spaun). The role of art as a contributor to the pursuit of lofty ideals (Spaun and Ottenwalt) was crucial to their thinking. Notable, however, is the absence in the letters of any reference to *Sehnsucht* (longing) which, although crucial to most Romantic thinking, evidently played no part in the philosophy of the circle. The friends were unhappy with various Romantic trends in the arts, especially where they perceived that a non-productive dream-world was taking over from reality, self-indulgent chaotic longings of the heart from well-ordered rational ideas. Indeed, in a passage of dialogue in his *Raphael*, Mayrhofer has his character profess the superiority of the art and aesthetics of Classicism to those of Romanticism. Schubert was accepted in this society of idealistic young men, who saw it as one of their duties to provide a supportive environment for young artists. Among these friends Schubert found not only texts to set but an intellectual and social context that could motivate and support his activity in a genre he would later transform. The circle of friends is hereafter referred to as the Bildung Circle. Spaun and Mayrhofer were senior members of the Viennese branch, and the aim and outcome of the meeting between Schubert and Mayrhofer engineered by Spaun in December 1814 was very probably a decision to invite the composer to join the circle.

The study and discussion of works of art of all kinds, and of aesthetics, was an important function of the circle. The younger participants, who were virtually 'in training', were encouraged to follow a concentrated programme of reading, translating, and writing. Anton von Spaun set out for them a list of topics suitable for essays and subsequent discourse on such subjects as: 'Which perceptions inspire in us response to the beauties of nature, and how do they differ from our responses to everyday surroundings?'; 'Which is communicated most easily in the context of intimate friendships, that which is Good or that which is Bad?'.[29] The abiding mistrust of inactivity and laziness, amongst older members of the circle, who believed that time was to be used gainfully for the advancement of knowledge and understanding, must have rubbed off on Schubert, whose productivity over the next few years was astonishing. Thus, for example, in the period from November 1814 to September 1816 while he was working as his father's assistant, Schubert composed in the time left to him after schoolteaching some 360 of his total of around 1,000 works. These included four symphonies, four works for the theatre, three Church masses and many shorter sacred works, two string quartets, and some 250 songs, all these compositions falling between Deutsch numbers 119 and 486. The large number of songs in particular is noteworthy, and calls for some explanation. At this point it is pertinent to explain exactly what is meant by *Lied*, or *Lieder*, and to consider the kind of *Lieder* that were written by Viennese composers in the first fifteen years or so of the nineteenth century. In the context of this book, a *Lied* is a solo song with pianoforte accompaniment written to a German text. It may be a strophic song (the same music accompanying each of several verses), a more continuous composition, sometimes with dramatic content, a ballad, or any combination of these forms.

Schubert was in no way the creator of the German *Lied*. Neither was he the only composer writing songs in Vienna. Considerable work has been done in recent years by, among others, Ewan West on the Viennese *Lied* genre which Schubert inherited and developed; and the following represents a summary of some of West's findings.[30] By 1815 Vienna was already established as a city of German *Lieder*, though perhaps as yet less so than Berlin, Leipzig, or Hamburg. In the first fifteen years of the nineteenth century, building on earlier developments at the end of the eighteenth century, there was a remarkable growth of interest in *Lieder*, accompanied by an outpouring of new songs written by Viennese composers. More than seventy collections of songs were published in Vienna during this period, amounting to some 675 individual songs.[31] Many more remained

---

[29] Gramit, *Intellectual and Aesthetic Tenets*, 380–1.

[30] E. West, *Schubert's Lieder in Context: Aspects of Song in Vienna 1778–1828*, D.Phil. diss., University of Oxford, 1989; id., 'The Musenalmanach and Viennese Song 1770–1830', *ML* 67 (1986), 37–49; id., 'Schuberts Lieder im Kontext: Einige Bermerkungen zur Lied-komposition in Wien nach 1820', *Brille*, 12 (1994), 5–19.

[31] West, 'Schuberts Lieder im Kontext', 8.

unpublished, a fair number of which circulated in manuscript copies. Songs were often published in sets, generally collections of songs by several composers, but also singly, the latter both by music publishing houses and as supplements to journals and almanacs. A new type of *Lied* peculiar to Vienna had emerged which was of distinctive character, very different from that of the *Lieder* of other German-speaking areas in the tradition of such composers as Zelter, Zumsteeg, and Reichardt. The difference was in large part due to the poetry which was at first available to Austrian composers. As a result of the political and cultural isolation encouraged by the Empress Maria Theresia in the mid-eighteenth century, Austrian literature, prose and poetry, had followed a direction of its own, diverging from those of other German-speaking areas. In Vienna, poems written with a view to musical setting were strongly influenced by operatic libretti, of both serious and comic operas and singspiels. The result was that, while further north the influence of the folk culture of songs and ballads predominated, in Vienna, even in the first decade of the nineteenth century, composers were still setting to music of quite widely varying character poetry of the charming, simple, but often somewhat superficial anacreontic kind based on themes of love, nature, and friendship long superseded in Germany. The 'anacreontic style' had been most popular in Germany in the 1760s, and the young Goethe had written in this style. However, Viennese composers were soon looking further afield for poetic inspiration, and the songs of their German contemporaries were increasingly becoming available in Vienna. The result was that by 1815 Viennese composers, with a rather different approach to the selection of texts as well as the manner in which they were set, were composing songs in a richer and more varied style than their German counterparts.

Towards the end of 1814, up to which time Schubert had completed perhaps only a mere two dozen or so songs and had shown no particular passion for song-writing, there came the first signs of his new-found enthusiasm for composing *Lieder*, an enthusiasm which was to have a radical influence on his future as a composer. He now composed, amongst other works, his first six Goethe songs. These he wrote in the essentially Viennese style which he had inherited from his older Viennese contemporaries, many of them respected composers of operas, orchestral and chamber music in their day, notably Beethoven, but also lesser composers such as Ignaz von Mosel and Konradin Kreutzer. Schubert's setting of 'Gretchen am Spinnrade', for example, shows that he had not only mastered the genre which he inherited by the age of 17, but also that his genius for song composition outstripped the talents of all his contemporaries.

No doubt it was easier for Schubert, now teaching in his father's school and living in the schoolhouse, to snatch a quiet hour or two to compose, or sometimes to dash off a song to a text which attracted him than to find the longer period necessary to plan and embark on the first movement of a quartet or symphony. The large number of short solo piano dances he wrote during this period confirms this habit. More importantly, however, Schubert's interest in contemporary literature, in particular poetry, was being stimulated by works he heard, read, and discussed at meetings of the Bildung Circle. Some of the poets whose works were read at these meetings he could already have come across during his last year at school, as they were represented in the 1812 edition of the *Institutio ad eloquentiam*. If he had not, those friends remaining at the Stadtkonvikt after he left, and who also became members of the Bildung Circle, would undoubtedly have done so. In the years 1814 to 1817 Schubert composed more than 320 *Lieder*, well over half of which were settings of poems by poets represented in the 1812 *Institutio*. These included in the three year period settings of Schiller (31 out of 44 in total), Matthisson (26 out of 29), Hölty (22 out of 23), all composed in 1815 and 1816; Klopstock (13), all in 1815 and 1816; Claudius (13), all between 1815 and 1817; Salis-Seewis (13), all in 1816 and 1817; and Friedrich Stolberg (7 out of 9), all in 1815 and 1816. Goethe with only one entry in the *Institutio* (as compared with Lessing's 52, for example), was considered unsuitable reading for young people; yet remarkably, Schubert composed 51 of his total of 74 settings of Goethe's poems in this same period. Poets he was introduced to by friends, especially at meetings of the Bildung Circle, accounted for most of the other *Lieder*: Jacobi (7), all in 1816; Körner (13 out of a total of 14), in 1815; Kosegarten (21), between 1815 and 1817; Macpherson's Ossian texts (10), between 1815 and 1817; and, of course, the circle's own poet, Mayrhofer (31 out of 47). For Schubert, this period was undoubtedly a time of great literary discovery and excitement, and of productive inspiration.

There is an additional dimension to this upsurge in Schubert's song composition from the end of 1814. Younger members of the circle were expected to prepare written material for discussion at their meetings. It is hard to imagine Schubert, after a day's or morning's teaching, relishing the prospect of writing essays on such themes as Anton von Spaun was suggesting. For him, the questions posed would be better answered through the setting of a poem to music. As the only composer in the circle, his contributions of new songs, the texts of which reflected the circle's interests and ideals, and which he would sing (accompanying himself) at their meetings, were especially valued. From the appreciative response of his friends to the songs he also gained great encouragement to compose and at the

same time, in the true spirit of self-education encouraged by the circle,
learned by experience a new craft. As the *Lied* genre, although popular for
domestic music-making, was not yet taken seriously as an art form in artistic circles, few if any serious teachers of composition were willing to help
him with it, least of all Salieri. He, throughout his years in Vienna, probably never mastered the German language, and was in any case primarily
concerned with Italian operatic settings. For Schubert, at a time when his
father was pressing him to accept his role as a schoolteacher, his friends'
positive reaction to his songs and his own cultivation of the aesthetic values
of the circle, which placed music ahead of all the other arts for its unique
ability to inspire 'the most noble feelings and intimations of eternal goodness, beauty and truth',[32] strengthened his conviction that his future lay in
the service of art through music.

For a while there was thus a certain shift in Schubert's compositional
focus towards the *Lied*, beginning with Spaun's help late in 1814, and at the
same time an abandonment of his former 'rather haphazard approach to
text selection', as he moved to 'one that resulted in numerous settings by
authors of recognized literary status'.[33]

If Schubert's membership of the Bildung Circle was largely instrumental in his composing a multitude of songs in 1815 and 1816, many of these
were written for particular meetings of the friends and were little more than
exercises in songwriting, or unpolished occasional pieces, which Schubert
never envisaged would be published. Those texts which were chosen
because they fitted with present concerns of the circle or were the work of
some of its members (and there were several part-time poets amongst
them) did not inspire Schubert's greatest response. The manuscripts of
many of these songs have survived only in rough first-draft form, the
sources for later published editions being neat copies (made by his friends)
of more polished versions. Other songs of this period, which may or may
not have begun as his offerings to the circle, are in a totally different cate-
gory. Some were settings of dramatic scenes or ballads. Schubert had for
several years been fascinated by, and experimented with, the dramatic song
forms he had inherited from older composers, including especially
Reichardt's Gluck-influenced *Deklamations-Stücke* (Declamatory Pieces)
and Zumsteeg's dramatic ballads.[34] The very first song he completed which
has come down to us, 'Hagars Klage' D5 of 1811, all 369 bars of it, was
closely modelled on Zumsteeg's setting of the same (Schücking) text.
Several friends from the Stadtkonvikt told how the composer, as a schoolboy, was captivated by a collection of Zumsteeg's ballads and used to sing

[32] Gramit, 'Schuberts "Bildender Umgang" ', 15.   [33] Ibid. 5.
[34] M. W. Hirsch, *Schubert's Dramatic Lieder* (Cambridge, 1993).

and play them through, sometimes with the help of one or other of their number. Beethoven's songs, especially 'An die ferne Geliebte', received the same enthusiastic treatment. He also enjoyed some lyrical strophic songs of earlier contemporary composers. Amongst the songs he composed in these early years, though many were of little interest, were a number of lasting masterpieces of the *Lied* repertory, such as 'Gretchen am Spinnrade', 'Heidenröslein' (Wild Rose) D257, and 'Erlkönig' (Erl-King) D328, each with text by Goethe. (On the last of these Schubert expended considerable care, revising it three times before its publication in 1821.)

Schubert's vast output of songs and ballads did not result in rejection or neglect of other compositional forms. On the contrary, the considerable quantity of, in particular, music for the theatre (singspiels) written during these years, complete with overtures and small and large vocal ensembles, is impressive. He also wrote orchestral, chamber, and church music. All the time he was learning from his forebears, developing new crafts and using them for his own expressive purposes. He was essentially a composer of the Viennese classical school, indeed, the last great composer of that tradition. Despite his enormous respect for, and awe of, Beethoven, in particular of the music of his middle period, and despite the influence this music had on him, Schubert's real roots and affections lay with the Austrians Haydn and Mozart. In fact, he rejected some of the more strident elements of Beethoven's later music. Throughout his early years he based his music on classical forms and structures, with classical textures and instrumentation.[35]

Classical clarity and discipline mark his string quartets and orchestral music; the early compositions for church and the theatre belong to the same tradition. By the age of 20 he had already completed five symphonies, each with a distinctive character and for which his orchestration, in particular for woodwind and brass, was carefully chosen. On the other hand, his teacher Salieri was a strong advocate of the Italian heritage and that of his own teacher, Gluck. Although Salieri spent most of his life in Vienna, the Austrian heritage remained foreign to him; and consequently, his ability to help Schubert in this direction was very limited. His young pupil had to learn for himself through study of earlier music and practice in his own compositions. The music of Schubert's early years may be that of a young man; but the evident skill with which he planned and structured those works in classical forms is symptomatic of self-discipline and a purposeful devotion to development of the tradition he inherited and loved. In two other fields of composition he was less restricted and less encumbered by a

[35] For a full discussion of Schubert's symphonic writing and development, see B. Newbould, *Schubert and the Symphony: A New Perspective* (London, 1992).

traditional approach. Here he could let his imagination run more freely: in *Lieder* and in dance music. And yet even here, there is plenty of evidence of careful structuring and planning. Schubert took these compositions seriously, although at this time, during the first two decades of the nineteenth century, songs and dances were usually the products of run-of-the-mill composers, and were published in volumes of collected works by many contributors, if published at all. Schubert saw himself not as a purveyor of trifles but as a serious composer. He knew that to make his mark and earn a living as such he must eventually succeed with instrumental or dramatic music. These in the end would constitute his bread and butter.

The interest and admiration that Schubert as a young man inspired in his friends can be understood. It is evident from the accounts many of them left of the particularly happy hours they spent with Schubert during this period of their lives that their admiration was accompanied by great affection for the modest, straightforward, appreciative young composer. Only a few years later much was to go sadly wrong for Schubert as he gradually came to reject many of the worthy, if naïve, ideals of the Bildung Circle, and, encouraged by Schober, to give free rein to the hedonism latent in his own nature. But by this time, from 1821 to 1822, the original group of friends was already drifting apart.

The piano which his father promised Schubert in the autumn of 1814 probably arrived only in early February (1815). Whereas until then Schubert had shown remarkably little interest in solo piano music, after the piano arrived and over the next two or three weeks, while still composing songs, he wrote several solo piano works, including the Variations in F D156, and his first sonata, D157. From these compositions it can be assumed that the compass of the instrument was five octaves + two tones. As Schubert's father and stepmother already had a year-old daughter and were expecting a second child (born on 8 April),[36] there were many calls on his modest earnings which would have limited the choice of instrument for his son. In consequence, the piano he bought was almost certainly not new, and Schubert rather quickly, over a year or so, wore it out.

Schubert's enthusiasm early in 1815 for solo piano music did not last very long, perhaps reflecting the disappointing quality of his instrument. On the other hand, in February he did compose ten songs with piano accompaniments, and thereafter music of many kinds flowed fluently from his pen. In the first week of March he produced his second mass, that in G D167, for the Lichtental church. Intended for general use at Sunday parish services,

---

[36] *Doc.* 48, *Dok.* 36.

it was a shorter work than the earlier festival Mass in F, and it made only moderate demands on the performers: chorus and soloists (including a high soprano part for Therese Grob), string and organ, trumpet and timpani parts being added later. On 25 March, the day after he completed his Symphony No. 2 in B flat, he began the String Quartet in G minor D173, which he finished in just over a week. Other songs and part-songs followed. In early May Schubert returned to music for the theatre, which he had neglected since finally completing *Des Teufels Lustschloss* in late October 1814.

Starting afresh on a work for the stage, Schubert chose first a lightweight comedy, *Der vierjährige Posten*, with text by Theodor Körner, his late friend and encourager, ten of whose poems he had set to music within the previous six weeks. The Symphony No. 3 in D D200 and a very disappointing little serious singspiel, *Fernando* D220, with text (owing much to Beethoven's *Fidelio*) by his Stadtkonvikt friend Albert Stadler, soon followed. He returned to the world of theatre again, setting Goethe's three-act singspiel *Claudine von Villa Bella* D239, which he finished in the first week of August. Sadly, all the music for the second and third acts of *Claudine* was burned as fuel by the servants of Josef Hüttenbrenner (Anselm's brother) during the 1848 revolution in Vienna. (It is possible that this very promising singspiel was performed at one of the many private theatrical evenings in Vienna soon after it was composed.[37])

Although the Säulengasse school was now flourishing, with a large number of pupils, Schubert's father saw an opportunity for a move which strongly appealed to him. He applied on 25 August 1815 for advancement in his profession in a letter to the prelate of the Scottish Order in Vienna, seeking the vacant director's position at the elementary school of the monastery, spicing his application with the situations of his four sons, who were all now themselves involved in some way or another in schoolteaching. He pointed out that two of them, Karl at the Academy of Drawing (Zeichnungs-Akademie) and Franz 'under the guidance' of Court Kapellmeister Salieri, would benefit from being 'nearer' their sources of further education if their home were in the city.[38] Once again he was not offered the post. He had to wait another two and a half years before he was successful in an application, and thus able to move from the Himmelpfortgrund schoolhouse to more salubrious surroundings in the Rossau district.

Between July and October Schubert was composing mostly vocal works. In November he began a new stage work, *Die Freunde von Salamanka* (The Friends from Salamanka) D326, a singspiel in two acts, on which he worked

---

[37] O. Biba, 'Schubert's Position in Viennese Life', *NCM* 3 (1979), 106–13.
[38] *Doc.* 49, *Dok.* 37.

for the remainder of the year. The libretto was by Mayrhofer who, after Schubert's death, destroyed the text of this singspiel, along with all his other attempts at theatrical pieces. Only the sung text of *Die Freunde* has survived, but from this the course of the plot is clear. The story, which focuses on the bonding of three pairs of lovers and is strongly influenced by the plot of Shakespeare's *Twelfth Night*, is light-hearted but not without drama. The plot is of particular importance, however, for the manner in which it presents the attitudes and beliefs of Mayrhofer, which were largely accepted in the thinking of the Bildung Circle and indeed had considerable influence on it as well as motivating much of Mayrhofer's own thinking and behaviour. In his dialogue *Raphael*, which was printed in the second volume of the circle's journal, *Beyträge*, in 1818, Mayrhofer expressed his beliefs about the artist in society and his attitudes to one of the circle's favourite topics, friendship. The content of *Die Freunde von Salamanka* and its title stress the importance and virtue he attached to true friendship. In Schubert's music, refinement and imaginative invention are evident as well as interesting signs of his ability to set comic scenes and situations in music.

In the summer of 1815 members of the Bildung Circle were shocked and alarmed to discover that the circle had been denounced to the police authorities as a suspect secret society. The ceremonies and diplomatic activities of the Congress of Vienna had been accompanied by much secret intrigue. When the congress ended, the chancellor, Prince Metternich, encouraged by Emperor Franz, was already alert to the dangers of dissidents and activists at home. Both were eager to establish and maintain a secure and safe state, one in which political and social unrest and destabilizing elements were effectively contained. In order to do this, Metternich, in 1815, embarked upon a policy of controls, restrictions, censorship, and police intelligence, not all of which were exactly new to Vienna, directed mainly against those he saw as enemies within the country, and specifically against all possible subversive activities.[39] He established a strong and loyal police force which, aided by a host of paid informers and an efficient censorship office, was given the task of preserving security. These authorities directed their attentions particularly towards students and young people, in whose ranks those with 'revolutionary' tendencies, radical and dangerous opinions, and freethinkers (such as Schubert's brother Ignaz) were most likely to be found. A group of young men with intellectual and artistic interests and idealistic motivations, encouraging the reading of a wide range of literature, determined on spreading its influence amongst a younger membership, was almost bound to attract the attention of the secu-

---

[39] E. N. McKay, *Schubert's Music for the Theatre* (Tutzing, 1991), 27–38.

rity officers. Such was the Bildung Circle, despite its proclaimed, if naïve, goal of 'betterment of youth by the inculcation of lofty idealism and delight in virtue and activity'.[40] The founder members, like Anton von Spaun, in their innocence, and probably because many of them had never lived in Vienna, could not understand the adverse police interest they were attracting, believing as they did that their 'noble' ideas could only benefit the state. The first intimations of trouble came from the Stadtkonvikt, where those connected with the circle found themselves the object of unpleasant attention and harassment. As a result, other members of the circle in Vienna were advised to keep well away from the boarding-school both for their own safety and in an attempt to ease the lot of their friends there. For Schubert the result, no doubt to the relief of the director, Dr Lang, was the curtailment of his Sunday afternoon visits to his friends. On 9 October Josef von Spaun wrote a long letter to Franz von Schober, already connected to the Linz branch of the Bildung Circle but still at school in Kremsmünster, strongly urging him not to enrol at the Stadtkonvikt when he came to Vienna to study law a month later, eager as the idealistic young man was to share in the hardships and fate of his friends already there.[41] However, Spaun's advice seems to have prevailed, and Schober stayed instead with his mother and sister in their home in Vienna. Not long after this, original members of the Bildung Circle in Linz approached their mentor and friend, Michael Arneth, a respected churchman at the St Florian monastery, who at their request wrote a favourable report on the activities of the circle to the Austrian authorities. The result was that the Vienna branch of the circle was permitted to continue its activities as before.[42]

Throughout 1815 Schubert lived at home in his father's house. He continued to teach at the school and to give some private musical instruction, earning sufficient money to clothe himself and keep himself in manuscript paper, pens, and ink; but there was little, if any, left over for luxuries. After his visits to the Stadtkonvikt were stopped, Stadler and Holzapfel visited Schubert in the schoolhouse on several occasions to sing and play through his new songs, and to join with him in singing male-voice trios (for two tenors and bass). At the regular orchestral rehearsals, at Frischling's until the end of the year and then at the home of Otto Hatwig in the Schottenhof, some of Schubert's orchestral music was played. He had good friends and enjoyed some stimulating company and, most importantly, he was in love with Therese Grob, and she, it seems, with him. His friendship with Mayrhofer was growing, and by the end of November two new friends who were nearer his own age, Schober and Anselm Hüttenbrenner, had entered

---

[40] Gramit, *Intellectual and Aesthetic Tenets*, 142.   [41] Ibid. 389–90.   [42] Ibid. 149.

his world in Vienna. Salieri no doubt delighted in his pupil's remarkable talent and some of the music he was composing; but he surely despaired at Schubert's lack of progress and interest in those musical areas closest to his own heart: Italian opera and oratorio.

1816 was another prolific year for Schubert. He composed around 100 songs (compared with 140 or so in 1815), a stack of church music (including the twelve-movement Stabat Mater D383, the Mass in C D452, and the Magnificat D486), two secular cantatas (including the 'Prometheus' Cantata D451), two symphonies, chamber music, and his first attempt at a serious opera on a classical theme, *Die Bürgschaft* (The Pledge) D435.

If early in 1816 Schubert and Therese Grob were contemplating marriage, then it was imperative that he earn a higher salary than that of an assistant in an elementary school. Whether intended marriage or merely the desire to escape from his present situation motivated him, by the end of April Schubert had sent off an application to Laibach in the hope that he might be appointed music instructor to the students of that town's teachers' training college. The requirements for the post were not inconsiderable:

a teacher is herewith sought, who, apart from excellent good conduct, must be a thoroughly trained singer and organist as well as an equally good violin player, and must furthermore not only possess an elementary knowledge of all wind instruments, but also be capable of instructing others therein.

This music master shall give instruction in music to his pupils for three hours daily during the school-year, with the exception of Sundays and the appointed feast-days, and in addition take the Country School candidates three times a week during their six-month preparatory course, for at least an hour at a time . . . in addition . . . he is to hold the rank of a Normal-School [college] teacher and to be at the same time allowed to devote his remaining hours to private teaching, but on no account to such occupations whereby the status of an official teacher might be endangered . . . [43]

Despite his youth and lack of experience, Schubert felt he stood a chance. In applying for the post, he supported his case with the comment: 'He has gained such knowledge and skill in all branches of composition, in performance on the organ and violin, and in singing that he is probably the most capable among all the applicants for this post, according to the enclosed testimonials.'[44] Testimonials recommending Schubert as suitable for the post were supplied by Salieri and Canon Josef Spendou, the Schubert family's patron. (Canon Spendou was a government councillor and German chief inspector of elementary schools.) This position was certainly more suitable to Schubert's talents and attainments than his present elementary school

---

[43] *Doc.* 52–3, *Dok.* 38.   [44] *Doc.* 54, *Dok.* 39.

teaching, and the salary was some six times the meagre payment he was then receiving. His youth and inability to teach wind instruments do not seem to have been held against him in the early selection process. He reached the final three out of twenty-one candidates before he was eliminated; and he received official information on or before 7 September that he had not been successful. Had he been appointed, his subsequent life might have been very different. Although he would have had opportunities to participate in musical activities in the area, such as those of the Laibach Philharmonic Society, his life would have centred on the college, with its academic routine, restrictions on his freedom, and—a problem for Schubert—limited time for composition. If the new situation had been accompanied by marriage to Therese Grob and thereafter domestic happiness, then his life would have turned out very differently.

Through the Bildung Circle Schubert's relationship with Mayrhofer was becoming closer, and was to develop to the point where, in 1818, Mayrhofer invited him to share his lodgings. This was at the time when the composer had finally rejected schoolteaching and felt the need to move out of his father's house. Mayrhofer was somewhat taciturn by nature, at times sarcastic, a hypochondriac, and pathologically depressive. He first attempted suicide in 1831, and succeeded in taking his life in 1836. Yet he was tolerant and kindly, a good man, loyal, idealistic, serious, and responsible. He was also intelligent and well educated. He was generous in his attitude to the young composer, and later won the respect and confidence of Schubert's father, and was sometimes able to ease the strain that existed between father and son.

Stadler and Holzapfel continued to visit Schubert at the schoolhouse, even though his father did not always welcome his son's visitors, especially if they were interfering with the private music tuition his son was supposed to be giving at the time. As long as Schubert's father was himself teaching, organizing the smooth running of his school or the welfare of deprived and orphaned children, or paying attention to his own two youngest children, then Franz, keeping out of his way, could find contentment. He composed music, and he welcomed his two friends, with whom he made music and frequently tried out his latest compositions. Together they sang male-voice trios, some of which he composed especially for them. From May 1816 dates a group of vocal trios (for two tenors and bass), D423–D428, several of the manuscripts of which were in Stadler's possession at the time of the composer's death.[45] Probably earlier in the year, and certainly again in the autumn, Schubert, in the company of Anselm Hüttenbrenner and Ignaz

---

[45] From this time also may date the Trios, *NGA*, app. I. 18–23, of which only the second tenor parts have survived, in contemporary copies formerly in the possession of Holzapfel.

Assmayer, was in the habit of visiting the tenor Josef Mozatti each Thursday evening to sing male-voice quartets.[46] All four were students of Salieri's, Mozatti a singing pupil and the others studying composition. They had become acquainted at Salieri's house, where he regularly gathered his pupils around him, male and female, composers and singers, for the purpose of singing through works at sight from Italian scores. At Mozatti's, those three of the quartet who were composers had an arrangement by which they each brought a newly composed quartet to every meeting. Hüttenbrenner told how on one occasion Schubert forgot his contribution, but immediately sat down and wrote one at great speed while they waited.[47] He added: 'Schubert attached very little importance to these small *pièces d'occasion* and scarcely six of them can still be in existence.'[48] He continued: 'On those Thursdays we four also used to sing the quartets for men's voices by C. M. von Weber, then very popular, as well as a number by Konradin Kreutzer, of whose compositions Schubert thought highly.'[49] As Hüttenbrenner was in Vienna only during the winter months, their quartet meetings were restricted to this period of the year.

At some time in the first three months of 1816 Spaun persuaded Schubert to prepare copies of some of his Goethe songs. Spaun then sent these to the poet in Weimar, along with a covering letter dated 17 April requesting that he would accept the dedication of the songs, probably sixteen in all, when they were published.[50] At the time, Spaun was heading a small group of the composer's friends and well-wishers in a plan to publish several volumes of his songs. According to Spaun's long, somewhat stilted letter to Goethe which he sent with the songs, the first two volumes were to have included Schubert's settings of Goethe's poems, hence his effort to win the poet's agreement to be dedicatee. Thereafter, six other volumes would follow, with poems by Schiller (volumes 1–3), Klopstock (volumes 4 and 5), Matthisson, Hölty, Salis-Seewis, and others (volume 6), and finally the Ossian songs (volumes 7 and 8), 'these last excelling all others'.[51] This comment of Spaun's on the pre-eminence of the Ossian settings seems rather tactless in the circumstances, and was unlikely to encourage a positive response from Goethe. In the event—and Goethe received many such

---

[46] *Mem.* 187, *Erin.* 215.　　　　　　　　　　　　[47] *Mem.* 179–80, *Erin.* 206.

[48] The few, 'scarcely six', unaccompanied male-voice quartets composed by Schubert for these occasions and which have survived may include 'Die Einsiedelei' (The Hermitage) and 'An den Frühling' (To Spring) D337–8, 'Fischerlied' (The Fisherman's Song) D364, and Goethe's 'Gesang der Geister über den Wasser' (Song of the Spirits over the Waters) D538.

[49] *Mem.* 180, *Erin.* 206.

[50] These included the DD368, 367, 216, 121, 161, 118, 138 in their first versions; DD247, 257, 260, 224, 226, 225, 142, 162, 328 in their second versions. See *Th.V.* under D118. This first manuscript volume of Schubert's Goethe songs is now in the German State Library in Berlin.

[51] *Doc.* 57, *Dok.* 41.

requests—it may have made no difference as the poet, according to his custom, left the letter unanswered, and returned the volume of songs without comment.

Spaun was concerned for Schubert's intellectual and his musical advancement, and he was in addition well aware that the young composer was discontented with his life at the schoolhouse, perhaps showing early signs of the depression which was to darken his later years. Early in May Spaun moved from his apartment in the inner city (the Landskrongasse) to a new home in the house of Professor Heinrich Josef Watteroth in Erdberggasse, in the Landstrasse suburb south-east of Vienna. Here Spaun joined his friend from student days, Josef Wilhelm Witteczek, who was then courting his future wife, Watteroth's daughter Wilhelmine. One of the first things that Spaun did after he settled into his new home was to invite Schubert to spend a few days with him, probably during the school's Whitsun holidays later in May.[52] During the visit Schubert was on one occasion, for a prank, locked in his room with the instruction that he was to complete a composition before his hosts would release him. He happily dashed off the *Six Écossaises* D421 for solo piano. The title-page (now lost) of these dances bore the inscription: 'Composed while confined to my room at Erdberg, May 1816'. The final page carries the sequel to this: 'Gott sei Dank!'[53] This was probably Schubert's first visit away from home or boarding-school. The comfort, high spirits, and cultural life of Spaun, Witteczek, and the Watteroth household must have been quite an experience for the young man, used to a much drabber existence in the Himmelpfortgrund schoolhouse.

Living close by Spaun's old home in the inner city, Franz von Schober (1796–1882) at this time shared an even more luxurious lifestyle, if a less cultured one, with his mother and younger sister. Schober and Schubert met in the autumn of 1815. Very slightly older than Schubert, Schober was born at Torup castle near Malmö in Sweden, where his father, a native of Saxony, was estate manager. Schober's mother, born Katharina Derffel, was Viennese. The owner of the Torup estate, Axel Stiernblad, was on close terms with the Schobers, who named their eldest son, Axel, after him. Franz von Schober's father died in 1802, leaving his widow with two sons and two daughters. On Stiernblad's death a year or two later, as he presumably left no family of his own, Katharina von Schober inherited his money and returned to Vienna a wealthy woman. From 1808 to 1815 the young Schober was educated at the Kremsmünster seminary, where he came into contact with the Linz-based Bildung Circle. His elder sister,

---

[52] *Doc.* 59n, *Dok.* 42n.   [53] Ibid.

Ludwiga, died in a shooting accident in 1812, which was never fully explained, two years after her marriage to Giuseppe Siboni, a successful opera singer at the Kärntnertor-Theater. According to Holzapfel, she was shot accidentally by her husband, with a pistol which he believed to be unloaded.[54] Schober was a lively-minded young man of some charm, gifted with artistic and literary interests and an ability to attract friends and attention. After his arrival in Vienna from Kremsmünster, he soon became a leading personality in the circle, and his home a popular meeting-place for the friends. The first such meeting, referred to by Anton von Spaun, then visiting Vienna, in a letter to his fiancée, took place on 12 April 1816.[55]

Although Schober's morality and aesthetics and his hedonism were far removed from the cherished ideals of older members of the Bildung Circle, his company was especially enjoyed by some of the younger members. Schubert, whose own deep sensuality had been largely suppressed until now under the influence of disciplines imposed by home, school, and the Bildung Circle, began to enjoy listening to his new friend, Schober, extolling other 'virtues' than he was accustomed to hearing about. The desirability of giving in to natural human passions, of seeking out pleasures rather than always concentrating the mind on intellectual and moral improvement as Mayrhofer and Spaun advocated, may have struck a chord within him, especially when he was sorely tried and depressed by his life in the Säulengasse school.

Despite new awakenings as a result of his contact with Schober, the influence on Schubert of Spaun and other older members of the circle remained strong throughout this year and for several years more. Not only was he working as hard as ever, but his choice of textual subjects (for example the 'Prometheus' Cantata (June) and the almost completed classical opera *Die Bürgshaft*, composed between May and late summer), was very much in line with literary tastes of the circle. Schubert had set Schiller's ballad 'Die Bürgschaft' D246 for solo voice and piano in August 1815. He composed the opera under Salieri's instruction. The story, drawn from classical sources and following Schiller's poem closely if not completely, is based on concepts of trust and self-sacrifice in the cause of true friendship, and their effects, in this case on a tyrant who eventually experiences a complete change of heart; a case of forgiveness and redemption through friendship and example. The circle's emphasis on the loving brotherhood of its members and the power this gave them to influence and change the lives of others for the better is thus strongly reflected in this story.

In June 1816 Schober left Vienna for a visit to Sweden with his uncle

[54] *Mem.* 62, *Erin.* 73.   [55] *Doc.* 54–5, *Dok.* 39.

(probably Josef Derffel[56]) as his legal adviser, on business associated with his mother's inheritance. Schober was now well aware of Schubert's distress and frustration in the Säulengasse schoolhouse, and began to plan how he could help his friend to achieve the freedom he longed for, should he be unsuccessful in his application for the position in Laibach. Much later, in 1876, Schober told Schubert's nephew Heinrich (his brother Karl's son), in typically grandiose style, that he felt partly responsible for persuading Schubert to give up schoolteaching, thus releasing him from 'the constraint of school', and of 'having led him on his predestined path of independent, spiritual creation . . .'.[57] It is indeed likely that, before he left for Sweden, Schober persuaded his own mother to take the penniless young composer into her home without payment, and that Schubert, with the promise of this arrangement after the school summer term was over, or after Schober's return to Vienna, lived through the following months with new hope.

Schubert did not keep a diary regularly. When he exercised his pen, this was more likely to be for the purpose of composing music than for keeping a daily record of his activities or thoughts. However, a few pages of a rare document in Schubert's hand, a notebook, in which he recorded events and thoughts over a five-day period between 14 and 18 June 1816, and again on 8 September, has survived, along with further entries in a notebook for March 1824. The June 1816 entries strikingly reflect a sense of impending release and freedom. On Thursday, 13 June, the date of the first entry, he described a visit to a Viennese musical salon, where he also had to perform (maybe for a fee). He gives no indication as to where this was, or how he came to be invited; but his reaction to a performance of a Mozart string quintet, which he described as 'so to speak one of his greatest minor works',[58] is illuminating. He enthused over the beauties of the music and the unforgettable impression it made and praised the playing of the leader of the quartet. In the context of his aesthetic approach to music, he wrote of its power to raise the spirits, to lighten darkness with hope and confidence, bringing 'comforting images of a brighter and better life . . .'. For Schubert this was, as he began his entry: 'A clear, bright, fine day' which 'will remain [with me] throughout my whole life . . . O Mozart, immortal Mozart . . .'.[59] These entries in his diary were private expressions of his own thoughts and feelings. His musical contributions to the evening were a performance of a set of Beethoven variations, probably those in F Op. 34, and singing to his own accompaniment (as was normal practice at this time) his setting of

---

[56] *Dok.* 45n.   [57] *Mem.* 208, *Erin.* 239.   [58] *Doc.* 60, *Dok.* 43.
[59] *Doc.* 60, *Dok.* 42–3.

Goethe's 'Rastlose Liebe' (Restless Love) D138 (first version) and of
Schiller's 'Amalia' D195, both written more than a year before.

On the next day, a Friday, Schubert described a summer evening walk
taken with his artist brother Karl in the fields between Währing and
Döbling, north-west of Vienna and not far from their Himmelpfortgrund
home. After the earlier frequent walks together to and from their respec-
tive colleges in the Annagasse (from 1813 to 1814), and because each was
intent on an artistic career, the young men were close. Schubert wrote in
his diary:

I took an evening walk once again, as I had not done for several months. There
can scarcely be anything more agreeable than to walk in the green countryside on
an evening after a hot summer's day, a pleasure for which the fields between
Währing and Döbling seem to have been especially created. In the uncertain twi-
light and in the company of my brother Karl, my heart warmed within me. 'How
beautiful', I thought and exclaimed, standing still delightedly. A graveyard close
by reminded us of our dear mother. Thus, talking sadly and intimately, we arrived
at the point where the Döbling road divides. . . .[60]

Schubert's diary entry for the next day was short, but may have had a connection with the walk on the previous evening. He attended an exhibition
of Austrian paintings at the Academy of Fine Arts, possibly in the company
of Karl, who was still a part-time student at that institution. Schubert was
disappointed with the exhibition, or rather with his own response to it,
which he explained by the comment: 'I admit that it is necessary to look at
such things [paintings] often and long, if one is to discover the proper
meaning and receive the full impact.'[61] The only picture which really
impressed him was a portrait of the Madonna with Child by Josef Abel. The
brothers' conversation about their mother on the previous evening may
have increased his sensitivity to this painting of the perfect, devoted mother
with her child: 'The Virgin Mary showing her sleeping child to four angels,
with motherly delight', as the 1816 catalogue described the painting.[62]

On the evening of Sunday, 16 June, Schubert attended a celebration of
the fiftieth anniversary of Salieri's arrival in Vienna. For Salieri, the day had
been a festive, ceremonious one, arranged by Imperial Court officials. On
the other hand, the evening celebration was a more relaxed affair in his own
home, with his pupils around him: fourteen women and twelve men. The
proceedings began and ended with performances of Salieri's compositions:
a thanksgiving chorus first, and finally an Italian oratorio. Between them,
works written especially for the occasion were played by each of his composition students in turn. Schubert's contribution was a cantata with piano

[60] *Doc.* 61, *Dok.* 43.   [61] *Doc.* 62n, *Dok.* 44n.   [62] Ibid.

accompaniment—'Contribution to the Fiftieth Anniversary of Herr von Salieri' D407—written in three parts, but altogether of only 110 bars length. (No doubt the composers were instructed to keep their works short for this occasion.) Schubert wrote the first section originally for male-voice trio, presumably for himself to sing with Assmayr and Mozatti, as the fourth member of their regular quartet, Hüttenbrenner, was in Graz for the summer months. But he must have found another bass singer to take part, and he rewrote the trio as an unaccompanied male-voice quartet. The second part is an aria for tenor (Mozatti?) with piano, and the piece ends with an unaccompanied short three-part canon with 8-bar piano coda. Later that night Schubert wrote in his diary:

It must be fine and enlivening for an artist to see all his pupils gathered around him, each one striving to give of his best for his master's jubilee, and to hear in all these compositions the expression of pure nature, free from all the eccentricity that is common among most composers nowadays, and is due almost wholly to one of our greatest German artists [i.e. Beethoven]; that eccentricity which combines and confuses the tragic with the comic, the agreeable with the repulsive, heroism with howlings and that which is most holy with harlequinades, without distinction, so as to goad people to madness instead of soothing them with love, to incite them to laughter instead of lifting them up to God. To see such eccentricity banished from the circle of his pupils and instead to look upon pure, holy nature, must be the greatest pleasure for an artist who, guided by such a one as Gluck, learned to know nature and to uphold it in spite of the most unnatural conditions of our age.[63]

Schubert in these thoughts was surely writing under the influence of an emotional celebration at which the music of Salieri and Gluck had been lauded. He was expressing on this occasion a rather surprisingly rigid preference for the nobility of the old classical style culminating in the style of Gluck in his reformed operas, in which one principal emotion or mood inspired the whole of a piece of music, giving it a 'natural' unity and flow; and he was criticizing the most recent works of the 'German' Beethoven. Clearly, there was some topical discussion along these lines after the evening's music; for in 1816, after enthusiasm for Beethoven's music had peaked and passed two years earlier, he was being attacked quite fiercely in Vienna for his most recent 'bizarre' or 'eccentric' compositions.

Schubert's entry in his diary for the next day was short and to the point: '17 June 1816. Today I composed for money for the first time. Namely, a cantata for the name-day of Professor Wattrot [Watteroth], words by Dräxler. The fee is 100 florins, W.W. [40 fl. KM]'.[64] This 'Prometheus' Cantata has long been lost, but Leopold Sonnleithner, who took part in the

---

[63] *Doc. 64, Dok. 45.*   [64] *Doc. 65, Dok. 45.*

performance, and through the occasion first became acquainted with the composer, left a detailed description of the work and how it came to be written.[65] Sonnleithner was also involved in a later performance of 'Prometheus', this time at a salon concert of his father's on 8 January 1819.[66] The text was written by one of Professor Watteroth's fourth-year law students, all of whom had planned a surprise celebration for the name-day of their popular professor: a serenade concert to include the cantata, to take place in the courtyard and garden of his house in the Landstrasse suburb where earlier in the year Schubert had been Spaun's guest. Spaun and Witteczek, lodging in the professor's house, were presumably responsible for Schubert's commission to compose the music. In the event, the performance planned for 12 July had to be postponed because of bad weather until 24 July. The one-act cantata, for soprano and bass soloists, chorus and orchestra, opened the programme and lasted three-quarters of an hour. According to Sonnleithner, the solos consisted largely of 'solemnly delivered recitatives, which recounted the tragic fate of Prometheus and its cause'.[67] There was one elaborate duet for the soloists, and for the rest, three choruses of considerable variety. The first of these was a cheerful piece; the second, in the form of a slow funeral march, was a chorus of Prometheus' pupils, a poetic allusion to the students of Watteroth, and the third an impassioned chorus of triumph. For several of the students taking part in this celebratory performance, the occasion was as memorable and exciting for the participants as the first performance of the Mass in F, towards the end of 1814. One of the law students present, most if not all of whom were of around the same age as Schubert, was Franz Schlechta. He recorded his appreciation of the cantata in an enthusiastic poem published in the Vienna *Allgemeine Theaterzeitung* on 27 September 1817, more than a year after the event, when he became a contributor to that paper. It was entitled: 'To Herr Franz *Schubert* (On the Performance of his Cantata *Prometheus*)'.[68]

The cantatas of 1816 in honour of Salieri and Watteroth were followed, in September of the following year, by a commission for yet another secular cantata, this time in honour of Canon Josef Spendou, the Schubert family's sponsor. The work was entitled Cantata in Honour of Josef Spendou D472. Spendou was the founder and president of the charity administering funds for widows of Vienna's elementary schoolteachers, for the benefit of which, on its twentieth anniversary, the cantata was written. It is another fairly short four-movement work to a topical secular text, including as characters in the story both widows and orphans. Meanwhile, in June and

[65] Sonnleithner: *Mem.* 443–6; *Erin.* 513–16.   [66] *Mem.* 343, *Erin.* 396.
[67] *Mem.* 443–4, *Erin.* 513–14.   [68] *Doc.* 68, *Dok.* 47–8.

July, Schubert had written a third mass, in C (D452) for the Lichtental church, which he dedicated to his former teacher Michael Holzer. This mass was not performed until 1825. Two short sacred works, each a Tantum Ergo in C (D460 and D461) and the Magnificat, also in C, D486, followed in August. C major was clearly his favoured key for church music at this time. Of other music he wrote during the year, the Piano Sonata in E D459 and the associated first set of *Drei Klavierstücke* D459A date from August, while songs continued apace, including the Goethe *Wilhelm Meister* songs, D478 and D481, in September.

In the autumn of 1816 Mayrhofer affectionately recognized the healing power of Schubert's music in a poem he wrote and dedicated to the composer, 'The Secret [*Geheimnis*]. To Franz Schubert': 'Say, who taught you to make songs so tender and sweet? When all around us seems shrouded in fog, you sing, the sun shines and spring is near . . .'. Coming soon after Schlechta's poem, this was the second to be dedicated to the composer that autumn. In October Schubert set it to music in an unpretentious but charming *Lied* (D491), along with several other Mayrhofer poems of this period.

Amongst his friends and acquaintances and in some churches and musical circles in the city, appreciation of Schubert's music was growing. With this widening reputation and some certainty that, if necessary with Schober's help, his escape from schoolteaching was imminent, Schubert could look forward to the coming months with some confidence. As a result, he may not have been too disappointed when he heard, early in September, that he had failed in his Laibach application, unless, that is, he was still desperately hoping for immediate marriage. His future, for the present at least, lay in Vienna, and he reacted to his rejection from Laibach with another burst of musical creativity. At the prospect of revival of the orchestral rehearsals at Hatwig's after the summer break, he composed three works, all in the key of B flat: the Overture D470, an extensive fragment of a string trio D471, followed by the Symphony No. 5 (D485), which he finished on 3 October and which Hatwig, from his position as leader of the rehearsal orchestra, directed. There was space enough in Hatwig's premises for a small audience, which on this occasion Schubert may have preferred to join, rather than leading the viola section, his customary role. Other performers included his brother Ferdinand, who sat behind Hatwig amongst the first violins, Heinrich Grob (Therese's brother), who played second violin, and the versatile Josef Doppler, probably playing bassoon.

The last entry in Schubert's diary for 1816 was written on Sunday, 8 September. This was immediately after a Saturday meeting of the usual friends of the Bildung Circle held at the home of Mayrhofer on 7 September, the same day that Schubert probably heard of his rejection for

the position at Laibach. Mayrhofer, writing to Schober earlier that Sunday
of the approaching meeting, expressed the hope that some music-making
would help to raise the spirits of the friends, and to lift some of the 'fogs of
this present leaden time'.[69] Events and conversations of the previous day
surely influenced Schubert's thoughts in the diary entry that followed.
These jottings in his notebook followed on directly from, and on the same
page as, the entry for 17 June: he had written no other entry between June
and September. It could be no coincidence that the September entry came
so soon after his realization that he would not be moving to a new professional life in Laibach, and that the possibility of marriage to Therese Grob
was now out of the question in the foreseeable future. He wrote:

Man resembles a ball in play, subject to chance and passions. . . . . He is like an actor on
a stage who plays his part as best he can. If the part suits him, he plays it well; but
his success in the eyes of others is of no matter, as their response is coloured by
their mood at the time rather than by the excellence of the performance. In heaven,
praise and disapproval depend on the Stage-Manager of the World. . . .

*The heart and mind of a man are determined by his natural temperament and upbring-
ing.*

*The heart is the ruler, but the mind ought to be. Take people as they are, not as they
should be.*

Moments of bliss brighten this dark life; over yonder these blissful moments coalesce and are transformed into continuous joy . . .

Happy is the man who finds a true man-friend; but happier still he who finds a true
friend in his wife.

These days matrimony is an alarming thought to an unmarried man; if he does not
marry, he has to settle for misery or gross sensuality. Monarchs of today, you see
what is happening and do nothing. Or are you blind to it? If so, O God, shroud
our senses and feelings in numbness; but remove the shroud again one day without lasting harm.

A man bears his misfortunes without complaint, but the less he complains the
more he suffers.—Why did God give us the power of empathy?

A light mind accompanies a light heart; yet too light a mind usually conceals too
heavy a heart.

Urbanity is the great antipode to sincerity in human relationships. The greatest
misfortune of the wise man and greatest good-fortune of the foolish man reside in
convention.

To be noble and unhappy is to feel the full depths of misfortune and of happiness;
likewise to be noble and happy is to feel both happiness and misfortune to the full.

[69] *Doc. 70, Dok. 48.*

That is all I can say! Tomorrow I shall surely think of something more.

Why is that? Is my mind duller today than tomorrow, because I am sated and sleepy?—Why does my mind not think when my body sleeps?—It goes for a walk, no doubt?—For surely it cannot sleep? . . .[70]

Some of this is very jejune stuff, particularly the first paragraph. But one might conclude that real personal concerns lie behind some of the formulations. To distinguish Schubert's original thoughts from ideas put into his head by others, by the Bildung Circle for example, is not possible; and yet the last paragraph in particular suggests that in the often rather naïve comments there is much that is Schubert's own. Several statements provide explanations for certain traits in his nature and aspects of his behaviour, notably his distrust of applause and praise, his belief that basic human nature cannot be changed by education, and that the heart rules the head. He refers with some intensity to the misery caused by the state's refusal to permit the marriage of men without means, forcing them instead into either unwilling celibacy or commercial sex; and he prays that the nation's rulers will see what they are doing to their people and relent, and that meanwhile God will help those faced with the wretched options open to them. He recognizes the role of suffering in life, and the different ways men deal with it; and he rejects the present conventions of 'polite' society, the conversation and conformist behaviour which permit man to hide behind convention. Finally, Schubert seems to admit his own extremes of emotion and of mood. Whether the extremes were noble or an early sign of an emotional instability beginning to manifest itself can only be conjectured.

Two of Schubert's friends during this period of his life referred to his love for Therese Grob. His brother Ferdinand mentioned her merely as 'his favourite singer'.[71] The only evidence that she may have returned his love, apart from Anselm Hüttenbrenner's comment to this effect (see p. 43 above), seems to be a group of autograph manuscripts of sixteen of his songs, all but two written in 1816 and the last three in November of that year, which he gave to her and which she, perhaps lovingly, kept together. She added a title-page 'Lieder (Manuscripte) von Franz Schubert, welche ich einzig und allein besitze' (Songs (manuscripts) by Franz Schubert which I, and I alone, possess), and kept them until her death when, childless, she bequeathed them to a nephew. For three of these songs, Therese had the only copy. Included in the set is one other manuscript, an unsigned copy of a song perhaps not even by Schubert, written in her hand. This is a second setting of an anonymous poem, 'Klage' (Lament): 'Nimmer länger

---

[70] *Doc.* 70–1, *Dok.* 49–50.   [71] *Mem.* 36, *Erin.* 46.

trag ich dieser Leiden Last' (No longer will I bear this suffering).[72] The first setting of the same poem, dating from May 1816, is a Schubert autograph also in Therese Grob's collection. The text is one of unmitigated sorrow and hopelessness, the only escape from which is death. The characteristically Schubertian melody of this May 1816 setting of 'Klage' (D432i) Schubert used again, at the end of 1823, as the theme for the second minor section of the B flat major entr'acte of his incidental music to *Rosamunde* D797. The song was originally written for a high soprano, presumably for Therese Grob to sing.[73] The setting copied out by Therese is of a completely new song, distinguished by its opening melody—basically a falling chromatic scale down an interval of a minor sixth, from E flat to G, the tonic, to be sung 'unruhig und etwas schnell' (restlessly and rather fast). From the moment the voice enters, this melody underlines the despair of the poem; and the very existence of the song opens up two possibilities: the first, that Therese was broken-hearted in the autumn of 1816 when she and Schubert were unable to marry, and she added this song to the collection as best representing her emotions at the time; the second, that together the young couple co-operated in this anonymous, sorrow-laden setting. However, the true facts may never be known either concerning the G minor setting of this poem, or, far more importantly, the intensity of the relationship between Schubert and Therese Grob.[74]

Schubert's final composition of the year was probably an Italian aria to a text by Metastasio, 'Vedi quanto adoro' (See how much I love you) D510, from his opera libretto *Didone Abbandonata*. This, and surviving preliminary sketches of the aria, bear the marks of Salieri's corrections, proof that Schubert was still studying with Salieri, and that his teacher must have retained a vestige of hope that he might yet make a composer of serious Italian opera out of him.

When Schober returned from Sweden to Vienna towards the end of the year, Schubert soon, and certainly by the beginning of December,[75] moved in with him and his family. Another phase of his life was about to begin.

---

[72] *NGA*, app. I. 28, formerly D512.

[73] Schubert wrote other songs to the same text (D432—'Der Leidende').

[74] An album-leaf entry by Schubert, signed and dated Aug. 1821, addressed to a 'Frl. [Fräulein] Therese' was not written for Therese Grob, who had married the previous Nov. This formerly unknown autograph manuscript was sold by auction by J. A. Stargardt in Berlin in Mar. 1995: *Brille*, 15 (1995), 143.

[75] *Th.V.*, D507–9.

4

OPPORTUNITIES
(1817–1819)

AT the end of January 1817 Schubert attained his twentieth birthday. Already a picture of the composer is emerging. He was short in stature and thick-set, an unassuming, unprepossessing, bespectacled young man who preferred the congenial company of intimate friends to what he judged to be more pretentious society. Reticent even with friends about his own feelings and aspirations, he was to a high degree absorbed in music, both composition and performance; yet his absorption was not exclusive, and he particularly enjoyed both high-spirited companionship and serious discussion about artistic subjects, literature, and politics. With family and friends he was affectionate and generous, warm-hearted, honest, and straightforward. At the same time, he was subject to swings of temperament and mood changes which sometimes restricted his ability to conform to the self-discipline demanded of normal society. He felt a strong sense of vocation to be a composer, and this was entirely in accord with the high-minded principles in art and morality propagated by the Bildung Circle. But here too his temperament, like that of many other great creative artists and writers, sometimes conflicted with his sense of vocation. At times he was unable to compose for days on end; at others he was spurred on to hyperactivity. Professionally he was naïve, incapable of planning his career and sometimes of seizing opportunities when they arose. Artifice, only a little of which might have helped him to a secure position in the musical establishment, was abhorrent to him. As a result, he was almost entirely dependent, and probably unconsciously so, on the concern and help of his friends to find him opportunities, to encourage him to follow them up, and thus to further his career.

From now on, and for several years, the manner and degree to which Schubert's friends and acquaintances opened up opportunities which he would never have found for himself become very apparent. For better or worse, and most would unhesitatingly agree for better, the help they gave not only influenced, but determined the course of his future life. Thus the generous hospitality of the Schobers from the end of 1816 until the autumn of 1817 enabled him to escape from the schoolteaching he detested and the unhappy restrictions in his father's home. An additional and very important service of Schober was to arrange for him an introduction to the distinguished opera singer Johann Michael Vogl (1768–1840), who was to become a valuable, influential, and attentive patron. For many years, ever since his early visits to the Kärntnertor-Theater with Josef von Spaun, Schubert had wanted to meet Vogl, whose many performances, especially as Orestes in Gluck's *Iphigenia in Tauris*, had made a very strong impression on him.[1] Schober, who had some connections with the Kärntnertor-Theater through his late sister Ludwiga and her husband Siboni, may have been slightly acquainted with Vogl; but it took some persistence, if not diplomatic pressure, on his part to persuade Vogl to meet Schubert and to look at his songs. Very much the grand artiste, Vogl, now approaching the early end to an operatic career in Vienna which had spanned twenty-two years, was far from happy with the changing attitudes and tastes of Vienna's opera-goers and music-lovers. On Schober's suggesting that he have a look at some of Schubert's song compositions, Vogl replied that 'he had heard about young geniuses hundred of times before and had always been disappointed . . . He wanted to be left in peace and to hear nothing more about the matter'.[2] The unassuming Schubert was neither surprised nor upset by this reaction; but after a few other friends had put in a good word for him and his music, in March 1817 Vogl agreed 'to see what all the fuss was about'.[3]

Vogl was a tall man of commanding presence, high intellect, and with considerable knowledge of classical culture, especially of Greek language and literature. His years of stardom had resulted in a certain haughty pride and affectation, which in later years was to attract some scorn from a section of Schubert's younger friends. But in 1817, for Schubert, he was a hero. On their first meeting the composer, little more than five feet tall and much in awe of the great man, initially made no impression. When, however, the singer was at length prevailed upon to try through the topmost song on a pile of manuscripts, accompanied by Schubert, he commented, rather coldly 'not bad!'.[4] As, with whetted appetite, singing *mezzo voce*, he tried more songs, including the recently completed 'Memnon' D541 and

---

[1] *Doc.* 32–3n, *Dok.* 25–6n.   [2] Spaun: *Mem.* 131–2, *Erin.* 154.   [3] Ibid.
[4] *Mem.* 132, *Erin.* 154.

'Ganymed' D544 (both on classical Greek themes), his enthusiasm and friendliness towards Schubert increased. He left the apartment giving the composer an encouraging pat on the shoulder with the comment: 'You have something special in you, but as yet are too little of the actor and showman; you have fine ideas but should make more of them.' Vogl's interest had been aroused, and from this time he went out of his way to help Schubert.

At the same time as Vogl was discovering the wealth and promise of Schubert's early songs, the composer was embarking on a period of concentrated work on piano music and mastery of the classical piano sonata. Between March and August 1817, at the end of which month he had to leave the home of Schober and the fine six-octave piano which had been at his disposal there, Schubert completed three sonatas for piano and worked on several others. He had already written at least ten or eleven string quartets and five symphonies in cyclical (three- or four-movement) form; and he was at last discovering the potential of the same multi-movement form for the piano sonata.

No doubt encouraged by Vogl, who was born in Steyr in Upper Austria and, like several of Schubert's friends, had attended the Kremsmünster seminary, Schubert remained closely in touch with members of the Bildung Circle in Vienna, and he was aware of the contributions of Mayrhofer in particular to the first edition of the circle's journal, *Beyträge zur Bildung für Jünglinge*, which was published during 1817. Although Schober was already recognized by the circle as something of a rebel, he was socially gifted, and their meetings were now frequently held in his comfortable and somewhat extravagantly furnished home. In correspondence which has survived between members of the circle in Linz and Vienna, the names of both Schubert and Schober feature, the former in connection with his songs (manuscript copies of which were already circulating amongst members of the circle), the latter often in the context of his wayward thinking. Despite the fact that in many respects the ideals encouraged by the circle had become a part of Schubert's thinking, it is possible that in 1817, living in close proximity to the rebellious Schober, who was still smarting with resentment at being forced by older members to abandon his attentions to Marie von Spaun (sister of Josef and Anton) with whom he thought he was in love, the first seeds of questioning of the circle's tenets were sown in the composer's mind.

At the end of August Schubert's hopes and immediate prospects of growing success, especially with the interest and encouragement of Vogl behind him, were cruelly dashed when he had to leave Schober's home in a hurry, ostensibly to make room for Axel von Schober, the eldest son of the family, then serving in the Austrian army in France. The family was informed that Axel had fallen sick and was now very ill. On 24 August Schober set out to meet his brother and escort him back to Vienna. Schubert bade him farewell in words and music of his own:

Abschied
[Farewell]

In das Stammbuch eines Freundes
[For the album of a friend]

Lebe wohl, Du lieber Freund!
Ziehe hin in fernes Land,
Nimm der Freundschaft trautes Band—
Und bewahr's in treuer Hand!
Lebe wohl! Du lieber Freund!

Lebe wohl, Du lieber Freund!
Hör' in diesem Trauersang
Meines Herzens innern Drang,
Tönt er doch so dumpf und bang.
Lebe wohl, Du lieber Freund!

Lebe wohl, Du lieber Freund!
Scheiden heisst das bitt're Wort,
Weh, es ruft Dich von uns fort
Hin an den Bestimmungsort.
Lebe wohl, Du lieber Freund!

Lebe wohl, Du lieber Freund!
Wenn dies Lied Dein Herz ergreift,
Freundes Schatten näher schweift,
Meiner Seele, Saiten streift.
Lebe wohl, Du lieber Freund![5]

[Farewell, dear friend! Go forth to a distant land, taking this cherished bond of friendship—and keep it faithfully. Hear in this mournful song the yearning of my inmost heart, muffled and anxious. Parting is a bitter word; alas, it calls you from us to the place decreed for you. If this song should stir your heart, my friendly spirit shall hover close by, touching the strings of my soul.][6]

This poem is written in the sententious mode of the current 'soul-friendship' poetry. Schubert bids a long farewell to Schober. He asserts the deep sincerity of the sentiments of sorrow expressed; he bewails the parting and the destiny which has decreed it; and he believes that if Schober recip-

---

[5] *Dok.* 53–4.
[6] Trans. from R. Wigmore, *Schubert: The Complete Song Texts* (London, 1992), 20–1.

rocates the sentiments uttered, then their souls will continue to touch and respond.

Schubert, with no regular income with which to pay for rented accommodation, was now forced to return to the schoolhouse and to pay his way there by re-entering, for the very last time as it turned out, the detested classroom. When Axel died on 6 September, before his brother reached him, Schubert did not return to Schober's apartment. Whether Schober came home, perhaps with Axel's valet Claude Étienne (who settled in Vienna and joined Schober's circle of friends) or travelled to Sweden, as Schubert's poem of farewell might suggest, is not known; yet there is nothing to prove that Schober was in Vienna over the next few months. Schubert's musical prospects in the first half of 1817 had seemed very promising, his life comfortable and stimulating. Now, once again, he had to settle back into the dreary routine of teaching, becoming increasingly demoralized both mentally and spiritually. Here he was to remain until the early summer of 1818, a period of frustration during which he realized that he could no longer tolerate the pedagogic existence. At first, as in 1815, he found his escape in composing music.

In October 1817 Schubert began his Symphony No. 6 in C D589, which he completed in February 1818. His intention was to compose a grander work than his exquisite little classical Symphony No. 5, which he had completed twelve months earlier. He headed the first movement of the new symphony 'Grosse Sinfonie in C'. In November he temporarily laid the symphony aside while he composed two Overtures in the Italian Style D590 and D591. These overtures, the second of which was most effectively 'Italian' in the manner of Rossini, reflect both Schubert's interest in Rossini's music and the enormous and growing popularity of the Italian's music in Vienna. Schubert may have felt it expedient before he proceeded with his new symphony to master to some degree the Italian idiom and in the last three movements, as in his other orchestral and theatre music of the next few years, the influence of Rossini is evident. At some time after completing it, Schubert dropped the 'Grosse' title, replacing it simply on the first page with 'Sinfonie von Franz Schubert 1818 Febr.'. During the final months of 1817, in addition to working on the symphony and two overtures, Schubert completed the last of some sixty-five songs he had composed during the year, including settings of poems by Mayrhofer (20), Schiller (8), and Goethe (7), many of them now composed for Vogl to sing.

At the end of 1817 Schubert's father finally succeeded in gaining a new school appointment, becoming director of the elementary school in the Rossau district, not far from the Himmelpfortgrund, but in a far pleasanter area, and closer to the city. The family moved at the beginning of January.

FIG. 3. The schoolhouse in the Rossau, the Schubert family home from 1818, now demolished and replaced by Grünetorgasse 11. *Anonymous sketch; taken from Ernst Hilmar, Schubert, © Akademische Druck- u. Verlagsanstalt, Graz, 1989, reproduced by permission.*

The Rossau school had opened in a new building only a year before but, after the first director had been dismissed in disgrace for some misconduct, Schubert's father faced the task of establishing a good reputation for the school and thereafter of building up afresh the attendance numbers, on which his own remuneration depended. Both tasks he accomplished with his customary single-minded zeal. Schubert was present during the move to the Rossau, perhaps sad that he would no longer be living only five minutes' walk from the Grob family home. He also suffered, along with other members of his family, the effects of his father's enthusiasm and pride in his new Rossau appointment, a subject to which I will return shortly.

After the move, and during the first six months of 1818, Schubert's output of completed compositions slumped. It is probable that he was suffering from some degree of depression, aggravated by lost aspirations and his despair in the schoolhouse atmosphere. Early in the year he applied for membership of the Gesellschaft der Musikfreunde des österreichischen Kaiserstaates (Society of Friends of Music of the Austrian Empire) in his capacity as composer and accompanist of songs. This society, later often referred to as the Musikverein, was the most prestigious and influential of several musical societies in Vienna. His application was supported by Josef Mozatti, who had hosted the evenings of vocal quartets they shared with Assmayr and Anselm Hüttenbrenner in 1816. The Gesellschaft was founded in 1812, and by 1815 was already at the centre of Vienna's musical life, attracting for the most part members from the middle and upper classes of society, along with many of the ablest amateur musicians in Vienna. It organized a very important series of three or four regular private concerts each year—*Gesellschaftskonzerte*—held on Sundays at midday in the large assembly hall (Redoutensaal) of the Imperial Palace. At these concerts major works involving orchestra and chorus were performed by 'performing members' of the society. On only three occasions, all between 1821 and 1822, were Schubert's works performed in these grand concerts, two of them, rather surprisingly in such programmes, being male-voice quartets (the other an orchestral overture). In 1818 the society instigated a new series of more frequent private concerts for its members, given by small groups of performers, under the heading *musikalische Abendunterhaltungen* (musical evening entertainments). The programmes included chamber music, instrumental solos, *Lieder* and part-songs, and also excerpts from operas sung with piano accompaniment. These took place on Thursday evenings, the first on 12 March 1818.[7] Schubert had high hopes that he would be elected a performing member of the society so that at the new evening concerts his music, especially the songs, could be performed. Ordinary membership was open to all who purchased season tickets for the series of *Gesellschaftskonzerte*. Performing membership was, theoretically, for amateur singers and instrumentalists of fair accomplishment who were capable of performing to an acceptable standard in society concerts. All members had to be elected by the committee of the society. An 'amateur' was somewhat ambiguously described for these purposes as anyone who sang or played for pleasure; this does not appear to have barred music professors and teachers at the Conservatoire founded by, and associated with the Gesellschaft der Musikfreunde, who were in fact encouraged to join.[8] Vogl, on the other hand, as an established opera singer employed by the Kärntnertor-Theater, was not eligible for membership.

Schubert's hopes of election were surely raised considerably when, early in 1818, he saw an announcement of the society's programme for the coming months in which his own name was on a list of composers, including Haydn, Mozart, and Beethoven, whose music was to be performed that season. His rejection thereafter by the committee was a huge disappointment

---

[7] O. Biba, 'Franz Schubert und die Gesellschaft der Musikfreunde', 24–5.
[8] Ibid. 24.

to him. As he was at the time employed as an elementary schoolteacher, the stated reason, that he was 'no amateur', was strange indeed. The real reasons for his rejection are more likely to have been social ones: his youth, his poor pay, and low social standing. Schubert had to wait another three years before he was recognized as a suitable candidate. In the mean time, the rejection had come as yet another in a series of major disappointments.

Fortunately Schubert's depressed spirits in the early part of 1818 were intermittently lifted by a few successes: publications, publicity, and public performances of his music. This period saw the first publication, towards the end of January, of one of his compositions, the song 'Erlafsee' (Lake Erlaf) D586. This song was a setting of one of two poems by Johann Mayrhofer which were included early in 1818 in a pocket-sized almanac edition of poetry and prose of a kind which had been popular for some forty years in Vienna and throughout Germany. The poems appeared in the sixth annual series of an illustrated publication called the *Mahlerisches Taschenbuch für Freunde interessanter Gegenden, Natur- und Kunst-Merkwürdigkeiten der Oesterreichischen Monarchie*, aimed at a readership of those interested in the 'picturesque scenery, beauty-spots and art-treasures of Austria'. Schubert's setting of the poem, here wrongly entitled 'Am Erlaf=See', printed on two sides of a loose sheet, was inserted according to the practice of the day between the pages of the almanac.[9] This sixth and last volume of the journal was advertised in the official *Wiener Zeitung* of 24 January 1818, when Schubert's song setting was described: 'as brilliant as it is lovely'.[10] 'Erlafsee' was the first of fifteen of Schubert's songs which were published in this manner almost every year after 1818 during his lifetime as supplements to almanacs and journals, especially in the *Wiener Zeitschrift für Kunst, Literatur, Theater und Mode*. Others were published likewise after his death. Such publications usually ensured a considerably wider circulation than was usual when songs were published by established publishing houses. The collections of poems which appeared periodically in Vienna in almanacs and pocket-books were a principal source of texts for Schubert's songs, and for the songs of most composers of *Lieder* of his day; and by the 1820s the great variety in the subjects and forms of these poems was having an important effect on the development of the *Lied*.[11]

The first public performance (outside a church, that is) of the first of the two Overtures in the Italian Style took place on 1 March 1818 at the Roman Emperor hotel. This performance was advertised in the Vienna press and was the first of his works to be reviewed in journals in Vienna and Dresden, and shortly afterwards in a Leipzig paper. And there were other concerts.

[9] *ND* 4.   [10] *Doc.* 85; *Dok.* 57; *ND*3.   [11] E. West, 'The Musenalmanach', 49.

Throughout this period Schubert looked forward to Saturday evenings, relaxing with the prospect of a free Sunday ahead, certainly without school commitments, and probably by now without church duties. To raise his spirits after a dreary week and to help him break out of any depression, there was no better companion than his Graz friend Anselm Hütten-brenner, a student colleague at Salieri's and an altogether entertaining comrade. Hüttenbrenner's contact with Schubert was originally entirely the result of their shared musical interests; he had not been at the Stadtkonvikt, neither was he a member of the Bildung Circle. To meet him, Schubert would walk in from the Rossau to the Kohlmarkt in the centre of Vienna, where Hüttenbrenner had his lodgings over Geistinger's bookshop. On one such Saturday, 21 February, Schubert, in his friend's words, 'helped him' to consume a few bottles of a rich red wine (Szegzard) 'a present from a distinguished family'.[12] As the young men talked, Anselm told Schubert of one of his younger brothers, Josef, who was hoping to find work in Vienna later in the year. On hearing that Josef liked his songs, Schubert decided to send him a present of a manuscript copy of one of these and he promptly, in a distinctly tipsy state, wrote out 'Die Forelle' (The Trout) D550 from memory (in the third of an ultimate five versions of the song). A note in his own hand in the manuscript explains its rather messy state and bespeaks the alcoholic *bonhomie* which occasioned the familiarity and expressions of affection towards someone Schubert had never met:

Dearest Friend,
It gives me extraordinary pleasure to know that you like my songs. As a proof of my devoted friendship I am sending you another, which I have just now written at Anselm Hüttenbrenner's at midnight. I trust that I may become closer friends with you over a glass of punch. *Vale.*

Just as, in my haste, I was going to send the thing, I rather sleepily took up the ink-well and poured it calmly over it. What a disaster![13]

Of course Schubert had not just composed the song, merely made a copy of it; and his intention had been to pour sand, not ink, over the manuscript. It was now well after midnight and, as he often did, he stayed the night with his friend.[14] Three weeks after this episode, on 14 March, they again spent a Saturday evening together, and on this occasion Anselm himself was the recipient of a Schubert manuscript: the 'Trauerwalzer' (Mourning Waltz) D365/2, composed in 1816. Again the waltz was written down from memory, and in the dedication he added jovially: 'Written down for my coffee-, wine- and punch-brother Anselm Hüttenbrenner, world-famous

---

[12] *Mem.* 181, *Erin.* 208.   [13] *Doc.* 86, *Dok.* 57–8.
[14] Hüttenbrenner: *Mem.* 184, *Erin.* 212.

composer, Vienna, 14 March in the year of Our Lord 1818, in his very own exalted lodgings at 30 florins W.W. [12 fl. K.M.] a month.'[15] In fact Schubert did not supply the title 'Trauerwalzer', nor did he give names to any of his waltzes; all were added by publishers, usually without first consulting him. According to Spaun, when he was told that the title 'Trauerwalzer' had been appended to this piece, Schubert commented: 'what ass would compose a mourning waltz?'.[16]

Schubert and Hüttenbrenner were seeing much of each other during this winter of 1818, and clearly enjoying each other's company. Leopold Sonnleithner wrote, in February 1829, in an obituary notice of Schubert for the monthly report of the Gesellschaft der Musikfreunde: 'Anselm Hüttenbrenner . . . had an enlivening effect and encouraged him [Schubert] at the beginning of his career.'[17] Hüttenbrenner completed his final law examinations that summer, while Schubert was away from Vienna, after which he returned to his home in Graz and did not reappear in Vienna until the autumn of the following year. By this time, Schubert's life had taken a new direction yet again.

During January and February Schubert had worked on his sixth symphony, and at the same time, and in March and April, had composed a handful of songs and piano works. In May, only three months after completing this Symphony in C D589, a classical work with touches of Rossini's brush, Schubert started again on another symphony, now in D (D615). This he left as a fragment consisting of some 120 bars of each of two movements: the first, an *allegro moderato* movement (with D minor slow introduction), the second, probably the last movement, a rondo. Important developments in his life and career may have interrupted his interest in this fragment. The first could have been serious problems in his relationship with his father. Another, and related, development was the opportunity which arose for him to escape from the schoolhouse, to win independence, and to earn sufficient money to keep himself in some comfort over the next few months.

According to Josef Hüttenbrenner[18] and Baron Schönstein,[19] both of whom entered Schubert's life later in 1818, at some time during the spring or early summer of the same year Schubert was introduced by Johann Karl Unger to Count Esterházy of Galánta. Unger, who himself wrote and published poetry, acted as tutor in various noblemen's households while also holding a teaching appointment at the Theresian academy (a prestigious school for the sons of the nobility). He was the father of the future young

[15] *Doc.* 88, *Dok.* 60; *Mem.* 184, *Erin.* 212.   [16] *Mem.* 367, *Erin.* 422.
[17] *Mem.* 12, *Erin.* 16.   [18] *Mem.* 78n, *Erin.* 91n.
[19] *Mem.* 100, *Erin.* 116.

operatic soprano Karoline Unger, with whom Schubert was to work at the Kärntnertor-Theater for a short time early in 1821. (In 1843 Karoline Unger published a volume of songs of her own composition.) The Esterházys of Galánta were descended from the Altsohl line of the Esterházys,[20] and only distantly connected with the Esterházys of Eisenstadt, where Haydn was for long employed. Galánta, the ancestral seat (and later the source of Kodály's 'Dances of Galánta'), is now in Slovakia, but in the early nineteenth century was part of Hungary. It lies approximately due west of Pressburg (now Bratislava) and approaching half-way to Zseliz. Count Esterházy was looking for a music tutor in piano and singing for his two teenage daughters for the summer months, which the family spent each year in their summer residence at Zseliz in Hungary (now Zeliezovce in Slovakia). Schubert, depressed and having a serious disagreement with his father, was desperate to escape from his present existence in the family home, and leapt at the opportunity to join the count's household in Hungary for the summer months. Interestingly, despite his intense unhappiness while living and working in his father's school and the by now very tense relationship between father and son, Schubert retained his affection for all members of his family. For most—brothers and sisters, stepmother, aunt and cousin—he felt deep and generous love; for his father, Schubert's feelings were more dutiful and respectful than warm.

On 7 July Schubert received a passport valid for five months which enabled him to visit and to work in Zseliz. Soon after this he said goodbye to his family and friends and set out on the 125-mile carriage ride to Hungary. He was now 21 years old, and this was the first time he had been away from Vienna and its surroundings. Travellers usually broke the thirteen-hour journey by mail-coach (*Postwagen*) in Pressburg for an overnight stop at the hostelry the Brown Stag, before setting of again in an easterly direction for the final eighty miles through the region of Galánta, where Count Esterházy's estates were situated, and on through Nitra and Levice to Zseliz. On arrival in Zseliz, situated on the right bank of the river Gran (Hron in Slovakia) some twenty miles north of its confluence with the river Danube, Schubert found a once-flourishing small town, of around 1,000 inhabitants, still somewhat depressed by economic decline after the wars against France, but with an important market for cattle and dairy produce serving a wide area, and a population which included many skilled artisans: leather-workers, weavers, smiths, tailors, wagon-makers, and wheelwrights.[21] The summer residence of the Esterházys was a

---

[20] *Doc.* 92n, *Dok.* 62n.
[21] Z. Viňálová, 'Schubert in Zseliz', *Brille*, 8 (1992), 93–102; id., 'F. Schubert und Zeliezovce', *Občasnik*, 1 (1994), 3–8.

comparatively modest baroque palace or country house (schloss), built some thirty years earlier and surrounded by a fine park and gardens. The four wings of the building, which was one storey high, faced inwards on a central courtyard. The schloss also had its own farm. Schubert was enchanted by his new surroundings, charmed and soothed by their beauty, and happy at the prospect of teaching his two pupils, the musical countesses Marie (aged 16) and Caroline (who had her thirteenth birthday during the summer). Both played the piano, and they sang soprano and contralto respectively. In addition to tutoring the young pair, Schubert was expected to provide musical entertainment as required for the family and their guests, whether in the form of musical performances or as an accompaniment for their dancing. For this none-too-demanding labour he was to receive accommodation and food, along with an adequate basic salary of around 75 fl. KM each month,[22] a sum which compared well with what he would have received had he been appointed in 1816 to the Laibach college. On this visit to Zseliz, as one of the count's employees he was first given a small room of his own in the main building, but one adjoining the kitchen. This he may have found too noisy, possibly also too hot in July, and after a short while there, he moved to a larger and more congenial room in the house of the estate manager, where he lived with several of the estate workers.

At first Schubert was content with his life in Zseliz. Unfortunately for posterity, his earliest two letters home to his family, of 1 and 8 August, have not been preserved; but four others have survived. Between them, these provide a fair if incomplete picture of his time there, and his reaction to it. In the first, a short letter dated 3 August, he wrote jointly to Spaun, Schober, Mayrhofer, and Senn in Vienna with some enthusiasm: 'I am very well. I live and compose like a god, as though that were as it should be.' In a reference to the life he had recently been leading in the Rossau and his inability to complete any compositions over the past months there, he continued: 'Thank God I live at last, and it was high time, otherwise I should have become nothing but a thwarted musician'.[23] In his second letter to the same friends and others, all members of the Bildung Circle, written on 8 September after two months in Zseliz, he gave a detailed description of the country house and the people he was with:

Our castle is not one of the largest, but very pretty. It is surrounded by a most beautiful garden. I live in the manager's house. It is fairly quiet, save for some forty geese, which at times cackle so lustily together that one cannot hear oneself speak . . . Good people around me, all of them. It must be rare for a count's ret-

---

[22] *Doc.* 96n, *Dok.* 64–5n.   [23] *Doc.* 93, *Dok.* 63.

inue to fit so well together as these do. The inspector, a Slavonian, is a good fellow, and has a great opinion of his former musical talents. He still blows two German dances in 3/4 time on the lute, with great virtuosity. His son studies philosophy, is here on holiday just now, and I hope I shall take to him. His wife is like all women who want to be ladies. The steward fits his office perfectly: a man with an extraordinary insight into his pockets and bags. The doctor, who is really accomplished, ails like an old lady at the age of 24. A lot of oddity around! The surgeon, whom I like best, is a venerable old man of 75, always cheerful and happy. May God give everyone as happy an old age! The magistrate is a straightforward, nice man. A companion of the count, a merry old fellow and a capable musician, often keeps me company. The cook, the lady's maid, the chambermaid, the nurse, the manager, &c. and two grooms are all good folk. The cook a bit of a lad; the lady's maid 30 years of age; the chamber maid very pretty and often my companion; the nurse a good old thing; the manager my rival. The two grooms are more fit for the company of horses than human beings. The count is rather rough, the countess haughty but more sensitive; the little countesses are nice children. So far I have been spared dining with the family. Now I cannot think of any more; I hardly need to tell you, who know me, that with my natural candour I hit it off quite well with all these people.[24]

The first letter to his brother Ferdinand dates from 24 and 25 August. Schubert enclosed this with a copy of the German Requiem D621 which he had just completed for Ferdinand, who was to perform it in the following month in the chapel of the Vienna orphanage, where he was employed as a teacher. After making a few suggestions for the performance of the requiem and some personal messages, he continued:

I have a request to match yours: give my love to my parents, brothers and sisters, friends and acquaintances, not forgetting Karl in particular. Did he not remember me in his letter? . . . Kick my city friends mightily, or have them kicked, to make them write to me. Tell Mother that my laundry is very well looked after, and that her motherly care greatly touches me. (But if I could have more things, I should be extremely glad if you were to send me an extra supply of handkerchiefs, neckerchiefs and stockings. Also I am much in need of two pairs of—cashmere trousers, for which Hart may take the measure where he will. (I should send the money for them at once.) My receipts for the month of July, including the travelling expenses, amounted to 200 florins W.W. [80 fl. K.M.]It is beginning to get cold here already, yet we shall not leave for Vienna before the middle of November. I hope next month to go for a few weeks to Freistadtl, which belongs to Count Erdödy, my count's uncle. They say the country there is extraordinarily pretty. I also hope to go to Pest, as we are going for the grape-harvest to Pócs-Megyer, which is not far from it. It would be uncommonly agreeable for me if I were to meet the administrator Daigele

---

[24] *Doc.* 99–100, *Dok.* 67.

there. But altogether I look forward to all the grape-harvests, about which I have been told a lot of such nice things. The grain-harvest too is very fine here. The corn is not put into barns here, as in Austria, but enormous stacks are erected, which they call *Tristen*. They are often some 80 to 100 yards long and 100 to 120 feet high. They are stacked with such skill that the rain, which is made to run off, can do no damage. Oats and the like is buried in the earth, too.—Well and happy as I am here, and kind as the people are . . . I look forward with immense pleasure to the moment when the word will be 'To Vienna, to Vienna!' Indeed, beloved Vienna, thou holdest all that is most dear and cherished in thy narrow space, and nothing but the sight of this, the heavenly sight, will appease my yearning . . .[25]

(The Daigele mentioned here was the cousin of Schubert's stepmother, clearly a man loved by his family who, as a priest, had conducted the marriage service of his father and stepmother.) Ferdinand answered this letter, or perhaps a later one of his brother's, in mid-October,[26] beginning with a shame-ridden confession the he had passed off the German Requiem as of his own composition. There then followed details of various musical activities in Vienna and of a concert Ferdinand had organized at the orphanage. He ended with a request that he might buy Schubert's fortepiano as he was selling his own, and then he offered an affectionate invitation to his brother to visit him in his apartment at the orphanage in the Alser suburb on his return to Vienna, and if he so wished, to spend the winter with him and his wife. (Ferdinand had married in 1816.)

Earlier in the letter Ferdinand had written: 'Your city friends could not be found, as they were all in the country. But Papa let Mayrhofer read your letter, and the secret that Schober is devoting himself to landscape painting is no longer a secret.[27] From this it appears that Schubert had asked his parents, in another lost letter, to pass on greetings to his friends in the Bildung Circle in Vienna. That Schubert's father gave his son's letter to Mayrhofer to read confirms the trusting relationship that had developed between the two men. Soon after his arrival in Zseliz Schober had told Schubert of his then still secret decision to train as a painter, and to this Schubert referred in the first part of his sixteen-page letter to the Bildung Circle friends of 8 September, already quoted. This began with an expression of delight and thanks to them all for their individual messages in their previous joint letter (which has not survived). This he received while attending a local cattle-market:

I cannot tell you how enormously the letter from you, each and all, delighted me. I was just attending a deal in oxen and cows when your nice, fat letter was handed

---

[25] *Doc.* 95–6, *Dok.* 64.   [26] *Doc.* 105–7, *Dok.* 72–3.   [27] *Doc.* 106, *Dok.* 72.

to me. As I broke it open, loud cries of joy burst from me on beholding the same of Schober. I read it in a neighbouring room, with continual laughter and childish pleasure. It was as though I were hand in hand with my dear friends themselves. But I will answer you all in good order.[28]

The next section was addressed to Schober alone and dealt with his friend's artistic ambitions:

Dear Schobert,
All right—we'll have to stick to that altered name. So, Dear Schobert, your letter was very welcome and precious to me from beginning to end . . . You are a capital fellow (in Swedish, of course), and believe me, my friend, you will not fail, for your understanding of art is the purest and truest imaginable. That you should have regarded this change i.e. Schober to Schobert, as a small one pleased me very much for after all you have long had one foot in our hell . . .

Schubert went on to bemoan the musical isolation he was experiencing, betraying early signs of restlessness half way through his summer sojourn in Hungary:

Here in Zseliz I am obliged to rely wholly on myself. I have to be composer, author, audience, and goodness knows what else. Not a soul here has any feeling for true art, or at most the countess now and again (unless I am wrong). So I am alone with my beloved [Muse] and have to hide her in my room, in my pianoforte and in my bosom. Although this often makes me sad, on the other hand it elevates me the more. Have no fear then, that I shall stay away longer than is absolutely necessary.[29]

Here, to reassure the friends that he was not idle, he added: 'Several songs have materialized recently—very good ones, I hope.'

The fourth and last of the surviving letters which Schubert wrote in Zseliz is dated 29 October, some three weeks before he returned to Vienna. The first part of this letter was again to his brother Ferdinand, an answer to his letter of a couple of weeks or so earlier. The second part was addressed to his eldest brother Ignaz, with a note added to his sister Theresia, both of whom were still living in the Rossau schoolhouse. With Ferdinand, Schubert remonstrated affectionately over what he considered a surfeit of conscience in a brother, firstly over his claiming as his own work the music of the German Requiem Schubert had composed for his use, and finally over possible payment for the fortepiano he was prepared to let him have. In his generosity and love for his brother, he was totally unaffected by Ferdinand's plagiarism of his compositions if it was to his advantage in his

---

[28] *Doc. 98, Dok. 66.*   [29] *Doc. 99, Dok. 66.*

profession; and he was not interested in any payment, or not at this stage, for his old piano, for which he seems to have had no use. He also expressed a longing to return to Vienna:

Dear Brother Ferdinand,

The sin of appropriation was forgiven you from the time of the very first letter, so that you had no cause to defer writing so long, except possibly your tender conscience. So my German Requiem pleased you, and you cried over it, perhaps at the very word over which I wept myself. Dear brother, that is my greatest reward for that gift: on no account mention any other.—*If I did not day by day get to know the people around me better, things would be as well with me as at the beginning.* But now I see that *I am lonely among them after all*, with the exception of a couple of really kind girls. My longing for Vienna grows daily. We shall be off by the middle of November. Affectionate remembrances and kisses to those dear little creatures, Pepi and Marie [Schubert's half-sisters], as also to my excellent parents. The city friends are the limit! Now that Schober's wish is no longer a secret, I breathe again.

The musical affairs [in Vienna you described] left me pretty cold. I merely marvel at the blind and wrong-headed zeal of my rather clumsy friend Doppler, whose friendship does me more harm than good. As for my feelings, I shall never be calculating and politic: I come straight out with what is in me, and that's that.

Do take my fortepiano; I shall be delighted. The only thing that troubles me is that you imagine your letters to be disagreeable to me. It is too terrible even to think your brother capable of such a thing, let alone to write about it.—I hate your always talking about payment, reward and thanks—to a brother, fie, for shame!— Kiss your dear wife and your little Resi [Ferdinand's daughter, b. 1816] for me. And so good-bye.[30]

All the evidence points to a breach between Schubert and his father in the summer of 1818, presumably occasioned by the composer's decision once and for all to turn his back on schoolteaching. As he had no immediate, let alone permanent, prospect of earning his living as a musician and seemed impervious to the realities of his situation, his father no doubt deplored this decision. Although latterly Schubert had been enjoying the company of his friends in the Bildung Circle and of Hüttenbrenner, at home he was depressed and increasingly desperate. The letters that passed between him and his family and friends while he was in Zseliz show the likelihood that there had been an angry scene between father and son, either before or shortly after the Zseliz visit was mooted, at which either the father had turned his son out of the family home or had told him he would not be welcome on his return from Zseliz. Another possible con-

---

[30] *Doc.* 109, *Dok.* 74–5.

clusion is that Schubert decided for himself that it would be better for all concerned if he lived elsewhere. Both Ferdinand and, particularly, Mayrhofer worked hard for a reconciliation between father and son, and it is apparent that some sort of peace was restored. Mayrhofer's role in this might be deduced from the remark in his obituary notice of Schubert written in February 1829: 'I often had to console Schubert's worthy father about his son's future . . .'.[31] This surely applied very much to the period in 1818 when Schubert was in Zseliz, and it is probable that Mayrhofer, in order to alleviate the father's anxieties, at this point offered to take Schubert into his own home on his return, and keep an eye on him. In any case Schubert agreed to this arrangement before Ferdinand, who well understood the problems for his brother during the last tense weeks he had spent in the Rossau home, affectionately offered him hospitality for the coming winter. Correspondence between Schubert and his family shows that some tension remained, but also reveals considerable efforts at reconciliation on both sides. Thus on 24 August Schubert asked Ferdinand to give 'love to my dear parents';[32] their father wrote to his son Karl on 27 August 'he [Franz] speaks in a very cordial tone, full of feeling and affection';[33] and Ferdinand in his last letter to Schubert, already quoted, told him that, according to their father, his little half-sisters were missing him.[34] A final postscript to this same letter of Ferdinand's suggests that part of the conciliation process was Schubert's acceptance of his father's advice that he save as much money as he could while he was in Zseliz. He was going to need it.

In the context of Schubert's relationship with his father, a letter he received in Zseliz from his eldest brother Ignaz, now 33 years old and still forced to teach in their father's school, is revealing. Ignaz painted an unhappy, even unwholesome picture of life at home over the previous weeks. The writer's own uneasy relationship with his father is very much in evidence here as Ignaz, a strong personality and a man who was ever ready to question authoritarian views and impositions from wherever they came, described the scene:

You happy creature! How enviable is your lot! You live in a sweet, golden freedom, able to give free rein to your musical genius, may let your thoughts stray where they will; you are loved, admired and idolized, while the likes of wretched scholastic beasts of burden are abandoned to all the brutality of wild youngsters and exposed to a host of abuses, not to mention the further humiliations to which we are subjected by an ungrateful public and a lot of dunderheaded bigwigs. You

---

[31] *Mem.* 14, *Erin.* 19.   [32] *Doc.* 95, *Dok.* 64.
[33] *Doc.* 97, *Dok.* 65.   [34] *Doc.* 106, *Dok.* 72.

may be surprised when I tell you that it has got to such a pitch in our house that no-one dare laugh any more when I tell them a really funny yarn about superstitious beliefs that have surfaced in the Scripture Class. You can easily imagine how, in these circumstances, I am often seized by secret anger, and that I experience liberty only by name. You see, you are now free of all these things, you are delivered, seeing and hearing nothing of all these goings-on, much less of our pundits [government and church officials]. . . .[35]

He continued with a description of the celebrations for their father's name-day on 4 October:

The next day, the feast of our holy patron-saint Franciscus Seraphicus [St Francis of Assisi], was kept with great solemnity. All the scholars had to be taken to confession, and the bigger ones had to gather at 3 o'clock in the afternoon at school before the saint's image; an altar had been erected, and two school banners were displayed right and left; a short sermon was preached which several times reiterated that it is needful to learn to 'make up one's mind' between good and evil, and that much gratitude was due to the 'boring' teacher . . . Also, a litany was addressed to the saint—a litany the oddity of which astonished me not a little. At the end there was singing, and a relic of the saint was given to all present to kiss, whereupon I noticed that several of the adults crept out at the door, having no desire, perhaps, to share in this privilege.

Ignaz, the freethinker, well knew his younger brother's loathing of such occasions and views on the insincerity of forced devotions. There can be little wonder that Schubert answered Ignaz' letter two weeks later (29 October) with a tirade against the local priests in Zseliz, probably based on verbal translations of the sermons in Hungarian he was given by some of the count's staff:

I was most sincerely pleased to receive letters from you, Ignaz and Resi. You, Ignaz, are still quite the old man of iron. Your implacable hatred of the whole tribe of bigwigs does you credit. But you have no conception what a gang the priesthood is here: bigoted as mucky old cattle, stupid as arch-donkeys and boorish as bisons. You may hear sermons here to which our most venerated *Pater Nepomucene* can't hold a candle. They chuck about blackguards, riffraff, &c. from the pulpit, something lovely; they put a death's head on the pulpit and say: 'Look here, you pockpitted mugs, that's how you will look one day.' Or else: 'There, a fellow takes a slut into the pub, they dance all night, then go they to bed tight, and when they get up there are three of 'em,' &c. &c.—Whether you thought of me while you were guzzling I don't know.[36]

Schubert's letters from Zseliz are informative, entertaining, carefully designed for each recipient, direct and unegotistic. He comes over as per-

---

[35] *Doc.* 103–4, *Dok.* 70–1.   [36] *Doc.* 110, *Dok.* 75.

ceptive, sensitive, humorous, affectionate, and warm-hearted. He shows some signs of varying temperament, but not in a manner likely to cause his readers alarm. Indeed, it is the letters of Ferdinand and Ignaz which arouse sympathy. For Schubert, life and work in Zseliz was, at least at first, for the most part satisfying and pleasant. Whether his references to the chambermaid, Josefine (Pepi) Pöckelhofer, indicated a brief love affair, a flirtation, or an enjoyable friendship the ever-reserved composer was unlikely to reveal in any letter his parents might see, or collectively addressed to his friends in the Bildung Circle. Whatever feelings he may have retained for his fist love, Therese Grob, it is probable that they had now parted company; for, if Anselm Hüttenbrenner was correct in his recollections of their relationship, the three years during which Therese maintained hopes of marrying Schubert were now over. His recent decision to abandon a teaching career must have been for her the final straw. In this case, it is possible that Schubert sought and found consolation for the loss of Therese in some short-term relationship with the cheerful chambermaid, in modern parlance, in a holiday romance. Another possibility also arises that Schubert had found that he was unable to love Therese, or any woman, sufficiently to seriously contemplate marriage, a subject to which I shall return later. What is certain is that two years later Therese Grob married her master baker.

After his musically unproductive last few months at the Rossau school, in Zseliz Schubert found again the will and ability to compose. During the four months he spent there he wrote, in addition to the German Requiem for Ferdinand, a host of piano music for four hands, solo piano music, and songs. The piano duets were sometimes written with a more difficult *primo* part for himself to play while one or other of his young pupils was expected to play a simpler *secondo* part.[37] Some of the marches, of no great difficulty in either part, may have been written for the sisters to play together. In addition they performed songs to Schubert's accompaniment. The Esterházys' piano was a good grand which had been made to order for the count by Karl Schmidt in Pressburg.[38] This was kept in the dining-room, where Schubert and his pupils had freer access to it than they would have done had it been permanently positioned in the main salon. The dining-room was also a better venue for the dancing which sometimes took place in the evenings.

While in Zseliz Schubert, as was his custom, explored some of the surrounding countryside on foot. On some of these walks he may have called in at a nearby mill, about half a mile from the schloss, where the miller and

[37] As e.g. in the Theme and Variations on a French Air D624 and the Four Polonaises D599.
[38] Schmidt was a former pupil of Konrad Graf in Vienna.

his family were German-speakers and with whom, unlike most of the townsfolk of Zseliz, he could converse in his own language.[39] Although a fair number of German-speakers had been encouraged by Count Esterházy to settle in and around Zseliz, the majority of the local population was Hungarian. In the course of this summer, Schubert surely experienced some of the local folk music and dancing in the town; and he may have heard Pannonian gypsy bands. How much influence this music had on him is uncertain. Even in the *Divertissement à l'hongroise* D818 for piano duet, which he composed after his second visit to Zseliz in 1824, there is little real native Hungarian influence. Whatever there is could easily have been acquired in Vienna where there were already many Hungarian musicians, as well as Czechs and those from other central European areas in the Austro-Hungarian empire.

Schubert was well pleased with his stay in Zseliz, but after four and a half months on an estate on the edge of a country town, he was tiring of the company and, despite the kindness shown to him by his two pupils, he began to long for Vienna, for the stimulation of his friends and family, and the music and culture of the city. He returned on 19 November, at the same time as the Esterházy family, no doubt to a warm welcome from his friends. With sufficient money saved to see him through the next few weeks, he moved directly into his new abode with Mayrhofer.

One of the first things to cheer Schubert further after his return to Vienna was the news that Vogl had negotiated a commission for him. He was to compose the music for an operetta, *Die Zwillingsbrüder* (The Twin Brothers), for the Kärntnertor-Theater, in the production of which Vogl himself would sing the leading double role of the twin brothers. The text, based on a French model, was by the resident librettist of the opera house, Georg von Hofmann. Schubert's initial excitement on receiving the commission was tempered by disappointment when the libretto arrived. To the one-act length common in theatres at this time he was resigned; but he was very disappointed by Hofmann's frivolous treatment of the subject and the poverty of the text. However, despite this disappointment, he knew that to compose for the Court Opera House was, for a young man not yet 22 years old, an opportunity not to be missed. Thanks to Vogl, here was a chance for him to break into the theatre world and perhaps to achieve a success which would assure his future. He set to work at once on the score.

Schubert lived with Mayrhofer in the same house in the Wipplinger-strasse in which in 1813 the poet Theodor Körner, one of Schubert's heroes, had lodged. Here he remained until the end of 1820, shortly after

---

[39] Vitálová, 'Schubert in Zseliz', 98.

Mayrhofer was appointed to a permanent position with the Central Book Censorship Office as third censor. Between 1818 and 1819 Mayrhofer, who was neither temperamentally nor physically robust, suffered unspecified ill health, which aggravated his difficulties in finding suitable employment. Like many educated young men of the day without regular employment, for a while he earned a modest living as a private tutor; but it was now financially to his advantage to share his lodgings with Schubert. The one room they occupied was rather long, narrow, and dark. In Mayrhofer's words: 'Both the house and the room have felt the hand of time: the ceiling somewhat sunken, the daylight reduced by a large building opposite, a clapped-out pianoforte, a narrow bookshelf . . .'[40]—a somewhat sombre description.

From the autumn of 1819, Schubert was frequently visited in this room by Anselm Hüttenbrenner, after the latter's return from Graz to Vienna. Hüttenbrenner recorded his impressions of these visits and of the apparently well-ordered and contented life Schubert was now leading: 'Schubert . . . sat down at his writing desk every morning at 6 o'clock and composed straight through until 1 o'clock in the afternoon. Meanwhile, many a pipe was smoked.'[41] If Hüttenbrenner visited him during the morning while he was working, and there is no suggestion that Mayrhofer was ever at home on these occasions, Schubert played through his latest composition and asked for his opinion. 'Schubert never composed in the afternoon but went rather, after the mid-day meal, to a coffee-house where he would sit over a small cup of black coffee for an hour or two, smoke and read the newspapers . . . In the evenings he would sometimes go to the theatre.'[42] From this account it seems probable that the two men had arranged to apportion the time during which they occupied their room during the day: Schubert to compose music in the mornings, Mayrhofer to write poetry in the afternoons. Without such an arrangement, it is hard to imagine how they could have lived comparatively happily together for so long in such cramped conditions.

Mayrhofer claimed that he wrote much poetry while Schubert lived with him. Schubert certainly composed a great deal of music, including six settings of his friend's poetry. Fortunately for their relationship, Mayrhofer was musical; he sang and played the guitar and (according to Spaun) had 'an exceptionally good [musical] ear and great love of music'.[43] Schubert for his part loved poetry and avidly absorbed all that Mayrhofer could impart about poetry and, after Vogl had sparked his interest in Greek antiquity, about classical literature. Thus the two men had much to share and learn from each other. However, with two creative artists, both subject to

---

[40] *Mem.* 13, *Erin.* 18.   [41] *Mem.* 182, *Erin.* 209–10.
[42] *Mem.* 183, *Erin.* 210.   [43] *Mem.* 130, *Erin.* 151.

depression, living at such close quarters in one cramped and dark room, some tensions were inevitable. Mayrhofer described their lives together, and some of the ways in which they endeavoured to deal with disagreements:

While we shared a room our idiosyncracies could not but show themselves; we were both richly endowed in this respect, and the consequences could not fail to appear. We teased each other in many different ways and turned our sharp edges on each other to our mutual amusement and pleasure. His happy outgoing nature and my introspective one were thus thrown into higher relief and gave rise to names we called each other accordingly, as though we were playing parts assigned to us. Unfortunately I played my very own! . . .[44]

Money was sometimes a problem for both of them, but in 1819 Vogl came to Schubert's rescue. According to the poet, Vogl could be regarded as Schubert's second father: he 'not only took care of Schubert materially, but in truth furthered him also spiritually and artistically'.[45]

One of Schubert's few sources of earned income in the winter months after his return from Zseliz was his continued tuition to the young Esterházy countesses. He may occasionally have visited them in their winter palace in Penzing, a rather distant south-western suburb of Vienna; but most usually he attended them in their town house in the city. When the family returned to Zseliz in the following April, Schubert did not accompany them. If he was invited to do so, he probably declined because he was expecting his operetta, *Die Zwillingsbrüder*, which he had finished already in the previous January, to go into production later in the year; and of course he wanted to be in Vienna when this happened. Alternatively, or coincidentally, he was aware of burgeoning career opportunities in Vienna which he could ill afford to sacrifice by accepting a further long spell of employment in Zseliz.

Schubert had completed *Die Zwillingsbrüder* in the space of a few weeks on 19 January 1819, and thereafter anxiously awaited news of its projected performance. Meanwhile he enjoyed a stream of minor musical successes. On 8 January there was a second performance of his secular cantata 'Prometheus', as the final item in one of now fortnightly Friday evening musical 'rehearsals' for members of the Gesellschaft der Musikfreunde held in the home of Ignaz Sonnleithner in the 'Gundelhof', where there was ample space for some 120 guests.[46] At this performance of the cantata, a piano replaced the original orchestral accompaniment. The suggestion that 'Prometheus' should feature in one of these meetings came from the Sonnleithners' son Leopold, who in the summer of 1816 had taken part in

---

[44] *Mem.* 14, *Erin.* 19.   [45] Ibid.   [46] *Mem.* 342, *Erin.* 395, *ND* 17.

the highly successful first performance of the cantata in the garden of Professor Watteroth's house. Leopold saw this second performance of the cantata as a way of drawing the attention of influential members of the Gesellschaft der Musikfreunde to Schubert's talent, of boosting his reputation with them, and hastening the time when he would be welcomed as a performing member. In the first four months of this year, and apart from the private performance of 'Prometheus', there were four public concerts in Vienna, all in different venues, at which a composition of Schubert's was included. Three of these included the same song, 'Schäfers Klagelied' (Shepherd's Lament) D121 and attracted press mention in Vienna and Berlin. The fourth concert, on 14 March, in the Müller's Hall (Josef Müllerscher Kunstsaal am Rothen Thurm), was given by the Society of Amateurs (Dilettanten-Gesellschaft), of which Ferdinand Schubert was now an honorary member and orchestral director. Included in the programme was a performance of an orchestral overture by Schubert, probably the Overture in E minor D648 which he had completed the previous month.[47] For the awaited première of *Die Zwillingsbrüder* Schubert had to wait until the summer of 1820.

Schober was probably out of Vienna for much of 1819, supposedly studying landscape painting. This did not stop him from visiting Atzenbrugg castle, some twenty-five miles west of Vienna, as he had for the past two years, to enjoy there the three-day summer festival, or house-party, hosted by his uncle Josef Derffel, who was both manager of the Atzenbrugg estate owned by the Klosterneuburg monastery near Vienna, and legal representative of the same monastery. For this house-party Derffel and his wife opened up the castle to their nephews and nieces, Franz and Sophie von Schober and Franz and Therese Derffel and their young friends, many of them from Vienna. Schubert, although living with Schober at the time of the festival in 1817, did not attend; nor did he until 1820.

Anton Holzapfel, to whom, early in 1815, Schubert had confided his love for Therese Grob, was now a qualified lawyer. He continued to refer to Schubert in letters to their mutual friend Albert Stadler, living first in Linz and then in Steyr, but admitted that they now saw little of each other. The distance between them was widening rapidly, and so much so that three years later Holzapfel told Stadler: 'I rarely see him, nor do we hit it off very well . . .'.[48] In similar vein he wrote in recollections of Schubert many years later (in 1858):

---

[47] *Doc.* 115, *Dok.* 78.   [48] *Doc.* 211, *Dok.* 148.

The things we had in common grew noticeably fewer, he attached himself to a circle of friends quite foreign to me, while at the same time the pattern of my life, now devoted wholly to law, followed a path so divergent from his that for years on end I did not see him, and when I did, it was only by chance.[49]

Holzapfel surely knew Spaun and some members of the Bildung Circle. The 'friends quite foreign' to him were those of Schober's personal circle. Neither Holzapfel nor Anselm Hüttenbrenner were members of the Bildung Circle, and both kept their distance from Schober and his circle. Hüttenbrenner's relationship with Schubert was a private one and, where it involved other people as well, was usually connected with music. After he returned to Graz in the autumn of 1818 on his appointment to a position in the district court there, the two young men exchanged some lively letters, continuing the relaxed and carefree friendship they had enjoyed. Their meetings resumed when both returned to Vienna in the autumn of 1819, Schubert from a holiday in Upper Austria with Vogl, Hüttenbrenner to take up a new appointment.

Throughout the first half of 1819 Schubert attended many of the meetings of the orchestra which had formerly met at Hatwig's, but which, since his illness that spring, now assembled in the similarly spacious home of Anton von Pettenkofer, a wholesale grocer and landowner living near the Bauernmarkt.[50] The nature of these orchestral meetings, which had begun in 1814 as chamber music evenings in the Schubert family home, had changed beyond recognition. They now attracted some of Vienna's finest amateur and some professional players, so that by 1819 the orchestra was able to put on performances of the orchestral repertoire to a respectable standard, and also, on occasion, oratorios. The meetings continued on Thursday evenings, but the rehearsals now prepared the way for performances for invited audiences by a good ensemble, which included many well-known musicians.[51] Here, for example, on 6 April Schubert joined in a performance of Haydn's *The Seven Words of Our Saviour* (*Die sieben Worte unseres Erlösers*). No doubt at these 'rehearsals' he met many old acquaintances, some of them excellent musicians, with whom for some years now he had been making music, and who had already given first performances, if only private run-throughs, of many of his recent orchestral works. Most of these players, while known personally to Schubert, were not however his intimate friends. Nor were most of those he met at the fortnightly Gesellschaft der Musikfreunde musical salons (also known as 'rehearsals'), held on Friday evenings during the winter months at the home of Ignaz

---

[49] *Mem.* 61, *Erin.* 71.   [50] *Doc.* 116n, *Dok.* 78n.
[51] Sonnleithner: *Mem.* 339–40, *Erin.* 391–2.

Sonnleithner. Schubert was not yet a member of the society, but he was sometimes invited to attend these salons. Here he mingled with eminent musicians such as Ignaz Schuppanzigh, Karl Maria von Bocklet, Hugo Worzischek (Vořišék), Ferdinand Bogner, and Karl Czerny, some of whom later become good friends and colleagues who played in performances of his music. But the greatest influence on him at this time came from Vogl and Mayrhofer. With their encouragement, and with the access to a far wider range of literature that accompanied their friendship, Schubert became increasingly involved with difficult poetic texts and their musical possibilities. For a while he broke away from the more usual lyric poetry or story-telling ballads and dramatic scenas for inspiration, attracted now to poems of greater intellectual complexity by authors whose works previously had rarely, if ever, been set to music. When the intellectual demands or musical realizations caused him to falter, or if he was dissatisfied with a finished product, or, as he described it to Anselm Hüttenbrenner, he produced only 'boring stuff',[52] Schubert discarded his work and started again, either with the same text or with a fresh one.

Until this time Viennese song composers had been writing songs exclusively for a domestic market, choosing for the most part lyrical poems with simple themes or subjects that were quickly recognizable and understandable to the average amateur performer and listener. When Schubert in January 1819 selected both Ludwig Tieck's 'Abend' (Evening) ('Wie ist es den'—How does it come about) D645, which he failed to finish, and K. W. Friedrich von Schlegel's 'Die Gebüsche' (The Thicket) D646 from the cycle of poems *Abendröte*, in the setting of which he experienced considerable difficulties, he was attempting a new kind of song for a new class of performer and audience. Both poems (which had appeared together in the *Musenalmanach für das Jahr 1802*, edited by Tieck and A. W. von Schlegel, brother of Friedrich) express difficult Romantic concepts at a literary level which make it unlikely that the poets themselves ever imagined that their poems would be set to music. For Schubert here was a challenge, a new concept of the *Lied*, and one which exercised him far more than could be imagined from the limited number of his completed song compositions during this year—some twenty-six. Of these, six poems were by Mayrhofer, five by Novalis, four by Goethe, and between three and five by Friedrich Schlegel. Vogl almost certainly put him in the way of Novalis's poetry, of which the singer was particularly fond. When in May Schubert picked out four of Novalis's *Geistliche Lieder* (Sacred Songs), the 'Hymnen I–IV' DD659–62, and notably the first of these, 'Wenige wissen das Geheimnis

---

[52] Hüttenbrenner: *Mem.* 182–3, *Erin.* 210.

der Liebe' (Few know the secret of love), he was attempting to represent in music a difficult poetic and theological world of mysticism and paradox. This first poem in particular contains a stream of passionate and sensuous love imagery in a context of mystical religious feeling which, in a musical setting, almost precludes unity of form. In 1815 Schubert had found he sometimes needed several attempts, or at least several revisions, when setting poems by Goethe before he was satisfied with the result. With the complex poems of Novalis and the complex ideas of Friedrich von Schlegel, he was on virgin soil; he was attempting a novel kind of song in which verbal philosophical thought and rare kinds of imagery were translated into music. If he did not completely succeed with these songs in 1819, his efforts surely opened his mind and spirit, and stretched his creativity. At the same time, he was pioneering the development and potential of song and of all vocal writing, through a process of transforming both understanding and techniques. As a result, when in October he came to set Goethe's heroic poem 'Prometheus' D674, not to be confused with the cantata of the same name, in which the poet examines man's conflict with the gods and his destiny on this earth, he found the task far more manageable than that of setting Novalis's 'Wenige wissen' (Hymne I) five months earlier. Nevertheless, it presented Schubert with a considerable challenge. In this magnificent setting of 'Prometheus', he responded to the poem's powerful imagery, stretching the genre to new dramatic expressiveness, and showing that he was now fully equipped intellectually and technically for such a task.

During the 1819 opera season, Vogl was singing at least eight major roles at the Kärntnertor-Theater. Although the theatre was closed for the summer vacation for only the month of August, Vogl was able this year to take eight full weeks' holiday, from mid-July until mid-September. As was his custom for his annual vacation, he returned to his roots in Upper Austria; and on this occasion he invited Schubert to accompany him, presumably at least in part at Vogl's expense. However, shortly before they left Vienna, and probably as the result of Vogl's negotiations with the Kärntnertor-Theater management in an effort to ensure that the young composer had some money of his own for the holiday, the singer received on 9 July and on behalf of Schubert, an advance of 150 fl. on his fee of 500 fl. WW (200 fl. KM) for the music of the singspiel *Die Zwillingsbrüder*.

The two men travelled directly to Steyr, Vogl's birthplace, where the singer had arranged lodgings for Schubert in the home of Albert Schellmann, a cultured barrister,[53] father of eleven children and uncle of

---

[53] Berggerichtsadvokat: *Dok.* 83.

Schubert's old friend from their schooldays, Albert Stadler. (One of Schellmann's sons, also Albert, a year younger than Schubert, later became a friend of the composer in Vienna.) Schubert had a room on the second floor of the house, where Stadler and his mother also had an apartment. Thus Schubert was living in close proximity to his old friend. The Schellmanns occupied the first floor. Schellmann's three sons and only five of his eight daughters were then at home, but next door lived three daughters of the Weilnböck family, one of whom, Antonie, later married Albert Stadler. This complement of eight young ladies in the immediate vicinity inspired Schubert to write to his brother Ferdinand on 13 July, soon after his arrival in Steyr: 'At the house where I lodge there are eight girls, nearly all of them pretty. Plenty to do, you see.'[54] In the room made available to him Schubert slept and worked with the aid of the Schellmanns' own piano, generously lent to him for the duration of his stay—with the result that, as one of the daughters complained, 'during his visit [we] had to do without dances and things like that'.[55] Vogl had arranged for Schubert to meet him for meals at the home of another cultured friend, the iron-merchant Josef von Koller, whose daughter Josefine was a talented pianist and singer. The evening meal was frequently preceded by a walk in what Schubert termed the 'heavenly' country surrounding Steyr,[56] followed by private music-making 'behind closed doors' as Albert Stadler, who was usually present, described it.[57] On one such occasion the song 'Erlkönig' was sung to 'odd effect' as a trio,[58] and 'only among ourselves, of course'. Josefine Koller sang the role of the boy, Schubert the father and Vogl the erl-king, while Stadler accompanied. At other times the younger three would exchange roles as singers and accompanists, also playing solo piano works by Schubert. In his turn, Vogl added variety by singing through operatic arias that were currently much in vogue. In his July letter to Ferdinand, Schubert did not mention these musical evenings; the pattern of events had not yet settled into its ultimate pleasurable form; but he did refer to Josefine Koller as 'very pretty, plays the piano well and is going to sing several of my songs'.[59] Again according to Stadler, Schubert showed his appreciation to the Kollers for their kindness to him during his stay and his admiration for the daughter by presenting her on his departure with the manuscript of a new solo piano sonata which he had recently completed (presumably that in A D664).

Other musical events in Steyr of a more public nature took place in the home of a wealthy bachelor, music-lover, and generous patron of the arts,

[54] *Doc.* 121, *Dok.* 82.
[55] Ebner: *Mem.* 47, *Erin.* 55–6.
[56] *Doc.* 124, *Dok.* 84.
[57] *Mem.* 152; *Erin.* 178.
[58] Stadler: *Mem.* 153, *Erin.* 178.
[59] *Doc.* 121, *Dok.* 82.

Sylvester Paumgartner. He was by profession a mining official (manager), and an amateur wind-player and cellist. Paumgartner lived by himself in a sizeable house in the central square of the town, using the first-floor set of rooms, complete 'with its own decorated music-room',[60] as his own apartment. This music-room was used very frequently for chamber music rehearsals and small private evening music parties. There was a larger and grander salon on the second floor, with symbolic emblems and portraits of musicians decorating the walls, various musical instruments, and a plentiful collection of music. Here Paumgartner hosted midday concerts for larger invited audiences, but these too were of an informal and friendly kind. And here Schubert and Vogl delighted many of the music-lovers of Steyr with their performances although, as Stadler described, 'it was not uncommon for the good Paumgartner to have to almost go down on his knees to persuade Vogl, who was not always in exactly the right mood and temper to take part'.[61] At the smaller private evening parties at Paumgartner's they again performed. On all these occasions Vogl, the local hero, led proceedings, while Schubert sat inconspicuously at the piano, following his partner's every whim. With a singer of such eminence, reputation, and temperament, there was little else Schubert could do; and if most of the praise and acclaim was directed at Vogl, Schubert, while in any case preferring his 'back seat' at the piano, still had the satisfaction of recognizing that his songs were warmly appreciated. At Paumgartner's request Schubert, on his return to Vienna, composed the five-movement Piano Quintet D667 (the 'Trout' Quintet) for violin, viola, cello, double bass, and piano, the fourth movement of which is a set of variations on his song of that name. There is uncertainty as to which of Schubert's three visits to Steyr—in 1819, 1823, and 1825—resulted in the composition of this quintet.[62] However, an analysis of the style suggests that the quintet dates from the period after Schubert's return to Vienna from Steyr in the autumn of 1819.

While they were in Steyr, on 10 August, Vogl celebrated his fifty-first birthday. The young friends who had been making music with him over the previous weeks decided to celebrate with a new musical offering written especially for the occasion. First Stadler produced a eulogistic poem in six verses, of the kind fashionable at the time; Schubert followed by setting it to music for solo soprano, tenor, bass, and piano in three sections (D666). This was then rehearsed and performed for Vogl at the Kollers' home by Josefine Koller, Bernhardt Benedict (a local tenor), and Schubert, accom-

---

[60] Stadler: *Mem.* 152, *Erin.* 177.   [61] Ibid.
[62] A. Feil, *NGA*, ser. 6, vol. vii, pp. xiv–xv.

panied as usual by Stadler. The evening was described by Schubert in a letter to Mayrhofer of 19 August, as 'quite a success'.[63]

Schubert was happy in Steyr. He wrote to Mayrhofer: 'At Steyr I had an excellent time, and shall again. The country is heavenly.'[64] After their stay there, Schubert and Vogl moved on, during the second or third week of August, for a short visit to Linz. Here Schubert again met old friends from the Stadtkonvikt, such as Spaun and Josef Kenner. He deepened his acquaintance with Anton von Spaun, whom he had met briefly in Vienna in 1816,[65] and got to know Anton Ottenwalt. Both these men, as founders and leaders of the Bildung Circle in Linz, had already heard much about Schubert and his music, and he of them. In Linz Schubert discovered the charm of the popular Castle inn and its garden situated in public woodland on a high ridge overlooking the town, and with fine views of surrounding mountains and the twisting pattern of the river Danube below. When he returned to Linz in later years, he was to spend many happy evenings here with friends. But, on this first visit, these were infrequent. He was content to visit Spaun and his mother in their home, to get to know a few new friends, and to make music for them with Vogl. A planned visit to Salzburg did not materialize (he and Vogl were there together later, in the summer of 1825), and they returned to Steyr for the final days of their holiday.

In the third week of September, Schubert left Upper Austria in good spirits, refreshed by the clear air, and with many happy memories of events, scenery, and the new friendships he had enjoyed. Back in Vienna and his room with Mayrhofer, he found the poet now in better health and at last at work on the new libretto he had promised Schubert some months earlier, his first since *Die Freunde von Salamanka* of 1815. *Adrast* was based on the classical Greek legend of Adrastus as told by Herodotus, a subject of which Vogl too would surely have approved. Schubert's father realized finally that his son had no intention of returning to schoolteaching, and, for the first time since 1814, declined to register him officially as an 'assistant' in his school. Schubert may have presumed by now that his short stature, already given by his father in January 1818 as '4 Schuh 11 Zoll 2 Strich' (around 157 cm, or 5′ 1″) in the government conscription form, would for the time being make him ineligible for the dreaded military service.[66] In the longer term he trusted that his success as a composer would permanently exempt him; for established composers and performing musicians were among those who were excused.

---

[63] *Doc.* 124, *Dok.* 85. For Herr Koller's next name-day, on 19 Mar. 1820, the precedent having been set, Stadler and Schubert collaborated in another celebratory cantata (D695), this time for solo soprano (Josefine) and piano (Stadler) alone.

[64] *Doc.* 124, *Dok.* 84.   [65] *Doc.* 54–5, *Dok.* 39.   [66] *Dok.* 56n.

On holiday in Upper Austria Schubert had composed or completed very little music; and not one song appears to date from the months July to September. As was now usual for him in October of each year, he soon settled again into a productive period, working on some nine songs, the Mass in A flat D678 (begun on 19 November but not completed in its initial version for another three years, until September 1822, and in its final version until late 1825 or early 1826), probably the 'Trout' Quintet, and the new opera *Adrast* D137. (The early Deutsch number for the opera is the result of former false dating of this work to 1815.) Schubert was composing this opera, which he left unfinished, from the autumn of 1819 until January 1820, when he put it aside to concentrate on an Easter oratorio, *Lazarus, oder: Die Feier der Auferstehung* (Lazarus, or the Festival of the Resurrection) D689. To compose great classical operas may not have been Schubert's destiny, or that of any of his contemporaries in German-speaking countries, but *Adrast* is of special interest not only for many passages of original and striking music, but for some revolutionary advances Schubert made in vocal and orchestral sonorities. A new imaginative quality in both the vocal lines and accompaniment is as remarkable in this opera as is, for example, his innovative contrapuntal writing for strings often divided in their lower registers.

Thus 1819 passed, for Schubert a year of some successes, of rewarding friendships, and of rich advances in his intellectual and musical thinking and its application. His genius and promise were being noticed and appreciated by more than a few. He was beginning to be accepted in middle-class cultured society. Schubert seemed to be in control of his life, and had much to look forward to.

5

LA DOLCE VITA
(1820–1822)

WITH reliable and supportive friends like Josef von Spaun, Johann Mayrhofer, and Anselm Hüttenbrenner, and influential patrons of the calibre of Johann Michael Vogl and Ignaz Sonnleithner, the outlook for Schubert at the start of 1820 was promising indeed. Helped by his friends, his reputation in musical circles was growing, particularly as a composer of songs, but also of orchestral and church music; and by the end of 1820 he had already made some impression in Vienna with his music for the theatre. In 1821 he was to enjoy remarkable advances in his profession, with more, and some prestigious, concert performances of his music, publications, and press reviews and notices. By the end of 1822 his situation had changed totally.

Composers, like all creative artists, need both stimulation and solitude. Schubert's closest friends understood this. They knew when it was necessary for him to be alone, and they were ready when he needed them to listen to his latest compositions, to discuss poetic texts, to share his current concerns, or just to relax with him and enjoy his company. This was the apparently happy situation for much of 1820, but over the next two years his attitudes were to change, and for a while during this period he rejected some of the affection he had shared with former companions. He became impatient or lost touch, through no fault of theirs, with such as Spaun and Holzapfel, was downright neglectful of those wishing to help him, including Vogl and Leopold Sonnleithner, and quarrelled with his publisher. A period of capricious sensuality and irresponsibility ceased abruptly at the end of 1822 when he developed the first symptoms of venereal disease.[1]

---

[1] Eric Sams has suggested early 1823 for the onset of the disease. I prefer the earlier date, for reasons that will become apparent below. E. Sams, 'Schubert's Illness Re-examined', *MT* 121 (1980), 15–22.

It was no coincidence that the change in Schubert, which was particularly apparent from the latter part of 1821, began soon after Schober's return to Vienna early in 1821 (or perhaps the very end of 1820) after an absence of more than a year, and the strengthening of their friendship. Since the early days of this friendship in 1816, Schober had both travelled widely and indulged himself with some extravagance. At the kind of experiences he may have enjoyed and attitudes he had adopted we can only guess. Back in Vienna, he soon collected around him a circle of young male admirers. However, his ability to wheedle his way into their affections, to excite their adulation, to win their loyalty both collectively and individually, seldom resulted in long-term close relationships. Schubert, whose most intense emotional relationship with Schober was probably restricted to 1821 and 1822, remained a loyal friend until his death, although, not surprisingly, they sometimes had disagreements. As the period of their closest involvement coincided with the gradual decline in Schubert's social behaviour, it is likely that Schober played some part in the change in his friend, or at least that he did little, if anything, to oppose it. On the positive side, however, this time of sowing wild oats and self-discovery was essential to Schubert as an artist. In fact, he may not have seen the resulting breakdown of his previously sturdy physical health at the end of 1822 as total disaster. The Romantic concept of the suffering artist was by this time widely accepted, and presumably by Schubert himself, to judge from an entry in his notebook of 1824: 'Pain sharpens the understanding and strengthens the mind . . .'.[2] However, in the music he wrote from 1823 onwards when the full force of his illness struck him, there was a new element born of experience, physical suffering, and anguish of mind occasioned by the misery of the present and uncertainty of the future. The innocence, charm, high-spirited joy, zest, and humour frequently found in his earlier music disappeared for ever, to be replaced by earnestness, brooding melancholy, resignation, severity, and determination, even forceful energy and violent anger but little charm or joy of a personal nature. It is this change in the content of his music which enables us to conclude with some certainty that the 'Trout' Quintet, for example, dates from the period before Schubert developed syphilis.

Schubert's professional fortunes in the three years from 1820 to some degree mirror the changes that took place in his private life and the responses these occasioned in his friends and acquaintances who had initially been eager to help him. During 1820, the number of his public successes and his professional prospects improved considerably, but now

[2] *Doc.* 336, *Dok.* 232.

almost entirely in the world of theatre. In that year, two of his stage works were produced in Vienna, both commissioned. *Die Zwillingsbrüder* ran for six performances at the Kärntnertor-Theater (Hofoper) in June and July. The full-length magic extravaganza *Die Zauberharfe* (The Magic Harp), a play for which he composed extensive music, opened in August at the Theater an der Wien, and received eight performances before it was finally withdrawn in October. On the other hand, apart from these fourteen theatre performances, his music was heard in a public venue apparently only once during the year, and then in a concert in Graz, when one of his orchestral overtures was played. In addition, on Friday, 1 December at a private evening concert of the Gesellschaft der Musikfreunde at the home of Ignaz Sonnleithner, Schubert's song 'Erlkönig' was included in the programme, the first of his songs to be performed before an audience other than of his friends alone.

Significantly 1821, when Schubert was at last accepted as a performing member of the Gesellschaft der Musikfreunde, saw a remarkable growth early in the year in the number of performances of his music. Eight concerts at which his music was heard were private occasions of the society, either Thursday evening chamber concerts or other evening entertainments (usually on a Friday), most of these in the early part of the year. From the frequency of these performances at Gesellschaft concerts, Schubert's music was obviously popular, and his reputation with the members quickly grew. Some of these, notably Ignaz and Leopold Sonnleithner, had considerable influence on the affairs of the society. As a result, one of his works, different on each occasion, was included in three major concerts of the Gesellschaft.[3] Two of these were in the Redoutensaal of the Imperial Palace: in April a male-voice quartet and in November an orchestral overture. Also in November, at a smaller venue, his song 'Der Wanderer' (the Wanderer) D489 was included in the programme. Even more prestigious were the invitations he received to provide music for three important public concerts in the Kärntnertor-Theater. The first two were charity concerts (*Akademien*) given on Ash Wednesday and Easter Sunday. The third was a benefit concert in October. In addition, there were eight performances at the same theatre of Hérold's opera *Das Zauberglöckchen* (The Magic Bell) in which two numbers by Schubert were inserted. Announcements and notices of all the major concerts and some of the private ones were published in the Vienna press, and mention made of them in several newspapers and journals of Leipzig, Dresden, and Berlin and, perhaps for the first time, Hamburg.

---

[3] *Doc.* 173, 198, 199, *Dok.* 122, 141, 142; *ND* 83, 129, 130.

In 1822, thanks to the advance in his professional standing and the popularity of some of his songs, his name was becoming generally known amongst music-lovers in Vienna, and in some areas beyond. How else could it be that a song of his was to be heard on the equivalent of the modern juke-box—a mechanical clock—at the Hungarian Crown inn, one of the favourite haunts of Schubert and his friends?[4] In the course of the year there were seven concerts that we know of in public venues in Vienna, several of them charity concerts, apart from those organized by the Gesellschaft der Musikfreunde. In addition, there were three in Graz and one in Linz. All except one of these included a vocal quartet by Schubert, a genre for which he was becoming increasingly well known. However, none of his operas was staged during this year, and there was an appreciable fall in the number of performances of his music in private concerts of the Gesellschaft: from a total of twelve in 1821 to a mere four in 1822. For this fall in his popularity with members of the Gesellschaft, Schubert was entirely to blame. By his unco-operative attitude and unreliability he was making it difficult for his friends and acquaintances, on whom his progress depended, to help him. Indeed, their patience ran out. A decrease in the number of his songs published in 1822 as compared with the previous year is less significant. Whereas all except one of the twenty appearing in 1821 had been written several years before, more than half of those appearing in 1822 had been composed within the last two years. However, despite this alleviating factor, Schubert's personal life during 1822 was proving both socially and professionally damaging. Its effect on his creative genius, on the other hand, was quite the opposite.

At the end of 1822 Schubert was just one month away from his twenty-sixth birthday. He had served his apprenticeship as a composer, already written minor masterpieces in each of the principal musical genres, except perhaps opera, where he hoped still to prove himself. He was now a master craftsman. We will now turn to look in detail at Schubert's life and development as man and composer in these three vital years of his life.

Until the end of 1820, Schubert shared with Mayrhofer the long, dark room in the Wipplingerstrasse, rented from Frau Sansoucci, the widowed mother of Franz Sansoucci who had been a student with Schubert at the Stadtkonvikt. Writing of the partnership of Schubert and Mayrhofer, the good-natured Spaun, who tended to see the best in all his friends, suggested that '[their] friendly relationship . . . and years of living together had a most favourable effect on both of them, on the poet as well as the composer'.[5]

---

[4] *Doc.* 213, *Dok.* 149.   [5] *Mem.* 21, *Erin.* 28.

Holzapfel, on the other hand, after referring first to Mayrhofer's recurring states of 'emotional exultation' and contrasting periods of melancholy and depression which were later to drive him to suicide, was aware of the difficulties the two men experienced in their 'day-to-day relationship . . . perhaps on account of small differences of opinion regarding money matters, in which Schubert may well have often been to blame'.[6] Schubert was anything but practical, and he could be impatient. Mayrhofer, ten years older, was an unusual man of few words and with a strange sense of humour which Schubert did not always appreciate. Yet throughout the time they lived together, whatever the minor quarrels and a general cooling in their relationship, they retained respect and affection for one another. Before the end of the year both had made sufficient progress in their careers for them no longer to need to share accommodation. Mayrhofer was appointed a book censor, despite the incongruity of the appointment to such a position of a poet obsessed with literary freedom. Despite his personal feelings, he kept the position and served with integrity until his death, although that may have been hastened by his unhappiness in his employment. Schubert meanwhile had seen two of his stage works produced in the principal theatres of Vienna, and received payment for them. Thus his prospects for earning a living as a composer were improving. Towards the end of the year the two men agreed to separate, and Schubert moved out to a room of his own, only a few blocks away in the Wipplingerstrasse.

In moving into new lodgings, Schubert was particularly glad to get away from the pestering Josef Hüttenbrenner, younger brother of his good friend Anselm, to whom two years earlier he had sent the ink-stained copy of his song 'Die Forelle'. Josef had moved early in 1819, soon after his arrival in Vienna from Graz, into a room in the same house as, but on the floor below, Mayrhofer and Schubert. Coincident with this move, it had seemed an ideal arrangement that Josef, with time on his hands, should act as Schubert's factotum, relieving the composer of professional, business, and financial affairs and worries for which he had little stomach or capability, and so leaving him more time for composing. Josef, for his part, was ardent in his admiration of Schubert and his music, and soon proved so zealous in his tasks that the composer was prompted to complain: 'Why, that man likes everything I do.'[7] By now Schubert was seriously irritated by Josef's constant attention and was anxious to avoid contact with him as much as possible. This was not easy while they lived under the same roof. Schubert's growing impatience was to culminate in ever more curt messages, acid verbal responses, and resort to extreme means to escape personal meetings.

---

[6] *Mem.* 63, *Erin.* 73.   [7] Kreissle, *Schubert*, i. 130.

According to one of Schubert's friends, Hüttenbrenner 'became almost an object of aversion to the musician; he often put him off rudely, and treated him so harshly and inconsiderately that we nicknamed Schubert "The Tyrant"—of course good-naturedly'.[8] If the friends' response to Schubert's behaviour was good-natured, this was perhaps far more than Schubert deserved.

Moritz von Schwind, the painter who became a close friend of Schubert a few years later, made a pen-and-ink drawing of a corner of the composer's second home in the Wipplingerstrasse, showing a bare wooden floor, an old-fashioned piano without foot-pedals possibly dating from the beginning of the century and covered with a clutter of books and manuscripts. The room was frugal, comfortless, but no more so than he had been accustomed to at home, at the Stadtkonvikt, and with Mayrhofer. Here, in a building which had once been a Theatine monastery, paying his rent probably with the assistance of Vogl, Schubert lived, slept, composed, and entertained his friends.

Very few details are known of his life during 1820, but some facts stand out as being of special interest or importance. A few weeks into the year he laid aside unfinished his excitingly experimental opera on a classical subject, *Adrast*, with a libretto by Mayrhofer, when already well into the second act, in order to start on another and pressing venture. That he never returned to *Adrast*, as he rarely did to unfinished works, may have upset Mayrhofer, especially after Schubert had pressurized him into writing the text for him. The new composition which replaced the opera, the three-act dramatic oratorio, *Lazarus* (to a text by August Hermann Niemeyer published in 1778) was intended for performance as an Easter cantata at the church in the Alt-Lerchenfeld suburb of Vienna where his brother Ferdinand, who had resigned his position as organist at the Lichtental church, had recently been appointed choirmaster. *Lazarus* is another innovative work, through-composed and with fine characterization, containing some strikingly beautiful, even sublime music, written with fastidious care. Alas, the oratorio too was never completed. (Two acts were finished, but of these the final part of the second act was lost before it was published.) In its place, on Easter Sunday Haydn's 'Nelson' Mass (also known as the 'Imperial' or 'Coronation' Mass) was performed.

One reason for Schubert's failure to finish the cantata in time for Easter may have been his involvement during March in an unpleasant episode with the police, one which was of sufficient seriousness to result in a report of the occasion, including his own name and profession, being sent to the head of

---

[8] Kreissle, *Schubert*, i. 130.

police in Vienna, the notorious Count Josef Sedlnitzky. The affair concerned the activities in student politics of his friend Johann Senn, three years older than himself, whom he had come to know and admire for his idealism and sense of justice at the Stadtkonvikt. Senn, now a private tutor, had been on the police suspect list ever since his support for a student colleague, Johann Bacher, who was in trouble at the end of the school year in 1813, and thereafter on account of his activities in radical student politics. He had been a much loved member of the Bildung Circle; but this group, having first attracted the attention of the police as early as 1815 and then adverse official reaction to the publication of its annual journal, *Beyträge zur Bildung für Jünglinge*, was already under threat when in 1819 there was a new repressive response to the assassination in Mannheim of the outspoken conservative dramatist, August von Kotzebue, by a radical student. This response of the police authorities may well have caused the circle, already in decline, finally to abandon its formal activities in Vienna. Although Kotzebue's plays were enormously popular and much performed (even as far afield as London), his political allegiance to ideals of absolute power in government was anathema to a growing number of intellectuals, artists, and students eager for more democracy and greater individual liberty. Kotzebue's death resulted in the introduction of the infamous Karlsbad decrees, draconian attempts to eliminate in many German-speaking states opposition to absolute government and to destroy all movements that might propagate ideas of democracy, notably through the strict surveillance of student associations (*Burschenschaften*) and of their members. Senn, highly intelligent, idealistic, and courageous, was now a leading light of one such group which met regularly. The authorities had been watching the group for some while and had compiled a list of its members. In the second or third week of March 1820 they took action, swooping on and searching the homes and lodgings of the members. They arrived at Senn's lodgings in the early hours of the morning to find not only Senn, but also Schubert and Josef von Streinsberg, a law student and companion of Schubert since their final years at the Stadtkonvikt. The three young men were in boisterous spirits after a convivial evening's drinking at a farewell party for a fellow Tyrolean friend of Senn's. When the police demanded a search of the premises, Senn replied angrily that he 'did not care a hang about the police', and 'the government was too stupid to be able to penetrate his secrets'.[9] He was backed up loudly by his two companions, and then also by two late arrivals, Johann Ignaz Zechentner and Franz von Bruchmann, who had also been at the party, and all of whom were good

---

[9] *Doc.* 128, *Dok.* 87–8.

friends. Bruchmann (who was a pantheist for a while in the 1820s under the influence of Senn, but in 1826 experienced a reconversion to Roman Catholicism, and thereafter tried to convert Senn to his way) wrote to the poet in 1827 of the police raid in his 'confessions' (*Selbstbekenntnis*): 'After a hectic night, when we concentrated on enjoying ourselves without a care and with no inkling of the impending disaster, you were torn from our midst in the early morning, never to return.'[10] After the search, all five were taken directly to the police station for questioning. A report of the evening's events, drawn up by the high commissioner of police and sent to Count Sedlnitzky, began:

Concerning the stubborn and insulting behaviour evinced by Johann Senn . . . on being arrested as one of those involved in the Students' Association [Burschenschaftlicher Studentenverein], on the occasion of the examination and confiscation of his papers carried out by order in his lodgings . . . It is also reported that his friends . . . chimed in against the authorized official in the same tone, inveighing against him with insulting language . . .[11]

Senn was arrested immediately on arrival at the police station, and detained for fourteen months before he was released and deported to his home district in the Tyrol, exiled for ever from Vienna, his career prospects totally destroyed. For many years after this, he was remembered with great affection and as a hero and noble martyr by his friends in Vienna; he was corresponded with enthusiastically; his health was drunk at their New Year and other celebrations, and he was visited in the autumn of 1823 by Bruchmann and Doblhoff. The other four young men were released, Schubert sporting a black eye; but the highly respectable fathers of Streinsberg and Bruchmann were informed of their sons' misconduct and all four, according to the high commissioner's report, were called back for a severe reprimand. Neither Schubert, who was falsely described in the first report as 'the school assistant from the Rossau' (was this his cover for respectability?), nor Zechentner were mentioned by name in Sedlnitzky's response dated 25 March 1820,[12] but it can be assumed that they were also cautioned and were aware that from now on they must keep well inside the law if they were to avoid serious consequences.

Schubert turned for comfort and support after this frightening experience to his brother Ferdinand, perhaps even spending a few days with him and his wife at their home in the orphanage in the Alsergrund suburb. Here, shortly before Palm Sunday on 26 March, Schubert composed in a mere thirty minutes the six short Antiphons for Palm Sunday D696, which were performed at the Alt-Lerchenfeld church on that day. Ferdinand, as their

---

[10] *Doc.* 130, *Dok.* 88.   [11] *Doc.* 128, *Dok.* 87–8.   [12] *Dok.* 89n.

new musical director, was meeting with some opposition from musicians at the church, and Schubert wrote the antiphons for him to present as his own work, in an effort to help win support for his brother. One week later, on Easter Sunday, he directed the same musicians in the Haydn Mass in place of his own *Lazarus*, as already mentioned.[13] Ferdinand perhaps stood down from directing not only in deference to Schubert's greater musical abilities, but also in an effort to take his brother's mind off his recent experience with the police and his concern for Senn.

Already Schubert's reputation as a composer was spreading outside Vienna. As mentioned above, in Graz on 7 April Eduard Jäell, formerly leader at Hatwig's orchestral evenings, who had directed performances of Schubert's music in Vienna, led a performance of his 'New Overture', presumably again that in E minor, in a concert of the Styrian Musical Society in the assembly hall of the Landständisches Theater. This was the first public or semi-public concert to include work by Schubert outside Vienna. Schubert must have known of the event, although he was of course unable to attend. In fact, throughout his life he seems to have been remarkably uninterested in attending performances of his music even in Vienna, and singularly unconcerned about their reception, placing little value on the reactions of audiences in general. As he had written in his diary in September 1816, it was his belief that whether a performer 'receives applause or not will depend on a public subject to a thousand moods'. After his death, several of his friends referred to this lack of interest in performances of his music; and their efforts to help him by publicizing his work were made the more difficult by his unwillingness to show interest in, or support for, what they were doing. He showed a careless want of co-operation and lack of ambition, perhaps touching as an aspect of character, but infuriating to those trying to advance his career. His behaviour at the first night of his comic singspiel *Die Zwillingsbrüder* at the Kärntnertor-Theater on 14 June of the same year illustrates his natural shyness and his reluctance to step into the limelight. This was for Schubert an important occasion: his theatrical and operatic début, with the renowned Vogl in the dual role of the twin brothers. The admirable virtuoso violinist, Josef Mayseder, who in 1814 had led the orchestra in the performance of Schubert's Mass in F at the Lichtental church, was leading the Court Opera orchestra. The conductor was the Court Opera's Kapellmeister, the then much acclaimed Czech composer, Adalbert Gyrowetz. There is nothing to indicate whether Schubert attended any rehearsals of his singspiel. If he did, he may have realized too late that he had miscalculated the kind of

---

[13] *Doc.* 131–2n, *Dok.* 90n.

music required for this play. Under the influence of Rossini's successful operas when he composed it early in 1819, he had adopted too highbrow, too operatic a tone when easygoing, typically Viennese light theatre music would have been more appropriate to the text. Schubert attended the first performance, sitting in the top gallery in the company of the amiable Anselm Hüttenbrenner. Although the operetta was received with no great enthusiasm by the majority of the audience, some of Schubert's friends and supporters seated in different parts of the theatre were carried away in their enthusiasm, 'making a lot of noise', as one diarist expressed it,[14] with the result that others became annoyed and hissed their opposition. Under these circumstances Schubert, who was embarrassed, refused all calls for the composer to take a bow, despite Hüttenbrenner's pressing him to exchange his humble frock coat for his wealthier friend's evening tailcoat. Instead Schubert listened with a smile as Vogl stepped forward to thank the audience for their response and to announce that the composer was unfortunately not in the house to take a curtain call for himself.[15] After the performance Schubert joined friends at the nearby wine shop of Achatius Lenkay to celebrate his début, where they drank several pints of cheap Hungarian wine. The reviews that followed were for the most part thoughtful, favourable to the music, and in several cases encouraging about Schubert's potential as a composer for the theatre. Interestingly, the theatre's income from the sale of tickets for the second performance two days later, on 16 June, was almost double that of the first night, and for the third even more. Thereafter the sales flagged and, after the sixth performance on 21 July and the summer-holiday closure of the theatre Schubert's *Die Zwillingsbrüder* fell from the repertory. The composer never attempted to revise his score or to raise interest in the work again. As with much of his early music, after it was completed he had no further concern for it.

At some time in the early part of July, during the run of his operetta, Schubert made his first appearance at the Atzenbrugg festival, or summer house-party, in the arrangements of which Schober played an important part, together with his sister Sophie and their Derffel cousins, Franz and Therese. Here Schubert was one of twenty young men and women enjoying what had become an annual event at Atzenbrugg since its inception in 1817. The days were spent in outings, picnics, and games; the evenings presented an opportunity for further games, theatricals, and dancing. Schloss Atzenbrugg was, and still is, a charming L-shaped country house, surrounded by a fine park, then rather larger than it is today. A miniature hill

---

[14] *Doc.* 135, *Dok.* 91.   [15] *Doc.* 135n, *Dok.* 92n.

at the back of the building, now covered in shrubbery, is capped by a delightful summerhouse where Schubert could escape for solitude if he so chose. If he did, it is rather unlikely that he composed more than an occasional song or dance. For he was at Atzenbrugg, like everyone else, for a brief holiday. By now, the summer months, especially June and July, had become for him creatively the least fertile period of the year. Thus, in these months between 1819 and 1822 he may have completed no other work than just two songs, although it is possible that during some of this time he was engaged in the composition of more extended works.

Soon after his return from Atzenbrugg, rehearsals of the melodrama *Die Zauberharfe* began at the smart and beautiful Theater an der Wien. This was another play based on a French model and created by the same Georg von Hofmann who had written the libretto of *Die Zwillingsbrüder*. That Hofmann's name did not appear as author on programmes of either of these works is indicative of the low status of librettists, the insignificance attached to the libretto genre and the poverty, even banality, of many texts at this time, in their content, language, and structure. The plot of *Die Zauberharfe* was so complicated and muddled that audiences and critics alike were unable to follow the story. As the critic of the Vienna *Theaterzeitung* wrote on 26 August, a week after the première: 'unfortunately, with the best will in the world, nothing very edifying may be said about it. Alas! though the witchery might pass, with what distressing tedium does it overflow, as it were, still affecting one's memory and paralysing even the most fluent critical pen!'.[16] And another comment, this time in the diary of one of Schubert's acquaintances (Josef Karl Rosenbaum): 'Wretched trash, failed to please, the machinery jibbed and went badly, although nothing remarkable. Nobody knew his part; the prompter was always heard.'[17] The performance was designed as a spectacular, with a large cast and elaborate staging, of the kind in which the Theater an der Wien had formerly excelled. At the second performance, on 21 August, all performers gave their services for the benefit of the scenic artist, Hermann Neefe, the stage engineer designing and operating the elaborate machinery, Andreas Roller, and for the costume designer, Lucca Piazza. (Neefe was a son of Beethoven's teacher in Bonn, Christian Gottlob Neefe, and was married to Regina Lutz, sister of Leopold Kupelwieser's future wife, Johanna. The sisters were also cousins on their mother's side of Leopold Sonnleithner, who again may have had a hand in obtaining this commission for Schubert.) Despite near-disastrous moments at the première and a general atmosphere of chaos, Schubert's music occasioned some high praise but also some

[16] *Doc.* 144, *Dok.* 101; *ND* 50.   [17] *Doc.* 144, *Dok.* 101.

qualification: 'what a pity that Schubert's wonderfully beautiful music had not found a worthier subject';[18] and, adversely, 'the *Magic Harp* music is often thin, insipid and stale in taste',[19] and 'the score shows talent here and there; but on the whole it lacks technical resource and wants the grasp which only experience can give; most of it is much too long, ineffective and fatiguing, the harmonic progressions are too harsh, the orchestration overdone, the choruses dull and feeble'.[20] The melodrama ran for a total of eight performances. There are singing roles for only one soloist (tenor) and male and female choruses. Otherwise the music is purely instrumental, except for melodramatic passages in which it accompanies or punctuates passages of spoken dialogue. Contemporary critics attending performances of the melodrama were unable to appreciate, or recognize, the striking technical advances that Schubert made in his music for this demanding large-scale work. The outstanding overture (which he later attached to his *Rosamunde* score), the symphonic writing in some of the melodramatic numbers, the unity he built into the whole by use of recurring motifs, and his imaginative development of non-melodic material, are all examples of Schubert's progressive thinking in 1820. Indeed, his three dramatic compositions of this year—*Adrast*, *Lazarus*, and *Die Zauberharfe*—are proof of exciting developments in Schubert's compositional technique which help to bridge the gap between his more formal, classical compositions of the early years and the robust Romanticism he introduced into classical structures in his later years. At the same time, moving ahead of his contemporaries, he was in the forefront of the development of music theatre, creating forms and orchestral sounds which anticipated the musical world of Wagner. Unfortunately, so little of his theatre music was heard that he had no influence whatsoever through these works on the development of German Romantic opera. Where he did influence the development was through his *Lieder*, in the setting of German poetic texts to music.[21]

Between the premières of *Die Zwillingsbrüder* and *Die Zauberharfe*, a period of a little over nine weeks, Schubert may have composed no other music than revisions for the melodrama. His autograph score, surviving sketches, and alternative versions indicate that the work underwent a multitude of changes, some of them major, in the course of rehearsals, which proceeded chaotically right up to the opening night. Even the sequence of events in the drama was changed, thus involving alterations to the score, both moving a whole section of music from one act to another and creating bridging passages to accommodate the change, removing other sections

[18] *Doc.* 148, *Dok.* 106–7; *ND*54.   [19] *Doc.* 147, *Dok.* 105; *ND* 52.
[20] *Doc.* 149, *Dok.* 109, *ND* 62.   [21] McKay, *Schubert's Music for the Theatre*, 175–82.

and adding new ones. It is likely that Schubert was present at some of these rehearsals; and he must have worked closely with the musical director, pro-ducer/stage-manager, and designers in order to register their new musical requirements. It is even possible that some changes were introduced after the first performance. Thus Schubert was kept busy working on this score over a considerable period. After it was all over, he realized that *Die Zauberharfe*, a play in a magic genre already fast falling out of fashion, would never be revived; and he did not hesitate to use some of the music again in different contexts. In October he was to start again on yet another major operatic venture, *Sacontala*; but this he left unfinished (part of the autograph score is now lost). For this opera, which had its roots in an ancient Sanskrit dramatic poem, Schubert composed some exciting music of unusual vision, continuing along the lines he had explored in *Lazarus*, especially in the balance and relationship between vocal and orchestral ele-ments. This music was, in different ways, as forward-looking as had been his music for *Die Zauberharfe*. He continued working on *Sacontala* until early in the following year. The Quartettsatz in C D703 also dates from this exploratory period. A small masterpiece, it is a single movement of a quar-tet which he never completed.

In September, during a period of rich musical creativity, Schubert took time off from composing to write a three-verse, twelve-line poem, 'Der Geist der Welt' (The Spirit of the World), which he did not set to music. Two autograph copies of this poem have survived, both written in pencil, one of which Ferdinand inherited, the other passed to the family of a friend, Josef Huber, with whom Schubert later lived, from 1823 until 1824. As poetry, it is poor: the content is ambiguous and unclear; the form and scansion are inconsistent. The poem, however, is of interest in its presentation of an aspect of Schubert's thinking in the autumn of 1820, after a year of exciting experiences, both pleasant and distressing:

> *Der Geist der Welt*
> [The Spirit of the World]
>
> Lasst sie mir in ihrem Wahn,
> Spricht der Geist der Welt,
> Er ists, der im schwanken Kahn
> So sie mir erhält.
>
> Lasst sie rennen, jagen nur
> Hin nach einem fernen Ziel,
> Glauben viel, beweisen viel
> Auf der dunkeln Spur.

Nichts ist wahr von allen dem,
Doch ists kein Verlust;
Menschlich ist ihr Weltsystem,
Göttlich, bin ich's mir bewusst.[22]

[Thus speaks the World Spirit: Let men remain in their delusion; that is what keeps them in my power in the frail barque of life.

Let them rush headlong seeking some distant goal; let them find much to believe in, much they can prove, as they grope ever onwards.

None of it is the truth, but that does not matter. Their world system is human; it becomes divine through my consciousness of it.]

The *Weltgeist* was a concept which had for some while been engaging the minds of intellectuals and artists. The idea of *Weltgeist*, or 'absolute spirit', was introduced by Hegel in an attempt to bring philosophical understanding to the dichotomy between the Ideal and the Real, the relationships between man and nature, man and man, man and artistic creation. The *Weltgeist* was seen as a universal spirit experiencing itself in every form of creation and thought, growing in knowledge and awareness of itself through ever-new creations, each of which is an inadequate, transient 'achievement' that must make way for another as its inadequacies are revealed.[23] Schubert's musical creations could be explained as transient manifestations of that spirit, and in the poem he seems to be admitting equally to their importance and their imperfections. They are all part of the discovery of truth. But there may be another explanation for this poem: it is possible that the 'speaker' is not the *Weltgeist* of the title but Schubert himself. Further, in associating or confusing the idea of *Weltgeist* with the divine spark, Schubert seems to be saying 'man's capacity of awareness is the divine spark within him, which can make him aware in turn of the divine world system'. If the poem is really a statement of Schubert's understanding of the creative spirit in the artist, then it suggests a degree of spiritual vanity in the composer. As a young man, he was seen by those who knew him as modest and reserved. The essential confidence in himself as a creative artist was always with him, but was a trait of personality inconsistent with his observed nature. Perhaps 'Der Geist der Welt' provides a clue to an inner nature which may have escaped his friends, and in its affirmation explains some insensitivity and arrogance in his behaviour.

On 21 November 1820 Schubert's first love, Therese Grob, married the master baker Johann Bergmann in the Lichtental church. Although the

---

[22] *Dok.* 110.

[23] P. Gardiner, 'The German Idealists and their Successors', in M. Pasley (ed.), *Germany: A Companion to German Studies* (London, 1972), 403.

paths of Schubert and Therese had probably diverged decisively some
years earlier, maybe in 1818 before the composer went to Zseliz, the marriage of Therese cannot have left him unmoved. They had shared many
hours together in each other's company and making music; and her voice
had for some while been an inspiration to him. He surely wished her happiness in her married life, and may have had some regrets that, for whatever
reason, he had never been able to marry her himself. In marrying
Bergmann, she had now cut any ties of intimacy that may have lingered on
between them. Only ten days later, on 1 December, at a musical salon of
Ignaz Sonnleithner, the first semi-public performance of any of his songs,
the 'Erlkönig', was given. The first version of this song, written in the
autumn of 1815, was one of those which Schubert, after composing it, had
taken straight to Therese, sung and played it to her, and anxiously awaited
her response. If he remembered this earlier occasion, he knew it was part of
his past. He was now moving into another, more complex and dangerous,
world.

Until now the restrictions inherent in his conventional early upbringing,
the expectations of the respectable part of Biedermeier society, had
restrained him from excesses. Despite these constraints on his behaviour,
he had already begun to grasp at spiritual freedom and, as is evident
from 'Der Geist der Welt', he experienced growing independence and
confidence in the process. His move at the end of 1820 from the room that
he had shared with Mayrhofer for more than two years was also symptomatic of his need for more physical as well as spiritual freedom.

Schubert now believed that his greatest hopes of success as a composer
lay in music for the theatre. For more than a year most of his creative
energy had been directed at stage music, and two of his works had already
been performed in Vienna's principal theatres. Their impact may have been
small, but it was sufficient to bring his name to the attention of theatre
directors. Vogl was now encouraging him to push for a position at the
Kärntnertor-Theater, to learn more about the world of opera and to make
himself available for any work that might arise as coach, conductor, or
composer. Vogl may well have had a hand in his requesting and receiving
testimonials of his suitability for employment there from some of the most
influential figures in the theatre's hierarchy: Ignaz von Mosel, at the time
acting Court secretary, himself a capable writer and composer, who had
taken an interest in Schubert since his days as a chorister in the Court
chapel; Count Dietrichstein, Court music count, shortly to be appointed
supreme Court theatre director with Mosel as his secretary, and dedicatee
of Schubert's first published work, 'Erlkönig'; Josef Weigl, musical director of the Court Opera; and Salieri, Court Kapellmeister. Schubert had met

the first two in the previous year at the house of the poet Matthäus von Collin, a cousin of Spaun, when he performed songs (including 'Der Wanderer') with Vogl and a piano duet with Anselm Hüttenbrenner.[24] The result of the efforts of both Schubert and Vogl to get him installed in some capacity at the theatre was that, for a brief period in February, he was employed as a coach (*répétiteur*). He was given the task of coaching the soprano Karoline Unger (daughter of Johann Karl Unger who, in 1818, had introduced Schubert to Count Esterházy of Galánta) in the role of Isabella for her début in the German version of *Cosí fan tutte* on 24 February. On 9 April 1821 he received payment for this work. Alas, Schubert showed in his coaching work that he was 'incapable of keeping punctually to the rehearsal schedule, and the mechanical side of the work irked him'.[25] After this experience, he was never again employed on the music staff of this or any other theatre. It was at this time, however, that he was commissioned to compose two numbers for insertion in the German version of Hérold's opera *Das Zauberglöckchen* (The Magic Bell) based on the story of Aladdin from the *Arabian Nights*, in which Vogl was to sing the role of the Sultan. Once again Vogl may have helped Schubert to win this commission. His contributions were a comic duet, which was much praised by the critics, and a tenor aria which was less enthusiastically received. (This was long and, being pitched high in the tenor range, put the singer under undue strain.) There were eight performances of the opera between June and October. Meanwhile, in addition to performances of his songs at Sonnleithner's musical entertainment and in the chamber music concerts, all of the Gesellschaft der Musikfreunde, on 7 March there was another prestigious première for him when, through the good offices of Leopold Sonnleithner, no fewer than three of his vocal works were included in the Ash Wednesday *Akademie* (public concert) in the Kärntnertor-Theater. This was a charity concert organized by Josef Sonnleithner, Ignaz's brother and Leopold's uncle, on behalf of the Society of Ladies of the Nobility for the Promotion of the Good and the Useful. According to Anselm Hüttenbrenner, Schubert was too reticent and aware of his limited ability as a pianist to accompany his songs himself on this occasion, or indeed at any grand public concert. Instead, he was content merely to turn the pages for Hüttenbrenner, who accompanied Vogl in a performance of 'Erlkönig' on the theatre's new Konrad Graf grand piano.[26] Such an occasion as this, and the encouraging response to his compositions both in performance and in reviews after the event, were bound to advance Schubert's reputation in Vienna.

---

[24] *Mem.* 181–2, *Erin.* 208–9.   [25] L. Sonnleithner: *Mem.* 109, *Erin.* 128.
[26] *Mem.* 186, *Erin.* 213–14.

In the spring of 1821, Anselm Hüttenbrenner rather unwillingly left Vienna to return to the family home near Graz where, after his father's death and as the eldest son, he had to take over the management of the family estate. For some years he had had an eye for the girls, and Schubert complained to him in a letter of May 1819: 'You are a rogue, and no mistake!!! . . . First one girl, then another turns your head: well then, may the deuce take all girls, if you allow them to bewitch you in this manner. For heaven's sake get married and have done with it!'[27] In November 1821 Anselm married the daughter of a Russian government official who spoke not one word of German. (Hüttenbrenner wrote that she spoke only Russian and French, 'was not in the least musical but had a heart of gold and I lived very happily with her until 1848, when death took her from me . . .'.)[28] By now, his brother Josef was working hard as Schubert's factotum, seeing to his business affairs and thus relieving him of the necessity of communicating directly with those who might want to employ or pay him, such as publishers and dedicatees. The latter were important to Schubert. Not only did their support, if they were sufficiently grand, add credibility to his compositions but, unless they were personal friends to whom he felt indebted, they provided him with welcome additional income. In appreciation of the dedication proffered, they paid him on publication (and on a voluntary basis) an honorarium commensurate with their personal wealth. The process was not entirely a simple one, and Schubert was glad to leave the tedious negotiations to Josef Hüttenbrenner. Having first obtained the formal letter of acceptance from the dedicatee, he was obliged to apply to the censors' office with the proposed text of the dedication, which in turn had to be approved before it could be passed on to the publisher.

In February 1821, Schubert's brief trial as a music coach at the Kärntnertor-Theater ended abruptly, and in March there were further indications that he was becoming unashamedly thoughtless and negligent in many of his professional affairs. Leopold Sonnleithner, who for some while had been making considerable efforts to further his career, wrote to Josef Hüttenbrenner, clearly irritated by Schubert's failure to make an appearance at prearranged rehearsals with those who were to perform his music at Sonnleithner's concerts, adding: 'Indeed, I am surprised that Schubert never appears at our house at all, although I urgently need to speak to him about [publication of] his "Erlkönig" and other matters.'[29] Schubert was clearly guilty of discourtesy as well as negligence. Whether such lapses were the result of temperamental disorder, artist's licence, or character defect cannot be known for certain. And yet there was another important

---

[27] *Doc.* 177, *Dok.* 79.   [28] *Mem.* 69, *Erin.* 80.   [29] *Doc.* 169, *Dok.* 120.

contributory factor in the decline in Schubert's behaviour: his increasing intimacy with Franz von Schober.

Schober returned to Vienna early in 1821 after abandoning all idea of being a painter. He was older; he had more experience of life; and he was probably none the wiser. From this time Schubert for a while came increasingly under his spell. The first intimation that Schober was 'back in town' came at the end of January in a letter written by Josef Huber, another former student at the Kremsmünster seminary and member of the Bildung Circle, to his fiancée. In this he described an evening he had recently spent at Schober's home, in the company of some fourteen others, at which Schubert sang and played many of his songs. This is the first extant reference to a 'Schubertiad'. Huber continued: 'After that, punch was drunk, offered by one of the party, and as it was very good and plentiful the party, in a happy mood anyway, became merrier, so [that] it was 3 o'clock before we parted.'[30] It could have been immediately after this that Schubert wrote to his brother Ferdinand apologizing for not having finished an offertory which he had promised: 'As I was seedy to-day on account of yesterday's dissipations . . .'.[31] During the following months there were many meetings of the friends, some at Schober's apartment and others at the more auspicious venues demanded by the singer, at which Schubert and Vogl made music together. The Hungarian Crown inn and Wasserburger's coffeehouse[32] were now favourite meeting-places; and here Schubert was often to be found in the company of such as Schober and his cousin Franz Derffel, Huber, the painter Leopold Kupelwieser, the poet Mayrhofer, Spaun and his special friend Gahy, and Zechentner (who had been with Schubert when Senn was arrested). In July, Schubert returned with Schober to Atzenbrugg for his second visit to the annual house-party for three days of light-hearted entertainment and conviviality with other young men and women. His male friends there this year included Spaun, Gahy, Derffel, Kupelwieser, Zechetner, and Claude Étienne (formerly Axel Schober's valet).

Early in 1821 Schubert had worked on all four movements of the Symphony in D major D708A. He had composed hurriedly, leaving the manuscript, without date or title, in piano score with only six indications as to which instruments were playing. However, he planned a symphony of large structure, one employing more contrapuntal material than appears in his earlier finished symphonies.[33] All the earlier works were written with a view to performances at the orchestral rehearsals which were held regularly (after their humble beginnings as chamber music evenings in the Säulengasse schoolhouse in 1814) first at the home of the merchant

---

[30] *Doc.* 162, *Dok.* 115.   [31] *Dok.* 163, *Dok.* 116.   [32] *Doc.* 178n, *Dok.* 126n.
[33] Newbould, *Schubert and the Symphony*, 146–58.

Frischling, then at the end of 1815 at that of the violinist Hatwig (in first the
Schottenhof and then the Gundelhof) and, finally, in the spring of 1819, in
the home of the businessman Pettenkofer. These rehearsals came to a complete end in the autumn of 1820. Thereafter, when composing orchestral
music Schubert was anticipating, or hoping for, grander orchestras, musical establishments, and venues for performances. His first such work was
the D major Symphony, which he laid aside for reasons that cannot be
ascertained. Six months later, in August 1821, he set to work on another
major orchestral composition: the Symphony in E major D729. This he
completed in sketch form, but one which for him clearly represented a
finished work, requiring only the completion of the orchestration. This
symphony, which calls for a large orchestra including three trombones, has
been described not only as signalling 'tantalisingly, a dramatic leap forward
in style', but also as providing 'a fascinating link, reflecting the familiar
middle-period Schubert, assimilating . . . his current interest in Rossini, and
anticipating . . . several facets of the sound-worlds' of the masterpieces to
come: the 'Unfinished' and 'Great' C major symphonies.[34] The reason for
his failure immediately to complete the orchestration of the Symphony in
E major could have been the excitement engendered by his next musical
project: a collaboration with his friend Schober.

    Schubert and Schober left Vienna in September 1821 with this major pro-
ject in mind: the composition of a grand three-act romantic opera, for
which Schober was to write the libretto. They had hoped in vain that
Leopold Kupelwieser would join them for at least part of the time they were
away. These three had become sufficiently close for Spaun to refer to them
some five months later in a letter: 'I am so very anxious to know all that
the poetic–musical–painting triumvirate has produced.'[35] Schubert and
Schober travelled first to Atzenbrugg, early in September and, after a day
or two, moved on to St Pölten, some thirty miles south-west of Vienna,
where the bishop, Johann Nepomuk von Dankesreither, was a relative of
Schober's mother. Both she and her daughter Sophie were frequent visitors
at the bishop's residence; but Schober and Schubert most likely stayed at the
guest-house the Three Crowns in the principal town square. Schober
described their accommodation in a letter to Spaun: 'our room . . . was particularly snug: the two double beds, a sofa next to the warm stove, and a
forte-piano . . . '.[36] In the town they were invited to the homes of friends of
the Schobers', to balls, and concerts. The balls, or private dances, would
have had little appeal for Schubert, who did not dance, but he may have
been engaged as pianist on these occasions. Whether at the concerts he was

[34] Ibid. 178.   [35] *Doc.* 212, *Dok.* 149.   [36] *Doc.* 195, *Dok.* 139.

a member of the audience or was invited as a performer is unclear; but according to Schober there were three Schubertiads, two of them at the bishop's residence, at which he sang and played. Despite an apparently busy social life they, and especially Schubert, worked hard, as Schober assured Spaun in a letter. Later, the two friends moved out from St Pölten to the bishop's country residence, the castle of Ochsenburg, which stands on a high ridge overlooking the river with a fine linden tree in the garden at the rear of the castle. Here they enjoyed walks in the countryside around, and the work on their opera continued. By the time they returned to Vienna early in November, Schober had almost completed the third (and last) act of the libretto and Schubert the music of the second.

Schubert's professional experience of German texts for the musical theatre, those of *Die Zwillingsbrüder* and *Die Zauberharfe*, had left him with no exalted ideas about their literary quality. There was at this time an acute and recognized dearth in Vienna of good librettists and libretti. Would-be serious composers of operas had to make the choice between such inadequate texts as Hofmann had written, or finding others through friends and contacts or, as later became fashionable, writing their own. The latter would not have entered Schubert's head; but when Schober offered him a libretto on a medieval Spanish theme, *Alfonso und Estrella*, he readily accepted. However, it is difficult to comprehend how he could have been so naïve as to agree to begin composing music for the first act of what he envisaged as his first great operatic triumph before he had read the complete libretto, unless perhaps the two men had first together worked and decided on details of the plot and the characters and their voice-types, and had carefully planned the shape of each act within the whole, the number and positioning of arias and solo- and chorus-ensembles. Whether they had or no, Schubert proceeded with the composition and, with a trust bordering on stupidity, completely confident in Schober's abilities as a librettist. Sadly this confidence in his friend was misfounded; for Schober, a poet of very modest talent and accomplishment, was a complete novice as a dramatist. At first Schober spoke with enthusiasm and pride of the opera he and Schubert created. In 1876, when a very old man, he described his contribution to *Alfonso* in terms quite different from those he had used years before while seeking production of the opera: 'as an opera libretto . . . such a miserable, still-born, bungling piece of work that even so great a genius as Schubert was not able to bring it to life . . .'.[37] This was written twenty-two years after Liszt, for whom Schober had worked for a while as secretary, strongly criticized the whole work. Liszt adapted and performed, indeed

---

[37] *Mem.* 208, *Erin.* 239.

premièred, *Alfonso* in Weimar in 1854 as, he claimed, 'an act of piety to the composer', the opera being 'of historical interest only' in his opinion.

The text of *Alfonso und Estrella* has an authentic eighth-century historical background in the ancient kingdom of Leon in north-west Spain. The plot has some similarities to Shakespeare's *As You Like It*: the children, Alfonso and Estrella (= Orlando and Rosalind) of a usurping King of Leon, Mauregato (= Duke Frederick) and the usurped King Froila (= the Duke), who has been living incognito for many a year in idyllic pastoral exile (= Forest of Arden), bring reconciliation to all through their love for each other. There are, however, fundamental flaws in the construction of the libretto which make it very difficult to perform: many static scenes with romantic effusions, the inclusion of only one female principal role, with resulting limitations in the range of ensemble available, and a preponderance of duets. But composer and librettist seem to have recognized none of these inadequacies, were delighted with their opera, and very optimistic about its future. When they left Vienna that autumn, they may have known already that the Kärntnertor-Theater was shortly to be under new management. Soon after they returned, just in time for the Viennese première of Weber's *Freischütz* on 3 November, both Weber and Schubert among others were asked by the Italian impresario Domenico Barbaja, recently arrived manager-elect and leaseholder of both this theatre and the Theater an der Wien, to submit new German operas for consideration for performance in the theatre's 1822–3 season. By thus promoting the cause of native German opera, Barbaja hoped to appease those critics who saw his appointment as a takeover of Vienna's opera theatres by Italians planning to exploit the current enthusiasm, even craze, in the city for Rossini's operas. As soon as Schubert was approached, he and Schober were convinced that *Alfonso* was exactly what was needed, and with its imminent production in the forefront of Schubert's mind, he was soon back at work on the opera. He finished it on 27 February of the next year, 1822.

The through-composed format of *Alfonso*—there is no spoken dialogue—may have been a consequence of the influence of both Salieri and Ignaz von Mosel.[38] Mosel, who had himself turned his hand to writing libretti,[39] also wrote a treatise on the aesthetics of opera (*Versuch einer Ästhetik des dramatischen Tonsatzes*, 1813). Mosel and Schubert were now occasionally meeting socially at musical gatherings, both private and of the Gesellschaft der Musikfreunde. Mosel took it upon himself to advise Schubert on the composition of opera, recommending old-fashioned Gluckian principles of structure as best representing the ideals of Greek

---

[38] T. G. Waidelich, *Franz Schubert: 'Alfonso und Estrella'* (Tutzing, 1991), 72–81.
[39] Ibid. 65.

theatre, with through-composed format and the restriction of solo numbers for the most part to heights of expressive feeling. It seems likely that he would have seen to it that Schubert had access to a copy of his short treatise on the aesthetics of opera, and this despite the poor reception of his own operas by Viennese audiences. Be this as it may, in *Alfonso* Schubert broke away for the first time, except for in his oratorio *Lazarus*, from the singspiel format of spoken dialogue; and Mosel seems to have approved the result.[40] If he did, he was one of very few. Vogl, whom Schubert intended for the role of the noble King Froila, was singularly unimpressed with the opera. Schubert had handed him the completed score expecting an enthusiastic response. Instead, Vogl reacted with severe criticism of the opera and was resentful and angry, with some justification, that Schubert had chosen to compose it without any reference to himself. For the last four years he had given the young composer valuable and generous help with his career, advised him on vocal compositions, and supported him financially when necessary. Now, when working in the field of opera where Vogl had so much experience, Schubert had turned his back on him. Vogl told him in no uncertain terms that his opera was a disaster; but Schubert did not, and would not believe him. Instead he decided that Vogl's judgement was at fault; for in his own opinion *Alfonso* was, if not the finest, at least one of the best works he had written. Spurred on by Schober, in whose libretto he could find no fault and whose opinions and advice he now accepted unquestioningly, Schubert displayed a callous conceit, even cockiness, towards Vogl which was not attractive to his own friends. Vogl, in his turn, did not keep his views on Schubert's behaviour entirely to himself. In July 1822 Spaun's brother Anton wrote to his wife after a meeting in Steyr with the singer: 'Vogl . . . says Schober's opera is bad and a complete failure, and overall Schubert is on quite the wrong track.'[41] It is very probable that, when approached by Barbaja or one of his staff for his considered opinion of the opera, Vogl had voiced the same judgement.

Despite repeated efforts in various directions to excite interest in *Alfonso*, by the autumn of 1822 Schubert knew for certain that it would not be performed in Vienna. Still obstinately, even arrogantly, convinced of its worth, he continued for some years in attempts to get it accepted outside Vienna. In this he had the help of Mosel and allegedly of Weber in Dresden, though one must wonder with how much enthusiasm. In 1825 Schober tried again in Dresden,[42] and Schubert in 1827 worked on Karl Pachler in Graz,[43] but all to no avail. The opera contains strikingly beautiful music, especially in the lyrical sections, while Schubert's ability to write continuous arioso-

[40] Spaun: *Mem.* 366, *Erin.* 421.   [41] *Doc.* 230, *Dok.* 161.   [42] *Doc.* 444, *Dok.* 308.
[43] *Doc.* 671, *Dok.* 452.

like recitative between the set numbers advanced to such a degree in the course of composing the opera that, by the final act, the music flows with easy continuity. But to stage it successfully as a financially viable venture or repertory opera is impossible. There are too many deficiencies in the dramatic elements of the play and too few dramatic highlights in Schubert's music.

When Schubert left Vienna for St Pölten in the autumn of 1821 he gave up the tenancy of the room in the Wipplingerstrasse, where he had been living alone for almost a year. On his return from his holiday with Schober after some six weeks away, he moved directly into the Schobers' family home. One of their first engagements thereafter was a visit to the Kärntnertor-Theater on 3 November to see the first Viennese performance of Weber's much acclaimed opera *Der Freischütz*. This proved to be an unexpected disappointment. Unfortunately, in order to be acceptable to the Austrian censors, the opera was emasculated to a degree which shocked and horrified Weber when he saw this 'version' in the following February. After Weber complained bitterly, the censors were persuaded to drop their objections, and the opera was restored to its original form, complete with magic bullets, the firing of which on stage had formerly been thought subversive. *Freischütz* then proved very popular in Vienna. Its initial failure to excite Viennese audiences does not appear to have dampened the hopes of Schubert and Schober for their own opera in the same theatre.

Euphoria over their opera and their contentment at living again under the same roof in Vienna after nearly four years apart were however dampened, if not entirely extinguished, for a while by the way their friends had behaved in their absence. Without the core members—Spaun and Schober in particular—the meetings of their circle of friends had lost their sparkle. Spaun had left Vienna shortly after themselves, at the end of September, to take up a new appointment in Linz.[44] In a letter to him of 4 November, Schober told him that the Hungarian Crown, their former meeting place, was now 'utterly desolate'. Of the rest, Schober wrote first of his cousin Derffel:

Derffel is now wholly obsessed by the demon whist: he has established two regular days for it at home, yet plays as usual at Hugelmann's, at Dornfeld's, at the coffee-house—in short, all the time. Waldl [Mayrhofer] too, as well as Huber, is a prey to the same devil, and they are both kept away by living out in the suburbs. Gahy is quite lost without you. I found him desperately sad. He does not know what to do, and in despair watches the gambling. I shall try to look after him again.

---

[44] *Doc.* 190n, *Dok.* 135n.

Kuppel [Kupelwieser] is always at the Belvedere [Belvedere Palace], where he is copying the *Io* [Correggio's, *Jupiter and Io*]; so he hardly ever comes . . .[45]

At the start of 1822 Schubert's professional prospects must have seemed excellent. As a member of the Gesellschaft der Musikfreunde he was now in contact with many, if not most of the leaders of Vienna's concert life, and with distinguished performers, many of them teachers at the Gesellschaft's Conservatoire. In the early part of the year he became acquainted with Karoline Pichler, an important literary hostess in Vienna, and he attended several of her lunchtime salons in the role of self-accompanying singer. He also came to know Carl Maria von Weber, but not yet very closely, on the German composer's four-week visit to Vienna from February to March. He was now living in high hopes that *Alfonso* would soon go into production. Other music of his was being performed, published, and reviewed. Indeed, the first detailed review, rather than short report, of his songs appeared in the Vienna *Allgemeine musikalische Zeitung* on 19 January, and an even longer one in the *Wiener Zeitschrift für Kunst, Literatur, Theater und Mode* on 23 March. His personal life, however, was moving increasingly in a socially less admirable direction. The thoughtlessness and impatience he had shown towards associates on a few occasions in the previous year were increasing; he quarrelled with some friends, others he neglected. The same probably applied also to his family, for there is no evidence whatsoever of contact between them. In fact, there are scarcely any personal recollections of Schubert at all in this year, and most of those that have survived show him in an unfavourable light. Three of his own letters show impatience, ill-temper, and discourtesy. Added to this, his worsening social behaviour was to have serious repercussions in the development of his career during the year, as some of those who had been helping him finally lost patience. Schubert had changed, certainly as a result of Schober's influence.

The two friends were now intimate, Schubert captivated by his friend's worldly charms and apparent brilliance, his hedonism and social self-assurance. Schober, in turn, enjoyed Schubert's company and soon found that the composer, in his present vulnerable state of mind, was easily dominated. The friendship between them might suggest a homosexual relationship, although there is no evidence that it was. In fact, there is considerably more evidence of heterosexual proclivities in both of them. Whatever their personal relationship, Schober certainly encouraged Schubert in his hedonistic tendencies, to free himself from unwelcome responsibilities and inhibitions, and to follow his own inclinations regardless of the conse-

[45] *Doc.* 195, *Dok.* 139.

quences. In the process of his 'release' and his willing entanglement with Schober, Schubert tended to behave badly in public places, was careless in his relationships with other friends, and lost respect for their views whenever these conflicted with those of Schober. Holzapfel, who in 1815 and 1816 had been such a good friend to him, was one of the first to point to the change in Schubert, in a letter to Albert Stadler, now living in Linz, on 22 February:

Schubert has, as they say, made a splash and no doubt will also, as they say, make it in the world. I rarely see him, and we do not hit it off very well, his world being a very different one [from mine], as it is bound to be. His somewhat uncouth manner stands him in good stead and will make a man of him and a mature artist; he will be worthy of his art . . .[46]

Soon after this, on 5 March, Josef von Spaun wrote to Schober from Linz, complaining that he had received no letter or news of his friends: 'It hurts me deeply that Schubert has drifted away from me.'[47] Soon afterwards he must have given up all hope of receiving a letter from Schubert, who was in any case known to be a poor correspondent, when he wrote again to Schober in May: 'It gave me much pleasure to hear so much about you all from him [Kandler]; I am very glad that so many of you still gather together and have such a good time at the "Crown". But do let me hear something about you, from yourselves . . . What has Schubert done and Kuppel painted?'[48]

Spaun had for many years now been a tower of strength for Schubert, helping him on many occasions when he was in trouble, practical or mental, personal and professional. Schubert's neglect of him during 1822 was as heartless and ungracious as was his treatment of Vogl. Anton von Spaun, in a letter to his wife of 20 July, wrote: 'I like Vogl very much. He told me all about his relationship with Schubert with the utmost frankness, and I am afraid I can find now no excuse for the latter. Vogl is very much embittered against Schober; it was he who made Schubert behave most ungratefully towards Vogl . . .'.[49] Although the doting but wearisome Josef Hüttenbrenner may have occasioned irritable responses from 'The Tyrant', Schubert's behaviour towards him shows an intolerance and streak of brutality which had not been evident before, and does not fit with the general picture passed down by some friends and members of his family of Schubert's kind and generous nature. The brusque, discourteous tone of two of his notes to Hüttenbrenner show this other side to his nature, but should be assessed in the context that the recipient could be very trying: 'Have the goodness to bring me the opera [copyist's score of *Alfonso*] out

[46] *Doc.* 211, *Dok.* 148.   [47] *Doc.* 212, *Dok.* 149.
[48] *Doc.* 223, *Dok.* 156.   [49] *Doc.* 230, *Dok.* 160.

here act by act for correction. I should be glad if you would also deal with my account to date with Diabelli, as I need money. Schubert';[50] and: 'As I have to make very important alterations to the songs I handed you, do not give them to Herr Leidesdorf yet, but bring them out to me. If they have been sent already, they must be fetched back immediately.'[51] The request for delivery 'out here' and 'out to me' when Schubert was presumably still living with the Schobers may imply that Hüttenbrenner was to deliver material for his attention to Schubert's father's house in the Rossau. Thus the composer was trying to avoid personal meetings with Hüttenbrenner. To his publisher Diabelli, with whom Schubert was also losing patience, he wrote excitedly and irritably in connection with the dedication of a group of his songs to Count Esterházy: 'As Baron Schönstein was not to be found, and I do not know of any other way in which I might obtain a formal authorization [from the count], for goodness' sake take this letter as a substitute.'[52] These examples of Schubert's unamiable treatment of Holzapfel, Spaun, Vogl, Josef Hüttenbrenner, and Diabelli all date from 1822. Individually they may not add up to much; but taken collectively they suggest that a boorish, unpleasant side of his nature was now emerging, along with an arrogance, perhaps first hinted at in his poem 'Der Geist der Welt' of 1820.

There is another comment in Anton von Spaun's letter to his wife which reveals a fresh dimension to the bond between Schober and Schubert, and the former's integrity, or lack of it: '[Schober] takes full advantage of Schubert in order to extricate himself from financial embarrassments and to defray the expenditure he has incurred which has already exhausted the greater part of his mother's fortune.'[53] In this context, it is noteworthy that the Schobers had recently moved from their former handsome home in the house 'Zum Winter' (The Winter) in the Landskrongasse to a less grand apartment on the second floor of the 'Göttweigerhof' (The Gottweig House) in the Spiegelgasse. Schober had extravagant tastes and enjoyed the good things of life; he was also lazy, lacking the determination to earn a living and happy to be a parasite. Schubert, while financially incompetent, was generous with money when he had it, a combination making him vulnerable to the whims of unscrupulous friends. Anton von Spaun's reference to his financial entanglement with Schober raises the possibility that Schober's motivation in his apparent devotion to Schubert was at least partly, though not necessarily entirely, selfish. Schubert's prospects in mid-1821, when the two men became almost inseparable, were considerable. Schober may have

---

[50] *Doc.* 226, *Dok.* 158.   [51] *Doc.* 239, *Dok.* 167.   [52] *Doc.* 219, *Dok.* 153.
[53] *Doc.* 230, *Dok.* 160–1.

hoped to share in any fame and financial advantages that his friend's success, as perhaps with their opera, might occasion.

Schober's attachment to Schubert, whatever its nature, was of a kind unlikely to survive for long at the same intensity. For Schubert it lasted longer than with some others who, having at first basked in the apparent exoticism of Schober's tastes and opinions, soon began to see through his affectations. Eduard von Bauernfeld, the dramatist, who met Schober a year or two later, saw through the pretensions from the start. He wrote of Schober in his diary soon after their first meeting in the summer of 1825: 'He is five or six years older than we, also a sort of man of the world well endowed with the gift of the gab . . . and a ladies' man, despite being a bit bow-legged.'[54] Despite this, the two men 'at once began an agreeable friendship'. Moritz von Schwind, the artist, was at first quite as gullible as Schubert had been. After their intimacy ended, however, Schwind tended to quarrel with Schober, while in later years the former friendship became a source of considerable embarrassment to him. Schubert, on the other hand, throughout his short life remained loyal to Schober, genuinely fond of him as well as grateful for his support.

Whenever he was in Vienna Schober was at the centre of the circle of friends, arranging reading-parties and Schubertiads. Thanks to Schober's leadership, the gatherings at the Hungarian Crown, which had dwindled during the previous autumn, were resumed early in 1822. In these congenial and comparatively spacious surroundings the friends enjoyed each others' company. For more intimate and private companionship they now began to meet at Wasserburger's café in the Seilerstätte, where they reserved a small, cosy, private room for themselves alone. It is possible, even likely, that here Schober encouraged the smoking of opium.

As Bauernfeld recognized, Schober was a man of the world. If he had not already savoured the delights of opium in Vienna, it is likely that he did so on his travels in northern Europe. Here, posing as an aesthete, he would have mixed with others with artistic pretensions who enjoyed the social taking of opium, a practice which was then widespread and socially acceptable. On his return to Vienna, his social instincts and preferences for the exotic would have encouraged him towards smoking opium, sharing the Turkish hookah pipe, rather than the simpler consumption of liquid laudanum. Turkey's flourishing trade in coffee with Vienna resulted in the easy availability of opium and hookah pipes, also imported from Turkey. Although opium is never mentioned by name in literature appertaining to Schubert

[54] *Doc.* 428, *Dok.* 294.

and his friends, there are reasons for supposing that, for a period around 1822, they may have been smoking it. There is one clear reference to the 'Turkish pipe', another name for the hookah, in a letter from Anton Doblhoff, written to Schober from Moravia in the spring of 1823. In this letter Doblhoff described with nostalgia the cosy scene, as he remembered it, in Wasserburger's café:

We have the vilest weather—rain, snowstorms, the roughest of north winds— and we are in the country! How else could I effectively defy all this blustering than by taking my bit of imagination by the hand and transferring myself nicely and pleasantly to the Wasserburg and my dearly loved friends? For was it not cold winter then too? Yet in that small room my heart always opened so warmly, nay glowingly and bloomingly, so that now I want to be with you again for good and not to part from you until the sun shines sweetly and lures me into the pine forest.[55]

Now, in his imagination, Doblhoff continued: 'Josef, a black coffee and a long Turkish pipe!' (Josef was the waiter at the coffee-house.) The language of Doblhoff's description of his heart opening so 'warmly . . . glowingly and bloomingly' is not dissimilar to that of perhaps the most famous opium-eater of the time, De Quincey, who wrote in 1821: 'of chronic pleasure . . . a steady and equable glow' and the illusion of 'moral serenity . . . and over all is the great light of the majestic intellect'.[56] A further piece of evidence, though by no means conclusive, that Schubert and Schober were sharing the hookah pipe in the period 1821–2 and that Spaun was aware of this, comes in a letter Schober wrote to Spaun on 4 November 1821. Describing his days of contentment in the room he and Schubert were sharing while together in St Pölten, Schober wrote to Spaun: 'In the evenings we always compared notes on what we had done during the day, then sent for beer, smoked our pipe [*rauchten unsere Pfeife*], and read . . .'.[57] In the English translation of this passage, 'our pipe' is translated as 'our pipes'. In the original singular version, it is likely, but not certain, that Schober was referring to a shared pipe—perhaps the hookah.

On 3 July 1822 Schubert wrote out in pencil a strange tale in the first person usually referred to as 'My Dream' ('Mein Traum'). Such was the name given to the original copy of the tale by his brother Ferdinand. It has attracted much attention over the years. Different psychological explana-

---

[55] *Doc.* 271, *Dok.* 187.
[56] T. De Quincey, *Confessions of an English Opium Eater and Other Writings*, ed. G. Lindop (Oxford, 1985 edn.) 40–1.
[57] *Dok.* 139.

tions, nearly all Freudian and some no longer acceptable, have resulted in a variety of interpretations of the passage.[58] A quite different explanation, until now probably never seriously considered, is that Schubert wrote this unique piece of prose as part of an experiment on the understanding of dreams perhaps under the influence of opium. Dreams were revered by the Romantics both as aesthetic experience and for their importance in understanding the creative process. Many artists in Europe, and especially writers, while in no way addicted to the drug, took opium to encourage conscious reveries. They were aware that the drug, acting on subjects like themselves who were sensitive to reverie, could intensify, prolong, and help them to understand dreams.[59] Some English writers, such as Byron and Keats, took laudanum occasionally and in small doses to 'exhilarate the mind'.[60] Coleridge, on the other hand, became a crippled addict suffering from the terrifying nightmares associated with addiction. In Germany, Jean Paul, Novalis, and E. T. A. Hoffmann in the early years of the century expounded the value of dreams for enlightenment and for re-establishing the right balance between Man and Nature. Their thinking on this and on the importance of dreams in the process of literary creation would have been known to Schubert and his friends. The next generation of writers and artists, like their colleagues in England and France, chose to further their understanding of dreams with the help of opium. Because the use of the drug by Romantic writers to induce a more controlled and conscious inspiration was an established practice, the possibility that Schubert's allegorical dream sequence, 'Mein Traum', was the result of an opium reverie cannot be ruled out. The tone, language, and, for the most part, subjectively imaginative substance conforms to the pattern of such. The fact that he wrote it in pencil, rather than with quill pen and ink, points to the occasion as being away from home, perhaps in a coffee-house or inn. The complete dream is reproduced here in translation:

I was the brother of many brothers and sisters. Our father and mother were kind. I was deeply and lovingly devoted to them all.—Once my father took us to a feast. There my brothers became very merry. I, however, was sad. Then my father approached me and bade me enjoy the delicious dishes. But I could not, whereupon my father, becoming angry, banished me from his sight. I turned my footsteps and, my heart full of infinite love for those who disdained it, I wandered into far-off regions. For long years I felt torn between the greatest grief and the

[58] e.g. G. Grove, 'Schubert', *Groves Dictionary of Music and Musicians* (1883), 336; W. Dahms, *Franz Schubert* (Berlin, 1912), 19; M. J. E. Brown, 'Schubert's Dream', *MMR* 83 (1953), 39–43; A. Mayer, 'Der Psychoanalytische Schubert', *Brille*, 9 (1992), 7–31; M. Solomon, 'Franz Schubert's "My Dream" ', *American Imago*, 38 (1981), 137–54.

[59] A. Hayter, *Opium and the Romantic Imagination* (London, 1968), 334.

[60] Ibid. 76, 102.

greatest love. And so the news of my mother's death reached me. I hastened to see her, and my father, mellowed by sorrow, did not hinder my entrance. Then I saw her corpse. Tears flowed from my eyes. I saw her lie there like the old happy past, in which according to the deceased's desire we were to live as she had done herself.

And we followed her body in sorrow, and the coffin sank to earth.—From that time on I again remained at home. Then my father once more took me to his favourite garden. He asked whether I liked it. But the garden wholly repelled me, and I dared not say so. Then, reddening, he asked me a second time: did the garden please me? I denied it, trembling. At that my father struck me, and I fled. And I turned away a second time, and with a heart filled with endless love for those who scorned me, I again wandered far away. For many and many a year I sang songs. Whenever I attempted to sing of love, it turned to pain. And again, when I tried to sing of pain, it turned to love.

Thus I was split between love and pain.

And one day I had news of a gentle maiden who had just died. And a circle formed around her grave in which many youths and old men walked as though in everlasting bliss. They spoke softly, so as not to wake the maiden.

Heavenly thoughts seemed for ever to be showered on the youths from the maiden's gravestone, like fine sparks producing a gentle rustling. I too longed sorely to walk there. Only a miracle, however, can lead you to that circle, they said. But I went to the gravestone with slow steps and lowered gaze, filled with devotion and firm belief, and before I was aware of it, I found myself in the circle, which uttered a wondrously lovely sound; and I felt as though eternal bliss were gathered together into a single moment. My father too I saw, reconciled and loving. He took me in his arms and wept. But not as much as I.[61]

The text itself is probably of no great importance, but it has attracted considerable attention because of the paucity of source material written in Schubert's own hand. A further and less speculative explanation for its content, indeed perhaps the most convincing so far, first mooted by Otto Erich Deutsch[62] and very recently particularized by I. Dürhammer,[63] is that this was an allegorical tale written in the style of Novalis. Dürhammer sees close parallels between Schubert's story and that of the fable 'Hyazinth und Rosenblütchen', which appears in the unfinished novel 'Die Lehrlinge zu Sais'. It would seem that Schubert was experimenting with story-telling in the manner of Novalis, perhaps with some slight autobiographical dimension concerning his relationship with his parents. The result is very undistinguished as literature; and whatever the circumstances under which Schubert wrote it, whether with or without the aid of opium, it is rather

---

[61] *Doc.* 226–8, *Dok.* 158–9. [62] *Doc.* 228n, *Dok.* 159n.
[63] Dürhammer, 'Zu Schuberts Literaturästhetik', 20–2.

unlikely that 'Mein Traum' can explain or point to anything of appreciable significance about the composer's psychology.

A week or so after writing 'Mein Traum', Schubert attended his last Atzenbrugg festival. He then returned to Vienna, and stayed there for the remainder of the summer.

Schubert was 25 years old, for the most part healthy and energetic, his sensibilities continually stimulated by poetry and music. During the following weeks many of his friends and associates were away from Vienna, on vacation or working elsewhere. Most musical activities, concerts, and rehearsals and meetings of the reading-circle had stopped for the summer months. He was suffering great disappointment, even despair and a strong sense of injustice at the rejection of *Alfonso* which, encouraged by Schober, he still believed to be eminently suitable for production in Vienna. He needed consolation. Although he may have been working on the final stages of the first version of his Mass in A flat (begun almost three years previously), from June through to August he completed no major works, and probably only one minor one: the female-voice quartet 'Gott in der Natur' (God in Nature) D757. With time on his hands and in a depressed state while many of his friends were out of Vienna, his sensuality stimulated by his new hedonism, it would not be surprising if he turned to easy excitements, to the seedier side of city life, including visits to prostitutes of whatever persuasion he preferred. It seems probable that, in a devil-may-care mood, he indulged in sexual activities which put him at very real risk of contracting venereal disease. Having once succumbed to this pattern of behaviour, it probably became a habit which continued into the autumn months. By this time, Vienna's social and musical life had returned to normality, and Schubert was experiencing his now customary surge of creative musical activity at this time of year. But his sexual appetites were soon to seal his fate.

Schubert was heartened by news from friends in Graz that he was to be proposed for honorary membership of the Styrian Musical Society. Whether this spurred him to write a new symphony or he was already working on the Symphony in B minor, he now decided to present the work to the society in Graz in appreciation of the honour they had bestowed on him. Much has been written about the composition of this symphony, the title-page dated 30 October 1822, why he left it 'unfinished', and how the two completed movements came to remain in the hands of Anselm Hüttenbrenner in Graz rather than being passed on to the society. What is certain is that the recommendation of Johann Baptist Jenger, the society's secretary, that he be honoured was passed by its committee of management early in the following April (1823), and Schubert was duly notified:

Sir,

The services you have so far rendered to the art of music are too well known for the Committee of the Styrian Musical Society to have remained unaware of them. The latter, being desirous of offering you a proof of their esteem, have elected you as a non-resident honorary member of the Styrian Musical Society. A diploma to that effect as well as a copy of the Statutes is enclosed herewith.

On behalf of the Committee:
Kalchberg   Jenger[64]

This was the first official honour Schubert had received. It was not an especially exclusive one—there were three others appointed with him, including the popular Viennese poet Ignaz Castelli and well-established violinist Eduard Jäell. Yet for a young composer it was a very considerable honour.

His next major composition, in November, was the complete antithesis of this unfinished symphony: the Fantasia in C for solo piano D760, which much later came to be called the 'Wandererfantasie'.[65] This work stands out amongst all Schubert's piano music for its aggressive character and virtuosic demands, as well as for its remarkably forward-looking structure. Nothing is known of Schubert's connection with the dedicatee, Emmanuel Liebenberg de Zsittin, except that he was a wealthy nobleman, able pianist, and one of Hummel's pupils. (The wealth of Liebenberg was most likely the attraction for Schubert, who hoped for a generous gratuity.) Whereas the 'Unfinished' Symphony is spacious, the first two movements in slowish tempi, at the same time both lyrical and dramatic, the Fantasia is in fast tempi, and even the slow second movement (Adagio) includes extended passages of very rapid notes. This music is energetic, self-confident, passionate, even egoistic, angry, and uncompromising. There is no other music for solo piano amongst Schubert's compositions comparable in content, so atypical of its composer in its pianistic demands, and one may wonder whether its composition marked some particular, traumatic experience in his life.

That something momentous had recently happened to him might be suggested by two handwritten documents of this period, and of very different kinds. The first is a few lines written by Schubert on a single sheet of paper for Albert Schellmann, a young lawyer and fine amateur pianist, with whose family Schubert had lodged in Steyr so happily in 1819. It is dated 28 November:

> Who loves not wine, girls and song,
> Remains a fool his whole life long.

[64] *Doc.* 275, *Dok.* 191.
[65] M. J. E. Brown, 'Schubert's "Wandererfantasie" ', *MT* 92 (1951), 540–2.

                    Martin Luther
        For eternal remembrance   Franz Schubert[66]

The 'girls' (*Mädchen*) here is a misquotation for 'women' (*Weiber*). On the reverse side, Schubert wrote:

> One thing will not do for all.
> Let each man find his own place in life,
> And he who standeth
> Take heed lest he fall.
>   Goethe
> (As a reminder).[67]

Here are no regrets for anything that has happened, and Schubert is repeating the hedonistic philosophy which had motivated him for some while. The sting in the tail comes in the final 'take heed lest he fall'. The second document is the letter he wrote to Spaun on Saturday 7 December,[68] after he had decided to dedicate three songs to him. It begins: 'I hope that my dedicating these three songs to you will give you some small pleasure, though I am so indebted to you for all your kindness that I truly and *ex officio* would wish to make it very much more if only I could . . .' He continues with the kind of news of his life and compositions for which Spaun had longed earlier in the year, and then makes a significant comment: 'I have told you all the news that I could of me and my music.' Does the expression 'that I could', suggest Schubert was holding something back? After concernedly asking after the well-being of Spaun and his family, he continues: 'I would be quite well were it not for vexation over the shameful business of the opera.' In all his letters to friends until now, he had always used 'recht' in qualifying the state of his own health: 'recht gut', 'recht gesund', 'recht wohl'. Why, one may wonder, does he now modify the qualification to only 'ziemlich gut'?; from 'very well' to 'quite well'? Further, the tone of the whole letter is more typical of the Schubert of earlier years than of the self-centred, neglectful man of the past fifteen months. The letter to Spaun was written, surprisingly and without explanation, from his father's home in the Rossau; and he indicates that he had only recently left Schober's apartment. Both the suggestion of change in his state of health and his return to the family home suggest that Schubert was already ill.

Schubert attended a performance of a comedy in the popular Viennese style *Aline, oder Wien in einem anderen Erdteil* (Aline, or Vienna on another Continent), a long-popular magic play by Adolf Bäuerle, with music by

---

[66] *Doc.* 246, *Dok.* 172.   [67] *Doc.* 247, *Dok.* 172.   [68] *Doc.* 247–9, *Dok.* 172–3.

Wenzel Müller[69] at the Leopoldstadt suburban theatre on 19 October (in the company, rather surprisingly, of Josef Hüttenbrenner), and the revival at the Kärntnertor-Theater of Beethoven's *Fidelio* on 3 November. Apart from these two occasions, there are no further recorded appearances of Schubert in company during this period, except for a Schubertiad at Bruchmann's on 10 November and the reading-parties at Schober's which Schubert mentioned in the letter to Spaun. Of course, this does not mean that he was definitely restricted in his movements in the period around these dates. However, all evidence points to the very end of November as the time when Schubert may have recognized the first symptoms of syphilis. In this condition he could not remain in the home of Schober, his mother and sister. He hurriedly returned to his own family home, soon afterwards to be nursed through the second and highly infectious stage of the illness. In this case, his letter to Spaun, in which he carefully withheld the shocking news of his health, was a cry from the heart of a lonely young man facing illness and isolation to a dear and loyal friend. He was seeking a renewal of that friendship, affection, and support which for the last months, or even year or so, he had rejected.

The past year and a half had seen the gradual ascendency of a second and disturbing side of Schubert's nature. To the two sides of that nature we now turn.

[69] *Doc.* 236–7n, *Dok.* 165n.

6

TWO NATURES

THE notion of two souls in one breast has been part of German thinking about the artist ever since Goethe's classic formulation of it in *Faust*, part I:

> Zwei Seelen wohnen, ach! in meiner Brust.
> Die eine will sich von der andern trennen;
> Die eine hält, in derber Liebeslust,
> Sich an die Welt mit klammernden Organen;
> Die andre hebt gewaltsam sich vom Dust
> Zu den Gefilden hoher Ahnen.

[Two souls live, alas, in my breast | The one seeks to sever itself from the other; | The one, in vulgar lust, holds on to the world, | Clinging with every organ; | The other forces its way up out of the mists | To the uplands of our noble ancestors.]

Descriptions of Schubert's nature written after his death by two of his friends from the Stadtkonvikt days provide a starting-point for an attempt to understand the character and personality of the composer. Josef von Spaun, his first benefactor, was one of Schubert's most reliable, kindly, and generous friends, both throughout his life and long after he died in November 1828. His loyalty to, and affection for, Schubert led him in the spring of 1829 to write in an obituary of his friend: 'He was uncommonly frank, sincere, incapable of malice, friendly, grateful, modest, sociable, communicative in joy but keeping his sorrows to himself . . . free from all bitterness . . . his attachment to his home, to his friends and to his native city was so great . . .'.[1] With tolerance and frankness he continued:

Altogether public opinion will criticize him on many counts: for refusing to be bound by social convention when he saw no reason to do so, and for having an

---

[1] *Mem.* 25, *Erin.* 33.

elastic conscience in regard to such duties; also for breaking his promise to attend functions given by important patrons if there was a chance of spending time at a party got up meantime by his friends or even merely out of doors on a summer's evening. In this way he gained a reputation in some quarters as a man with no social instinct or social training and one whose personality, discounting his genius as an artist, was entirely insignificant.[2]

Josef Kenner, who also knew him at the Stadtkonvikt and was a leading figure in the Bildung Circle for several years, later (while living in Linz) kept in touch with Schubert only intermittently and through mutual friends. Writing in 1858, he first described the 'idyllic' music-making of the group of friends, inspired by the young Schubert's genius, during their Stadtkonvikt days, a group in which 'Schubert's genius attracted the most gifted amateurs of art', including 'von Spaun and the friends of his noble family'.[3] However, on Schubert's behaviour in later years Kenner continued:

his body, strong as it was, succumbed to the cleavage in his—I would like to say souls, of which the one pressed heavenwards and the other wallowed in slime; perhaps, too, it succumbed to frustration over the lack of recognition which some of his larger efforts suffered and to bitterness at the meanness of his publishers.[4]

Three weeks later he added: 'Anyone who knew Schubert knows how he was made of two natures, foreign to each other, how powerfully the craving for pleasure dragged his soul down to the slough of moral degradation.'[5] This suggests that amongst Schubert's friends and acquaintances there had been much disquiet and distress about the way his life was developing. The critical comment continued after Schubert's death, also in Kreissle's biography of 1865, and was to result in a defensive, maybe even testy response from the elderly Spaun. Thus, on the subject of Schubert's supposed love from 1824 on for Countess Caroline Esterházy, Spaun wrote:

things that are included could actually give rise to a wrong view of Schubert as, for example, the assertion that at the time when he was aflame with love for the young Countess Esterházy he was having a secret affair with someone else on the side.

I ask, what is the point of such gossip? I am absolutely convinced that during the time . . . Schubert had no relations of any kind with any other girl; but even in the quite inconceivable event of the above assertion being true, was it really necessary

---

[2] *Doc.* 877–8; *ND* 717.   [3] *Mem.* 82, *Erin.* 95.
[4] *Mem.* 82, *Erin.* 96.   [5] *Mem.* 86, *Erin.* 100.

to make it known to the world? The biography [Kreissle's] contains too little light and too much shade regarding Schubert as a human being.[6]

(Spaun used a similar expression when he complained about the way in which Kreissle discussed the songs: 'Too much shadow and too little light.'[7]

In writing about the life and personality of any creative artist, there is an inherent danger of stressing the darker side of his nature at the expense of the lighter. Maybe the lighter side tends to be underplayed because it is generally less interesting and less spectacular, while the creator's wrestling with his darker side often seems to inspire the greatest creations. With some understanding of his own two extremes of nature and emotional experience, Schubert, as mentioned above, wrote in his notebook on 25 March 1824: 'Pain sharpens the understanding and strengthens the mind, whereas joy seldom troubles about the former and softens or trivializes the latter.'[8] Similarly, Spaun wrote (in 1858) of Schubert's composition process: 'those who knew him know how deeply his creations affected him and that they were conceived in suffering.'[9] Eduard von Bauernfeld, the dramatist, some five years younger than Schubert, who only came to know him in his last years but then spent much time with him, wrote in 1857 of the two natures: 'Schubert had, so to speak, a double nature, the Viennese gaiety being interwoven with and ennobled by a trait of deep melancholy. Inwardly a poet and outwardly a kind of hedonist . . .'.[10] In 1869 Bauernfeld continued:

in Schubert there slumbered a dual nature. The Austrian element, uncouth and sensual, revealed itself both in his life and in his art . . . If there were times, both in his social relationships and in his art, when the Austrian character appeared all too aggressively in the vigorous and pleasure-loving Schubert, there were also times when a black-winged daemon of sorrow and melancholy sought his company— not altogether an evil spirit, it is true, since, in the dark consecrated hours, it often brought out songs of the most agonizing beauty.[11]

In the songs referred to here, written in the 'dark consecrated hours', Bauernfeld may have been thinking specifically of the two parts of *Winterreise*, which Schubert composed in February and October 1827.

When Schubert was a young man, in good health and neither composing music nor walking for pleasure in beautiful countryside, he was probably at his happiest engaged in lively conversation with a group of congenial friends discussing intellectual and artistic subjects. Several of his companions refer to his sociability on such occasions and the active part he often played in the exchanges, stimulated into contributing his own thoughts and ideas in a manner often spiced with humour. After the banning of the

[6] *Mem.* 362, *Erin.* 417.   [7] *Mem.* 363, *Erin.* 419.   [8] *Doc.* 336, *Dok.* 232.
[9] *Mem.* 138, *Erin.* 161.   [10] *Mem.* 45, *Erin.* 53.   [11] *Mem.* 233–4, *Erin.* 267.

Bildung Circle's annual literary journal in 1818, the group began to break
up. Some of the original members moved away from Vienna to take up professional positions (in Linz or Steyr, for example), or were precluded from
attending evening meetings, which often continued late into the night, by
professional or familial duties. Some of those who remained stayed in contact and were joined by other, younger men. When Schober, the original
heretic in the Bildung Circle, was in Vienna, he eventually became the
leader of the group, with the result that the high moral element in the thinking of the early circle was soon lost, and discussions and arrangements took
on a more haphazard form. Towards the end of 1822, with their interest in
literature supposedly still to the fore, the friends formed a reading-circle,
which flourished for a while. They met to begin with on three evenings
each week in the home of the charismatic Schober, where they read many
works of importance by renowned authors. In his letter to Spaun of
7 December Schubert wrote: 'We hold readings at Schober's three times a
week, as well as a Schubertiad',[12] thus suggesting that the composer was
present at many of these gatherings. When Schober was away, the meetings
faltered without the strong control he exercised, and which he so enjoyed.
Later, in 1823 and 1825 respectively, two young men, the artist Moritz von
Schwind and dramatist Eduard von Bauernfeld, both of whom Schubert
had met two or three years before, were to join the close circle of friends
which still centred on Schober, and would prove especially good companions of Schubert.

Although Schubert was introduced to Schwind by Josef von Spaun in
1821[13] when the painter was only 17, they did not become close until some
little while after Schwind joined Schober's circle. The friendship blossomed
especially in the two years when Schober was away from Vienna from 1823
to 1825, trying to establish himself as an actor in Breslau. The then charming, good-looking, boyish Schwind, a favourite with the women, seven
years younger than Schubert, was an exuberant and youthful companion,
valued by Schubert not only for his friendship and personality but also for
his not inconsiderable musical talents and perceptions and, no doubt, for his
amusing and extravagant enthusiasms. Bauernfeld became increasingly
close to Schubert and Schwind while completing his law studies in Vienna
in the summer of 1825.[14] By the end of that year (when Bauernfeld was in
fact lodging with Schober) the three men—Schubert, Schwind, and
Bauernfeld—were spending a fair amount of time in each others' company,
bound by shared artistic interests and increasing mutual affection. The letters which passed between them in the summer of 1825 betray the immature

---

[12] *Doc.* 248, *Dok.* 173.   [13] *Dok.* 132n.   [14] *Doc.* 444n, *Dok.* 308n.

high spirits of Schwind and Bauernfeld, and maybe a touch of irritation or impatience with them on the part of the older Schubert. Schober, Schwind, Bauernfeld, to some extent Spaun, and the composer's older brother Ferdinand, to whom we return later, were probably closest to Schubert in his last years, although several others, such as Jenger, Gahy, Bocklet, and Lachner, each of them a talented musician, whether amateur or professional, were also good friends of considerable importance to him. Of them all, Bauernfeld, who may have been less inclined to, or less capable of deep emotional involvement with friends than some, later wrote with a degree of objectivity, openness, and understanding of Schubert's changing moods, despite his own comparative youth at the time of their friendship.

The composer's friends loved him not only for his creative genius but also, as they have recorded, for his generosity of spirit, affectionate and unassuming nature, his modesty, frankness and honesty, love of sharing thoughts and ideas, sensitivity, and sense of fun. They put up with a certain gaucheness, his unwillingness to conform to accepted social standards, his intolerance of affectation and impatience with boredom, and some boorishness and vulgarity. These characteristics were all part of the 'normal' Schubert they loved. Latterly, it is probable that some of his friends were unable to tolerate his unpredictable behaviour, embarrassed by his abusive outbursts or rages under the influence of alcohol, irritated by his unreliability and ill manners, dismayed or disgusted by some of his sexual activities. His younger friends, Schwind and Bauernfeld, were more tolerant; but for many former friends, Schubert's life occasioned considerable despondency. The faithful Spaun in 1829 ended his obituary of his friend: 'This heart, as rich in kindness as in music . . . how much we loved him . . . Our gratitude and our love . . . follow the dear departed beyond the grave.'[15] He made no mention of the bouts of wretched behaviour, whether of noisy vulgarity or of angry despair, witnessed by others towards the end of Schubert's life. Elsewhere he even denied the suggestion that the composer was at times a heavy drinker, for which there is ample evidence in the reports of others who knew him well. In fact Spaun, who in any case saw far less of Schubert after his marriage in April 1828, had a rich private life of his own after his return to Vienna in the summer of 1826 with his devoted family and with friends other than those of the Schober–Schubert circle. Those now close to Schubert continued to enjoy the composer's company while he was acting 'normally', but they were aware of the increasing intensity of his 'moods' and the associated behaviour. Such changing moods bear the stamp of a manic-depressive disorder, from which so many creative

---

[15] *Mem.* 28–9, *Erin.* 37.

artists and writers have suffered. On the evidence from Schubert's life over the following years it becomes a virtual certainty that he suffered from cyclothymia.

Cyclothymia is defined medically as a mild form of manic depression characterized by pronounced changes of 'mood, behaviour, thinking, sleep, and energy levels'.[16] In adults, periods of depression, hypomania (mild mania), and complete normality alternate, the latter lasting no more than two months at a time.[17] The condition at this level of severity is not debilitating, but the severity is liable to increase with the years, in many cases into full-blown clinically definable manic depression. However, even when psychotic illness is severe, many individuals are normal for most of the time, and are able to reason and function without impairment of the faculties in both personal and professional capacities. Common early symptoms of cyclothymic depression are dark moods manifested by apathy, lethargy, pessimism, self-deprecation, and irritability, and loss of interest in things usually enjoyed. Such moods may last for days, weeks, or months, although two to four weeks is common for each episode in the early stages, and three to ten weeks for the complete cycle of depression and hypomania.[18] In hypomania the symptoms are to a considerable degree the opposite of those of depression. The subject is in an excited or elevated mood, energetic and requiring less sleep. His thinking is fast as he moves rapidly from one topic to another, speaking quickly and often intrusively. He has inflated self-esteem and grandiose ideas of his own abilities and importance, and poor judgement—all to the detriment of personal and professional relationships. In a creative artist hypomania may lead to periods of high productivity. It may also result in unevenness in quantity and quality of the production, as powers of self-criticism are decreased. Those suffering from cyclothymia often feel the need to be with other people—they indulge in 'uninhibited people-seeking'; but when with companions they may behave in an embarrassing fashion, laughing and joking loudly and inappropriately.[19] In this context, Holzapfel's description of Schubert's behaviour already in 1822, that he 'made himself conspicuous' in company by his loud manner, is relevant. Other accounts of his social and practical inadequacies fit well into the cyclothymic pattern of irresponsibility in personal affairs: spending money prodigally (when he had any), showing extreme impatience, and, in Schubert's case, presumably indulging in unrestrained romantic or sexual activities, as suggested by Kenner's reference to his fall into the 'slough of moral degradation'.

[16] K. Redfield Jamison, *Touched with Fire* (New York, 1993), 13.
[17] Ibid. 263.   [18] Ibid. 15.   [19] Ibid. 295.

All manic-depressive illness is recurrent and, if ineffectively treated, as was the case in early nineteenth-century Vienna, liable to worsen in the intensity of mood changes and length of the attacks, with commensurate shortening of periods of normality. In many instances, there is a seasonal rhythm to the cycle of moods, and this can be deduced from the dates of commencement and cessation of high productivity. In Schubert's case, from 1818 until venereal disease struck, his periods of most intense productivity tended to be in April and May and again in October and November. During the midsummer months of June, July, and August he composed very little. The first symptoms tend to appear in adolescence or late teens, although today's average of around 18[20] may have been delayed in the early nineteenth century, when physical maturity was reached a few years later than now. The condition has always been rare in children, and for this reason Schubert's loneliness and unhappiness during his first year at the Stadtkonvikt were unlikely to have been caused by clinical depression; they were most probably a normal and far from uncommon reaction in a child sent to boarding-school to face a new way of life amongst strangers, and undergo forced separation from the support of familial love and affection. Although there is very little surviving documentation concerning Schubert's personal life before 1818, it is likely that by 1817, and perhaps earlier, he was beginning to experience some swings of mood from mild depression, or 'melancholia' as it was often called, to mild mania (hypomania). Thus, as early as 1816 (on 13 June), at the age of 19, he made reference to extremes of mood, 'continual joy' and 'dark life' in his diary: '*Moments of bliss brighten* this dark life; over yonder these blissful moments coalesce and are transformed into continuous joy, and happier ones still will turn into visions of yet happier worlds, and so on.'[21]

Initially Schubert's cyclothymia followed the normal pattern; but after he contracted syphilis at the end of 1822, problems with his general health and changed habits seem to have increased the usual modest rate of degeneration to more acute and longer episodes of mental disturbance and shorter periods of normality. For Schubert, affected by syphilis, both alcohol and nicotine abuse may have been manifestations of his cyclothymia, hastening the deterioration in his mental health: a vicious circle of cause and effect. It is even possible that, by the time of his death, Schubert's condition had already deteriorated into a more severe form of manic depression.

Any manic-depressive condition, whether of an acute psychotic kind or the milder cyclothymia from which Schubert suffered, is genetic, and there

---

[20] Ibid. 17.   [21] *Doc.* 71, *Dok.* 49.

must be evidence of similar disturbance in close relatives of the subject.[22]
Behaviour patterns in the lives of immediate members of his family, his
first-degree relatives, and especially of his sister Maria Theresia (Resi) provide sufficient evidence of a familial tendency to depressive disorder, probably on his mother's side, to make this assumption with confidence.

Maria Theresia, Schubert's only surviving sister (apart, that is, from two
half-sisters born in 1814 and 1815), suffered a serious mental breakdown
after the birth and death of her first child in the summer of 1824. She had
married Matthias Schneider, some twelve years her senior, in the Rossau
parish church on 31 August of the year before. Schneider was a secondary
schoolteacher at the orphanage in the Alsergrund suburb, where Ferdinand
taught from 1810 until 1820 and conducted the school orchestra. Schneider
was also musical, and gave singing and cello tuition to boys at the orphanage. He was later appointed headmaster of the secondary school in the
St Ulrich (or Maria Trost) suburb, and here Ferdinand also lived with his
wife and family from 1824, when he took up a teaching post at the teachers'
training college in the Annagasse. Four years later, a requiem mass for
Schubert was sung in the parish church of St Ulrich where Ferdinand, and
presumably Schneider, were active in a flourishing musical society. Thus
Ferdinand was responsible for introducing his friend and colleague
Schneider to his sister, and the two men remained closely in contact after
the wedding. Maria Theresia's breakdown caused her family great concern.
In reply to Schubert's cheerful enquiry in a letter from Zseliz of 18 July asking whether Resi had 'yet blessed the world with a new citizen???',[23] his
brother Ferdinand wrote on 6 October:

Resi, who gave birth to a strong and healthy girl, was not granted that happiness
for long, for the infant lived only twelve or fourteen days. Grief at the death of her
first-born nearly turned into raving madness and confined her to the sick-bed for
several weeks. Fortunately she has now got past the danger of serious trouble and
seems to be resigned to her fate.[24]

Mental breakdown and severe depression after childbirth or the loss of a
child are quite common, but it was more likely to occur in young women
from families with manic depressive tendencies or a history of melancholia, mania, or suicide.[25]

The artistic talents of Schubert and his family are believed to have come
from his mother's side—the Vietzes. For Elisabeth Schubert there is some
reason for suspecting ill health or depression around the time of the composer's birth in 1797. The suspicion springs from a surprising gap of almost

[22] Jamison, *Touched with Fire*, 192–237.   [23] *Doc.* 364, *Dok.* 251.
[24] *Doc.* 378, *Dok.* 261.   [25] Jamison, *Touched with Fire*, 156.

three years between the birth of Franz and the next child, Aloisia Magdalena (who lived only twenty-four hours). Elisabeth Schubert was 40 when Schubert, and 44 when her last child, Maria Theresia, was born—the latter twenty-one months after Aloisia. Unless she suffered miscarriages during her three childless years, her health in this period might be suspect; for, in the light of the less than two-year gap between the birth of her last two children, there is no evidence for more than a steady, slow decline in her fertility between January 1796 and December 1799. A further pointer to her possible ill health, whether of a physical or mental kind, may lie in Schubert's father's efforts to obtain other school appointments during the years immediately before and after Schubert's birth. At least once in 1796 (in January) and twice in 1797 (during March and December) he applied unsuccessfully for positions which would have necessitated his family moving from the overcrowded and unhygienic conditions of their Himmelpfortgrund home.[26] Here his wife had given birth every year before Schubert was born at intervals of eleven to fourteen months, and had seen seven out of eight of her children die in infancy in the five years between 1788 and 1793.[27] It would not be surprising if in 1797, now 40 years old and perhaps worn out by continuous childbearing, she was fearful for the lives of her surviving infants, and unwilling to bear more only to watch them die. The possibility that she suffered a period of depressive illness accompanied by a decline in sexual appetite cannot be ruled out. However, such depression was probably more likely to have been of a reactive nature than an inherited disorder. Schubert's father, on the other hand, showed in his strenuous, over-conscientious working life both physical and mental robustness.

Ferdinand, who was three years older than Schubert and enjoyed an especially close relationship with him, was probably mildly depressive, as the letters they exchanged suggest. Franz, when he was in Zseliz in 1818, received a letter (now lost) from Ferdinand showing the writer to be in particularly low spirits. Schubert responded affectionately and supportively on 24 August:

Things are not well with you: I wish I might change with you, so that you might be happy for once. You would find all heavy burdens cast off your shoulders. I could wish this for you with all my heart, dear brother.—My foot is going to sleep, much to my annoyance. If the dolt could write it could not go to sleep . . . Good morning, dear little brother: I have now slept, foot and all, and continue my letter at 8 am on the 25th . . .[28]

---

[26] *Doc.* 3n, 4n, *Dok.* 5n, 6n.   [27] *Doc.* 1–3, *Dok.* 4–5.   [28] *Doc.* 95, *Dok.* 64.

He continued with an informative description of his life at Zseliz, of the kind with which Schubert blessed and cheered Ferdinand more than any other of his correspondents. Only eight weeks later, on 29 October, he tried to allay Ferdinand's dismay over his 'sin of appropriation [purloining]' of music, the German Requiem with which Schubert had supplied him for performance in Vienna at the orphanage where he was then employed, and which Ferdinand had then passed off as his own composition.[29] Ferdinand was an able musician, first violinist of the family string quartet, organist at the Lichtental church from 1810 to 1820, and chorus-master at the Alt-Lerchenfeld church (a western suburb of Vienna) from early 1820.[30] In 1838 he was appointed professor of organ at the Conservatoire associated with the Gesellschaft der Musikfreunde,[31] and he applied unsuccessfully in 1822 for the position of assistant Court organist.[32] But he was a composer of only modest accomplishment, and on several occasions was helped out by his younger brother, who willingly presented him with works which, not entirely without misgivings, Ferdinand sometimes claimed as his own. (With or without a bad conscience, and long after Schubert's death, Ferdinand continued to appropriate quite large sections of his brother's music in his own compositions.) In the same October 1818 letter, Schubert affectionately rebuked Ferdinand for his fears that his letters to him were inadequate: 'The only thing that troubles me is that you imagine your letters to be disagreeable to me. It is too terrible even to think your brother capable of such a thing, let alone to write about it';[33] and in reference to imagined financial obligations which Franz found totally uncalled for from a brother, he continued: 'I hate your always talking about payments, rewards and thanks—to a brother, fie, for shame!'

These communications between the brothers suggest that Ferdinand was often in low spirits and suffered from a sense of inadequacy, both possibly symptoms of mild depression. However there is no firm evidence of his self-deprecation being other than situationally, rather than medically based; and whatever the cause, the depressions were not sufficiently serious to preclude his successful pedagogic career, which included prompt promotions from schoolteacher to member of the staff of the teachers' training college and, in 1851, to the prestigious appointment of director of that establishment.[34] His musical career was far from undistinguished.[35]

Ignaz Schubert, the eldest child of the family, was born seven weeks after his parents' marriage. Like his brothers, he was a musician, second violinist in the family quartet, and Franz's first piano teacher, although less

[29] *Doc.* 107n, 109; *Dok.* 73n, 74.   [30] *Doc.* 131n, *Dok.* 89n.
[31] I. Weinmann, 'Ferdinand Schubert', *MGG* (Kassel, 1965).   [32] *Doc.* 452n, *Dok.* 310n.
[33] *Doc.* 109, *Dok.* 75.   [34] *Doc.* 43n, *Dok.* 34n.   [35] Weinmann, 'Schubert'.

talented and enthusiastic than Ferdinand. He remained an assistant elementary schoolteacher, working for his father until the latter's death in 1830, at which time Ignaz took over the headship of what was now a flourishing school in the Rossau district. His remaining at his father's schools and his consequent lack of promotion until he was 45 may have been partly the result of his deformity: he was a hunchback.[36] It was also no doubt because, as a radical and a freethinker, he was politically suspect in Metternich's Vienna. To the authorities potentially a dangerous militant, he would have been kept under close surveillance by the police and their spies. In the family home he was clearly something of a rebel; yet he had little choice but to stay with his very respectable father if he wished to remain in work and perhaps out of prison. His discontent and impatience with his father come out clearly in the letter he wrote, with some irony, to his brother Franz in Zseliz at the start of his own autumn school vacation on 12 October 1818, his only surviving complete letter. Ignaz first bemoaned the sorry position of a schoolteacher (see above, pp. 85–6), and then attacked the narrow-minded government and church officials who made their lives such a misery:

You see, you are now free of all these things, you are saved, you now see and hear nothing of all these evils, nor of our pundits, about whom it is surely unnecessary to recall Herr Bürger's consolatory verse to you:

> Nay, envy not the massive skulls
> Of consequential people,
> For most of them as hollow are
> As knobs upon a steeple![37]

Schubert replied to this: 'You, Ignaz, are still quite the same man of iron you always were. Your implacable hatred of the whole tribe of bigwigs does you credit',[38] and he continued with a colourful and vitriolic attack on the absurdities of the local Catholic priests in the Zseliz area.

Ignaz was temperamentally strong, the 'man of iron', inheriting his father's mental stability and, like him, vigorously holding on to his own views and philosophies. His father and Ignaz living and working under the same roof would have led to tempestuous times had the authority of the strict Biedermeier father not been sacrosanct in their home. It is strange that Ignaz, an eldest son, did not inherit the headship of the younger generation (a position that fell instead to Ferdinand); nor did he receive a share of the inheritance from the sale of the Himmelpfortgrund schoolhouse.[39] This could have been due either to his radical freethinking tendencies or to

---

[36] *Doc. 83, Dok. 56.*   [37] *Doc. 104, Dok. 71.*   [38] *Doc. 110, Dok. 75.*
[39] *Doc. 25, Dok. 20.*

the disapproval of the state or church authorities. Whether he moved out of the Rossau schoolhouse or brought his wife into it on their marriage in 1825 is not known. As we have mentioned, she was a widow, Wilhelmine Hollpein, née Grob, born the same year as Ignaz, and the aunt of Therese Grob.[40] An example of Ignaz' freethinking, and of a sense of humour not very different from Schubert's own, is found in a note he wrote at the foot of a letter of 14 August 1824 from their father and stepmother to Schubert: 'The latest is that a rabid suicide-mania is the fashion here [in Vienna], as though people were quite sure that once over yonder, they'd jump straight-away into heaven.'[41]

For Karl, just fifteen months older than Schubert, life in the Himmel-pfortgrund home as he grew older may have been as uncomfortable and alien as it was for Schubert, perhaps even more so; for while Schubert's great passion, music, was a communal activity in the home and something shared, Karl, as a painter, could not so easily share his passion for painting and drawing. He was a gifted young artist who in later life established a good reputation for himself as a landscape painter, engraver, lithographer, and calligrapher. Both his sons, Ferdinand and Heinrich, became profes-sional painters. Franz and Karl were good friends, perhaps at their closest during the period 1813 to 1814 while the composer was studying at the teachers' training college and Karl still at the Academy of Fine Arts, both colleges being situated in the same building. After this, Karl referred to Franz as 'his two-fold brother',[42] possibly because they were both creative artists as well as blood-brothers. By the end of 1818 Karl, at the age of 23, was already engaged,[43] although he did not marry until 1823.[44] Of Karl's temperament, nothing is known. The four brothers seem to have remained close, both Ferdinand and Karl serving as godfather to each other's eldest son (neither Schubert nor Ignaz, both no longer willing churchgoers, served in this capacity).

Although there is no clear or dramatically obvious strain of serious men-tal illness in the Schubert or Vietz families, there is sufficient evidence, par-ticularly through the experience of Maria Theresia, that depression was present in at least one member of the family apart from Schubert. There is also some evidence that both Ferdinand and their mother Elisabeth (Vietz) had depressive tendencies. The diagnosis of Schubert as cyclothymic on this basis is highly likely, and we now turn to a closer look at how this affected his behaviour.

According to descriptions of his youth by his contemporaries at the

---

[40] *Doc.* 436–8, *Dok.* 300–1.   [41] *Doc.* 368–9, *Dok.* 254.   [42] *Doc.* 94, *Dok.* 63.
[43] *Doc.* 110, *Dok.* 75.   [44] *Dok.* 96n.

Stadtkonvikt, during the first four years of his education there, Schubert was a well-behaved student who conformed to the rules and caused no trouble. In his final year, his passion for music and impatience with the dreary education he was expected to pursue were aggravated by a perfectly normal adolescent questioning of prescribed values and criticism of authority. His friends in the Bildung Circle during his late teens, when the first indications of mild mood swings may have occurred, provided him with intellectual and aesthetic stimulation and also with an idealistic ethical code which at this time helped to curb his pleasure-loving tendencies. As the activities of the circle, as originally conceived, began to decline after 1817, the influence of Franz von Schober on Schubert increased. Schober's hedonism was soon to take a more dangerous form when, after a year's absence from Vienna, he returned from Sweden towards the end of 1820 and became in effect the charismatic leader of Schubert's circle of friends. Here he encouraged a new ethic and extravagances which were totally antipathetic to the high and worthy ethics of the original Bildung Circle. Unfortunately for Schubert, who was especially susceptible to hedonistic suggestion, and less in control during cyclothymic periods, Schober encouraged and fuelled his natural inclination towards pleasures and vices, and induced attitudes which would have been unthinkable within the confines of the schoolhouse morality in which he had been reared. As already described, by late 1822 when the 'Wandererfantasie' was composed, Schubert had probably developed the first symptoms of syphilis. From then until early 1825 his life and thinking were much affected by this distressing illness, and it becomes impossible to disentangle his depressions resulting from venereal disease and those associated with cyclothymia.

For two years or more after the autumn of 1824 his physical condition greatly improved, and he may well have hoped that, as for a fair proportion of those who developed syphilis at that time, his health might eventually be almost fully restored. (As understood today, this restoration of health, coming after the first two stages of syphilis, would have meant that the disease was now latent. He would be free of symptoms, except perhaps for some residual damage from earlier stages of the disease, and uninfectious; and he might escape further and possibly fatal developments associated with the late, or tertiary stage. Extreme caution regarding sexual activities would be advisable for anyone suffering from syphilis.) However, between this time and 1827, when he began to complain of recurring headaches, an ominous sign that the syphilis was not latent, he was living a normal life. Johanna Lutz wrote to her fiancé Leopold Kupelwieser on 7 March 1825: 'Schubert is now very busy and well behaved, which pleases me very much'.[45] Anton Ottenwalt in letters to his brother-in-law Josef von Spaun referred to Schubert's stay with him and his wife in Linz in July 1825, at the start of Schubert's travels that summer in Upper Austria, Salzburg, and Gastein with Johann Michael Vogl: 'Schubert looks so well and strong, is so nice and cheerful and so genially communicative that one cannot fail to be sincerely delighted about it . . .'.[46] Eight days later he wrote: 'Of Schubert—I could almost say of *our* Schubert—there is much I should like to tell you . . . Schubert was so friendly and communicative . . .'.[47]

In Schubert's letters written between July and September during these travels to his parents, Ferdinand, Spaun, and Bauernfeld, Schubert gave no indication that he was other than in good health and spirits. In August, shortly after he arrived back in Vienna, Schober returned after a second prolonged absence from the city, this time of two years' duration. For a while after this, Schubert's creative activity seems to have declined, and by the summer of 1826 he was complaining that he was seriously short of money, and this despite a fair number of publications during this year.[48] His lodgings in the Fruhwirthaus near the Karlskirche were, by the standards of the day, not inexpensive; and maybe for this reason he left his pleasant home here and moved in again, though at first temporarily, with Schober. On 10 July he wrote to Bauernfeld: 'I cannot possibly get to Gmunden or anywhere else, for I have no money at all, and altogether things go very badly for me. I do not worry about it, and am cheerful.'[49] Schubert was short of money in the summer of 1826 because over the previous months he had mismanaged his income, small though it may have been. His friends described him as generous to a fault when he had money, and also as irresponsible in financial matters. If he had paper money or coins in his pocket, he spent them readily on himself and on his friends rather than putting some aside for future necessities. He ran up bills at inns and coffee-houses, with tradesmen (such as his tailor) and sometimes with his landlord. Some of his recent carelessness with money and excessive expenditure could be explained by a deteriorating mental state. Financial extravagance and the resort to hypersexual activity and alcohol, apparently two of Schubert's particular weaknesses, as a 'means of self-treatment or augmenting excitement' are common symptoms of advancing cyclothymia.[50] Schubert was in reasonably good physical health during the first half of the year, and there is no evidence to suggest that he was paying doctor's bills. On the other

[45] *Doc.* 406, *Dok.* 278.   [46] *Doc.* 429, *Dok.* 295.   [47] *Doc.* 441–2, *Dok.* 303–4.
[48] Publications included the piano sonatas in A minor D845 and in D major D850, seven piano duets (DD 733, 773, 818, 823, 824, 859, 885) and many songs, including the Walter Scott 'Lady of the Lake' songs and settings of poems by Schiller, Goethe, Hölty, Rückert, and Mayrhofer.
[49] *Doc.* 538, *Dok.* 366.   [50] Jamison, *Touched with Fire*, 264.

hand, doctor's fees and medical treatment were certainly at least partly responsible for the shortage of money of which he complained in July 1828,[51] and again soon afterwards when he was forced to put off a planned autumn visit to Graz,[52] although he had managed to visit the Pachlers there in the previous autumn.

There are various accounts of Schubert's anti-social behaviour during these last years, in particular his failure to appear at various functions after promising to attend[53] and of drunkenness accompanied by vulgar and abusive language.[54] Wilhelm von Chézy (son of the authoress of the play *Rosamunde* for which Schubert wrote incidental music in 1823) described much later, in 1841, a form of Schubert's behaviour which, if true, points to advanced cyclothymic disorder. Chézy, a minor author and journalist, moved with his mother to Baden, south of Vienna, in 1823 and remained in the area until after Schubert's death. He was acquainted with Schubert, though not one of his closest friends. (His younger brother Max, a painter, came to know the Hartmann family and Anton von Spaun in Linz.[55]) Under the influence of alcohol, Schubert was subject to uncontrollable and aggressive rages. Chézy wrote of these:

As soon as the blood of the vine was glowing in him, he liked to withdraw into a corner and give in to a quiet, comfortable anger during which he would try to create some sort of havoc as quickly as possible, for example, with cups, glasses and plates, and as he did so, he would grin and screw up his eyes tight.[56]

In this description of Schubert's behaviour in the last years of his life, Chézy suggests that the composer's destructive behaviour was malicious, but not directed against people. If this was the case, then it is comparable with the 'violent rages and dark moods' associated with the drinking sessions of Byron, another renowned and serious sufferer from manic depression;[57] and Schubert's destruction of glass and crockery was a manifestation, if a less expensive one, of the same dark rage experienced by Byron when he threw a much-loved watch into the ashes in the hearth and ground it into small pieces with a poker.[58] Hugh Macdonald has drawn attention to what he has described as examples of 'volcanic temper', a 'streak of violence and distemper' in Schubert's music.[59] Such musical passages occur in compositions throughout his life, and Macdonald cites one in

---

[51] *Doc.* 789, *Dok.* 525. [52] *Doc.* 807, *Dok.* 537.

[53] *Mem.* 136–7 (Spaun), 229 (Bauernfeld), 252–3 (Breuning), *Erin.* 159, 262, 289.

[54] Bauernfeld: *Mem.* 230, *Erin.* 264. [55] WL ii. 95; *Doc.* 293n, *Dok.* 202n.

[56] W. von Chézy, 'Erinnerungen aus Wien: Aus den Jahren 1824 bis 1829', *Deutsche Pandora* (Stuttgart, 1841), 183. (I am indebted to T. G. Waidelich for drawing my attention to this article.)

[57] Jamison, *Touched with Fire*, 176. [58] Ibid. 182.

[59] H. Macdonald, 'Schubert's Volcanic Temper', *MT* 99 (1978), 949–52.

the slow movement of the String Quartet in B flat D36 of 1812 as a very early example. However, they are most frequent in the slow movements of Schubert's later works, where sudden rage shatters an established mood of, for example, quiet reflection, suggesting an increase in the violence and desperation in Schubert's inner world. Macdonald describes the 'most violent of all passages in Schubert' as that leading up to and including the climax of the second movement of the 'Great' C major Symphony (in bar 248). This climax occurs on the frenetic *FFF* diminished seventh chord on D sharp (after a harmonic shift up a semitone from the preceding harmony) which precedes 1¾ bars of silence before the 'cellos lead the music back' to the gentle 'Elysian lyricism of A minor, as though some great evil force has been exorcized'.[60] Other striking examples of the demonic element in his music are found in the slow movements of the string quartets in A minor D804 and G major D887, the Octet D803 (in the coda) and the String Quintet in C D956. In the piano sonatas and duets there are many others: in the Sonata in A minor D845 (the first and last movements) and in the first movement of that in B flat D960; in slow movements of the unfinished Sonata in C D840 (the 'Reliquie'), in D major D850 and G major D894, and the late Sonata in A D959. Examples in the piano duets are, in the opinion of Macdonald, richer, more numerous, longer, and more frenetic, as exemplified in the wilder sections of the Divertissement D823 and 'Lebensstürme' D947, and also in the Fantasia in F minor D940. Similarly, the slow C-minor movement of the Piano Trio in E flat D929 contains a disturbing and violent section in F sharp minor, subsequently transformed by a Neapolitan modulation to the dominant (G) and then to C major. The early part of the development section of the first movement of the 'Unfinished' Symphony is described by Macdonald in terms of hysteria and narrowly avoided dementia. The power and insistence of all these passages, and many more, come as a shock to the listener more familiar with Schubert's lyrical moods; but they are dominant features in much of Schubert's music.

One early work surprisingly stands out in its entirety in the context of musical evidence of Schubert's disturbed moods and the aggression of which he was capable: the Fantasia in C for Piano ('Wandererfantasie') of November 1822, almost contemporary with the 'Unfinished' Symphony. This quasi-four-movement sonata is unique amongst Schubert's compositions in several ways. First, written when he was 25 years old in a grandiose style for which there was no identifiable model, it anticipated to a remarkable degree in form, style, and techniques developments in piano music

---

[60] H. Macdonald, 'Schubert's Volcanic Temper', *MT* 99 (1978), 950–1.

later in the century. This is Schubert's only strikingly virtuoso composition for the piano, and it was written before he came to number among his friends such virtuoso pianists as Karl Maria von Bocklet, who was the pianist in all public performances of his piano music in the last years of his life, both solo and chamber music. Schubert himself did not have the technique (or large enough hands) to play the Fantasia himself, as Leopold Kupelwieser made clear: 'Once when Schubert was playing the Fantasia . . . to a circle of friends and got stuck in the last movement, he sprang up from his seat with the words: "Let the devil play the stuff!" '[61] This is a pianistic show piece, richly textured, finely structured, and wildly energetic. Anthony Storr has described as 'manic defence' the condition when:

a man reverses and denies his depression. Instead of being sensitive to the needs and wishes of others, he becomes inconsiderate, irritable, demanding; often riding roughshod over people or attacking them without consideration . . . [he] triumphantly proclaims his ability to overcome every obstacle . . . he omnipotently claims complete self-confidence.[62]

This Fantasia is the music of such a man; subjugating his despair with assumed over-confidence, selfishness, and boasting, to produce a striking piece of music of somewhat sinister exuberance. These characteristics are not to be found to the same degree in any other work Schubert wrote. Was this composed at the very time of his discovery of the ugly lesion that signified the onset of syphilis, and of his realization that he must now pay the price for the irresponsible life he had probably been leading for the past two years?

It is not always easy to distinguish between normal personality traits and mild mental disorders. From early on Schubert's dislike of smart society and formal gatherings, which we are told 'he only frequented in order to accompany his songs, more or less as a favour' (i.e. with or without payment),[63] could have been the result either of his normal nature or else a symptom of depressive shyness. He was certainly uncomfortable in fashionable salon circles, and totally out of sympathy with the affectations of thought and musical taste which were sometimes to be found there. His reaction could be boredom, discomfort, or irritation, all of which he was liable to mask by withdrawal from conversation or near-silent boorishness. Anselm Hüttenbrenner described how Schubert, when not performing:

usually sat in a corner, or even in a neighbouring room, and listened. One evening he whispered in my ear: 'Look here, I can't stand these women with their

---

[61] *Mem.* 194–5, *Erin.* 224.
[62] A. Storr, *The Dynamics of Creation*, 2nd edn. (London, 1976), 112.
[63] L. Sonnleithner: *Mem.* 121, *Erin.* 141.

compliments. They understand nothing about music, and the things they say to me they don't really mean. Go along, Anselm, and bring me a glass of wine on the sly!'[64]

A disinclination to enter the limelight was part of his nature; hence his refusal to take a composer's bow at the Kärntnertor-Theater in June 1820 after the first performance of *Die Zwillingsbrüder*. After performances of his music, he preferred the reasoned and valued judgements of friends whom he trusted to uncritical popular acclaim. Schubert in society would choose a back seat, sit apart, or move inconspicuously with the crowd. At house-parties and balls he was content to sit at the piano, perhaps for several hours during an evening, playing pieces for friends and acquaintances to dance to. Similarly, in salons in Vienna and elsewhere he was happier performing his songs than entering into conversation with people he scarcely knew, putting forward his compositions, and his music, rather than himself.

In those early days (from 1815 to 1817) his depressive and hypomanic moods may have passed almost unnoticed—Mayrhofer was surely more depressive than he was—and certainly caused little concern amongst his friends. All references to his 'melancholy' or attacks of 'melancholia' in sur-viving records have come from friends closely associated with Schubert in the final years of his life, and were concerned particularly with that period. In her old age, Leopold Sonnleithner's sister remembered Schubert as 'an extremely simple, natural man with a tendency to severe melancholy'.[65] Mayrhofer referred to Schubert's melancholy in the simple context of opposites in his character: 'tenderness and coarseness, sensuality and can-dour, sociability and melancholy';[66] Bauernfeld, as mentioned above, wrote of his double nature: 'the Viennese gaiety being interwoven and ennobled by a trait of deep melancholy.'[67] Spaun described Schubert's gloom as he composed the *Winterreise* song-cycle in 1827: 'For a time Schubert's mood became gloomy.'[68] Bauernfeld elaborated on his descrip-tion when writing of Schubert's behaviour in company from 1825 onwards, a time when he was much in contact with the composer:

he suffered from a genuine dread of commonplace and boring people, of philistines, whether from the upper or middle classes, of the people, that is, who are usually known as 'educated'; and Goethe's outcry:

> Lieber will ich schlechter werden,
> Als mich ennuyieren!
> [I would rather die than be bored.]

[64] *Mem.* 182, *Erin.* 209.   [65] *Mem.* 281, *Erin.* 323.   [66] *Mem.* 14, *Erin.* 19–20.
[67] *Mem.* 45, *Erin.* 53.   [68] *Mem.* 137–8, *Erin.* 160. See Ch. 10.

was and remained his motto, as it was ours [their friends']. Among commonplace people, he felt lonely and depressed, was generally silent and apt to become ill-humoured as well . . . So it was no wonder if at table he sometimes drank himself into a state of thorough going tipsiness and then tried to free himself from his oppressive environment by using some coarse expressions, which shocked people and made them shrink away from him.[69]

Bauernfeld here showed his awareness both of Schubert's situational depressions, and, when these were intensified by cyclothymic and later perhaps by psychotic moods, how he attempted to alleviate his misery with alcohol and abusiveness. Bauernfeld later explained depression with a situational cause as a normal condition: 'But things are not always rosy. No mortal is immune from melancholy and occasional low spirits.'[70] On Schubert's later, deeper depressions he was also clear when he wrote of the 'black-winged daemon of sorrow and melancholy', and 'at times he felt absolutely without courage and without hope, filled with gloomy visions of the future'.[71]

Schubert's depressions were worsening with the years, and the rapid deterioration in his temperament was aggravated not only by his poor physical health from syphilis but also by his continued abuse of alcohol and nicotine. At the same time, his resort to creative work which, as Anthony Storr has so convincingly argued, 'tends to protect the individual against mental breakdown',[72] may have saved him from serious psychosis.

After 1822 it is impossible to establish any sure seasonal pattern for Schubert's creativity, such as a regular cycle of annual or biannual hyper-creativity or the lack of it, which can be readily associated with seasonal episodes of cyclothymia. Indeed, there is no pattern, after his apparent barren periods during the summer months in the years up to 1822, except that he began a major composition in the June of each of three years: 1825 (the 'Great' C major Symphony), 1827 (the opera, *Der Graf von Gleichen*—The Count of Gleichen D918) and 1828 (the Mass in E flat). He also wrote the String Quartet in G major D887 in the June of 1826. Possible reasons for the lack of a basic pattern are threefold. First, any usual cyclothymic pattern was liable to be upset by periods of serious syphilitic illness and any accompanying depression resulting from this; he was also affected by the often debilitating medical treatment he received, including fasting, purging, and mercury applications. Secondly, in each year from 1823, except for 1826 and 1828, he travelled or toured outside Vienna and its environs, when professional, social, and practical commitments could interfere with

---

[69] *Mem.* 230, *Erin.* 263–4.   [70] *Mem.* 233, *Erin.* 267.
[71] *Mem.* 236, *Erin.* 270.   [72] Storr, *Dynamics of Creation*, 51ff.

compositional habits and inclinations. Thirdly, various commissions or planned concerts made it necessary for him to compose as far as he was able, within prescribed time limits. However, despite no obvious cyclical pattern, his periods of heavy drinking, dissoluteness, and laziness and his episodes of offensive behaviour, were all linked to his mental condition.

In early adulthood, most of Schubert's serious drinking was probably social, enjoyed in the company of friends in a city where the consumption of alcohol was very much part of the culture. His comment to his brother at the end of January 1821 that he was 'seedy today on account of yesterday's dissipations',[73] very probably at a lively party of some sixteen young people given by Schober, need cause no special concern unless we take it to herald the start of a new decadence, encouraged by Schober, in his way of life. Anselm Hüttenbrenner, among others, referred to the normal drinking habits of his friend: 'Schubert was at his most communicative over a glass of wine or punch; his musical judgements were acute, concise and to the point.'[74] Schubert had certainly been drinking in March 1820 when he was taken with his unfortunate friend Johann Senn and three others for police questioning. His drinking habits became more serious after the onset of syphilis, when he was seeking relief from his worsening depressions or, if in an exalted hypomanic state, further excitement. Leopold Sonnleithner claimed to having seen him intoxicated on several occasions, and referred in disapproving terms to a particular gathering in one of the suburbs of Vienna where Schubert disgraced himself at a private party 'in a house where he had not long been known and where he had only been introduced a short time previously'.[75] Gerhard von Breuning referred to Schubert's having drunk too much at the home of a 'middle-class family in the Landstrasse' (perhaps the Schmerling family with whom Bauernfeld was living at the end of 1825)[76] and having to be carried to another room.[77] Josef Hüttenbrenner mentions another occasion when he was drunk, or may have arrived already intoxicated, at the home of the president of the Supreme Court of Justice, probably Karl Josef Pratobevera von Wiesborn who lived near the Kärntnertor[78] between 1826 and 1828.[79] Whether the first two of these occasions were the same or not, they were well remembered by those of Schubert's friends who were present as examples of his deplorable and embarrassing conduct while a guest at private functions in respectable family homes. Bauernfeld tells of another occasion at a Grinzing hostelry when Schubert, in a drunken state, was overcome by an

---

[73] *Doc.* 163, *Dok.* 116. [74] *Mem.* 185, *Erin.* 213. [75] *Mem.* 110, *Erin.* 128.
[76] *Mem.* 240, *Erin.* 275. [77] *Mem.* 255, *Erin.* 291–2. [78] *Doc.* 509n, *Erin.* 346n.
[79] *Mem.* 191, 193n, *Erin.* 220, 222n.

attack of totally unprovoked rage, of volcanic temper, resulting in a tirade of noisy abuse being directed at two orchestral players with whom he was slightly acquainted.[80] He had shown a tendency to volatile temper as early as 1813 when at the Blumenstöckl inn in Vienna in the company of the poet Theodor Körner and Spaun, after a performance of Gluck's *Iphigenia in Tauris*, he became involved in a violent exchange of words which nearly led to blows with older men sitting at the neighbouring table. He was just 16 at this time.[81] Wilhelm von Chézy's description of his destructive, drunken though silent rages later in his life, are vivid, and seem to confirm Schubert's seriously deteriorating condition as his cyclothymic cycles showed signs of changing into a more distressing state of manic, depressive, and 'mixed' episodes. His behaviour was becoming so unpredictable that, although he was probably clinically 'normal' for much of the time, some of his older friends may have tried to distance themselves from him whenever the consumption of alcohol was a possibility, fearing his outbursts—volatile, outrageous, and inevitably distressing—which were becoming ever more embarrassing to them. Against this varied evidence of alcohol abuse and Schubert's loss of self-control, Spaun's protective protestation that Schubert was a moderate drinker and that accusations of his drunkenness were false cannot be accepted.[82] It may be that the often unreliable Schober was nearer the mark when he claimed (in 1868) that 'Schubert let himself go to pieces; he frequented the city outskirts and roamed around in taverns'.[83]

As a postscript to this picture of Schubert's drinking habits drawn from the reports of those who witnessed certain events in his life, the mention again of the domestic comedy, or harlequinade, *Die Verwiesenen* (The Outcasts), written by Bauernfeld for performance by Schober and his friends on 31 December 1825, is surely pertinent. (In the event, Schubert was unable to attend this celebration as he was unwell, his role presumably being taken by another of the revellers.) Bauernfeld drew particularly convincing caricatures of two of the leading actors in the roles they were playing: Schober, as Pantaloon, and Schwind as Harlequin.[84] In the light of what we know of Schubert's life at the end of 1825, and in particular that he appears to have completed virtually no compositions in the October and November of that year (although he may have been working on his 'Great' C major Symphony and the final version of the Mass in A flat), Bauernfeld's depiction of Schubert in the role of Pierrot as lazy, alcoholic, and pipe-smoking, much under the influence of an equally lazy and

---

[80] *Mem.* 231–2, *Erin.* 264–6.   [81] *Mem.* 129, *Erin.* 151.

[82] *Mem.* 137, 360–1, *Erin.* 159–60, 415–16.   [83] *Mem.* 266, *Erin.* 304.

[84] *Doc.* 486–501, *Dok.* 331–41.

amorally dissolute Schober, may not have been far from the truth at this time.

By the age of 21 Schubert was well on the way to becoming a heavy smoker of tobacco. Anselm Hüttenbrenner intimated this when he described Schubert's well-ordered life while he was living with Mayrhofer in the Wipplingerstrasse, between the autumn of 1818 and the end of 1820. During this period, he started composing every morning at six o'clock and continued 'straight through until one o'clock in the afternoon. In the mean time a few pipes were smoked'. After the midday meal 'he went to a coffee-house, drank a small portion of black coffee, smoked for an hour or two and read the newspapers at the same time'.[85] When Hüttenbrenner and he met for a drink in the evenings, Schubert drank Bavarian beer rather than the more expensive wine, and 'smoked a great deal'.[86] He appears, no doubt characteristically, with a long pipe in hand in the Mohn–Schober–Schwind etching of 1820 or thereabouts, entitled *Game of Ball at Atzenbrugg*. After this, there are many more documentary and pictorial references to his being a pipe-smoker, at work and at play.

Johanna Lutz, who lived opposite Schubert's lodgings in 1824, wrote to her fiancé Leopold Kupelwieser in Rome in May of that year: 'he [Schubert] must be gone now [to Zseliz], for the windows of his lodgings, which were always closed, are now wide open.'[87] The state of his lodgings after months of heavy smoking, and the degree to which the smoke would have impregnated everything in the room, can well be imagined.

Smoking was almost a male preserve, rarely indulged in, except out-doors, in the presence of ladies. As a result, most inns, ale-houses, and cof-fee-houses were frequented by men alone, and could become oppressively smoke-filled. A few Viennese establishments banned tobacco altogether; one at least, the Café Josef Leibenfrost, encouraged the patronage of ladies by providing for them a special room in which smoking was forbidden.[88] In respectable private homes, when parties or house-balls were held, those men who wished to smoke might be permitted to do so in a separate room set aside for this purpose; otherwise they had to wait until all the ladies had departed.[89] The von Hartmann brothers, Fritz (b. 1805) and Franz (b. 1808), were studying in Vienna from November 1824[90] until the autumn of 1827,[91] during which time they were frequently in the company of Schubert and his friends. Franz returned to Vienna in November 1827 for the new university year, and remained there until the end of August 1828, just three months before Schubert's death. Both brothers kept diaries and reported on

[85] *Mem.* 182–3, *Erin.* 209–10.   [86] *Mem.* 181, *Erin.* 208.   [87] *Doc.* 347, *Dok.* 240.
[88] *Doc.* 404n.   [89] *Doc.* 609–10, *Dok.* 411.   [90] *Doc.* 383n, *Dok.* 264n.
[91] *Doc.* 660n, *Dok.* 445n.

many gatherings of the friends, with numerous references to smoking. However, they were not among the party of young men and women celebrating the arrival of the New Year of 1826 when Bauernfeld's *Die Verwiesenen* was performed. It becomes evident from this play that by the mid-1820s, Schober, Schwind, and Schubert were the most addicted smokers in the circle of friends. In the play, they are continually smoking, lighting pipes, or encouraging others to do so; and the play ends significantly with the entry of Pierrot (Schubert) heading a 'silent chorus of smokers', all of whom, at a given signal and accompanied by background music, ceremoniously and at the same moment light up their pipes. Franz von Hartmann recorded that, on 31 January of that year, Schubert's birthday was celebrated in style at Spaun's home, complete with an expensive luxury which had become available only recently in Vienna: genuine American cigars.[92] Schubert would not have been aware of the increased dangers to his health, already weakened physically by syphilis and deteriorating cyclothymia, that his addiction to nicotine was causing. In the case of mental health, Kay Redfield Jamison has explained:

Secondary problems are . . . created by the use of alcohol, laudanum, cocaine, nicotine and many other drugs that artists and writers have used over the centuries to mediate or induce the moods associated with manic-depressive illness. Clearly these drugs . . . cause both short- and long-term damage to the brain and other parts of the nervous system, and compromising the functioning of the pulmonary and cardiovascular systems . . .[93]

Anselm Hüttenbrenner referred again to Schubert's smoking habits later in his life: 'He neglected his appearance, especially his teeth, and smelt strongly of tobacco; and for this reason, he was quite unfitted for the role of Lothario (the merry seducer in Rowe's play *The Fair Penitent*).[94] Earlier Schubert had been rather careful about his appearance, as various portraits painted during this period and the comments of friends suggest. Clearly, since then his standards had deteriorated. The cause of the deterioration could well have been linked with worsening mental problems, in which case, both the desire for nicotine and alcohol and a total disregard for his physical unacceptability (even marginalization in society) would have been expected. Throughout this commentary on Schubert's smoking habits, it has been assumed that his addiction was to nicotine. As I have already suggested it is possible that he enjoyed smoking opium, although it is likely he was never addicted to it.

The taking of opium for pleasure, for inducing a state of serenity, happiness, and heightened awareness, rather than for medical reasons, was not an

[92] *Doc.* 599, *Dok.* 404.   [93] Jamison, *Touched with Fire*, 250.   [94] *Mem.* 70, *Erin.* 82.

offence against the law in the early nineteenth century. Although laudanum, the 'tincture of opium' (opium dissolved in dilute alcohol) was the
most usual method of consumption, the practice of smoking opium, often
mixed with tobacco, was not uncommon. Both methods were widely
employed socially, when small quantities of the drug were taken in the company of friends to induce a 'calm euphoria . . . a serene self-assurance . . . an
exquisite don't care attitude'.[95] As at this level of comparatively infrequent
low consumption there were no unpleasant after-effects (like the hangover
after alcohol) but merely a state of exceptional well-being 'once generated
. . . stationary for eight or ten hours',[96] the experience was usually entirely
pleasurable. Among the people most likely to choose to experiment with
opium in the early part of the century were those with 'restless mental
curiosity about strange and novel mental experiences'.[97] At a time of
Romantic searching and exploration for new understandings and different
levels of consciousness, many artists, writers, intellectuals, and those, like
Schober, who posed as aesthetes, sought the inspiration of drug-induced
states, particularly dreams and reveries, in the belief that there existed a link
between dreams and artistic or literary imagination. Several members of
Schober's circle, including Schubert, fitted into one or other of these categories, and it is perhaps more probable than not that, in line with the fashion of the day, the young men experimented together with opium. If they
did, the practice was most likely introduced by Schober on his return to
Vienna after a long absence from the city at the end of 1820.

Between 1821 and August 1825 there are some half-dozen known refer-
ences to gatherings, apparently occurring regularly at Wasserburger's café,
of Schubert and male friends: Schober, Schwind, Spaun, Doblhoff,
Bruchmann, Kupelwieser. After 1823, those present included Bernhardt
(Schubert's doctor during his syphilitic illness in 1823–4), Smetana, and
Karl Hönig. These last three, along with Schubert, were mentioned by
Doblhoff, again in a letter to Schober (now in Breslau), of April 1824 as 'the
only faithful Wasserburgians . . . Bruchmann and the others [come] only
rarely'.[98] Assuming that opium was smoked on a regular basis in the café,
it is likely that Schober, when in Vienna, also shared the hookah with
friends in the secluded but seductive atmosphere of his family home, surrounded by 'Arabian carpets, Turkish upholstery and Persian pipes'.[99]
Maybe it was also smoked after a small Schubertiad, attended only by men,
at Spaun's on 8 December 1826. Franz von Hartmann wrote of this occasion in his diary: 'to Spaun's . . . All were very lively and wide awake. At

[95] Hayter, *Opium and the Romantic Imagination*, 20, 42.   [96] De Quincey, *Confessions*, 40.
[97] Hayter, *Opium and the Romantic Imagination*, 39.   [98] *Doc.* 342, *Dok.* 237.
[99] *Doc.* 231n, *Dok.* 161n.

the end everybody began to smoke. Spax, naturally enough, very often dozed off. At 12.45 we parted. We saw Schober home.'[100] Spax was Max von Spaun, younger brother of the host. Even if Schubert over a period of a few years sometimes smoked opium in small quantities in a social context, and perhaps with Schober when they were living together, there is nothing to suggest that he was addicted. If he had been, the medical effects of opium consumed over a long period on his physical health and temperamental well-being would have been very detrimental. Since Schubert was at most never more than an occasional smoker of opium, during a short period of his life, such effects can be rejected.

The possibility that Schubert was homosexual, even a pederast seeking young male partners under the cover of a secret society in Vienna, has been exhaustively aired and argued since the idea was first mooted in 1989.[101] As there is no definitive evidence either for or against Schubert's homosexual or bisexual tendencies, the possibility must remain unless or until such evidence emerges. However, whatever his persuasion, his sexual extravagances were an embarrassment to his family and many of his friends; and they were responsible after his death for the suppression or destruction of evidence for the dark side of his character.

Amongst Schubert's young male friends, all of whom had been educated at single-sex schools and colleges, many of them as boarders in monastic institutions, it is likely that there was some kind of homosexual activity; and yet such youthful encounters have never precluded the possibility of successful marriages in later years. The strongest suggestions of a physical relationship between two members of Schubert's circle of friends comes in the frequent and somewhat erotic letters that Schwind (aged 20) wrote in 1824 to Schober, who was then working in Breslau. The uninhibited prose style and overt declarations of affection were exaggerated even for the early nineteenth century; but they do not prove that a physical relationship existed between the two men. In any case, Schwind was a young man of unrestrained enthusiasms and manners. Thus Bauernfeld commented in July 1825 that Schwind worshipped Schober 'like a god';[102] yet at the same time it is known that he was besotted with the lively-minded, though now very sick, opera singer Katherina Lászny (1789–1828), also worshipped the young Therese Clodi (of Ebenzweier castle, on Lake Traun) and was deeply and jealously in love with, and courting, Nettl Hönig. In his turn, Schober in 1825, after earlier showing more than casual interest in several

---

[100] *Doc.* 568, *Dok.* 386.
[101] M. Solomon, 'Franz Schubert and the Peacocks of Benvenuto Cellini', *NCM* 12/3 (1989), 193–206; various authors, *Schubert: Music, Sexuality, Culture, NCM* 17/1 (1993).
[102] *Doc.* 428, *Dok.* 294.

young ladies, was secretly engaged to Justina von Bruchmann, the sister of his friend Franz. In the light of Schwind's obvious affection for Schober, perhaps Anthony Storr's comment on the close friendship between Tennyson and Hallam at about the same time is relevant here: 'Their friendship was intimate and passionate, but neither overtly nor covertly homosexual. Pre-Freudian generations were more fortunate than our own in being able freely to admit "love" for a member of the same sex, without the implication that love is necessarily sexual in origin.'[103] Whatever their former relationship, some years later Schwind, having long outgrown his earlier exuberance, quarrelled with Schober and, now an established and respected painter, a happily married and contented father, finally broke off all contact with him. Schwind wished to forget this short episode in his past. He could not have foreseen that, after his own death in 1871, Schober, the recipient of his letters, would make them public.

Schubert's world in his early days at school and college, as for many young men of his time, was almost entirely male-dominated. On the other hand, at home he had plenty of female company: his mother, stepmother, sister, aunt, and female cousin, and neighbours such as Therese Grob and her mother. His relationships with female members of the family and neighbours seem to have been good, as were those he had with the young lady musicians whom he met or collaborated with at various times in his life. His friends said that he was shy, even gauche, in female company; but this was no more so for Schubert than for many a reserved young man, diffident in the company of the opposite sex. For a year or two from 1814 to 1816 he was apparently in love with Therese Grob, and a frequent visitor at her home. After this, for a while no other female companion seems to have featured in his life, but later he enjoyed many friendships and social relationships with other young women, such as Josefine von Koller, Sophie Müller, Josefine (Pepi) Pöckelhofer, and Countess Caroline Esterházy. With none of these is there any positive reference to a sexual relationship, although with Pepi Pöckelhofer (in Zseliz, in 1818) comments are more suggestive. The fact that he contracted syphilis at the end of 1822 makes it abundantly clear that before this he was sexually active. Further support for the argument in favour of Schubert's heteroerotic persuasion comes as a result of recently discovered material, formerly in the possession of Caroline Esterházy. This reveals a closeness between her and the composer, a sharing of musical experiences, which seems to confirm the views of a mutual friend, Baron von Schönstein, that Schubert fell deeply in love with the unattainable young countess and retained his feelings for her up

---

[103] A. Storr, *Solitude*, 2nd edn. (London, 1989), 130.

until his death, and that she became the inspiration for all his greatest music, whether or not she returned his love. In any case, there was no possibility of a physical relationship between the well-brought-up young countess and the syphilitic composer. A yet more recent discovery which supports the argument is the comment of Wilhelm von Chézy in his *Memoirs* of Vienna: 'Schubert loved girls and wine, but this inclination [towards both] had unfortunately taken wrong turnings from which he was unable to extricate himself alive.'[104] Later, in his autobiography (1863), Chézy expressed this slightly differently, omitting the specific reference to 'girls': 'Schubert, with his liking for the pleasures of life, had strayed into those wrong paths which generally admit of no return, at least of no healthy one';[105] however, the first quotation makes his meaning, his understanding, clear: Schubert was heterosexually profligate.

While the arguments so far, based on various contemporary or near-contemporary commentaries, point clearly towards Schubert's heterosexuality, there are a few significant pointers towards a different scenario. Schwind advised Schubert, obviously with some humour, in a letter of 14 August 1825: 'If you apply for the court organist's post . . . you will have to satisfy your fleshly and spiritual needs—or rather, your need of pheasants and punch—in a solitude that can stand comparison with life on a desert island, à la Robinson Crusoe.'[106] A year later, in August 1826, Bauernfeld wrote in his diary in similar vein: 'Schubert ailing (he needs "young peacocks" like Benvenuto Cellini).'[107] Solomon has suggested that this reference may imply that Schubert shared with Cellini a preference for young male sexual partners, possibly transvestite.[108] Cellini's *Memoirs*, translated by Goethe and published in Vienna in 1806, would have been known to many of Schubert's circle; and, indeed, they were in many cases family reading-matter. (Thus Anna von Hartmann wrote to her fiancé, Anton Count von Revertera, on 15 October 1823 that her father was reading them to his family: 'Papa las uns im Benvenuto Cellini vor [Papa read to us from Benvenuto Cellini]'.[109] If the assumption is correct, however, it could explain Schubert's embarrassment when discovered and approached in the summer of 1827 by friends and acquaintances, including Hoffmann von Fallersleben, in a Grinzing inn where Fallersleben variously described him as 'surrounded by several young ladies',[110] 'with a girl',[111] and 'with his girl'.[112] Maybe the 'girls' were not what they appeared to be, although this

[104] Chézy, 'Erinnerungen aus Wien', 183.
[106] *Doc.* 451, *Dok.* 309.
[108] Solomon, 'Schubert and the Peacocks', 202.
[110] *Mem.* 285, *Erin.* 327.
[112] *Doc.* 658, *Dok.* 444.

[105] *Mem.* 261, *Erin.* 299.
[107] *Doc.* 548, *Dok.* 372.
[109] WL ii. 33.
[111] *Mem.* 286n, *Erin.* 328–9n.

seems a far-fetched explanation. On the other hand, it is possible that there was no hidden innuendo in the references to Cellini, that Schwind and Bauernfeld may have discussed Goethe's translation of Cellini's memoirs with Schubert, and that they understood the references, which may have had no bearing whatsoever on homosexual activities, but merely on pleasure and conviviality.

In the light of these arguments, chosen as the most sustainable from several put forward by protagonists on both sides of the discussion on Schubert's sexuality which followed the publication of Solomon's first article, it is in my view more likely that Schubert was heterosexual in his adult life. However, healthy sexual desires and drives of either persuasion, or both, can be accepted as 'normal' and belonging to Schubert's 'light' and happier nature. To the sexual passions of his 'dark', guilt-ridden nature we now turn.

After Schubert's illness in 1823, he must have known that it was inadvisable, if not impossible, for him ever to marry or to have sexual relationships, for fear of infecting his partner or partners. To have contracted syphilis in the first place he must have engaged in risky sexual activities. Thereafter Schubert's intense sensuality and strong passions may have driven him to seek satisfaction in disreputable circumstances, whether he had done so before or not. Of all the comments that cause concern about Schubert's darker nature, only one that has survived in writing was made during his lifetime. Anton Ottenwalt, with whom Schubert stayed in Linz in the summer of 1825, wrote to his brother-in-law and friend, Josef von Spaun, some three months later: 'Of Schubert I could tell you nothing that is new to you and to us; his work proclaims a genius of divine creation, unimpaired by *the passions of an eagerly burning sensuality* . . .'[113] (my italics). This letter assumes that the recipient was well aware of Schubert's passions, but as neither Ottenwalt nor anyone else explained their nature, that must remain conjectural. After Schubert's death, his friend from the Bildung Circle Josef Kenner was the most outspokenly critical. Kenner, though rather younger than Josef von Spaun, had been a friend of his since their youth together in Linz, at Kremsmünster and then at the Stadtkonvikt in Vienna. Later he became a lawyer and much loved and admired family man in Linz. He had no reason to be bitter about, or unfair to Schubert, although he was clearly outraged by Schober, and the harm he had done to the composer and to other young men who came under his influence. He also obviously deplored the side of Schubert which led him into 'the slough of moral degradation',[114] leaving him 'bathed in slime'.[115] In no uncertain

---

[113] *Doc.* 476, *Dok.* 326.   [114] *Mem.* 86, *Erin.* 100.   [115] *Mem.* 82, *Erin.* 96.

terms, Kenner blamed Schober, the 'seducer', for leading Schubert to this slough; and yet, as the proverbial horse led to the water cannot be made to drink, so neither Schober nor anyone else could have forced Schubert against his natural inclination into the slough.

At a time when prostitution was rife and homosexual relationships were neither uncommon nor a serious criminal offence,[116] Schubert's sexual activities as insinuated by Kenner, must have taken some particularly debauched form; or else Kenner was very easily scandalized. (Only such debauchery could have warranted the defamatory label of unmentionable vice, that he was 'enslaved by *passions mauvaises*', as the music historian Oulibicheff described it in 1857,[117] albeit without first-hand knowledge of the circumstances. Whatever the vice, Schubert's proclivity to outrageous behaviour was surely increased not only by the restrictions on normality imposed by his syphilitic condition, but also by his steadily advancing cyclothymic swings of mood. Yet to indulge in base sexual practices, assuming this was the form his vice, whether hetero- or homosexual, took, was his own choice. He was probably leading a double life—the one seen by most as open, honest, and direct, socially and morally tolerable if not always gracious; the other, one in which he sought satisfaction for dark cravings. Whether his sexual adventures were known to many of his friends and acquaintances or no, Schober must have been aware of what was going on. He may even have encouraged it. After Schubert's death, the marked silence of those closest to him on his debauchery, especially those in Vienna, is understandable. It also points to a conspiracy of silence, with the associated destruction of evidence that might later have resulted in attacks on his name and his music, with the consequent results for their own reputations.

Schubert, whether in normal or cyclothymic periods, had two natures: one of light, the other of darkness. The man of light was the much loved Schubert: 'simple, confiding and honest', loving 'mirth and sociable pleasures . . . a stranger to pride and vanity . . . modest';[118] 'falsity and envy were utter strangers to him . . . modest, open, childlike';[119] with 'a faithful heart for friends'.[120] His reputation and public image in Vienna must have been sufficiently high and respectable for him to have been elected first a performing member of the illustrious Gesellschaft der Musikfreunde in 1821, and then a deputy member in 1825, then a full member of the committee in 1827. The man of darkness was very different, disturbing,

[116] Solomon, 'Schubert and the Peacocks', 199.

[117] A. Oulibicheff, *Beethoven: Ses critiques et ses glossateurs* (Leipzig, 1857), 14.

[118] L. Sonnleithner: *Mem.* 11, *Erin.* 15.　　　　　[119] Mayrhofer: *Mem.* 14, *Erin.* 19–20.

[120] Ottenwalt: *Doc.* 476, *Dok.* 326.

sometimes unpleasant when motivated by self-interest, especially when driven to excess by mood swings and intoxication. The picture could then become an ugly one: neglectful of his appearance, uncaring and unreliable; reeking of stale tobacco, or alcohol or both, drinking alone in seedy inns or seeking sordid sexual satisfactions; a vulgar little man, drinking himself into a rage or stupor in a public hostelry, or, more embarrassingly, in the homes of respectable friends and acquaintances. It was no wonder that many decent people, including members of the professions, dignitaries, civil servants, patrons of the arts, writers, painters, and other musicians, all of whom might have enjoyed his company in earlier days and were eager to encourage and help the young composer, now distanced themselves socially from Schubert, and to a great extent, he from them. Such were probably Mosel, Leopold Sonnleithner, Josef Weigl, Salieri, Nestroy, Grillparzer. There were still some smart occasions when they appeared together and Schubert, on his 'good' days, would be much the same as they remembered him. But he could not be relied upon. Those intimate friends left to him were either exceptionally tolerant and understanding, like Spaun and Gahy, and from 1825 Lachner and Jenger, or they were much younger than himself, students who had not yet outgrown youthful ardours, like Schwind, Bauernfeld, Doblhoff, and the Hartmann brothers; and of course there was always Schober. The one 'friend' on whom he could always depend was his brother Ferdinand.[121] How much Ferdinand knew about the dark, sordid side of Schubert's life is not known; but he could not have been entirely ignorant. In sickness, Schubert more than once turned to his family for help, and, with all his failings, he retained and returned familial love and affection. It was to Ferdinand that he went when his health was failing in the autumn of 1828. Neither of them, nor Schubert's friends, had any idea that he was soon to die. His syphilis was worsening, and it was to play a part in his end far earlier than anyone, least of all Schubert himself, expected.

Schubert's two natures were observed and expatiated on by some of those who knew him best; but there was another part of him, his innermost self, his soul, which he bared to very few. Ottenwalt was one of those who was left in amazement and wonder by some of the composer's most uninhibited revelations, as he described to Spaun an intimate conversation they shared during Schubert's visit to Linz in 1825. Schubert had bared his soul as he spoke about art, literature, the relationship between idealism and reality. But Schubert had talked endlessly of art, poetry and ideals with several friends long before the occasion referred to by Ottenwalt, especially with

---

[121] *Doc. 363, Dok. 250.*

those who were creative artists like himself. Some of the ideas he expressed in Linz were common thinking amongst these friends; but others were born of his own imagination, understanding and concerns, aspirations, hopes, and acute sensitivities. Later his concerns included also the manner in which he coped with his dual nature, mood swings, and the pain and distress of syphilis. Ottenwalt was not alone in enjoying at least one occasion of Schubert's intimate and personal revelations. Spaun, Mayrhofer, Kupelwieser, Schober, and later Jenger, as well as his brother Ferdinand are likely also to have had some knowledge of the very private man behind the more obvious personality. To them, the intensity and range of feelings evident in his greatest music, the products of his innermost being, would have come as no surprise.

7

FIGHT AGAINST ILLNESS
(1823–1824)

'Pain sharpens the understanding and strengthens the mind.'

1821 and 1822 were years of crisis in Schubert's personal life; in the years 1823 and 1824 he had to come to terms with the deterioration of his health, both physical and mental, and specifically the destabilization of his position in society which resulted from syphilis. It was almost inevitable that, as a creative artist of great sensuality living in an artistic and intellectual climate in which the importance and the spiritual freedom of the individual were especially valued, he would find it necessary eventually to break free from the restrictive disciplines and morality in which he had been nurtured. Only then was he in a position to develop his independence and personal identity, to fulfil his artistic promise, to create his own musical language, style, and sounds and, through them, to express in music his genius. Before turning to a detailed look as Schubert's life during 1823 and 1824, it is worth pausing to establish an overall picture of his health, his professional career, and his relationships with friends.

After the onset of venereal disease, probably in November 1822, Schubert was seriously ill for several months, and most of this time unable to compose. For several weeks he was in no condition to attend public places or private musical salons. Prior to this, for two or three years his career had progressed satisfactorily. From the start, although he had appreciated the company of close friends in the informal surroundings of local hostelries and coffee-houses, he had never been at ease in smart social gatherings. And yet these more formal occasions were professionally important to him. They presented opportunities for his music to be heard; and his performances and his presence there brought his work and his name to the notice of people who could help him. By 1821 his music was fast becoming an attraction in semi-public and private concerts in Vienna. By 1822, when his social, or rather anti-social, attitudes were making him increasingly unwelcome in polite society, there was a commensurate falling off in the number of performances of his music. In 1823 illness was to take its toll. There were few performances of his music; and the number certainly did not increase as it should have done if his career had been progressing satisfactorily. However by the summer, probably in early July, his health had improved and he was able to attend the brief Atzenbrugg festival, for the last time. He also felt well enough to take up the invitation he had received for a holiday in Upper Austria, in Steyr and Linz, where he had been so content in the summer of 1819. The holiday may have done him good, but his friends saw a great change in him. He was no longer the bright, enthusiastic if shy young man, ever ready to make music or go for walks with friends, enjoying their companionship, returning their affection and admiration with good humour. Shortly before his return to Vienna from Steyr, he suffered some kind of ill health, either a recurrence of syphilis or, and more likely, a serious depression. This both surprised and alarmed him in its intensity.[1] A few weeks after his return to the city it was deemed necessary for him to receive treatment in hospital, after a further episode of infectious secondary syphilis.[2] While in hospital, and driven now by his habitual autumn urge to compose, he was able to continue work on some of the songs of the *Schöne Müllerin* song-cycle. By late November or early December, having completed the song-cycle, he was ready to compose with some urgency the incidental music for Helmina von Chézy's four-act play *Rosamunde*, which he completed just in time for its first performance five days before Christmas.

In the early months of the following year Schubert's spirits were often low, and he was probably ill again in February. Either because of illness or on account of the treatment he was undergoing, he was again confined to the house, but by May he felt better and probably bore no visible signs of his recent illness. Thus he was able to accept another invitation: to return to Zseliz, this time as resident musician and guest of Count Esterházy and his wife. Their two daughters, whom he had taught for some years during the winter months after his first visit to Zseliz in 1818, were now young ladies, no longer requiring regular musical tuition. Schubert was invited to help the young countesses when required, and to enrich the musical activities of the family and their guests. For this he received adequate

---

[1] *Doc.* 363, *Dok.* 250.

[2] There has been uncertainty as to when exactly in 1823 Schubert entered hospital. In the light of his known state of health and movements in 1823, including his stay in Hütteldorf in the early summer, an autumn date seems most probable.

remuneration. He needed money badly, some of it to pay his doctors' bills; and as financial prospects in Vienna during the summer months were virtually non-existent, the obvious solution was a further period of employment in Zseliz. He consoled himself with the thought that there he would be amongst people who knew him and appreciated his music; and he would have ample time for composition. He also trusted that the fresh country air would be beneficial to his health. In the event, the visit was not very happy. At 27, and after the severe illnesses of the past two years, he was not as adaptable as he had been six years earlier. The letters he wrote in Zseliz on this second visit suggest that he may have suffered a further relapse in health, but whether this was serious or prolonged, physical or mental, is not made clear. Whatever his situation, he was often very homesick for Vienna, its music and its culture, and especially for the company and support of his family and friends.

Schubert's bouts of despair and depression occasioned by illness were exacerbated by his fears for his future health and for the threat posed to his ability to compose. He apparently experienced two episodes of secondary syphilis within a year or so from recovering from the primary attack; and it is probable that after only two or three years of comparatively good health, in 1826 or 1827, symptoms associated with tertiary syphilis developed. Any hopes he may have nurtured that he would be one of those fortunate victims of syphilis who, as he saw it, would recover almost completely, or at least for a period of many years, were soon dashed. His letters to his brother Ferdinand are the most intimate and revealing of all his correspondence, and those which the brothers exchanged in July 1824 while Schubert was in Zseliz are indicative of the degree of their mutual affection and understanding. Thus Schubert, after reminding Ferdinand of the many times he had seen him weeping during the worst periods of his sickness and mental anguish during the last two years, continued: 'You, and you alone, are my truest friend, bound to my soul with every fibre!'[3] It was to Ferdinand that he turned more and more for support in hard times, as many of his former friends, some with families of their own and careers to concern them, became increasingly inaccessible to him.

In 1824 Schubert's surviving friendships in Vienna were thin on the ground. His closest friend was Schober; but he left Vienna in August 1823 in order to pursue his latest inclination to study for a career on the stage in Breslau, where he remained for the best part of two years. In a letter of 30 November 1823 Schubert wrote to his friend: 'only you, dear Schober, I shall never forget; for what you meant to me no one else can mean, alas!'[4]

---

[3] *Doc.* 363, *Dok.* 250.   [4] *Doc.* 301, *Dok.* 207.

Spaun was now working in Linz and Anselm Hüttenbrenner in Graz. Schubert's relationship with Mayrhofer had cooled. To Kupelwieser he might have turned, but at first the artist was intent on courting his future wife, the admirable Johanna Lutz, and then in November 1823 he left Vienna for a two-year visit to Italy. Of Bruchmann, Schubert wrote (in the letter to Schober of 30 November already quoted): '[he] has returned [to Vienna from his vacation in Upper Austria] . . . is no longer the same. He seems to be adapting to the forms of society, and by that alone he loses his halo, which in my opinion came precisely from his determined disregard of all worldly affairs.'[5] Bruchmann was a changed man. He had first left Vienna after his brush with the police in Schubert's company at the time of Senn's arrest in March 1820, and did not return to Vienna until after 1822, when he re-entered the artistic circle of friends, at first with some enthusiasm. At this point he was persuaded by his father to settle down and prepare himself for marriage to his recently betrothed, Julie von Weyrother (whom he eventually wed in June 1827). Bruchmann began law studies at the university in Vienna. He took these very seriously and lived quietly outside the city in the family's summer residence in Hütteldorf, only rarely meeting with his old friends.[6] Moritz von Schwind, seven years younger than Schubert almost to the day, was not yet a close companion of the composer, but the friendship was to strengthen towards the end of 1824. Early in 1823 Schwind, a rather frivolous 19-year-old art student, fell under Schober's spell. It was the shared affection of Schubert and Schwind for Schober that initially formed the basis of their own friendship. Schubert's life and behaviour had grown to be incompatible with the influential and socially correct but generous and musical Sonnleithners, although Leopold seems to have retained affection and concern for the composer.

The importance in later years of the inner circle of friends in which Schubert moved has in many ways been overrated. The Bildung Circle was indeed very influential in his development and education from 1814 until 1818. The reading-circle, founded with a very different ethos by Schober towards the end of 1822 at the time of the onset of Schubert's illness, did not play a lasting part in his life. At first he was eager, but often too sick or too busy to attend many of the meetings. Latterly, and some time before the meetings were suspended in April 1824, he showed little interest in what had deteriorated, after Schober's departure, into rather tasteless and disorganized evenings of boredom. Back in 1822, at the peak of his period of *dolce vita*, at Wasserburger's café he had acquired the punning nickname 'Canevas' (canvas or sacking). When any new companion was to be

---

[5] *Doc.* 300, *Dok.* 207.

[6] W. Litschauer, 'Unbekanntes zur Schubert-Ikonographie', *Brille*, 6 (1991), 58.

introduced to the gathering, Schubert was in the habit of asking 'Kann er was?' (can he do anything?), by this meaning: had the person concerned either artistic or intellectual gifts as writer, poet, painter, sculptor, or musician, whether professional or amateur, which would interest him.[7] He made no apology for his social intolerance of those whom he deemed boring, and probably never lost the arrogance, which for him was a matter of principle, that the 'Canevas' suggests. After his illness Schubert for some while was less gregarious. When he was feeling well and not restricted by the medical treatments he was receiving, he sometimes felt the need in the evenings for congenial company. Then he joined any friends who might turn up to relax with a drink and a pipe at one or other of the appointed meeting places, the Hungarian Crown or Wasserburger's café. He was now drinking very moderately, and while under medical treatment not at all.

Thus a picture of the composer, prematurely aged by illness, begins to come into focus. His physical well-being, even his life, was under threat. His cyclothymic mood changes were at present probably little affected, if at all by the syphilis. He had grown more independent-minded, and lived for the most part the self-centred existence usually necessary for a creative artist.

We turn now to a more detailed look at Schubert's life in these years, and to how the events of this period affected his character and personality and, of course, his musical achievements.

Schubert was either ill or to some degree unwell throughout 1823. The symptoms from which he suffered are now recognized with certainty as those of syphilis. Because disease patterns tend to change over a period of time, it cannot be assumed that Schubert's syphilis followed a course identical with that of the twentieth-century version of the disease. However, Schubert knew that if he were unlucky and the disease progressed inexorably to its final stage, then it would probably be fatal. If he were very fortunate, after a year or so he would return to something approaching normal life for an indeterminate period. When he left Schober's apartment and returned to his parental home in the Rossau district towards the end of 1822, his condition was infectious but relatively painless. The symptoms of secondary syphilis, which appeared early in 1823 when the disease was at its most infectious, may have included fever, headaches, general malaise, an ugly rash, and aches in joints, muscles, and bones. Other possible symptoms at this stage included loss of hair and laryngitis. In the first part of 1823 for several weeks he was confined to home by the disease. (In his article

---

[7] *Doc.* 178n, *Dok.* 126n.

'Schubert's Illness Re-examined'[8] Eric Sams has suggested that Schubert developed syphilis in January 1823. His conclusion was based on the false premiss that Schubert 'was seen out and about in company during early January' of that year. Sams deduces this from a report written by the Viennese correspondent of the Leipzig *Literarisches Konversations-Blatt* published on 18 January 1823 concerning musical salons held at the home of Ignaz von Mosel.[9] The customary time-lag between such reports being written and their publication in foreign newspapers was at least four weeks and often much longer, and the events there described took place some weeks or months earlier, in 1822.)

A major disappointment for Schubert in early 1823 must have been his inability, because of illness, to conduct or play any part in a performance of his recently finished Mass in A flat D678, which he had begun more than three years earlier on 19 November 1819. In his letter to Spaun of 7 December 1822, Schubert indicated how important this work was to him: 'My Mass is finished, and is to be performed before long. I still hold to the original idea of dedicating it to the Emperor or Empress, as I consider it has turned out well.'[10] Plans were made for a performance early in 1823; vocal and orchestral parts were copied, the organ part written out by Schubert himself in October or November,[11] others by a professional copyist.[12] Despite these preparations, it is unlikely that the performance took place. Without Schubert to guide the singers and instrumentalists through the rehearsals, they may have found the work too difficult to perform. If this was the case it would explain why in 1825 and 1826 he extensively revised and simplified sections of the mass. Although the early months of 1823 saw Schubert rejecting requests for compositions which he had earlier promised but now felt unable to provide,[13] by late February he found the energy and will to compose the Piano Sonata in A minor, D784. This is one of the darkest of all his compositions, autobiographical in the emotions it expressed of pain, distress, anger, and ill temper, and certainly the grimmest music he had written to date.

On the last day of February, now that the worst of his symptoms had abated, Schubert sent to the influential Ignaz von Mosel the last act and the overture of his 1821–2 opera *Alfonso und Estrella*. Accompanying the score was a carefully written letter, but anxious in tone, in which he apologized for sending a letter rather than making a personal visit, which was then an impossibility owing to 'my state of health still forbidding me to leave the

---

[8] *MT* 121 (1980), 15–22.   [9] *Doc.* 261, *Dok.* 180; *ND* 190.
[10] *Doc.* 248, *Dok.* 173.   [11] *Catalogus*, 6.
[12] See J. Hüttenbrenner's second account of financial expenses incurred on Schubert's behalf presented to the composer in Feb. 1823: *Doc.* 266, *Dok.* 184.
[13] *Doc.* 264–5, *Dok.* 182–3.

house'.[14] He sought Mosel's honest opinion of the opera, and reminded him of his earlier promise to encourage Carl Maria von Weber to perform it in Dresden now that its rejection by the Kärntnertor-Theater in Vienna seemed almost irrevocable. After requesting Mosel to put in a good word for the opera also with the directorate of the Dresden theatre, Schubert made one last appeal: 'humbly and in God's name . . . whether you would be so kind, Sir, as to let me in the meantime have the libretto intended for my humble self, which I solemnly assure you will be faithfully guarded by me and shown to no-one.'[15] It is possible that Mosel responded to this appeal for a libretto which, as Schubert understood it, had been previously promised, with the suggestion that he turn to Castelli's *Die Verschworenen* (The Conspirators) which had appeared in print earlier in February. Whether or not this was how Schubert came across the play, within a week or two of writing to Mosel he had begun work on Castelli's one-act comic singspiel, a lively and humorous work. Ignaz von Castelli, then a very popular Austrian writer, based *Die Verschworenen* principally on Aristophanes' comedy *Lysistrata*, but transferred to a German setting at the time of the Crusades. He wrote the play in answer to current complaints, now that Italian operas were all the rage in Vienna, about the lack of good German libretti. 'Here is one, gentlemen! . . . Let us do something for true German opera, gentlemen!' was Castelli's challenge to German composers in the preface to his new play.[16] The original title of the play was thought by the Viennese censors to be politically too inflammatory, and it was changed to the safer *Der häusliche Krieg* (Domestic Warfare). By early in 1824, Schubert had once again given up all hope of performance at the Kärntnertor-Theater of this little one-act opera, which contains music of charm, humour, and pathos.[17] It has been suggested that an untitled fragment of another opera, dated May 1823, in which the principal character was a young knight named Rüdiger (tenor), was the beginning of an opera with the libretto promised by Mosel, who certainly wrote (in 1820) the text of a romantic opera *Rüdiger*, after Metastasio. (Mosel had sent this libretto first to Weber, in 1822, and Weber had rejected it.) Although the story of Schubert's short operatic fragment in no ways conforms to Mosel's version of the tale, there are some similarities between it and corresponding scenes written by Josef Kupelwieser for Schubert's last finished opera, *Fierrabras*.

In 1823 Schubert was soon seriously short of money. When he was ill, his only source of income was from sales of his published music. While he was

---

[14] *Doc.* 270, *Dok.* 186.

[15] *Doc.* 270, *Dok.* 186–7.

[16] McKay, *Schubert's Music for the Theatre*, 231.

[17] Ibid. 232.

unfit to appear in salons and musical gatherings in Vienna, the public tended to forget him, to lose interest in his music: a case of out of sight, out of mind. In that year there were performances of his music in Vienna at only four concerts for members of the Gesellschaft der Musikfreunde, each of them a Thursday evening chamber music concert, and one summer open-air event. At all these concerts only a single work of Schubert's, either a song or a vocal quartet, was included in a mixed programme. As far as is known, no other secular work by Schubert received a performance, public or semi-public, in the Imperial capital during the whole of 1823 except, shortly before Christmas, his incidental music to *Rosamunde*. Apart from a series of substantial notices of the two performances of *Rosamunde* in the December, the only review of his compositions published in Viennese journals was one, and a very favourable one at that, in the *Allgemeine musikalische Zeitung* on 30 April, of the Piano Fantasia in C ('Wandererfantasie'). In the *Rosamunde* reviews, the play and performances were almost unanimously condemned as inadequate, but the music was accorded some praise.

In the light of his illness and his already uncertain future in the early part of the year, Schubert must have been cheered to hear in April that he had been elected a non-resident honorary member of the Styrian Musical Society in Graz. The letter sent to him announcing this award was followed later by a handsome diploma certificate.[18] A similar honour was awarded by the Linz Musical Society in August of the same year.[19] But such honours, like performances of his music in concerts at the Gesellschaft der Musikfreunde, brought no financial reward; and he remained convinced that his future lay with opera and music for the theatre.

Schubert had been invited late in 1821 by Barbaja to submit a German opera for performance in the 1822/3 season at the Kärntnertor-Theater. When *Alfonso und Estrella* was rejected for this purpose, he was determined to try again. The secretary to the directorate at the theatre was an acquaintance of Schubert's, Josef Kupelwieser, the older brother of his artist friend Leopold; and it was soon agreed that Josef should provide Schubert with the text of a full three-act opera. Josef had literary pretensions but as yet had published nothing. However, having worked in the theatre for several years, he had some slight understanding of what made for dramatic effect. The subject chosen for the opera was Fierrabras, an invented heroic–romantic tale of Charlemagne's wars against the Saracens in the Pyrenees, taken from the Old French epic poem, the *Chanson de Roland*. The *Chanson* had been exciting some interest among early nineteenth-century Romantic writers in Germany, and the Fierrabras story was

---

[18] *Doc.* 274–6, *Dok.* 189–91.   [19] *Doc.* 288, *Dok.* 198.

already in circulation in print in Vienna in two different versions.[20] Kupelwieser devised an attractive plot with a variety of scenes and characters, but of considerable complexity and with several serious flaws. Notable among the flaws is the non-appearance of the titular hero, Fierrabras, in the second act and only a perfunctory part for him in the third. To cope with an over-wordy libretto, Schubert returned to the singspiel format in *Fierrabras*, leaving long sections of spoken dialogue, much of it essential to a full understanding of the plot, without music. This resulted in some imbalance in the dramatic economy of the opera. When Schubert received the libretto, in April or May 1823, he immediately put aside the fragmentary *Rüdiger* and set to work on the new opera with avid enthusiasm. Schubert dated the manuscript of his score of the first act '25 May–30 May', and of the second, '31 May–5 June'. The third act was begun on 7 June, but not completed until 26 September, the overture on 2 October. The reason for the long delay in completing the final act, and maybe some of the orchestration of the first two acts, will soon become apparent.

By the end of April Schubert's friend Bruchmann was already proposing, now that Schubert's health was much improved, that he and Schober should rent his family's summer residence in Hütteldorf for a few weeks. The house would otherwise be empty when Bruchmann (who, as previously mentioned, had been living there during the winter while studying at the university) went on holiday, and in the period before his parents moved there from Vienna for the summer months. In Vienna the winter season of concerts and entertaining continued until the end of April. In May and June, as Fritz von Hartmann described it in a letter to his sister Anna von Revertera, everything stopped. All who were able to do so moved out of the city[21] to their own or rented summer residences. Although such a move had never been possible for members of Schubert's family and their social circle, for Schubert himself, now convalescing satisfactorily, and hopeful that he was on the way to full recovery, to escape into the country, away from the Rossau schoolhouse, was an attractive prospect. Before he left Vienna, and with the memory of illness still much in his mind, on 8 May he wrote a four-verse poem, 'Mein Gebet' (My Prayer). This is a strange plea to an unnamed all-powerful Deity, written in poor poetic form and expressing a muddled mixture of thoughts and ideas. It is also Schubert's heartfelt prayer that the physical and mental torments of his illness may now be left behind, this part of his life 'thrown into the river Lethe', submerged; and

---

[20] A. W. von Schlegel's trans. of Calderón's *La Puente de Mantible* pub. in his *Spanisches Theater* as *Die Brücke von Mantible* and, the principle source of Kupelwieser's play, a prose version by Büsching and Hagen in their *Buch der Liebe*.
[21] WL ii. 88.

that out of the water might rise a much longed-for finer life of strength and purity, in which eternal love will surround him:

Mein Gebet
[My Prayer]

Tiefer Sehnsucht heil'ges Bangen
Will in schön're Welten langen;
   Möchte füllen dunklen Raum
   Mit allmächt'gem Liebestraum.

Grosser Vater! reich' dem Sohne,
Tiefer Schmerzen nun zum Lohne
   Endlich als Erlösungsmahl
   Deiner Liebe ew'gen Strahl.

Sieh, vernichtet liegt im Staube,
Unerhörtem Gram zum Raube,
   Meines Lebens Martergang
   Nahend ew'gem Untergang.

Tödt' es und mich selber tödte,
Stürz' nun Alles in die Lethe,
   Und ein reines kräft'ges Sein
   Lass', o Grosser, dann gedeih'n.[22]

[The holy dread which comes from deep longing seeks to attain finer worlds; fain would it fill dark space with an all-powerful dream of love. | Mighty father! grant your son now, at last, the eternal beam of your love as a deliverance from profound pains. | Lo, here in the dust, vulnerable to unspeakable depression, lies my life's Gethsemane, approaching its eternal demise. | Kill it, kill myself, throw all into Lethe, and then, o mighty one, bring a pure, strong life into being.]

Exactly when Schubert moved out to Hütteldorf is uncertain, but that he was there by early June seems highly likely. On 20 May Schober's sister Sophie was married in Heiligeneich near Atzenbrugg to Schubert's friend Johann Ignaz Zechenter, who with Schubert was one of the five friends involved in the affair with the police early in 1820. Zechentner was now a government surveyor; and because he had to make an imminent extended journey on business, his bride-to-be had been granted at six days' notice a special licence from the Atzenbrugg district court permitting the marriage to take place without the normally required three weeks' notice. Shortly after the wedding, Zechenter left on his business travels, and it seems that his bride moved out to the Bruchmanns' summer residence to keep house

---

[22] *Dok.* 192–3.

for her brother and Schubert. It is also likely that Josef Kupelwieser, the librettist of *Fierrabras*, visited them there and conferred with Schubert about their opera.[23] Evidence for this holiday lies in a recently discovered series of silhouette portraits of Schubert, Schober, Kupelwieser (Josef, not Leopold) and their 'Zehetnerwirtin' (*sic*) (Zechentner-hostess or house-keeper) made in Hütteldorf that summer. There are two versions of the *Fierrabras* libretto. The possibility arises that the creators of the opera discussed amendments and improvements to the first version during this month of June in Hütteldorf. The revised libretto was not submitted to the censors until 21 July, but was passed by them swiftly (with just nine small alterations) on 19 August. Schubert undoubtedly had a copy of the revised libretto with him when he left Vienna for a holiday in Upper Austria at the end of July.

Whenever Schubert was ill and unable to earn money in ways other than by his publications, he tended to turn to music publishers in an effort to encourage their interest in his music and its commercial value. These dealings, which began in earnest at the end of 1822, could be stormy. We look now to his relationships with some of these publishers.

The first works of Schubert's to be published were the three songs which appeared in February 1818 ('Erlafsee'), September 1820 ('Widerschein'—Reflection) and 9 December 1820 ('Die Forelle') in three different almanacs (the second in Leipzig) as music supplements. These brought no payment to the young composer, but they provided him with free publicity. The first composition to be published (with an opus number) by a firm of music publishers was another song, 'Erlkönig', which appeared on 2 April 1821, published in this case ostensibly by the firm of Cappi and Diabelli, but in fact financed in the first instance by Leopold Sonnleithner and friends. They paid for the engraving of the song, which was then issued and sold 'on commission' by the publishers, who thus avoided any risks to themselves if the sales slumped. In fact, far from failing to attract interest, several hundred copies sold rather quickly. Leopold Sonnleithner, the same age as Schubert, engineered the arrangements, while his illustrious father, Ignaz, helped to assure the success of his son's venture and of Schubert's songs by himself persuading the distinguished Viennese dignatory, Count Moritz von Dietrichstein, to be dedicatee. He also found another respected member of the higher establishment, Moritz Reichsgraf von Fries, who agreed to be the dedicatee of 'Gretchen am Spinnrade'. (Both Ignaz and Leopold were Court judges when they were ennobled to von Sonnleithner in 1828.)

[23] Litschauer, 'Unbekanntes zur Schubert-Ikonographie', 57–65.

Schubert was beholden to Ignaz Sonnleithner not only for acquiring such valuable patronage for his songs, but also for hosting many of the evening salons, in conjunction with the Gesellschaft der Musikfreunde, attended by some 120 people on each occasion, at which his songs and part-songs were first performed, and thus bringing his music to a wider public. Leopold Sonnleithner continued to advance Schubert's interests over close on two years by arranging with Cappi and Diabelli the publication on a commission basis of several small collections of his songs.[24] Schubert should have been immensely grateful to the Sonnleithners and other friends who facilitated these publications; sadly he seems to have accepted it all in a remarkably casual, even ungracious manner.[25] Long after Schubert's death, Leopold wrote of the advantage to the composer brought by his friends' efforts:

From the abundant proceeds we paid Schubert's debts, namely his outstanding rent, his shoemaker's and tailor's accounts and his debts at the tavern and the coffee-house, and handed over to him, in addition, a considerable sum in cash; unfortunately some guardianship such as this was necessary, for he had no idea how to manage his money and was often led by his tavern friends . . . into wasteful expenditure from which the others benefited more than he did himself.[26]

To Leopold Sonnleithner's dismay and anger Schubert, without consulting the friends who had been looking after his interests, and thus with considerable discourtesy, in 1822 sold the engraved plates, stocks of copies, and rights of publication of his most recently published songs to the same publisher, at rates very unadvantageous to himself.[27] Sonnleithner continued:

If his affairs had continued like this [as set up by his friends], Schubert would have received considerable profit from his works and remained the legal owner. But behind our backs, Diabelli offered him 800 fl K.M. for the plates and copyright of the first twelve works; this sum induced Schubert to accept the offer and then it was all over with his freedom. For those twelve works he got about 2000 fl K.M. in all, which makes an average of 166 fl for each work, a fee he never attained again later. This really rather ungrateful behaviour on Schubert's part did not cause a breach with us in any way; we regretted his weakness but continued to promote the performance and propagation of his works.[28]

By the end of 1822 Schubert was totally dissatisfied with Diabelli's treatment of him. Through Josef Hüttenbrenner, who was then looking after his

---

[24] Songs in Op. 1–7 and 12–14.
[25] Letter from L. Sonnleithner to J. Hüttenbrenner: *Doc.* 169, *Dok.* 120.
[26] *Mem.* 108, *Erin.* 126. [27] *Doc.* 267–8, *Dok.* 185. [28] *Mem.* 108, *Erin.* 126.

business affairs, he had already approached another publisher, Karl Friedrich Peters in Leipzig, but to no avail. Now suspicious that Diabelli was defrauding him, he turned to other reputable Viennese publishers, in particular the firm of Sauer and Leidesdorf. Early in April 1823, when he was well into the recovery stage of his initial attack of secondary syphilis, he sent an angry and trenchant letter to Diabelli demanding in no uncertain terms settlement of all money owed to him since their agreement was broken off, as well as manuscripts and copies of published works already promised to him. In the same letter he commented that 'Herr von Steiner has repeatedly conveyed to me an offer to publish my works'.[29] At the turn of the century Steiner and Co. had been the most important music publisher in Vienna; but now, with a large fall in interest in classical music, Steiner's was a declining business.[30] (In March 1826 Steiner's firm was taken over by his partner Tobias Haslinger, and was thereafter known by this name.) It was now Sauer and Leidesdorf who showed real interest in Schubert's compositions.

Schubert at first had great respect for Leidesdorf, whom he described in a letter to Leopold Kupelwieser as 'a really thoughtful and good man' but subject to depressions even more severe than his own.[31] A year later he became rather impatient with Leidesdorf's procrastinations. The publisher was himself a composer and arranger; his partner, Sauer, also a musician, had been involved in an art- and music-publishing business for more than twenty years.[32] Unfortunately neither of them had sufficient flair to prevent the company from getting into financial difficulties. Sauer withdrew after a while, and Leidesdorf eventually sold out to Diabelli, who by 1824 was running his own firm without Cappi, and with some success. Schubert and Diabelli were eventually reconciled in 1827.

Music publishers in Vienna were experiencing hard times, and the publication of new works by 'serious' composers was a particularly risky business. For a period of some twenty years, the demand for lighter music, especially dances, short piano pieces, and arrangements of popular operas written for amateurs of limited accomplishment, dominated the market. It was perhaps impossible for Schubert to achieve any success at this stage with his sonatas, chamber music, or symphonies. In this climate, Sauer and Leidesdorf decided to exploit the seasonal enthusiasm of the public for album collections of music by various composers—short pieces at Christmas and New Year and dances at carnival time (January to March). Schubert's first of seventeen contributions to these albums was for a collection of dances in

---

[29] *Doc.* 273, *Dok.* 189.

[30] E. Hilmar, 'Schubert und die Verleger', in id., *Franz Schubert in seiner Zeit* (Vienna, 1985), 32–42.

[31] *Doc.* 339, *Dok.* 235.   [32] Hilmar, 'Schubert und die Verleger', 39.

PLATE I. Franz Theodor Florian Schubert, father of the composer. *Oil painting by his son Karl; Historisches Museum der Stadt Wien*

PLATE II. Ferdinand Lukas Schubert, the composer's brother, painted shortly after Ferdinand's appointment, in 1851, as director of the Imperial Teachers' Training College in the Annagasse, where both he and the composer had been students. *Lithograph by Josef Kriehuber; Schloss Atzenbrugg Museum*

PLATE III. The Stadtkonvikt, a boarding establishment run by the Piarist Order for students of the
academic grammar-school and university. Situated in
the old Universitätsplatz (now Dr Ig. Seipelplatz), this
was originally part of the old Jesuit University of
Vienna. Schubert resided here from October 1808 until
September 1813. *Watercolour by Franz Gerasch;
Österreichische Nationalbibliothek, Vienna*

PLATE IV. Boy (Schubert?) in the uniform of the boy
choristers of the Court chapel. *Watercolour by Leo Diet;
reproduced from Ernst Hilmar*, Schubert, © *Akademische
Druck- und Verlagsanstalt, Graz, 1989*

PLATE V (*above left*). Josef von Spaun, good friend and patron of the composer. *Lithograph by F. Herr after oil painting by L. Kupelwieser, dated 1835; Historisches Museum der Stadt Wien*

PLATE VI (*above*). Johann Michael Vogl, the distinguished opera singer, who encouraged and supported Schubert in his career as a composer of operas and songs. *Lithograph by Josef Kriehuber, c.1830; Historisches Museum der Stadt Wien*

PLATE VII (*left*). Franz von Schober, one of Schubert's closest friends, if not the closest. *Pencil drawing by L. Kupelwieser; Historisches Museum der Stadt Wien*

PLATE VIII. Schloss Zseliz, the summer residence in Hungary (now Slovakia) of the family of Count Esterházy of Galánta, where Schubert was employed during the summer and autumn months of 1818 and 1824. *Photograph supplied by the Internationales Franz Schubert Institut*

PLATE IX. The Kärntnertor-Theater, Vienna, where, as a young boy and in the company of Josef von Spaun, Schubert enjoyed his first experiences of opera. Some of his music was later performed in the theatre in concerts (*Akademien*), and his own first attempt at opera, *Die Zwillingsbrüder*, was premièred in June 1820. *Watercolour by Elias Hütter; Historisches Museum der Stadt Wien*

PLATE X. The hotel 'Zum römischen Kaiser' (The Roman Emperor). The hall of this hotel was a venue for concerts in Vienna, notably of the Privat-Musikverein (Private Musical Society), of which Ferdinand Schubert was orchestral director for a while. Here several of Schubert's early compositions received their first performances. *Unsigned print; reproduced from Ernst Hilmar*, Schubert, © *Akademische Druck- und Verlagsanstalt, Graz, 1989*

PLATE XI. The Landhaus (Lower Austrian County Hall) in Vienna, whose grand hall was an important and more spacious venue for concerts in which, from 1818 onwards, Schubert's music featured on many occasions. *Reproduction of a copper-plate engraving by Elias Hütter, 1835; from Ernst Hilmar*, Schubert, © *Akademische Druck- und Verlagsanstalt, Graz, 1989*

PLATE XII. *Steyr; Teilansicht vom Tabor* [View from the Tabor]. Schubert visited this town in Upper Austria in 1819, 1823, and 1825. *Drawing and lithograph by Ludwig Czerny; Österreichische Nationalbibliothek, Vienna*

PLATE XIII (*above*). Leopold Kupelwieser, later a renowned ecclesiastical artist. Kupelwieser was one of Schubert's closest companions until his departure for Italy in 1823, and a friend thereafter. *Pencil drawing by Josef Tunner, 1817; reproduced from Ernst Hilmar*, Schubert, © *Akademische Druck- und Verlagsanstalt, Graz, 1989*

PLATE XIV (*above right*). Moritz von Schwind, the young Romantic artist who was much in Schubert's company from 1823. *Drawing by L. Kupelwieser; reproduced from Ernst Hilmar*, Schubert, © *Akademische Druck- und Verlagsanstalt, Graz, 1989*

PLATE XV (*right*). Eduard von Bauernfeld, dramatist, diarist, and close friend of Schubert from 1824, and librettist of his last opera, *Der Graf von Gleichen*. *Lithograph after a sketch by Moritz Michael Daffinger; Historisches Museum der Stadt Wien*

PLATE XVI. *Steyreck unter Linz an der Donau* [Steyregg Castle, near Linz, on the Danube]. Schubert spent some time here in the summer of 1825 as guest of the Count and Countess Weissenwolff. *Anonymous engraving, probably by J. and P. Schaffer; Österreichische Nationalbibliothek, Vienna*

PLATE XVII. *Gmunden am Traunsee 1850* [Gmunden on Lake Traun 1850]. Schubert stayed here for several weeks in summer 1825, working some of the time on his 'Great' C major Symphony. He had hoped to return in the summers of 1826 and 1828. *Steel engraving by G. M. Kurz after a drawing by Julius Lange, Österreichische Nationalbibliothek, Vienna*

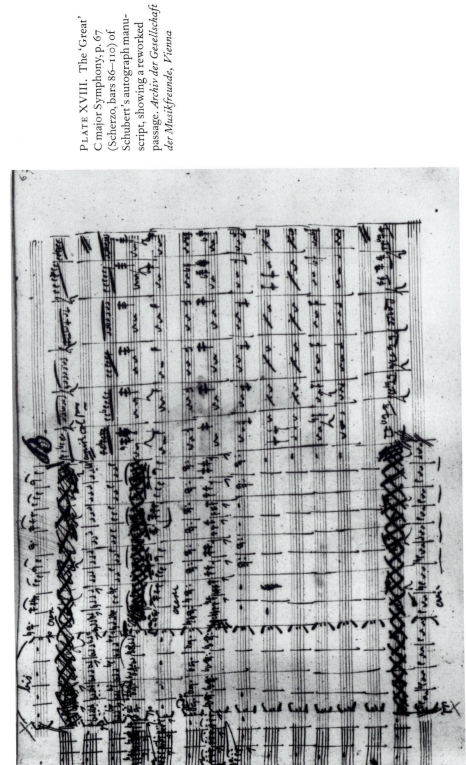

PLATE XVIII. The 'Great' C major Symphony, p. 67 (Scherzo, bars 86–110) of Schubert's autograph manuscript, showing a reworked passage. *Archiv der Gesellschaft der Musikfreunde, Vienna*

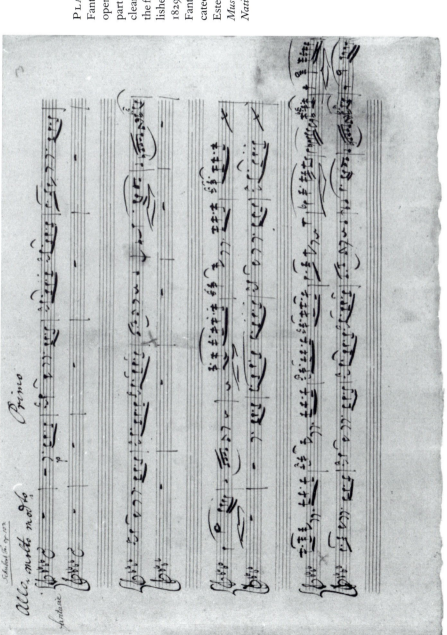

PLATE XIX. The piano-duet Fantasia in F minor D940: the opening, first side of the 'primo' part of the duet, taken from the clean copy Schubert prepared for the first edition, which was published after his death, in March 1829. Schubert completed the Fantasia in April 1828 and dedicated it to the Countess Caroline Esterházy. *Mus.Hs. 19,491 aus der Musiksammlung der Österreichische Nationalbibliothek*

PLATE XX. *Ein Schubert-Abend bei Joseph v. Spaun* [A Schubert-evening at Josef von Spaun's]. This 1868 retrospective sepia drawing by Moritz von Schwind depicts many of Schubert's friends and acquaintances, as known to Schwind. Vogl and Schubert are seated at the piano; to the right of them are Franz von Hartmann, Josef von Spaun, and Vogl's wife (Kunigunde). Schober alone appears uninterested in the music (middle row, right), and is flirting with his (then or future) fiancée, Justine von Bruchmann. *Historisches Museum der Stadt Wien*

PLATE XXI. *The Countess Caroline Esterházy.* Schubert is believed to have fallen more and more deeply in love with the young countess after 1824; early in 1828 he dedicated his piano-duet Fantasia in F minor to her. This portrait features prominently and pertinently on the centre back wall of Schwind's *Ein Schubert-Abend bei Joseph v. Spaun. After a lost watercolour by Josef Teltscher, 1828*

PLATE XXII. *Johann Baptist Jenger, Anselm Hüttenbrenner and Franz Schubert (c. 1827). Colour print after a lost watercolour by Josef Teltscher; Historisches Museum der Stadt Wien*

PLATE XXIII. *The 'Tuchlauben'*, a street in Vienna. The house 'Zum roten Igel' (The Red Hedgehog) in the Tuchlauben was, from autumn 1822, the premises of the Gesellschaft der Musikfreunde; beyond it is 'Zum blauen Igel' (The Blue Hedgehog), where Schubert lived with Schober and his mother from early 1827. *Reproduction from an unsigned copper-plate engraving; Österreichische Nationalbibliothek, Vienna*

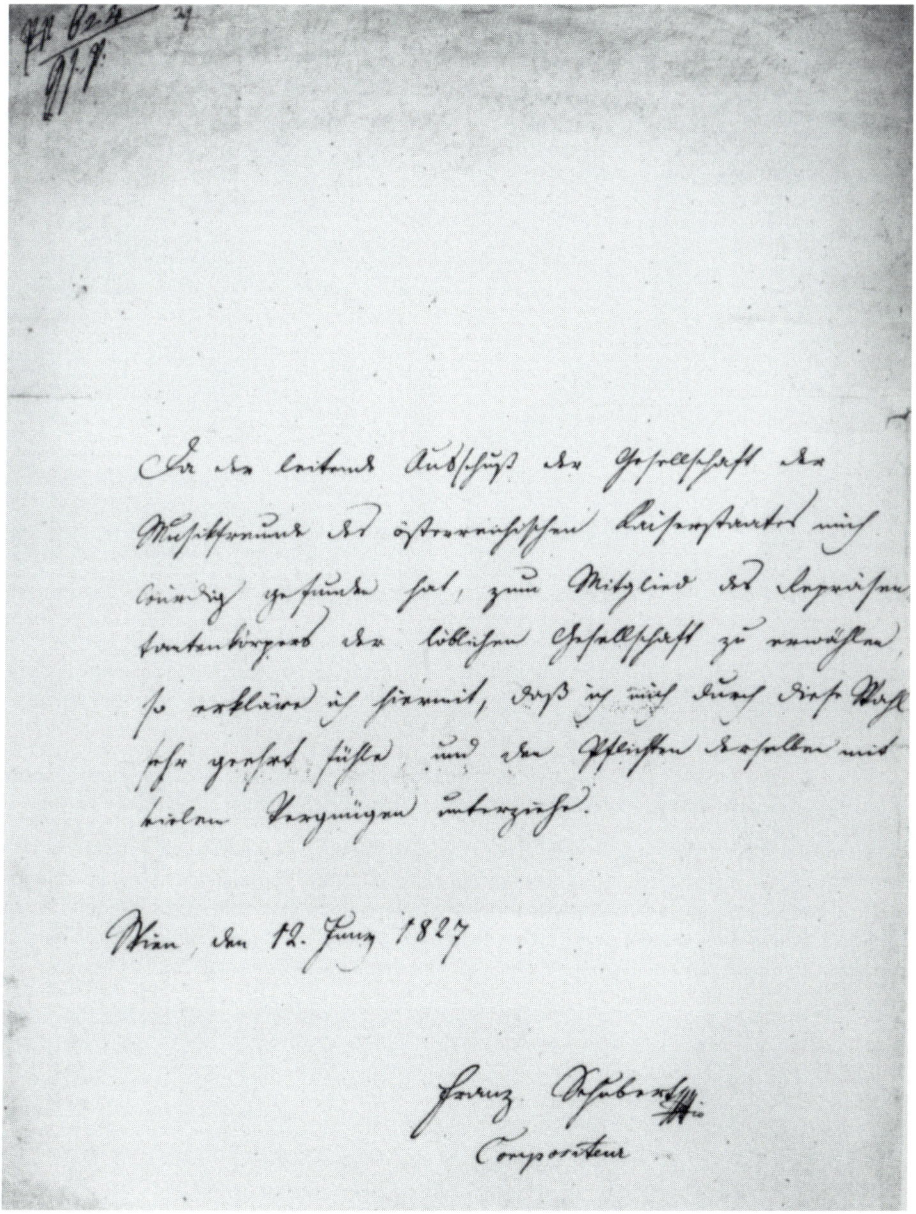
Da der leitende Ausschuß der Gesellschaft der Musikfreunde des österreichischen Kaiserstaates mich würdig gefunden hat, zum Mitglied des Repräsentantenkörpers der löblichen Gesellschaft zu erwählen, so erkläre ich hiermit, daß ich mich durch diese Wahl sehr geehrt fühle, und den Pflichten derselben mit vielem Vergnügen unterziehe.

Wien, den 12. Juny 1827

Franz Schubert
Compositeur

PLATE XXIV. Schubert's autograph letter of 12 June 1827 to officers of the Gesellschaft der Musikfreunde, confirming his readiness to serve as a full representative on the committee of the society. He was 'greatly honoured by his election'. *Archiv der Gesellschaft der Musikfreunde*

PLATE XXV (*above left*). The Lichtental parish church, where Schubert's parents married, and where he sang in the choir. Many of his early sacred choral works were written for and performed in this church, including the Mass in F in 1814. *Colour print after an unsigned engraving; Historisches Museum der Stadt Wien*

PLATE XXVI (*above right*). The Margareten parish church of St Josef, Neu Wieden, where Schubert's first funeral service took place. *Anonymous photograph; Österreichische Nationalbibliothek, Vienna*

PLATE XXVII (*below*). *Kirche St. Marien Trost oder bei St. Ulrich* [St Ulrich's church, or Maria Trost], where some of Schubert's sacred compositions were performed after Ferdinand Schubert became active in the lively musical society associated with the church. Here, on 27 November 1828, a requiem mass in memory of Schubert included a performance of Mozart's Requiem. *Engraving after a colour-washed pen-and-ink drawing by Salomon Kleiner, c.1724–36; Österreichische Nationalbibliothek, Vienna*

January 1823. According to Josef Hüttenbrenner, who was not always a reliable commentator, in addition to contributing to the albums, Schubert agreed with Leidesdorf to supply him with 'songs over a period of two years in exchange for 1,200 fl. WW [480 fl. KM] yearly'.[33] The result in 1823 was the publication of fourteen of Schubert's songs, in five sets, between April and November 1823. The publications culminated that year on 9 December with his piano duet Sonata in B flat D617, and in 1824 with the complete *Schöne Müllerin* song-cycle, in five separate parts. Distressingly for posterity, neither Sauer nor Leidesdorf had any idea of the importance or value of original manuscripts. As soon as Schubert's music was printed they destroyed, or at least made no attempt to preserve his original. The result was the loss not only of autograph manuscripts of the duet and song-cycle already mentioned, but also of the String Quartet in A minor D804, the piano duet Variations in A flat D813, and vocal numbers from *Rosamunde*.

As a postscript to this outline of Schubert's relations with publishers in the first half of the 1820s, we return briefly to the 'Wandererfantasie'. The publisher's engraving of this work raises the possibility that, after submitting the manuscript to Cappi and Diabelli and its acceptance late in November or December 1822,[34] Schubert may have been too sick to prepare a neat copy of the work. In the second movement (Adagio) the publisher arranged for a copyist to prepare just such a copy of a central section (from the second half of bar 44 to the end of bar 51) for the engraver to work from. Schubert's inability to do this work for himself seems to point to his being very sick in the months of January and early February, at the time when the engraving was in progress.

From Schubert's situation in early 1823, we move on again to the summer of that year. Soon after leaving Hütteldorf, Schubert set off again for Upper Austria at the end of July. He was certainly in Linz on 28 July when he was introduced by Vogl, Josef von Spaun, and Albert Stadler (who was now working in Linz) to their new friends, the family of Friedrich Ludwig von Hartmann. The Hartmanns were a very musical family and had come from Salzburg to live in Linz the year after Schubert's visit there in 1819. The eldest child, Anna, who became engaged in the summer of 1823 to the handsome and highly esteemed Count Anton von Revertera, was a much admired young lady of considerable musical talent, both as singer and pianist, and held in great affection by family and friends. She soon became

[33] *Mem.* 75, *Erin.* 87.
[34] Schubert's letter to Spaun of 7 Dec.: 'I have composed a Fantasy for piano, two hands, which is also to be engraved and published, dedicated to a wealthy person': *Doc.* 248, *Dok.* 172.

a great enthusiast for Schubert's music. The next two children, Fritz and Franz, later studied law in Vienna, where Spaun took elder-brotherly interest in their well-being and introduced them to Schubert's circle of friends. (Spaun was to remain a special favourite in the Hartmann and Revertera families.) On the occasion of Schubert's first meeting with the Hartmanns, he was sufficiently well to perform several of his songs with Vogl, an experience which Anna never forgot. She was already having singing lessons with Vogl who, impressed with her voice and musicality, and probably her charm, claimed that she was the finest amateur singer he had heard. In a letter to a friend, he opined that she had made 'the devil's own choice, to marry'.[35]

By 14 August Schubert, along with Vogl, had moved to Steyr, the town where he had been so contented in the summer of 1819. As he wrote to Schober, his relationship with Vogl, which had deteriorated badly in 1821 and 1822, was now mended. Unfortunately his health was not. After mentioning to Schober that he was in communication with his physician in Vienna (August Schaeffer), he admitted that he was only 'pretty well' (*ziemlich wohl*), and 'whether I shall ever fully recover I am inclined to doubt'.[36] Schubert continued: 'Here I live very simply in every respect, go for walks regularly, work much at my opera [*Fierrabras*] and read Walter Scott.' Soon after arriving in Steyr he may have succumbed to his first recurrence of secondary syphilis, which was not uncommon in the first year of the disease. This could have resulted in an anxious letter to his doctor, and it would account for Anton Doblhoff's comment in a letter (written three months later) about his visit during the summer to Steyr where he 'found Schubert seriously ill at the time'.[37] Schubert was also visited by Bruchmann (also on vacation) and Streinsberg (now employed in Linz). Before leaving Steyr, he wrote a brief inscription at the foot of a copy of one of his dances (the *Écossaises* D145/8) which he gave to Seraphine Schellmann, one of the dance-loving daughters of his host during his first visit to Steyr. He had done the same for Seraphine's brother Albert (junior) in Vienna at the end of November of the previous year. (The set of dances, D145, had already been published a few months earlier as his Op. 18.) Whether Schubert stayed with the Schellmanns again on this visit or no,[38] he must have been in touch with the family. It is probable that he also visited Herr Koller and his pretty daughter Josefine, with whom he and Stadler had made music in 1819. He met Sylvester Paumgartner again, but on this occasion he was not fit enough to take part in Paumgartner's formal musical entertainments.

[35] WL ii. 30.   [36] *Doc.* 286, *Dok.* 197.   [37] *Doc.* 296, *Dok.* 204.
[38] Stadler: *Mem.* 149, *Erin.* 174.

Schubert was sufficiently recovered from any indisposition he had suffered in Steyr to return towards the end of August with Vogl to Linz, where both musicians were invested with honorary membership of the Linz Musical Society, which had been founded only two years earlier. This was Schubert's second such honour in a six-month period. In Linz there were more parties and musical evenings, and on 23 August, in the company of Vogl, the von Hartmann parents, and their daughter Anna, he visited Anton and Marie (née Spaun) Ottenwalt, with whom the Spauns's mother was spending the summer. In the evening the Ottenwalts went with Schubert and Vogl to a local beauty spot, the Schlossberg (Castle Hill) gardens situated on a wooded hill with splendid views of the city and river. On this occasion they discussed and made arrangements for a further meeting two days later at the Ottenwalts', where the elderly Frau von Spaun, at her own request, was to host a small musical evening at which Vogl and Schubert would perform to a few friends. This occasion was described (retrospectively, in 1864) with some sentiment by Josef von Spaun:

A small sympathetic audience was invited and then began the songs, so fraught with feeling; these moved everyone so deeply that, after the performance of some melancholy songs, the entire female part of the audience, my mother and sister at their head, dissolved into tears and the concert came to a premature end midst loud sobbing. Nice refreshments and the good humour of Schubert and Vogl soon restored gaiety once more, and in the best of moods and glorious moonlight and starlight we made our way home through the lovely countryside.[39]

This particularly happy and successful occasion in the middle of a year fraught with pain, anxiety and distress, remained for Schubert a treasured memory. It was also one of the last parties which he attended in Linz. Schubert's time was so occupied during this Linz visit that Spaun was led to complain to Schober in a letter that 'I was sorry I was hardly ever able to be alone with Schubert'.[40] Spaun, who may not have seen Schubert since the onset of his illness, must have longed to talk confidentially with him, to find out how his health was affected and whether a cure really was possible. Although they had few opportunities for intimacy, it is likely that Spaun took an opportunity to give Schubert the name of a doctor he especially recommended, Dr J. Bernhardt, father-in-law of his cousin Matthäus von Collin.

On their way back from Linz to Vienna Vogl took Schubert to Kremsmünster monastery, where the singer and many of Schubert's friends who were members of the Bildung Circle had been educated at the seminary. This was Schubert's first visit to the monastery, where Vogl always

---

[39] *Mem.* 351, *Erin.* 405.   [40] *Doc.* 289, *Dok.* 199.

received a warm welcome. By mid-September they were back in Vienna. Schubert was now probably virtually penniless, although Vogl had helped to finance the Upper Austrian holiday, and their friends there had been generous in providing hospitality. Despite his precarious financial situation, he moved in with Josef Huber, a member of his circle of friends, in his lodgings at the Stubentor bastion. 'Tall Huber', as he was nicknamed, a particular friend of Mayrhofer, was physically ungainly and had an over-large nose. He was clumsy and awkward, rather boring in company, and was often teased, not always in a kindly manner, by such as Schwind. To take Schubert into his home when the composer was far from well and liable to recurrences of syphilis was generous, as was Huber's continuing kindness to his own fiancée, who over a number of years was slowly dying of consumption. Whether or not Schubert was able to pay Huber rent immediately, he could live here fairly independently, no doubt running up his customary debts while he awaited the theatrical success that he was still confident would soon come.

On 20 September Schubert wrote to members of the Styrian Musical Society thanking them for the diploma of honorary membership which Josef Hüttenbrenner had carried from Graz and recently delivered to him, and apologizing for the delay in his acknowledgement, caused by his absence from Vienna. Further, he expressed his intention 'before long of presenting your honorable Society with one of my symphonies in full score'.[41] As already mentioned, Schubert had received prior notice in the autumn of the previous year that this award was imminent from his friends Anselm Hüttenbrenner and Johann Baptist Jenger in Graz, where his music was attracting very favourable attention. Now, almost twelve months later, his Symphony in B minor was still unfinished, left as before with two completed movements and the first side of a Scherzo.[42] At some time, and maybe even a year or two after receiving the diploma, Schubert gave the manuscript of his unfinished symphony to Josef Hüttenbrenner, requesting that he hand it over to his brother Anselm in Graz. He must have expected Anselm then to pass it on to officials of the Styrian Musical Society, probably hoping that they would perform it, finished or no. Alternatively, he could have requested Anselm to hold it back until he sent the other movements. But, for whatever reason, the manuscript remained in Anselm's possession.[43]

---

[41] *Doc.* 290, *Dok.* 200.

[42] Some scholars and musicians see a strong case for arguing that the last movement was written by Schubert and then extracted to be used in his incidental music for *Rosamunde* as the *Entr'acte in B minor* (as argued by B. Newbould in *Schubert and the Symphony*, 294–6). I remain sceptical.

[43] M. Chusid (ed.), *Schubert: Symphony in B minor ('Unfinished')* (1st pub. New York, 1968; 2nd edn. 1971), 3–9.

Schubert failed to finish the symphony in 1822, or soon after, because he was ill. By April or May of 1823, when his health was improving, feeling the urgency to earn money as well as make his reputation, he turned promptly to the composition of what he hoped would be money-spinning music for the theatre. When, on his return from Upper Austria, he received the Graz diploma and was reminded of his plan to present the society with a symphony, he was intent first on completing his opera *Fierrabras*. By the time this was done, and feeling unwell again, he had discovered Wilhelm Müller's poems under the collective title *Die Schöne Müllerin*. In October and November he was absorbed in the composition of these songs. Meanwhile his symphony, begun a year earlier, remained on one side. As with the three other symphonies he had begun since 1818 (in D major D615 of 1818, also in D major D708A in 1820–1, and in E major D729 in 1821) and so many other compositions in which, after laying them aside, he seems to have lost interest, with no incentive to inspire him and with new compositions occupying his mind, he left the Symphony in B minor as it was, and never returned to it.

The *Schöne Müllerin* song-cycle was the first of Schubert's two complete cycles, the other being *Winterreise* of 1827. Both were settings of poems by the young German poet Wilhelm Müller. In the *Schöne Müllerin* cycle a youthful journeyman–miller (the singer) tells his story as it unfolds. He arrives at a new and busy mill, seeks employment and is accepted, falls in love with the miller's pretty daughter, woos her slowly and thinks he has won her. But she is fast and fickle, and soon rejects him in favour of a confident huntsman. The young miller, discarded, disillusioned, and broken-hearted, longs for oblivion and finally drowns himself in the stream. Throughout this cycle of twenty songs there is vivid scene-painting, especially in the piano accompaniment, as mill-wheels roar, stones dance, the wind blows, and branches rustle. The journeyman's confidant and friend throughout, the mill-stream, bubbles, ripples, and sings, is silent, is ruffled and fierce; and finally it brings supreme comfort to the young man as it embraces him and rocks him to calm, eternal sleep.

The theme of a miller's daughter, her suitors, and their unrequited love was already a favourite in literary circles and salons of north Germany when Wilhelm Müller began writing his cycle of poems in 1816. (He did not complete the cycle in the version that Schubert used until 1820.) How Schubert came across the poems is not known, but when he did they struck an immediate and sympathetic chord. However, he did not include all the poems in Müller's cycle. The poet, a somewhat sceptical late Romantic, included in his cycle of poems a prologue and an epilogue, 'Der Dichter, als Epilog' (The Poet, as Epilogue), in which, with more than a touch of irony, he distanced himself from the romantic emotions and passions expressed in his poems. These were, he explained, written for entertainment, and represented Art rather than real life: listeners/readers should be amused, but not deeply moved by, or involved with, the characters and events he portrayed. Despite this, in the prologue he added the moral: those who experience his tale will, he hopes, learn from it a few lessons in the art of living and loving well. Schubert rejected both the prologue and epilogue, and also three other poems which did not fit well into his own concept of the cycle, in which the young miller and the stream remain throughout the only active protagonists. His song-cycle tells a simple, romantic tale which moved him deeply and was intended likewise to affect performers of the songs and their audiences. In Schubert's song-cycle there is no irony, a quality which indeed is found rarely in Schubert's songs and operas.

Schubert's *Die schöne Müllerin* is not only richly romantic and emotional in its telling of the story, but also vivid in its symbolic depiction of the changing pastoral scene. Notable is the manner in which the composer combined in the cycle different forms of song—strophic, modified strophic, and through-composed—and included both dramatic and lyrical melody and scene-painting, as in the music of the stream both as confidant and companion, and as the power which turns the mill-wheel. The vocal writing varies from lyrical to recitative to dramatic-arioso. The integration of all his resources, of voice and piano, of poetry and music, represents an astonishing development of the *Lied* as a serious musical form, and the cycle as a concentrated musical monodrama of great power and emotional expression.

Early in October Schubert handed over his score of *Fierrabras* to the Kärntnertor-Theater in the expectation that it would be accepted and soon put into production, helped on its way if necessary by Josef Kupelwieser's good offices. This grand chivalric opera contains some of the finest music he had written to date. Schubert waited anxiously to hear when rehearsals would begin. Calamitously for his opera, on 25 October the première of Weber's *Euryanthe*, another large-scale heroic–Romantic opera also commissioned by Barbaja for the same 1822/3 season, was an expensive disaster. As yet unknown to Schubert, this operatic flop, closely following the dismissal of many of the leading German singers of the company to make way for Italian artists to perform Italian operas by Rossini and other Italian composers, was to destroy any chance *Fierrabras* might have had. Kupelwieser, ostensibly unable to work satisfactorily with the Italian singers, now left the theatre, perhaps taking with him any last vestige of hope for their opera. On 30 November, Schubert wrote to Schober:

With my two operas [*Die Verschworenen* and *Fierrabras*] things go very badly . . . Kupelwieser [Josef] has suddenly left the theatre. Weber's *Euryanthe* turned out wretchedly and its bad reception was quite justified, in my opinion. All this . . . leaves me scarcely any hope for my opera [*Fierrabras*]. Anyway, it would really not be a great piece of luck, as the productions are all done indescribably badly at present.[44]

Each of Schubert's operas of 1823, finished or unfinished—*Die Verschworenen*, *Rüdiger*, and *Fierrabras*—had a chivalric theme or a background of the crusader wars. These were popular themes at this time amongst forward-looking German composers and librettists, who were intent on developing a grander and more richly Romantic national German opera set to rival recent Italian operas, especially those of Rossini, which were sweeping the boards in Vienna. Such chivalric themes presented opportunities for a wealth of noble gestures, idealistic motives, romance, and, a subject especially close to Schubert's heart, the freedom of the individual to follow his own destiny. The operas required bigger and more expensive choral and orchestral resources, and stronger singers than some of the actor–singers who had played leading roles in the simpler, sentimental singspiels which had passed muster as 'serious' works with Viennese audiences for a while in the early part of the century. These theatrical resources were not yet easily available, as was evident from the ill-presented performances of Weber's *Euryanthe*.

Fierrabras is an opera in what was then the new grand style. It calls for a large cast, including several different choral groups, each playing a vital part in the development of the drama. Despite the spoken dialogue, Schubert composed long stretches of continuous music of variety and passion incorporating solos, small and large ensembles, narrative passages in recitative, and expressive and dramatic arioso. For moments of greatest dramatic tension he wrote melodramas, as in *Die Zauberharfe* of 1820, as also had Beethoven in *Fidelio* and Weber in *Freischütz*. As he had in *Zauberharfe*, he created unity in the opera by using reminiscence motifs, the forerunners of Wagner's leitmotifs. There is memorable music in the opera; but there are misjudgements, such as the long, repeated sections in big ensembles which hold up the action, and ineptitudes which point to theatrical inexperience, if not incompetence on the part of both librettist and composer. Had the work been performed or staged in his lifetime, changes in the structure of the play would undoubtedly have been made; and Schubert would have been required or advised to make cuts and alterations to his score. Whether these would have been sufficient to transform *Fierrabras* into an opera as popular as the third and final version of Beethoven's *Fidelio*

---

[44] *Doc.* 301, *Dok.* 207.

may be unlikely, but there must remain a strong possibility that, with adequate resources and rehearsal time for its production, the opera could have been successful in its day. For Schubert, despite bitter disappointment at the third rejection of an opera in a row, there was a new theatrical venture in the pipeline: he agreed to compose extensive incidental music for von Chézy's play *Rosamunde*. The prime mover behind the creation and presentation of *Rosamunde* was Josef Kupelwieser, the librettist of *Fierrabras*. Kupelwieser had met the Berlin-born Helmina von Chézy, a minor Romantic poetess, in connection with the première of Weber's ill-fated *Euryanthe*, of which she was the librettist. Kupelwieser, shortly before he resigned his position at the Kärntnertor-Theater, persuaded Chézy and Schubert (both suffering or about to suffer from the failure of their latest theatre work at the Court theatre) to collaborate on a new play with incidental music, to be performed towards the end of the year at the Theater an der Wien. The first performance was to be a benefit evening for the young actress Emilie Neumann, who played the title role. According to Chézy, and her meaning in her statement about it is not clear, either Schubert or Kupelwieser was in love with Neumann. If it was Schubert that was in love, then this is further evidence for his rather frequent infatuations with young women. For Kupelwieser this new Chézy–Schubert collaboration presented a chance to spread his theatrical wings in the period between his resignation as secretary from one theatre and his appointment to a similar position in the theatre in Graz. Early in October he watched anxiously as Schubert's health deteriorated. For a few weeks there must have been considerable doubt as to whether the composer would be well enough to work on the *Rosamunde* score in time for performances in December.

All the evidence points to Schubert being seriously ill in October with a recurrence of secondary and infectious syphilis. He could no longer remain with Huber; neither could he return to the schoolhouse, where on 7 November his stepmother gave birth to her third child, Andreas Theodor. Instead he probably entered the Allgemeines Krankenhaus (general hospital) in the Alsergrund suburb, still standing today almost opposite Dreifaltigkeitskirche (the church of the Holy Trinity) where a few years later the funeral service of Beethoven would be held. He left hospital, just in time for the première of *Euryanthe* on 25 October.

Three days after this première Schubert went with Weber, among others, to inspect a pianoforte by the Swiss maker Jakob Goll, who, in an effort to increase the loudness of the instrument (a problem with the instruments of this period), had placed the soundboard above the strings.[45] Schubert

---

[45] J. K. Rosenbaum: *Doc.* 294–5, *Dok.* 203.

was there at the behest of Anna von Hartmann in Linz, whose family were also friends of Weber. Her fiancée (Count Revertera) wanted her to consider carefully Goll's instruments, with their new technology, before she made any decision on what piano she should buy for their future home together. On 4 December Anna wrote to Revertera that she would seek Schubert's advice on the matter; there followed a delightful correspondence between the lovers about their choice of instrument which continued for several months, well into 1824.[46] After Schubert advised against Goll's piano 'of unproven excellence', preferring those of makers using well-tried methods of construction 'preferably a Viennese instrument',[47] he was asked to look out for something suitable, even though Anna's brother Fritz, then studying in Vienna, warned that the composer might take rather a long time over it. (Whether this was on account of Schubert's irresponsible time-keeping or of his health is a matter of conjecture.) Eventually Fritz himself, with or without Schubert's help, chose an instrument for his sister, one made by one of the Krämer brothers in Vienna.

Schubert had met Weber during the latter's visit to Vienna in March 1822 to conduct performances of *Freischütz*, at which time Weber offered to help him if he ever wanted an opera performed in Dresden, where he was then living. In 1823 the acquaintanceship was renewed when Weber arrived to conduct *Euryanthe*. On this occasion Schubert is supposed to have offended Weber by his critical reaction to the new opera in saying, in his usual blunt manner, that he considered it inferior to *Freischütz*. Whatever truth there was in this, there was no suggestion of strain between the two composers when together they inspected Goll's pianos.

Schubert must have been upset to miss the farewell party for his close friend Leopold Kupelwieser on 6 November when, according to Schwind, he was ill in bed again.[48] He now had two doctors, Schaeffer as before and, newly, Dr Bernhardt, attending him at Huber's lodgings. They assured him that, despite the setback, he was 'well on the way to recovery', and talked of 'a space of four weeks after which he might be quite recovered'. A few days after Kupelwieser's departure, Doblhoff wrote: 'Schubert seems at last to be making progress towards recovery'.[49] Thus his friends were still hopeful that his health would be restored.

Leopold Kupelwieser left Vienna on 7 November for Italy, where he eventually joined the Nazarene group of artists in Rome, not returning to Austria until August 1825, almost two years later. Shortly before he left he became engaged to Johanna Lutz, an observant young lady. Johanna wrote frequently to her fiancé, who preserved many of her letters (his to her are

---

[46] WL ii. 34–46.   [47] Ibid. 44.   [48] *Doc. 295, Dok. 203.*   [49] *Doc. 297, Dok. 204.*

rarer). In these she made a point of referring to Schubert, his health and well-being, and his compositions, understanding Kupelwieser's particular concern for his friend. She also kept him informed about other friends and the progress of the reading-circle, which was now a year old. By November she was able to write 'Schubert is already well again', and also: 'Last Saturday there was a meeting at Mohn's where readings were fixed for Mondays and Thursdays.'[50] (Initially there had been thrice-weekly meetings of this circle.) On 30 November Schubert himself wrote encouragingly in a letter to Schober of 'the state of my health, which (thank God) seems to be firmly restored at last'.[51] Throughout November, and probably since leaving hospital, he had been on a strict diet and health regime prescribed by his doctors; and by December he was hoping that he could soon begin to lead a normal life again. On Christmas Eve Schwind could write: 'Schubert is better, and it will not be long before he goes about with his own hair again . . . He wears a very nice wig . . . The dratted doctor [Bernhardt] is often with him, too.'[52]

From these various available snippets of information concerning Schubert's health it emerges as likely that, after a return of secondary syphilis in early October, he was first hospitalized and then embarked on a regime of fasting and dieting which, it was hoped, would lead to arrest of the disease. If the condition was not arrested, after an interval of time, which might be as long as ten or twenty years but was likely to be very much shorter, he would enter the tertiary phase. In this case his likely premature death could be preceded by debilitating physical and mental deterioration, incapacity, and possible madness associated with disorders of the nervous system. That the 'dratted doctor' Bernhardt so often accompanied Schubert on social occasions may well have been a ploy instigated by Spaun, ever concerned about his friend's well-being, to ensure that the doctor kept an eye on his patient and saw that he did not slip from his regime. Schubert's weakness for alcohol in particular was well known. In practice the doctor, despite his greater age, obviously enjoyed Schubert's company and that of the composer's friends in the reading-circle; for Bernhardt was also an amateur poet, of only modest accomplishment but with some literary ambitions. At this time he embarked on the writing of an opera libretto for Schubert, *Die bezauberte Rose* (The Enchanted Rose), which the composer was to reject.

Throughout November and the first weeks of December, whenever Schubert was fit enough to compose, he worked first at the *Schöne Müllerin* song-cycle and later at his music for *Rosamunde*. He was also seen about in

---

[50] *Doc.* 298, *Dok.* 205.   [51] *Doc.* 300, *Dok.* 207.   [52] *Doc.* 314, *Dok.* 219.

Vienna. There were at least two Schubertiads at which Vogl sang: at the Bruchmann family home (in Vienna) and at Enderes' and Witteczek's. On 23 November a supper party at the home of Schober's mother (Schober was still in Breslau), attended by some twelve or fifteen people including Schubert, Vogl, Étienne, Huber, Derffel, and Schwind, was followed by another short Schubertiad, and then dancing until midnight. Just occasionally Schubert attended a meeting of the reading-circle, now usually held at the home of Ludwig Mohn, and which, starting at 7 o'clock, went on for three or more hours.[53] Mohn was by profession a painter. (He was responsible for the coloured etching of the drawing by Schober—who drew the landscape and architecture—and probably Schwind—who drew the figures—entitled *Game of Ball at Atzenbrugg* or *The Feast at Atzenbrugg*.) He was first seen in the company of Schubert and his friends after he joined them at the Atzenbrugg festival in 1821. The initial meeting of the reading-circle under Mohn's leadership, on 17 December 1823, had begun promisingly with a reading of Goethe's *Tasso* (which had previously featured in meetings in 1822) along with excerpts from translations of Homer.[54] But without Schober and Kupelwieser, who were both out of Vienna, and only rare visits of Schubert, because he was either unwell or otherwise engaged, and Bruchmann, who was taking law studies very seriously and living at Hütteldorf, the heart had gone out of the meetings. The situation was not helped by the weak leadership of Mohn, nor by his introducing unsuitable new members to replace those who had left Vienna. Schubert, showing some of his old intellectual arrogance, complained in his letter to Schober of 30 November about the new members, who:

make the society only more insignificant instead of better. What is the good of having quite ordinary students and officials? If Bruchmann is not there or, worse still, ill, we go on for hours under the supreme direction of Mohn, hearing nothing but endless talk about riding, fencing, horses and hounds. If it goes on like this, I don't imagine I shall stand their company much longer.[55]

Schubert at first had valued the reading parties, both for their literary content and for the lively conversation inspired by the literature. As was not uncommon in circles and societies of male companions at this time, the members of the reading-circle were given pseudonyms. (The Ludlams Höhle club,[56] flourishing in Vienna with a membership which included distinguished writers, composers, musicians, actors, and singers, adopted the same procedure, as did many of the Burschenschaften student

---

[53] Bruchmann: *Doc.* 303, *Dok.* 208. [54] *Doc.* 303n, *Dok.* 209n.
[55] *Doc.* 300–1, *Dok.* 207.
[56] L. Porhansl, 'Auf Schuberts Spuren in der "Ludlamshöhle" ', *Brille*, 7 (1991), 52–78.

associations.) Amongst his closest friends Schubert had been variously known as 'Schwammerl' or 'Schwammelein', 'Bertel' or 'Bertl'. In the reading-circle, however, where many of the pseudonyms were the names of characters in the *Nibelungen Saga*, which was then fashionably a favourite with the members, Schubert was 'Volker the Minstrel'.[57] Like Schubert, Schwind was also dissatisfied with the changing tone of the meetings. On 2 December he wrote to Schober that he was on the point of resigning 'for reading is so drowned out by business affairs and horseplay that even to sit down together undisturbed is impossible. If you or Senn suddenly appeared in our midst, we should be truly ashamed of such company. Schubert will tell you the same.'[58] The reading parties were in fact suspended by general consent on 2 April 1824; but long before this Schubert had ceased attending, as had Schwind. Only in the New Year of 1828 was the circle reconstituted, now under the leadership once more of Schober.

Throughout much of 1823 there were suggestions in the press that an opera by Schubert was soon to be performed at the Kärntnertor-Theater, information which may have reached the editors through the offices of Josef Kupelwieser. When neither *Die Verschworenen* nor *Fierrabras* appeared, some confusion resulted as to whether Chézy's *Rosamunde*, to be composed 'by a young local tone-poet',[59] was to be a play or an opera. After Schubert had recovered his health sufficiently to be able to compose such a large score, he set to work first on the choruses and the one solo aria, so that these could go into rehearsal. For an overture, he took over one he had already written for *Alfonso und Estrella*, later replacing this for any projected future production of *Rosamunde* with the *Zauberharfe* overture of 1820. As the days of the première approached, he turned to the instrumental entr'actes. According to von Chézy, the 'dances were rehearsed for the first time forty-eight hours before the performance; the last musical pieces had arrived equally late, and to crown it all, a totally inexperienced prompter made his first trial run in *Rosamunde*'.[60] This comment appeared in the article 'Explanation and Thanksgiving', written by von Chézy, in the *Wiener Zeitschrift* of 13 January 1824, written in response to a series of damning reviews in various newspapers and journals. The complaints of the critics were that the text of the ambitious four-act play was ridiculous; and that, after a totally inadequate period of rehearsal, the players, singers, and dancers knew neither their parts nor the stage movements. One reviewer in Weimar went so far as to describe the performance as a 'fiasco'.[61] In the same reviews, however, the music was singled out for laudatory mention and some high praise. This theatrical score was the last

[57] *Doc.* 304, *Dok.* 209.   [58] *Doc.* 302, *Dok.* 208.   [59] *Doc.* 293; *Dok.* 202; *ND* 219.
[60] *Doc.* 321–2, *Dok.* 222; *ND* 237.   [61] *ND* 251.

that Schubert completed. Of his four such works of the last two years, only *Rosamunde* reached the stage; and it ran for only two performances.

For several years now, as the craze for Rossini's operas gathered momentum, so the tide had been turning against native German operas. Opera was, and always has been, an expensive art-form. In the 1820s the theatres of Vienna which presented operas were in serious financial difficulties. As hard-pressed theatre managers saw it, if audiences wanted Italian operas, then for practical reasons that was what they should be offered. Even so some, like the Kärntnertor-Theater, had to close their doors on many occasions. The situation augured ill for present and future Austrian–German serious opera in general, and in 1823 and 1824 for Schubert's operas in particular. For the next few years and for the foreseeable future, he abandoned hope of winning performances of his operas in Vienna, although he still aspired to success in German opera houses and, as will be seen, he nurtured some hopes in 1824 for incidental music for another play, although on this occasion for him the project never got off the ground.

Schubert's entrance just after midnight on the first day of 1824 at a New Year's Eve bachelor party hosted by Mohn was socially perhaps his most ostentatious move of the year, though not intended as such. Arriving at the party late, he and his companion Dr Bernhardt, unable to attract attention otherwise above the hubbub inside, announced their arrival in the street below by throwing stones at the window of the room in which the revellers were assembled. To the consternation of fellow guests, Schubert's stone hit its target fair and square and rather too violently, shattering the window. Fortunately no one was hurt. Most of the members of the reading-circle were present, including some of Schubert's particular friends and associates, such as Bruchmann, Doblhoff, and Schwind. In a letter to Schober describing this party, Schwind again communicated worry at the decline in quality of new members of the reading-circle, and in the standard of the meetings since Schober's departure: 'I got home at 4.30 am. It was all a bit crude and common, but better than we might have expected.'[62]

Schubert had few friends who were professional musicians during this period. Instead he was much with artists, in particular with painters. Kupelwieser had been a good friend for many years. After the recent departure of Schober from Vienna, Schubert and Schwind gravitated towards each other, at first drawn by mutual loyalty and affection for their absent friend, but thereafter by natural affinity. Two other artist friends who stand out but were not members of the reading-circle were Wilhelm August

---

[62] *Doc.* 319, *Dok.* 220.

Rieder and Ludwig Kraissl. Rieder, a year older than Schubert, was a fine portrait artist and painter, in 1825, of perhaps the most famous portrait of Schubert. The two men may have met through their brothers, for Ferdinand's closest friend in the early 1820s was Rieder's older brother Johann, also a schoolteacher. Kraissl, though less intimate with Schubert, attended the Atzenbrugg festival in 1822. He was a landscape painter (and Johanna Lutz's drawing teacher), but also a violinist of some ability, who played solo parts in the musical evenings at Ignaz Sonnleithner's.

Schubert had taken meetings of the reading-circle under Schober's leadership very seriously. His reaction to later developments is interesting. In early December Schwind had complained of uproariousness; Schubert wrote to Leopold Kupelwieser in March 1824: 'Our society [reading-circle], as you probably know already, has done itself to death owing to a reinforcement of that rough chorus of beer-drinkers and sausage-eaters, for its dissolution is due in a couple of days, though I have hardly visited it myself since your departure.'[63] From one who in 1821 and 1822 had sown some wild oats, was a hedonist at heart, and who latterly, under the influence of alcohol, had been capable of vulgar outbursts, this complaint might appear somewhat ironic. But in 1824, after his serious illness, Schubert was for a while moralistic and serious-minded. His response to the antics of young students is compatible with the message of 'Mein Gebet' (quoted above). In this poem Schubert recorded his intention to put his past errors behind him, to seek a finer world; it is a prayer for strength and purity in his new life. A year later he still retained these ideals, but not for very much longer.

For the first few weeks of 1824 Schubert's health still seemed to be improving and he was often in good spirits. He probably took part in a 'kind of Schubertiad at Mohn's' on 19 January,[64] and was certainly present at a merry 'feast' at the Hungarian Crown inn on 31 January for the joint celebration of his own birthday and of the news, false as it later transpired, that Schober had appeared for the first time as an actor in a Breslau theatre. By the end of the party all were tipsy, and Schubert asleep, if not unconscious. Soon after this drinking bout, Schubert was sufficiently unwell for his doctor to advise yet another period following a strict regime, which began with a fortnight's fast and confinement to his lodgings (with Huber). After this, a diet of alternate days of *Schnitzel* (cutlets) and *Panada* (a cooked and flavoured meal of bread and water), both washed down with vast quantities of tea, was prescribed for several weeks. During this 'cure', which included in addition frequent baths, Schubert composed with superhuman indus-

---

[63] *Doc.* 339, *Dok.* 234.   [64] Schwind: *Doc.* 324, *Dok.* 224.

try.[65] In appreciation of his doctor's ministrations, Schubert dedicated the first volume (nos. 1–3) of his *Six grandes marches et trios* D819 for piano duet to Bernhardt, with the words: 'en marque de reconnoissance [*sic*] à son ami Monsieur J. Bernhardt, docteur en médecine.'[66] Bernhardt looked after him from the final months of 1823 until Schubert left for Zseliz six months later, except for a short period when the doctor himself was ill.[67] On Schubert's return from Zseliz he chose another doctor.

Schwind described Schubert's powers of concentration during this last cure. On the occasions when he visited the composer during the day, his friend, not even raising his head, would greet him with 'Hallo, how are you? Good!',[68] while he continued writing. In the evenings—and Schwind claimed he visited him 'nearly every evening'—the welcome was very different.[69] Increasingly they enjoyed each other's company. Schwind, a fluent communicator and lively young man, could raise Schubert's spirits in the same way as had Anselm Hüttenbrenner some years before. Although an artist and art student by profession, he was also a fairly accomplished musician whose musical opinions Schubert valued. Alone together, they conspiratorially enjoyed the knowledge of Schober's secret engagement to Justina Bruchmann, sister of their friend Franz, who at first was totally unaware of the betrothal. Schwind was the confidential messenger between the young lovers. Of course, conversation between Schubert and Schwind did not stop at Schober's romantic intrigues; surely Schwind's paintings and drawings as well as Schubert's latest compositions featured in their discourse. The composer played excerpts from some of his current works, but these were more likely to be songs than some of his early chamber music masterpieces, each written in February or March of that year: the Octet D803 and the two string quartets, in A minor D804 and D minor D810.

Despite some improvement in Schubert's health after the latest treatment, five entries in a notebook he kept in the last week of March and a long letter he wrote to Leopold Kupelwieser on the last day of that month together point to a more complex situation. It is possible that Schubert never recovered at the end of 1823 from the relapse which forced him into hospital. Alternatively, he may have developed further symptoms of syphilis early in February 1824. Whatever the cause, he was going through a tense personal struggle as he tried to establish a balance between the physical and mental suffering resulting from his illness and its accompanying depressions, and the importance, as he saw it, of suffering for the creative soul. For it was through suffering that powers of inspiration and imagination could be heightened. On 29 March he had written in his notebook

---

[65] *Doc.* 331, *Dok.* 229. [66] *Doc.* 416n, *Dok.* 286n. [67] Doblhoff: *Doc.* 342, *Dok.* 237.
[68] *Doc.* 331, *Dok.* 229. [69] Ibid.

that pain, and not joy, sharpens the understanding and strengthens the mind.

Although some of the thoughts he jotted down in the notebook are not original, they reflect his continual searching, both in literature and within himself, for understanding and ideas which would help him establish the balance he was seeking. From his often-quoted letter of 31 March 1824 to Kupelwieser, then studying in Rome, it is clear that sometimes he was severely depressed:

In a word, I feel myself to be the most unhappy and wretched creature in the world. Imagine a man whose health will never be right again, and who in sheer despair over this ever makes things worse and worse, instead of better; imagine a man, I say, whose most brilliant hopes have come to nothing, to whom the joy of love and friendship have nothing to offer but pain, at best, whose enthusiasm (at least of the stimulating kind) for all things beautiful threatens to vanish, and ask yourself, is he not a miserable, unhappy being?—'My peace is gone, my heart is sore, I shall find it never and nevermore.' I may well sing every day now, for each night, I go to bed hoping never to wake again, and each morning only tells me of yesterday's grief.[70]

He continued with a remark confirming the help he was receiving from Schwind: 'Thus, joyless and friendless, I pass my days, except that Schwind visits me now and again and sheds on me a ray of those sweet days of the past!'

It has been customary to quote this letter as proof of Schubert's total despair about his illness, and of a death-wish comparable with that of his 'wanderer' in the *Winterreise* song-cycle of 1827. Looking at the passage in the context of the complete letter, a different picture emerges. Immediately after the expressions of hopeless misery (with the quotation from Goethe's poem 'Gretchen am Spinnrade', which he had set to music in 1814), and the tragic self-pity of these thoughts, he moves directly in the very next sentence to quite different matters. His comments on the reading-circle's 'beer-drinkers' and 'sausage-eaters', already quoted, are followed in quick succession by other, quite lively, comments: 'Leidesdorf [his new publisher] . . . is a really thoughtful and good chap . . . Your brother's opera [*Fierrabras*] . . . has been declared unusable'. He turns from opera to songs: 'I have not written many new ones', and to his recent instrumental compositions with some enthusiasm: 'I have tried my hand at several instrumental works . . . two Quartets . . . an Octet, and I want to write another Quartet; in fact that is how I want to work my way towards composing a grand symphony.' Thus Schubert grows more enthusiastic, and warms to

---

[70] *Doc.* 339, *Dok.* 234.

his task as he writes. He was thinking positively, planning for the future both compositions and, towards the end of the letter, a concert in Vienna in the following year to consist entirely of his own music, on the same lines as Beethoven's imminent concert (which was to include the first performance of the Ninth Symphony). Schubert ends the letter: 'I will close now, so as not to use too much paper, and kiss you 1,000 times. If you would write to me about your present enthusiastic mood and about your life in general, nothing could please me more!' The letter, seen as a whole, is not a happy one, but neither does it indicate unalleviated misery in the writer. It includes the constructive thoughts and promising plans for the future which led Kupelwieser, who knew Schubert intimately, to react on receiving it with no sign of serious concern for his friend's mental state. In the second week of May, some five weeks after receiving this letter, Kupelwieser dismissed his friend's state of health in one short sentence when he wrote to his fiancée: 'Poor old Schubert complains to me that he is ill again.'[71] However, it is probable that another letter had passed in each direction between the two men within these weeks, for Kupelwieser continued the May letter with: 'I wrote to him recently, and as I did not know whether, according to his indications, the letter would still find him in Vienna, since he intends to travel to Hungary with Esterházy, I enclosed the letter with one to Rieder.' Schubert had given no indication in the letter of 31 March that he was then planning a return visit to Zseliz that summer.

There were occasions after Schubert developed syphilis, and the first part of the letter to Kupelwieser could be one of them, when he seemed almost to revel in his illness. It is unlikely that this was his spontaneous reaction to physical suffering, but more likely a result of the personal philosophy he was working through in order to use his illness to positive effect. When some weeks later he was in Zseliz, his father wrote to him with schoolmasterly moralizing, he added: 'but we must not let our spirits sink in gloomy circumstances either, for sorrows too are a blessing from God and lead those who manfully endure to the most glorious goal. Where in history is to be found a great man who did not win the victory through suffering and unflinching perseverance?'[72] Biedermeier postulation this may have been, but it echoes some of Schubert's own thoughts of three months earlier, as entered in his notebook: 'There is no one who understands the pain or the joy of others! . . . What I produce is there because of my musical understanding and my sorrow; what sorrow alone has produced seems to give the least pleasure to the world.'[73] In musical terms, the recent rejection by Diabelli of his sombre Piano Sonata in A minor D784 of February

[71] *Doc.* 345, *Dok.* 238–9.   [72] *Doc.* 356, *Dok.* 245.   [73] *Doc.* 336, *Dok.* 233.

1823[74] created at a time of great physical and mental torment with 'sorrows alone', may have been in the forefront of Schubert's mind when he wrote this last comment. Later, in the early months of 1824, however, he was to compose chamber music which depended on his understanding of music and on his sorrow. This music included the Octet for wind and strings and the String Quartet in A minor, works which have surely given great 'pleasure to the world'.

The depressive mood swings from which Schubert suffered, now aggravated by serious illness, were becoming more severe. For him, as for many, one of the most attractive forms of self-medication to alleviate debilitating depression was alcohol. When a few years later he settled into a pattern of mental distress accompanied by excessive drinking, he embarked on a downward spiral. In 1823 and 1824 he recognized the dangers, not least the effect of alcohol on his physical condition as a syphilitic, and was frequently able to restrain himself from over-indulgence. What he is unlikely to have known was that excessive consumption of alcohol could result in severe neurological and cardiovascular damage.[75]

As late as April Schubert was still complaining of pains in his bones, particularly of the left arm, which prevented him from playing the piano. Neither could he sing, because of a laryngitic disorder also associated with syphilis.[76] His poor health early in 1824 may have come as a shock to him. He was born with a robust physique and had been a healthy child and young man and, knowing this, he pinned his hopes firmly on positive results from the medical régime he was following, trusting that for him there was a good chance of recovery. There were times when he was fit enough to meet friends; and he was composing chamber music of a fine quality, far superior to anything of the kind he had written before. Once again his music was heard in Gesellschaft der Musikfreunde concerts, though still restricted to solo songs or vocal quartets, and only one in each concert. And there were private performances of both the Octet and of the Quartet in A minor soon after they were composed, the latter played by the Schuppanzigh Quartet in the twelfth of its series of subscription concerts at the Gesellschaft der Musikfreunde.[77] Whether Schubert attended the première of his Octet at the house of Anton Spielmann (where Ferdinand Troyer, who commissioned the work, once lived) is not recorded. That he was present for the first public hearing of the Quartet in A minor is certain. Schwind, in a letter to Schober immediately after that performance, wrote that the quartet was performed, in Schubert's opinion, rather slowly, 'but very purely and sensitively'.[78]

[74] *Doc.* 274n, *Dok.* 189n.
[76] *Doc.* 342–3, *Dok.* 237.
[75] Jamison, *Touched with Fire*, 250; and see Ch. 6.
[77] 14 Mar.: *ND* 253.
[78] *Doc.* 333, *Dok.* 230.

Towards the end of May, now obviously much restored in health, Schubert bade farewell to his family and the few close friends left in Vienna, and set out for the second time for Zseliz. On this occasion he knew what to expect of the schloss and its park and the busy little town. Of the young countesses, Marie was now a rather accomplished pianist[79] and she had a good soprano voice. She was about to become engaged to her future husband, who spent some time at Zseliz that summer, and whom she married in 1827.[80] Caroline was a less advanced pianist than her sister, and her contralto voice was rather weak; but she was passionately interested in music, and already a useful accompanist.

On this visit, Schubert was treated more or less as a guest and friend of the family. He no longer lived with the estate workers in the manager's house, as he did in 1818, but in the 'Eulenhaus' (owl house), a building some 150 metres from the schloss and next door to the estate dairy.[81] But Schubert was not happy. Only three of his personal letters from this visit to Zseliz have survived. In these, while requesting news from the recipients of family and friends and of life in Vienna, he was markedly reticent about himself, recounting little of his life, companions, relationships with the Esterházys and their guests or with any acquaintances he had made six years earlier, or of the music-making during the five months he was away. To Schwind he summed things up: 'as my life here is as simple as could be, I have little material to write to you or others about'.[82] Just one reference in the same letter to the 'certain attractive star', while avoiding details of his feelings, points to a very important aspect of the Zseliz visit, and one that was to have an influence on Schubert for the remainder of his life: his infatuation with the Countess Caroline, whether this was of an erotic or platonic nature.

Although personal details were missing in his letters from Zseliz, Schubert made a point of referring to some of the music he had composed, notably two outstanding piano duets, the Sonata in C ('Grand Duo') D812, and Eight Variations in A flat D813. Both compositions, examples of his finest works for this medium, were proving popular in Zseliz.[83] (Schubert gave no indication whether they were played by himself with one of the young countesses, or by the sisters together.) With a monthly salary of 100 fl. KM,[84] Schubert was better paid than in 1818 (75 fl. KM) for his work both with the young countesses and as unofficial resident musician, performing as required both alone, with his pupils, and with Baron Schönstein.

---

[79] Her name appeared in a Viennese list of pianists in 1832—not in 1823, as given in *Doc.* 364 and *Dok.* 251.

[80] *Doc.* 690n, *Dok.* 466n.   [81] Vitálová, 'Schubert in Zseliz', 99.

[82] *Doc.* 369, *Dok.* 255.   [83] *Doc.* 363, *Dok.* 250.   [84] *Doc.* 933, *Dok.* 592.

The baron was a very musical and well trained amateur singer with a high-baritone voice, who stayed for several weeks at the schloss on the invitation of his friend, Count Esterházy (Schubert had first met him in 1818 at the Esterházys' home in Vienna). Apart from the musical activities in Zseliz, Schubert kept much to himself, avoiding company when he could and composing music, some of it inspired by his love for Caroline. Among these works were perhaps the three major duet compositions of this period, the sonata and variations mentioned above, and the *Six grandes marches* (dedicated to Dr Bernhardt).[85] Of these three duets, the sublime and intimate Variations in A flat D813 in particular has an intense emotional expression, exemplified in magical modulations and exquisite musical details, which might be explained by the awakening of Schubert's love for Caroline. However, this love and admiration for the unattainable countess could bring little emotional satisfaction, and he was often homesick and depressed, missing friends and the life he had shared with them in Vienna. To Schober he wrote in September: 'although I had an unpleasant disappointment, a repetition of what happened at Steyr, I am better able now to find happiness and peace in myself than I was then.'[86] This suggests that both in Zseliz and earlier in Steyr he suffered a period of serious depression rather than physical illness.

If Schubert left no informative description of his second visit to Zseliz, fortunately Baron Schönstein did. His account is therefore valuable, even if accuracy of detail may sometimes be subservient to the writer's feelings of affection and loyalty to his Esterházy friends:

The two daughters of the Count, Marie (afterwards Countess Breunner) and Caroline (later the wife of Count Crenneville) were already very good pianists when Schubert went there [to Zseliz]. In addition to this the former had a very beautiful soprano voice, trained by the best Italian masters. Schubert's task was more one of coaching than of teaching . . . The wealth of creative musical power in Schubert was soon recognized in the Esterházy household; he became a favourite of the family, remaining with them as music master during the winter in Vienna as well, and he also went with the family later for whole summers at their country estate in Hungary. Up to the time of his death, he was frequently in Count Esterházy's house. A love affair with a maid-servant, which Schubert started soon after he entered this house [in 1818] subsequently gave way to a more poetic flame which sprang up in his heart for the younger daughter of the house, Countess Caroline. This flame continued to burn until his death. Caroline had the greatest

---

[85] The duet *Divertissement à l'hongroise* D818, based on the solo 'Ungarische Melodie' (Hungarian Melody) D817, composed in Zseliz, was probably composed in Vienna in 1825— M. Domokos, 'Über die ungarischen Charakteristiken des "Divertissement à l'hongroise" D818', *Brille*, 11 (1993), 53–64.

[86] *Doc.* 363, *Dok.* 250.

regard for him and for his talent, but she did not return this love; perhaps she had no idea of the degree to which it existed. I say the *degree*, for *that* he loved her must surely have been clear to her from a remark of Schubert's—his only declaration in words. Once, namely when she reproached Schubert in fun for having dedicated no composition to her, he replied 'What is the point? Everything is dedicated to you anyway.'[87]

Schönstein went on to describe some of the music-making that went on at Zseliz in 1824, to the delight of performers and listeners alike. He told how the vocal quartet (SATB) with piano accompaniment, 'Gebet' D815, came to be written and performed. One morning at breakfast, which Schubert took with the Esterházy family and their guests, the Countess Rosina, who like her younger daughter sang contralto, invited Schubert to compose music for them all to perform, to a poem by Fouqué of which she was especially fond:

Schubert read it, smiled to himself, as he usually did when something appealed to him, took the book and retired forthwith, in order to compose. In the evening *of the same day* we were already trying through the finished song at the piano from the manuscript [full score]. Schubert accompanied it himself. If our joy and delight over the Master's splendid work were already great that evening, these feelings were still further enhanced the next evening, when we were able to perform the splendid song with greater assurance and certainty from vocal parts [individual], which had now been written out by Schubert himself . . . Anyone familiar with this opus and its not exactly small dimensions [209 bars long] will want to query that . . . Schubert produced this work in barely ten hours.[88]

On this occasion Schubert was the accompanist, while the Countess Marie sang soprano, the Countess Caroline joined her mother in the contralto line, Baron Schönstein sang tenor and the count, also not unmusical (despite Schubert's first impressions of him in 1818), joined in as bass. The count, like Schönstein, was an enthusiast for Italian opera. (Schubert's handwritten copy of Schönstein's tenor part of 'Gebet' has survived.) While they were in Zseliz they also sang through music by other composers, such as excerpts from Haydn's *Creation* and *The Seasons*, and Mozart's Requiem.[89] The changes could be rung amongst the performers, as the two young countesses and Schubert took turns as pianists and singers, in solos, duets, and other concerted music, both vocal and instrumental.

Ferdinand's letters to his brother in Zseliz provide some interesting pieces of information as well as shedding light upon the intimate and

[87] *Mem.* 100, *Erin.* 116–17.   [88] *Mem.* 102, *Erin.* 119.   [89] Ibid.

important role of Ferdinand in Schubert's life; for he had taken over, as far as he was able, the management of Schubert's business affairs in Vienna while the composer was away in Hungary. In the summer of 1824 Ferdinand had only recently been appointed to the staff of the teachers' training college, where he was involved in the routine of teaching and conducting examinations of the students, and also in inspecting schools over a wide area. For one such tour of inspection, Ferdinand travelled in the summer of 1824 to Hainburg, some fifteen miles west of Pressburg, and afterwards to Pressburg itself. He told Schubert how in Hainburg he was informed that his attentive host had arranged for him to attend mass on the following Sunday in the local church. On asking which mass was to be performed, he received the evasive answer: 'A very fine one, by a well-known and famous composer—only I can't think of his name at the moment'.[90] Ferdinand continued in his letter to Schubert:

And what do you think the Mass was? If only you had been there; I know you too would have been greatly pleased; for it was the B flat Mass [D324 of 1815] by—yourself!—You may well imagine how I felt, and also what kind and unusual people these must be that took the trouble to engage my feelings in such an agreeable surprising manner.—What is more, the Mass was performed with a great deal of enthusiasm, and really well . . .[91]

The fact that the mass, which was performed with orchestra and with Ferdinand himself playing the organ, was not published until long after this (in 1837), proves without doubt that handwritten copies of Schubert's music were circulating in his lifetime.

Ferdinand also informed his brother that he had handed over the manuscript score of the opera *Fierrabras* to its librettist, Josef Kupelwieser. The opera had by now finally been rejected by the Kärntnertor-Theater, who paid Schubert not one florin for his work. With this theatre under threat of closure at the beginning of December, Kupelwieser may have wanted to test its chances with other theatres in the German-speaking world, and most likely that in Graz, where he had recently been appointed secretary in the opera house. In Schubert's reply to Ferdinand, he commented: 'Did Kupelwieser not mention what he intended to do with the opera? Or where he was sending it?'[92] Schubert does not emerge blameless from another part of his reply to Ferdinand, where he reveals his negligence towards both his brother and a certain Josef Hugelmann. Hugelmann was a keen amateur musician who, among other things, had transcribed Mozart's string quintets for piano duet. The Hugelmann family was in touch with friends of

[90] *Doc.* 377–8, *Dok.* 260.   [91] Ibid.   [92] *Doc.* 363, *Dok.* 250.

Schubert, and the two men knew each other, if only slightly.[93] Schubert had borrowed the scores of the Mozart quintets from Hugelmann, intending to deposit them before he left for Zseliz with Ferdinand for later collection by the owner. Hugelmann visited Ferdinand first at his house, asking for the return of the scores as promised; but Ferdinand knew nothing of the matter and could find no trace of them amongst his brother's music. Hugelmann was impatient and justifiably angry that his valued property was not being returned to him. He visited Ferdinand twice more, first at work at the training college and then again at home, by this time 'inveighing so violently against your thoughtlessness, blustering, screaming and using such coarse expressions that I very much cursed the honour of his acquaintance. Please do let me know where the music in question might possibly be, so that I may pacify this raging monster.'[94] To be sure, Hugelmann behaved disgracefully towards Ferdinand, who was totally innocent in the affair, but Schubert's response was far from adequate. While rightly deploring the embarrassment caused to Ferdinand, he showed no sign of regret or concern at his own outrageous carelessness. At this time all printed music and copies were scarce and valuable; and the Mozart scores were understandably of especial importance to Hugelmann. That Schubert, who had carried them 'by mistake' with him to Zseliz, showed no trace of shame and offered no apology to the owner is likewise deplorable:

The quintets . . . belonging to that arch-donkey Hugelbeast have accompanied me here by mistake, and, by Heaven! he shall not have them back until he has atoned for his vulgar rudeness by a written or verbal apology. If, moreover, an opportunity arises to administer a vigorous scrubbing to this unclean pig, I shall not fail to give it him in a substantial dose. But enough of that wretch![95]

Empty words, foolish sentiments in a man of 27 and certainly no credit to the irresponsible borrower.

Until Baron Schönstein met Schubert his musical interests lay almost entirely in Italian songs and opera, while the German salon songs had no appeal for him. However, when he first heard Schubert's songs, he was quick to appreciate a new dimension in them, and from then on he took great pleasure in performing them. His tenor–baritone vocal range was rather similar to Vogl's, but the lyrical quality of his voice was very different from the dramatic grandeur of the opera singer. Schubert and Schönstein used to meet in Vienna to run through some of the composer's

---

[93] A Therese Hugelmann in 1824 married Claude Étienne, former valet to Axel Schober, to whom in c.1817 Schubert dedicated the Ecossaise, D511: *Doc.* 299n, *Dok.* 206n.

[94] *Doc.* 360, *Dok.* 248.

[95] *Doc.* 363, *Dok.* 250.

latest songs, although the singer stressed that, especially in early years, Schubert was beholden to Vogl, and never to himself, for technical help and advice. Anselm Hüttenbrenner recorded how Schubert took him (Anselm) to musical parties given by Schönstein in his Vienna home, at which the host and Schubert performed.[96] Schönstein wrote of their music-making: 'Schubert had grown fond of me and enjoyed making music with me, which he did often; he admitted to me repeatedly that from this time on, he generally had in mind only a voice of my range in his songs.'[97] The musical relationship of the two men was close, and the wide gulf in their social status which precluded social intimacy did not deter Schönstein from visiting 'our little Schubert', as he affectionately referred to him,[98] while the composer was living with Schober and his mother in the somewhat genteel Tuchlauben.[99] (This must have been between March 1827 and the summer of 1828, when Schubert moved to Ferdinand's home.) Schönstein also mentioned that they sometimes supped together: 'About ten days . . . before his death Schubert had supper with me together with several friends. He was very cheerful, indeed unrestrained in his gaiety, a mood which might have been induced by the large amount of wine he drank that evening, to which he was always rather partial.'[100] The kind of company they were in is not divulged, nor the venue, whether at Schönstein's home or at an inn.

Schubert's hopes of succeeding with his operas may have faded at the end of 1823, after two years of bitter disappointments, but his concern for theatre music did not die completely. According to Schwind,[101] he left for Zseliz in 1824 with an opera libretto in his luggage. Schwind believed this to be Dr Bernhardt's *Die bezauberte Rose*, but whether it was or no, the opera came to nothing. On the other hand, had he received when he should have done a promised copy of the text of a play by Johann Gabriel Seidl, it is possible that he would have composed another score of incidental music for a play. Through a series of misunderstandings and some negligence, he did not. The author of the three-act play, *Der kurze Mantel* (The Short Cloak), based on a popular fairy-tale, wanted Schubert to compose music which, like the *Rosamunde* score, was to include songs, choruses, and dances. On 1 July, when Schubert had already been in Zseliz for around six weeks, Seidl wrote to him requesting very prompt delivery of the score. As he explained, the play was almost certain to be accepted and performed, like Chézy's play, at the Theater an der Wien in the following autumn; indeed, this was likely to be 'the first autumn production'.[102] But at this time

[96] *Mem.* 182, *Erin.* 209.   [97] *Mem.* 101, *Erin.* 117.   [98] *Doc.* 346, *Dok.* 239.
[99] *Mem.* 333, *Erin.* 383.   [100] *Mem.* 101, *Erin.* 118.   [101] *Doc.* 347–8, *Dok.* 240.
[102] *Doc.* 357–8, *Dok.* 246–7.

Schubert had not even seen the script, let alone written any music for it. He had asked Ferdinand to hand over the play when he received it, along with a volume of Bach's 48 Preludes and Fugues, to his publisher, Leidesdorf, who would then send both out to Zseliz. This Ferdinand claimed to have done on 3 July.[103] By 18 July the play had still not arrived, and Schubert urged his brother to put some pressure on Leidesdorf, who seems to have been altogether rather slack in business affairs. (This may have been caused by the publisher's worsening depression over the financial affairs of his firm.) Had Schubert received the play in time, and despite his wariness at embarking on a new theatrical venture, then the prospect of payment for another score for the Theater and der Wien could have been sufficient incentive for him to accept Seidl's commission.

Although Schubert's composition of music for the play *Der kurze Mantel* never got off the ground, prospects for the *Rosamunde* music were not yet dead. Chézy continued to defend her play, and tried to create interest in it in theatres outside Vienna. She revised the text, a copy of which Schubert requested early in August 1824 (while he was in Zseliz), and asked the composer to sell her the rights to the music. He responded in customary (if not unfailingly) courteous terms:

Convinced of the worth of 'Rosamunde' from the moment I had read it, I am greatly pleased to find that you, Madam, have without a doubt succeeded in remedying in the most favourable manner a few insignificant faults which only an unsympathetic audience could have so conspicuously censured, and I account it an especial honour to become acquainted with a revised copy. As regards the price of the music, I feel it would be an insult to the music to fix it at anything less than 100 florins K.M. Should that nevertheless be too high, however, I should like to ask you, Madam, to fix it yourself, but without departing too far from what I have indicated, and kindly to forward it in my absence to the enclosed address. With the deepest respect . . .[104]

Both versions of the *Rosamunde* text were long lost, but in 1995 a copy of the revised text was found by T. G. Waidelich. Whether Schubert sold the rights, and if so, how much he was paid is not recorded. Indeed, the sale almost certainly never went through, and for this reason the composer was able to permit publication of the vocal numbers (by Sauer and Leidesdorf, and Leidesdorf respectively) in 1824 and 1828.

Schubert informed Schober in a letter of 21 September 1824 that he had written very few songs during the year, but had 'tried [his] hand at several instrumental things'.[105] In the previous March he had told Kupelwieser a similar story, adding his intention to 'pave my way towards grand

---

[103] *Doc.* 359, *Dok.* 248.   [104] *Doc.* 366, *Dok.* 252.   [105] *Doc.* 375, *Dok.* 258.

symphony . . .'.[106] The concept of a new symphony was very important to
Schubert. From the autumn of 1822, his instrumental compositions had
been constructed in less rigidly classical forms than his early compositions.
In several, a preponderance of these dating from the early months of 1824,
he used material from his own earlier vocal compositions—songs and
operas. Most of the longer and more obvious self-quotations occur in
movements in variation form. Already in November 1822 he had used a
theme taken from his song 'Der Wanderer' of 1816 in the *adagio* variations
of the 'Wandererfantasie'. From 1824 there are three similar examples. In
January, the melody of his song 'Trockne Blumen' (Withered Flowers)
from the *Schöne Müllerin* cycle (D795/18) provided the theme for the
Variations in E minor for flute and piano D802; the theme for the fourth
movement of the Octet D803 of February and March came from the Duet
no. 12 of the singspiel *Die Freunde von Salamanka* (1815); and likewise for
the second movement of the Quartet in D minor D810 he used music from
the song 'Der Tod und das Mädchen' (1817). (In December 1827, when
composing the Fantasia in C for violin and piano D934, Schubert was to use
his song 'Sei mir gegrüsst' (I greet you) D741 of 1821–2 as the theme for
variations in the third section, an *andantino*.) Other self-quotations of a different kind occur in the fourth and sixth movements of the Octet, and in a
particularly striking manner: he quotes from his setting of one verse of
Schiller's 'Die Götter Griechenlands' (The Gods of Greece) D677 (of
November 1819). He used the same excerpt again, but in less dramatic fashion, in the opening of the third movement of the String Quartet in A minor
D804, dating from the same period as the Octet.

   In the single verse that inspired Schubert's song 'Die Götter
Griechenlands', the poet (Schiller) looks back, lamenting the loss of ancient
Greece and Greek culture, the only traces of which he finds in the magic
land of song. He now observes a god-less world in which only the merest
shadow of a vanished divinity can be discerned. For Schubert early in 1824,
fighting to regain his health after his first year of syphilitic illness, the poem
had a new and intense personal meaning. The song begins very softly
pianissimo, but the tone swells rapidly during the opening vocal line,
'Schöne Welt, wo bist du?' (Fair world, where are you?) to a *forte* climax.
Schubert's use of material from this song, and from this desperate cry in
particular, in compositions of early 1824, is understandable. The manner in
which he integrated the quotation into the first theme of the Menuetto of the
A-minor quartet was masterly. Schubert's original approach to the integration of poetry and song into the previously predominantly abstract world

---

[106] *Doc.* 339, *Dok.* 235.

of instrumental music was vital in his own creative development, and it was to have an enormous influence on later generations of composers.

In his letters from Zseliz, as in the Hugelmann affair, Schubert shows definite signs of increasing intolerance, impatience, and tetchiness in his dealings with others. A fair amount of this is directed at his publisher, Leidesdorf, with whom at first he had got on well. At the end of March he had described Leidesdorf (to Leopold Kupelwieser) in friendly terms as a good man but 'hugely melancholic', adding to this: 'my affairs and his do badly, so that we never have any money'.[107] Schubert's chief complaint now lay with the slowness with which the *Schöne Müllerin* songs were appearing in print: 'It's a very slow business with the "Maid of the Mill" songs too: a fascicle comes dragging out once every three months.'[108] When, finally, they were all published, as Opus 25, he was greatly disappointed at the poor sales of copies and the lack of interest in the twenty songs of the cycle. To be sure, he had a good number of personal friends and acquaintances, notably such as Spaun, Schönstein, and Anna von Revertera (née Hartmann), who avidly sought and bought copies of all his newly published songs. The general public, however, showed little interest.

The public admittedly had little encouragement, since the *Schöne Müllerin* songs were totally ignored by critics in Vienna, Leipzig, Berlin, and Dresden. The Dresden *Abendzeitung* in early June mentioned the 'young, talented tone-poet Schubert' in highly complimentary terms, but referred to not one of his songs by name, let alone the existence of his cycle, the first two fascicles of which had appeared in print in Vienna three and four months previously. This neglect by the press, whether through their fault or that of the publisher, must have come as a great blow to Schubert who formerly, and as early as January 1822, had been attracting some enthusiastic and quite detailed reviews of his songs in Vienna,[109] and in June 1824 in Leipzig.[110] It seems likely that the lack of public acclaim for his *Schöne Müllerin* songs in 1824 was partly the result of a crisis in taste in Vienna. Quite apart from the fact that some of Schubert's songs were proving too difficult for the average amateur singer and pianist, the musical public was losing interest in so-called 'serious music', and for the most part sought the spectacular, light-hearted or frivolous. Schubert wrote from Zseliz to Schober on 21 September 1824, explaining how badly things were going for Leidesdorf's business: 'He cannot pay, and nobody's buying anything, whether my things or any one else's, apart from wretched modish stuff.'[111]

---

[107] Ibid. [108] *Doc.* 370, *Dok.* 255.
[109] *Doc.* 206–8, 214–18, *Dok.* 145–6, 150–3; *ND* 142, 146.
[110] *Doc.* 352–5, *Dok.* 243–5; *ND* 282. [111] *Doc.* 375, *Dok.* 259.

In the same letter Schubert summarized his thoughts on what he saw as a decline in aesthetic standards, 'the idle and insignificant life that characterizes our time', in a poem 'Klage an das Volk!' (A Plaint to the Nation). This is the last of his poems to survive. In it he bemoans the condition of his countrymen as he sees them: ordinary, wasted, bereft of ideals and nobility, the resigned victims of fate. Again Schubert perceives in art the last vestige of hope for man, the same idea that he had expressed in different form in his notebook in the previous March: 'O imagination! thou greatest treasure of man, thou inexhaustible well-spring from which artists as well as savants drink! O remain with us still, by however few thou art acknowledged and revered, to preserve us from that so-called enlightenment, that hideous skeleton without flesh and blood!'[112] Here, with enthusiasm and vigour, he extolled the virtue and value of artistic imagination and deplored the earth-bound mediocrity of the age. By July, and now to Ferdinand, he passed on similar thoughts in the context of his changed life since his illness: 'True, it is . . . a period of dire recognition of a miserable reality, which I endeavour to beautify as far as possible by my imagination (thank God).'[113] Now, in September, he sees sacred art as the only hope for overcoming the pain of recognizing the miseries of reality:

Klage an das Volk!
[Plaint to the Nation]

O Jugend unsrer Zeit, Du bist dahin!
Die Kraft zahllosen Volks, sie ist vergeudet,
Nicht *einer* von der Meng' sich unterscheidet,
Und nichtsbedeutend all' vorüberzieh'n.

Zu grosser Schmerz, der mächtig mich verzehrt,
Und nur als Letztes jener Kraft mir bleibet;
Denn thatlos mich auch diese Zeit zerstäubet,
Die jedem Grosses zu vollbringen wehrt.

Im siechen Alter schleicht das Volk einher,
Die Thaten seiner Jugend wähnt es Träume,
Ja spottet thöricht jener gold'nen Reime,
Nichtsachtend ihren kräft'gen Inhalt mehr.

Nur Dir, o heil'ge Kunst, ist's noch gegönnt
Im Bild' die Zeit der Kraft u. That zu schildern,
Um weniges den grossen Schmerz zu mildern,
Der nimmer mit dem Schicksal sie versöhnt.[114]

[O youth of our days, you have gone! Wasted is the strength of unnumbered folk. Not a single one stands out from the crowd; all pass by, insignificant. | Too great

---

[112] *Doc.* 337, *Dok.* 233.   [113] *Doc.* 363, *Dok.* 250.   [114] *Dok.* 259.

the pain, whose power consumes me, the last remnant left to me of that lost strength. For I too am left deedless and wasted by this time that will let none perform great deeds. | Sick and aged creeps the nation; the deeds of its youth seem a mere dream to it; indeed it foolishly scorns those golden verses, no longer having any notion of their powerful content. | Only to thee, sacred Art, is it given to depict the time of power and deed, to dull a little the great pain that will never let them [artists?] become reconciled to fate.

By the time he wrote this, Schubert had long been eager to return from Zseliz to Vienna. Finally, on 16 October, some weeks later than he had originally intended, he left Zseliz in the company of Baron Schönstein. They travelled in the Baron's own carriage, drawn as far as Pressburg on the second day by horses ('four bays') lent to his friend by Count Esterházy.[115] According to Schönstein, towards the end of his life Schubert 'was frequently seized with the notion that he had taken poison'.[116] During the 1824 visit to Zseliz 'this delusion dominated him to such an extent that . . . he no longer had a moment's peace in Zseliz, and on the evening before my return to Vienna . . . he begged me to take him with me'.[117] The symptoms Schubert associated with being poisoned could equally have come from the mercury ointments prescribed for syphilis; but whatever the cause of his physical and mental distress during his last weeks in Zseliz, he was an unhappy man. Ill health, loneliness, and presumably his fraught love for the Countess Caroline all played their part in causing his misery. Indeed, the hopelessness of this love, although it enriched his emotional experience and gave him inspiration, must have increased the sense of isolation which he felt as a result of his disease. At the same time, lack of sexual opportunities in the small country town of Zseliz may have added to his distress. Even on the journey back to Vienna, despite his relief at leaving and his expectations, Schubert was far from lively company in the carriage with Schönstein. On the first day of the journey, they slept; on the second, they froze. As Schönstein explained to Count Esterházy in a letter of thanks to his host after his holiday, and showing remarkable patience towards Schubert: 'To crown it all, the lackadaisical Schubert [*in seinem Phlegma*] managed to smash the rear window of the carriage as soon as we were out of Diószeg [where they spent the night], whereby the ghastliest of cold winds was given free play about our ears.'[118] But the journey was quick and otherwise easy, so that they were in Vienna by four o'clock in the afternoon. Schubert made straight for the Rossau schoolhouse. If Schubert's departure from Zseliz had been as sudden as Schönstein recalled, then his

[115] *Doc.* 380, *Dok.* 262.   [116] *Mem.* 101, *Erin.* 118.
[117] *Mem.* 101–2, *Erin.* 118.   [118] *Doc.* 380, *Dok.* 262.

arrival was equally unexpected by his family. But with them he was to
remain until early in 1825.

Schubert was delighted to be back in Vienna and soon recovered his spirits. According to his friends, within a week or two he was 'well' or 'very
well' and, according to Schwind, 'divinely frivolous'.[119] Schwind himself
only returned from Linz early in November, travelling with the young
Hartmann brothers, Fritz and Franz, who were to be seen in Schubert's
company often over the next few years. From now on too, Schubert was
frequently with Schwind who, immature and irresponsible for his twenty
years, was perhaps best able to recreate for Schubert some of the joys, as he
remembered them, of his own past youth, and to break up some of the
clouds which now oppressed him. Johanna Lutz, with her usual perceptiveness, wrote to her fiancé: 'If they [Schubert and Schwind] are not of
much use to each other, they do each other no harm, and even that is a good
deal in Schwind's case, since he is . . . so easily influenced by his environment. A male friend would be good for him.'[120] The final comment implies
that Schwind was unsteady. There was something feminine about him in his
youth,[121] and Johanna Lutz felt that he needed an older and wiser man for
company than Schubert. Yet it is important that she expressed no doubts at
this time about Schubert's integrity, his character and morality, and saw
him rather as a harmless associate of the young painter than as a bad
influence, unless that is she was sparing the feelings of her fiancé by avoiding too much criticism of his old friend.

As soon as Schubert had settled down again in Vienna, he had some reason to be encouraged by small developments in his musical prospects.
There were concerts which included performances of his music in Linz
on 15 November,[122] in Vienna on 2 December at a chamber concert of
the Gesellschaft der Musikfreunde,[123] and in the County Hall on
5 December.[124] Publications of his music included two short piano pieces
(from the *Moments musicaux* D780) in a Christmas album anthology published on 11 December by Sauer and Leidesdorf,[125] *Trois marches héroiques*
for piano duet D602 on 18 December by the same publisher,[126] and two of
his waltzes in a collection entitled *40 New Waltzes for Pianoforte* published
on 22 December by T. Weigl.[127] But perhaps the most exciting development for Schubert was the arrival of a letter written in Berlin on

---

[119] *Doc.* 383, *Dok.* 264.   [120] Ibid.   [121] *Doc.* 209n, *Dok.* 147n.
[122] His own concert version of his tenor aria for Hérold's opera *Das Zauberglöckchen. Doc.* 383–4,
Dok. 264; *ND* 289.
[123] A single song. *Doc.* 386, *Dok.* 266; *ND* 290.
[124] A vocal quartet. *Doc.* 387, *Dok.* 266; *ND* 292, 293, 294.
[125] *Doc.* 387–8, *Dok.* 267; *ND* 295.   [126] *Doc.* 390, *Dok.* 268; *ND* 297.
[127] *Doc.* 390, *Dok.* 269; *ND* 298.

12 December by the renowned and respected soprano, Anna Milder-Hauptmann, in which she enthused over his songs and expressed disappointment that she and Schubert were unable to meet in Vienna during the previous summer while she was there but he was in Zseliz. She looked forward to their meeting in the future, and asked whether, as he had already written several operas, he felt inclined to submit one of these for possible performance in Berlin. And she offered to use her influence with the management of the Berlin Königstadt-Theater (Court Theatre) to create interest in such an opera. In 1825, however, despite this encouraging invitation, Schubert was to turn very decisively away from music for the theatre and towards other pastures.

8

AN EXPANDING WORLD
(1825–1826, Part I)

'Schubert . . . Serious, Profound . . . *Inspired*'
A. Ottenwalt

IN 1825 Schubert seems to have shown few signs of ill health. In the year that followed there was a short spell in August and September when he was to some degree under the weather, a little sick (*halbkrank*) in August, according to Bauernfeld;[1] ailing (*kränkelt*) in September, as reported by Ferdinand von Mayerhofer.[2] This could have been due to syphilis, but might also have been a temporary indisposition, the result maybe of a long summer spent in the hot, unhealthy climate of Vienna. On the whole, the two years were good ones for him, 1825 particularly enjoyable, fruitful, and promising. On the other hand, any successes of 1826 were somewhat overshadowed by financial problems. Professionally, and this despite the public's declining interest in all classical music, Schubert was doing rather well; and his election in September 1825 to the prestigious position of one of the twenty 'deputies' of the committee of the Gesellschaft der Musikfreunde bore witness to his fast-growing reputation in Vienna. Slight fluctuations in his musical fortunes from one year to the next balanced out overall. Thus, a small decrease in the number of known performances of his music at public or semi-public venues from 1825 to 1826 (including six each at evening chamber concerts of the Gesellschaft der Musikfreunde) was compensated for by a small increase in the number of reviews or mentions of performances and publications of his music, especially in Germany. The number of publications of his music (including groups of two or three songs as one opus) in each year was more or less the same, around twenty, as was the number of private performances of his music, including Schubertiads. This,

---

[1] WL i. 51.   [2] Ibid.

however, does not take into account the allegedly weekly Schubertiads held early in 1825 in the home shared by Enderes and Witteczek, at which Vogl regularly took part, as reported by Schwind.[3]

In the early weeks of 1825 Schubert, no doubt with feelings of great relief, moved out of the Rossau schoolhouse and into pleasant lodgings in the 'Fruhwirthaus', next door to the beautiful baroque Karlskirche on the other side of the city. Here he lived comfortably and independently, on his own for only the second time in his life. The rather spacious house with a courtyard faced an open stretch of land separating Vienna from its suburbs, the 'glacis', towards the city and its walls. Schubert had 'a very pretty room'[4] on the second floor, which he rented from a cooper, Georg Kellner. He was only two doors away from the Schwinds' family home, where his friend Moritz lived with his widowed mother and sisters, and only a short and pleasant walk from the inner city. As by Viennese standards the lodgings were rather expensive, Schubert must have had money at the start of the year with which to pay rent, savings left over from Zseliz or, more probably, money from publication fees received at the end of 1824 (the String Quartet in A minor, for piano duet *Trois marches héroiques* and for solo piano two *Moments musicaux*, both published in the latter half of December).

For Schubert the highlight of 1825 was a four-and-a-half-month journey, from mid-May until early October, in the company of Vogl through Upper Austria to the Salzkammergut and Gastein. He was in good health, looking and feeling well. Much of the scenery was magnificent; and the tour was socially and musically a success. Stopping in several towns where Vogl had acquaintances, they were warmly welcomed for their performances of Schubert's songs. Vogl's operatic career was over, and from December 1821 he had been in receipt of a pension from the Kärntnertor-Theater. Now, at the age of 53, he was finding a new career for himself as a recital singer of Schubert's songs, at first mostly with the composer as his accompanist. Such recitals of German songs given in the private salons of wealthy local music-lovers must have been rare, if not unthinkable, before Vogl introduced them, as was the concept of a private recital tour. Undoubtedly both musicians received financial rewards or worthwhile gifts for their performances to help cover expenses,[5] and for Schubert there was perhaps something left over to see him through the first weeks on his return to Vienna.

By 1826, with no salaried appointment, either permanent or temporary, and no means of supporting himself either as in Zseliz (where he worked in 1818 and 1824) or with the help of Vogl (as in the summers of 1819, 1823, and 1825), and despite evidence that his musical career was burgeoning,

---

[3] *Doc.* 401, *Dok.* 275. See also *Doc.* 397n, *Dok.* 273n. [4] *Doc.* 401, *Dok.* 275.
[5] Schindler: *Doc.* 815, *Dok.* 543–4.

FIG. 4. The Fruhwirthaus, showing the dome of the Karlskirche, where Schubert lived from 1825 to 1826. *Anonymous drawing; taken from Ernst Hilmar, Schubert, © Akademische Druck- u. Verlagsanstalt, Graz, 1989, reproduced by permission.*

Schubert was short of money. This situation, and the worry about his long-term financial prospects, led him, on 7 April 1826, to apply for the vacant position of Vice-Kapellmeister (deputy musical director) of the Court chapel (he had to wait until January of the following year to hear that his application had been turned down). Financial need also forced him in September 1826, as it had in 1823–4, to write to music publishers, other than those with whom he was already in touch in Vienna, in an effort to stir up interest in his music. He sent letters in this case to Probst and to Breitkopf

& Härtel, both in Leipzig, then the music-publishing capital of the German-speaking world.

Schubert now numbered amongst his friends and acquaintances in Vienna several respected young government officials, such as Josef von Spaun, Gahy, Jenger, and Enderes, as well as a group of talented artists, musicians, and writers, some just embarking on their careers but others, like Schubert himself, already making their mark. The latter included the painters Kupelwieser, Rieder, Mohn, Schwind, and Teltscher; the musicians, notably Vogl, members of the Schuppanzigh String Quartet (renowned for their first performances of Beethoven's string quartets), the pianist Karl Maria von Bocklet, the flautist Ferdinand Bogner, and the young composer and conductor Franz Lachner; and writers such as Grillparzer, Ferdinand Sauter (Dinand), and Franz Schlechta. Another acquaintance and perhaps friend from early 1825 was the gifted young actress Sophie Müller, at whose home Schubert, sometimes in the company of Vogl, was a frequent visitor. He was also often with Schwind and Bauernfeld, both considerably younger than himself, who provided him with intelligent and high-spirited companionship, reminding him of happier days when he was their age, free of pain if not entirely of cares, rich in friendships, idealism, and purpose. Indeed, they reminded him of the lost youth for which he sometimes craved: 'O Jugend unsrer Zeit, Du bist dahin!' (O youth of our days, you have gone!), as he had begun his poem 'Klage an das Volk!' in September 1824.

Despite the apparent social respectability of Schubert's life and friendships at this time, the other side, the darker nature which he was not always willing or able to suppress, manifested itself after his return from the tour with Vogl and re-entry into Schober's now reviving circle. This was the period when Bauernfeld gained his knowledge of the characters of Schober, Schubert, and Schwind, and of their relationships with each other and the rest of their friends which inspired his New Year satire *The Outcasts* (see pp. 153–4 above). The personality of Schober was well represented; that of Schubert, alias Pierrot, almost as idle as Schober, was not entirely accurate. Although Bauernfeld may not have known it, Schubert was engaged at this time on the final touches to his Symphony in C major, on which he had been working throughout the summer. He was also amending and rewriting sections of the Mass in A flat, begun in 1819, completed in its first version in 1822, and then revised and completed in a second version at the end of 1825 or early 1826. Bauernfeld's image of Schubert as lazy and dissolute could have come partly from the composer's delighted reaction at again meeting, after some two years' separation with both Kupelwieser and Schober. In their company he may at first have thrown caution to the winds, enjoying their conversation and tales of their travels, to the accompaniment of many a pipe and a rather more frequent refilling of his glass than was advisable for him. Indeed, the indisposition which prevented him from attending the New Year's Eve party could well have been the result of over-indulgence. But he soon recovered and by 14 January was sufficiently well to play for an evening's dancing at a *Würstelball* (sausage-dance), hosted by Schober. This was a modest private dance, at which guests were sustained by a diet of frankfurter sausages and beer.[6]

The environment of his father's schoolhouse, where Schubert had been living since his return from Zseliz until early 1825, was not conducive to composing. He wrote little that was new, and was probably again beginning to suffer from depression. As in early 1818 when Anselm Hüttenbrenner frequently cheered Schubert through many a black period, so now Schwind was an enlivening companion. With Schwind Schubert occasionally visited the Hönig household, not far from St Stephen's cathedral, where lived the painter's beloved Anna, or Nettl, Hönig. She was a devout young lady of some charm, but of whose piety Schwind was to tire after a few years. Bauernfeld was now often with Schwind and Schubert. Although two years older than the painter, he had known him since they were at school together at the seminary of the Scottish monastery in Vienna (Schubert's father had applied unsuccessfully for the headship of the elementary school associated with the monastery in 1815.) Bauernfeld described Nettl Hönig in his usual perceptive and straightforward manner as 'not particularly pretty, but graceful, well-educated, domesticated and middle-class, rather than artistically gifted'.[7] The three men talked rather freely of their loves, but Schwind most freely of all.

The Schwinds' home, the Mondscheinhaus, was a fairly large split-level house built on a steep slope, three storeys and an attic high in the front, with one storey and attic at the rear.[8] 'Home' was now on the third floor, immediately over what had been, at the time of the Congress of Vienna, a very popular dance-hall. Here, in its one-time famous Langaussaal, there developed a particular version of the Viennese waltz known as 'Der Langaus' or 'Langaustanz', a dance later banned by police authorities when it degenerated into what was considered to be an improper exercise.[9] After a peak period during the Congress, the popularity of dance-halls declined, and the Mondscheinhaus dance-hall finally closed in 1824. In 1825 the hall was bought by Konrad Graf who opened, presumably in the former dance-hall

[6] *Doc.* 608, *Dok.* 410, Bauernfeld: *Mem.* 229, *Erin.* 262.   [7] *Doc.* 395n, *Dok.* 271n.
[8] K. Kobald, *Alt-Wiener Musikstätten* (Zurich, 1919), 353–5.
[9] Hilmar, *Schubert in seiner Zeit*, 78.

itself, one of the first piano factories in Vienna which were gradually to replace the old craftsmen's workshops. From here in 1825 Graf lent Beethoven his last piano. A few years later pianos were made for Chopin, Liszt, and Clara Wieck (Schumann). (In 1841 Graf sold the business to Carl Andreas Stein, grandson of Johann Andreas Stein, the great Augsburg fortepiano-maker whose instruments had been so admired by Mozart on his visit to Augsburg in 1777.) On the ground floor of the building was an inn, das Gasthaus zum Mondschein, which for Schubert and Schwind became their local hostelry, and where they and their friends often met.

In the Fruhwirthaus nearby, Schubert's accommodation was uncramped and he was contented. But he had no piano. He was disappointed when he found that another artist friend August Wilhelm Rieder, himself musical and the son of an organist and composer, did not have one either. Rieder lived only a short distance from the Karlskirche in the Wieden suburb, in a house once occupied by Gluck. When Schubert told him that he believed he would be especially inspired while composing in the 'Gluck-Haus', Rieder took pity on him and hired for the composer's use a fine square piano made by Anton Walter, whose instruments had been Mozart's favourites at the end of his life. Rieder's piano dated from the period between 1820 and 1825 and is still in existence today. It has a range of six octaves, and sustaining and *una corda* pedals. For the convenience of both of them, Rieder arranged with Schubert that if he arrived in the street outside the Gluck-Haus and found the curtains at a certain window were drawn back, then he was to enter directly, without knocking, and go straight to the piano. If, on the other hand, the curtains were closed, this meant that Rieder was working in his studio and did not wish to be disturbed by the sounds of the piano. According to Rieder's widow, when denied entrance to the apartment, Schubert would 'turn away sadly'.[10] Continuing with an explanation too sentimental to be wholly credible, she recorded that after Schubert's death her husband could not bear to be parted from the piano the composer had used while trying out his compositions and when accompanying Vogl at small Schubertiads and 'bought it as a valued memorial to his friend'. Rieder left another, much valued memorial to his friend: in May 1825, shortly before Schubert left for Upper Austria, he painted the watercolour portrait of Schubert which has remained the best known and most popular of all portraits of the composer.

Schwind wrote to Schober on 14 February that Schubert was now his neighbour and that he was 'well and busy again after an interruption'.[11] In the three months or so following his return from Zseliz, and while he was

---

[10] *Mem.* 221, *Erin.* 253.   [11] *Doc.* 401, *Dok.* 275.

living in the Rossau, Schubert had composed very little. Now, in addition to Rieder's piano and the Gluck-Haus setting, he had another source of inspiration: a poetic translation of Walter Scott's epic poem, 'The Lady of the Lake'. In August 1823, in a letter written while he was recovering from syphilis-related illness, Schubert had told Schober how he was attempting to control his life and convalescence, living simply, going for walks, working on his opera *Fierrabras*, and reading Walter Scott. The influence on European culture of Scott's narrative poems and novels was enormous, and already several different German translations were available. It is also possible, if not probable, that Schubert had attended one of the performances at the Kärntnertor-Theater of Rossini's opera *La Donna del Lago*, based on Scott's narrative, either in German (as *Das Fräulein vom See*—there were nineteen performances between 11 February 1821 and 10 March 1822) or else in Italian during the six-and-a-half month season of Italian opera in 1823. Although most of the performances in Italian were in the summer months of 1823 while Schubert was in Upper Austria, he could have seen one of the first performances on 3 or 25 July, immediately before his departure, or the last, on 28 September, after his return. But it is perhaps more likely that he celebrated his return to Vienna from Zseliz in the following year (on 17 October) by attending one of just two performances of *La Donna*, on 20 or 21 October, during the nine-month Italian opera season in 1824, and that this sent him in search of Scott's poem. In the 'Lady of the Lake', Schubert found dramatic situations and poetic utterances that sparked his imagination and were to result in some of his most beautiful and successful songs. He was awakened to a whole new world of romantic drama and emotion, in which tenderness and sensitivity coexisted with a larger, grander world of wide landscapes, nobility of mind, fateful action, and often tragic outcomes.

At the same time as Schubert was working on the Scott songs, he embarked upon his first piano sonata since the intense, grim Sonata in A minor which he had written while in the depths of the first devastations of secondary syphilis in February 1823. Now in 1825 he chose the key of C major associated with some of his most powerful music. Although he finished only the first two movements, he left the third (Menuetto e Trio) almost completed on paper, and presumably concluded in his head. He may have intended to rewrite the last movement, 272 bars of indeterminate form and of disappointing substance, on some later occasion, but in the event, as with many of his preserved but unfinished works, he never returned to it. Overall the sonata is fascinating on account of its epic character, of a kind not found in any of his music before 1825; there are moments that recall a melodic shape, a rhythmic motif, or an accompanying figure of one of the

Scott songs of the same period. But far more important in the context of Romantic expression and the influence of Scott is the dramatic nature of the whole, and suggestion of narrative content in the development section of the first movement, which is mirrored on a smaller scale in the second part of the minuet. In each case, Schubert builds up the tension to a mighty climax, following it with a passage of almost identical length, as the tension gradually subsides into a deathly calm. The whole section might be describing a battle scene followed by the bleak, tragic stillness of the battlefield after the fight. In 1861, when it was first published by F. Whistling of Leipzig, this unfinished Sonata in C D840 was given the title 'Reliquie'. Letzte Sonate (unvollendete). The 'last sonata' is of course wrong, but the 'Reliquie' nomenclature has stuck.[12] Schubert abandoned this sonata and instead immediately turned to another, the Sonata in A minor D845, a work which was more likely to appeal to contemporary audiences and amateur pianists. This sonata, unlike the earlier one of 1823, was accepted (by Pennauer) for publication soon after Schubert had finished it; and it appeared in March 1826, nearly a year after he had charmed audiences in Upper Austria with his performances of the slow variation movement.

As we have seen, Bauernfeld's diary is a useful source of information on Schubert and his friends. Although Schubert did not meet Bauernfeld until early in 1822,[13] Bauernfeld had been interested in the composer and his music for some years before this. In August 1820, when he was 18, he attended the first performance of *Die Zauberharfe* at the Theater an der Wien. He thought the music 'excellent'.[14] On 22 April 1821 he was present at the second big charity concert (*Akademie*) to be held early that year in the Kärntnertor-Theater at which a work by Schubert was performed: the male-voice quartet 'Die Nachtigall' (The Nightingale). Of this occasion he recorded: 'The best thing was a quartet by Schubert. A splendid fellow! I must meet him.'[15] Nine months later they met at a party at the home of Professor Vincentius Weintridt, a professor of theology but of unorthodox beliefs, on account of which he had been dismissed from his post in 1820. Bauernfeld arrived with his friend Josef Fick, with whom he shared lodgings in 1823–4. They were both members of a team of mostly young writers working on a new translation of Shakespeare's plays for a Viennese edition. Schubert was at the party as the guest of Schwind who, together with Bauernfeld, was a disciple of Weintridt. Among others present on this evening of no doubt lively discussion was Leopold Kupelwieser, who was later to become a distinguished ecclesiastical painter and religious

---

[12] E. N. McKay, 'Schuberts Klaviersonaten von 1815 bis 1825', in H.-J. Hinrichsen (ed.), *Franz Schubert: Reliquie Sonate, mit Beitragen* facs. edn. (Tutzing, 1992), 58–63.

[13] *Doc.* 208, *Dok.* 146.   [14] *Doc.* 143, *Dok.* 101.   [15] *Doc.* 175, *Dok.* 124.

conformist. In the course of the party, which did not finish until midnight, Schubert entertained the assembled company by singing several of his songs to his own accompaniment, in the manner customary at that time. On this occasion Bauernfeld's diary expressed no particular enthusiasm, or lack of it, for Schubert's music or the performances. His reaction was different when, after only rather distant acquaintance (as he described it) over the next few years, in February 1825 he spent an evening with Schubert and Schwind. This had begun in his own lodgings with his reading of a short play of his own, at their request, followed by his playing piano duets with Schubert and subsequently conversation, relaxation, and refreshment at an inn and a coffee-house.[16] This was the beginning of a close friendship between the three men, a second 'triumvirate' of artist, writer, and composer similar to the earlier group of Kupelwieser, Schober, and Schubert. Bauernfeld was intellectually gifted and musical, an observant witness and recorder of events and behaviour. He was also independent-minded and direct in his approach to others. Schwind was artistically gifted, enthusiastic, romantic, and often charming; but he was prone to selfish or thoughtless behaviour and sometimes quarrelsome. These two young men were to prove stimulating companions for Schubert for the remainder of his life.

There were now at least three different social strands in Schubert's life, in addition to his family, although some of these overlapped. First, he often met Schwind and Bauernfeld in one of their homes or in places of refreshment, such as the Mondschein inn. They made music together at Schwind's or Bauernfeld's, or smoked and enjoyed each other's company, discussed their work, and made plans. In a letter to Schober written on Easter Saturday, 2 April, Schwind told how at this time he was visiting Schubert early every morning in his nearby lodgings. For a short period over the schools' Easter vacation, the composer was 'much with his brothers',[17] but the close companionship of the three friends was soon re-established. Here was born the idea for a new opera which Schubert would write to a libretto by Bauernfeld. As Bauernfeld wrote in his diary in March 1825:

Am with Schwind and Schubert a good deal. He sang new songs here [the Walter Scott songs?]. The other day we slept at his place. As we were short of a pipe, Moritz fitted me up something of the kind from Schubert's spectacles-case. Fraternized with Schubert over a glass of sugar-water. He wants an opera libretto from me and suggested 'The Enchanted Rose' [the same subject as Bernhardt had agreed to the year before]. I said I kept thinking of the 'Count of Gleichen'.[18]

---

[16] *Doc.* 403, *Dok.* 276.   [17] *Doc.* 414, *Dok.* 284.   [18] *Doc.* 410, *Dok.* 281.

The 'fraternized' implies that Schubert and Bauernfeld took the necessary formal step towards intimate friendship, which was symbolized by the adoption of the familiar 'Du' rather than the more formal 'Sie' in their address to each other. Continuing the same diary entry, Bauernfeld gives an early indication of Schwind's intolerance of Vogl, in addition, that is, to Schwind's own comment to Schober on 14 February about the weekly Schubertiads at Enderes's: 'that is to say, Vogl sings'.[19] According to the blunt but not unkind Bauernfeld, the three friends visited Vogl: 'An odd old bachelor. He reads Epictetus and is a treasury of pleasant dandyism. Moritz behaved with studied rudeness towards him. Schubert is always the same, always natural.'[20]

The second group of people with whom Schubert was involved was the Lesekreis, the circle of friends, or the remnant of that circle after the departure of several of its central figures, which had at one time met regularly to read books and plays. Here, Schober, in Breslau, and Schwind acting on Schober's behalf were responsible for an irrevocable split in the membership. Neither behaved particularly well, and Schubert, in remaining loyal to both Schober and Schwind, himself behaved in a less than exemplary fashion. Whether or not Bruchmann in the early stages knew of the betrothal of his sister Justina to Schober, Schwind from February 1824 had been the intermediary through whom the betrothed exchanged letters.[21] Early in 1825 Bruchmann demanded that their engagement be broken off. He was of the opinion that Schober was a totally unsuitable husband for his sister, just as the von Spaun brothers in 1816 rejected him as suitor for their sister Marie. (There might be reason here for suspecting that Schober's sexual proclivities were as questionable as his moral attitude in general.) In doing this, Bruchmann made the matter of the engagement public, thus causing his sister some anguish, Schober considerable annoyance, and a total rift in the reading-circle. Schwind and Schubert remained on the side of Schober, as Johanna Lutz described to Kupelwieser:

[they were] in open feud with Bruchmann. The two of them seem to me like children, and indeed they give vent to their hatred like children. They have stopped meeting entirely, cut each other dead and behave like great enemies. It is true, Justina has been weak and vacillating, and Franz [Bruchmann] deliberately acted badly towards Schober, for of course he was quite aware of all the facts. And it's true that Schober's bad side was easier to see than the good. But after all, it is none of it their business.

If they [Schubert and Schwind] do not care for him [Bruchmann], that is their affair. But their conduct is infantile.

Yet their affection for Schober is good to see.[22]

---

[19] *Doc.* 401, *Dok.* 275.   [20] *Doc.* 410, *Dok.* 281.   [21] *Doc.* 326n, *Dok.* 225–6n.
[22] *Doc.* 406, *Dok.* 278.

Johanna received most of her information from the Bruchmanns and from Schwind who, as she admitted, 'no doubt both exaggerated a great deal',[23] and drew her own conclusions accordingly. Most of the friends retained a much more balanced view than the main protagonists; several of them, like Doblhoff, Hönig, and Rieder, walked away from the quarrel. Just two of them remained totally loyal to Bruchmann: Eichholzer, the painter and colleague of Schwind, whose loathing for Schwind (and vice versa) was obvious to all, and Smetana, who may already have had his own designs on Justina, whom he eventually married (on the day that Schubert died). With the collapse of the old reading-circle and the loss of intimate companionship this entailed, Schubert's increasing intimacy with the young Bauernfeld and Schwind, is understandable.

Schubert enjoyed a third, if as yet a small, social circle at the home of Sophie Müller and her widowed father in the Hietzing suburb. This was another world altogether, a more glamorous environment with a charming young hostess. At first, he and Vogl were often the only visitors, and after lunch the three made music together, singing and playing their way through many of Schubert's songs. The first such occasion was on 24 February, when Sophie wrote in her diary: 'Vogl and Schubert ate with us for the first time today.'[24] Born in Mannheim in 1804 she was barely 22 years old. Over the previous year she had been playing juvenile lead roles at the Burg-Theater, where she also sang musical numbers when required. For a short spell in early March Schubert visited the Müllers almost daily. Thus, on 1 March Sophie Müller wrote in her diary: 'Vogl and Schubert came in the afternoon and brought new songs'; new to her, that is, but not necessarily newly composed. On the next day, she wrote: 'After lunch Schubert came; I sang with him until nearly 6 o'clock, then drove to the theatre'; and on 3 March: 'After lunch Schubert came . . . later Vogl . . . Old Lange visited us too. We had music until towards 7 o'clock, when the gentlemen left.'[25] (Josef Lange, b. 1751, Mozart's brother-in-law, was re-engaged as an actor at the Burg-Theater from 1817 to 1821.) There is then a gap of four days before her entry: 'Vogl came before lunch, and . . . Schubert at 5 o'clock . . . they left at 7.30.'[26] On 30 March she wrote: 'Schubert and Vogl came for the last time today. Vogl leaves tomorrow for his country seat in Steyr.'[27] Schubert returned alone on 20 April, and again Müller 'tried several new songs' of his composition. Although each of Schubert's visits to the actress's home seems to have been primarily, or ostensibly, for the purpose of playing through some of his songs with Sophie, it is clear that there was a rapport between the pretty actress and the

[23] *Doc.* 405, *Dok.* 278.   [24] *Doc.* 403, *Dok.* 277.

[25] *Doc.* 404–5, *Dok.* 277–8.   [26] *Doc.* 407, *Dok.* 279.   [27] *Doc.* 411, *Dok.* 282.

composer. Sophie had a voice of some sweetness, and musical sensitivity. As these gifts were combined with physical beauty, charm, and a lively nature as well as apparently tireless enthusiasm for Schubert's songs, his willingness to travel out to Hietzing at her request on so many occasions is understandable. Indeed, in the light of his probable infatuation with Emilie Neumann and Caroline Esterházy, and the amount of time he was now spending with Sophie Müller, it is surely possible that, during these early months of 1825, Schubert was obsessed with Sophie Müller. Of her feelings for him and his behaviour towards her there are no records.

Schubert was variously described by his close friends as of short stature (or 'below average height' according to Lachner[28]), solidly built and thick-set rather than fat, and somewhat round-shouldered. His face was 'full', or 'rounded', with a domed forehead. His hair was curly and 'rather thin; his nose snub and lips pursed up' (Lachner again). Spaun wrote of his friend: 'one could hardly call Schubert handsome; but he was well formed and when he spoke pleasantly, or smiled, his features were full of charm, and when he was working full of enthusiasm and burning zeal, his features appeared sublime and almost beautiful.'[29] At the same time as Sophie and Schubert co-operated intensely and intently in performances of his songs, a bond of understanding and common response may well have developed between them. If Schubert fell in love with the 'bewitching Sophie', as Anselm Hüttenbrenner described her, it would not be surprising. And if he did, then he may have made some efforts with his appearance; his usual lack of concern for how he looked would not have enhanced his attractiveness in his hostesses eyes. As a successful actress, she was surely used to male admiration and well able to cope with it if the accompanying attention was unwanted or threatening. Whether there was a love affair or no, after Schubert's summer tour with Vogl, the relationship cooled. They saw less of each other, and were probably rarely, if ever, alone together again. (Sophie's early death in her late twenties in 1830 was mourned by Vienna's theatre-going public.)

In the following winter, now almost two years after her mother's death, Sophie Müller was holding larger music parties. Thus on 6 December when Schubert, back from his tour with Vogl, was again invited to the Müllers' home, it was not to a *tête-à-tête*. Among those present was Johann Baptist Jenger, a good pianist, formerly secretary of the Styrian Musical Society in Graz, who for some years had been an enthusiast for Schubert's music. In his capacity as secretary Jenger had communicated with Schubert in 1823 in connection with his honorary membership of that society. Jenger arrived

---

[28] *Mem.* 288, *Erin.* 331.   [29] *Mem.* 361, *Erin.* 416.

in Vienna towards the end of 1825, and was soon engaged with others in making music, sometimes playing duets with Schubert, but also working regularly with Baron Schönstein as his accompanist. On 6 December the musical programme included a piano duet by Schubert and some of the 'Lady of the Lake' songs. A few weeks later, on the evening of 11 January, there was another musical party at the Müllers', attended by several of Sophie's friends including a gifted young artist as yet unknown to Schubert, Josef Teltscher, who shortly afterwards was engaged to make a lithograph portrait of the composer, copies of which were soon circulating amongst his friends.

Before Schubert left Vienna for Upper Austria in May 1825, he went to some considerable trouble and expense to have prepared two handsome copies of settings of some of his Goethe songs. He asked his publisher to send the copies when they were completed to Goethe in Weimar, along with a letter which he left ready and signed. In 1816 Spaun had written to Goethe on Schubert's behalf. Now, nine years later, this was the first and only approach that Schubert himself made to the great man. In the letter, Schubert requested permission to publish the songs with a dedication to the poet. Goethe received the package on 16 June, the same day as he received another set of manuscripts, and wrote in his diary: 'Consignment from Felix [Mendelssohn] of Berlin, quartets. Consignment from Schubert of Vienna, compositions of some of my songs.' The 16-year-old Mendelssohn's piano quartets were duly acknowledged in a long letter of thanks, written on 21 June. Mendelssohn had been introduced to Goethe by the composer Zelter, and had taken part in a performance of one of these quartets for the poet only three weeks earlier. Schubert, on the other hand, had no such introduction, and was but one of many composers sending copies of their song-settings to the poet. As Goethe could see at a glance that Schubert's settings did not conform to his preferred strophic settings of the poetry, favoured also by his composer friends Zelter and Reichardt, the songs warranted no reply from him. He returned them without comment.

If Schubert's approach to Goethe in Weimar without an introduction was fruitless and disappointing, that to the singer Anna Milder-Hauptmann in Berlin, with an introduction from her former teacher Vogl, was more encouraging. On 8 March the singer wrote to him about both the songs and the opera he had sent to her.[30] She was very moved by some of the songs but regretted that 'all this endless beauty' would not be welcomed by her audiences. They would respond best to 'somewhat brilliant music for the voice', and to songs with many changes of mood and style. She had earlier (at the

---

[30] *Doc.* 408–9, *Dok.* 280.

end of 1824) sent Schubert a poem, 'Nachtschmetterling' (The Moth) which she still felt might inspire a song of suitable brilliance for her. He was disappointed by her reaction to *Alfonso und Estrella*; she saw no hope of its performance in Berlin, where audiences were 'accustomed to grand tragic opera or French comic opera'. She encouraged him to 'write something new, if possible, in one act, namely on an oriental subject with a principal part for the soprano' who, as she earlier suggested, might be 'a queen, a mother or a peasant woman'. She might have added that this should be a role for a dramatic soprano, suitable for herself. She also recommended just three principal characters, soprano, tenor, and bass, with chorus; and 'Should you find such a subject, I would ask you to let me know, so that we may negotiate further. I should then do everything in my power to get the thing staged. Please let me know what I am to do with your opera of *Alfonso*.'[31] Schubert must have been depressed yet again at the uncompromising rejection of *Alfonso*, and at Milder-Hauptmann's reservations about his music, especially after the encouraging letter she had written at the end of 1824. However, he replied to the latest letter, and it appears that a score of the opera was passed to the management of the Berlin Königstädtisches-Theater. As Milder-Hauptmann had predicted, it was rejected.

Communications between Schubert and Milder-Hauptmann did not stop here. At the end of June she wrote a letter to him describing the success of his songs with her Berlin audience in a concert on 9 June.[32] She sent this to her father in Vienna, requesting that he take it personally to the schoolhouse in the Rossau, and also show Schubert the highly complimentary reviews of the Berlin concert, in which the critic singled out for special praise the two songs by Schubert she included in her programme. Schubert's father sent the letter on to his son in Upper Austria, and stressed the civility of the great singer's father. Unfortunately, he had to hand back the reviews to the carrier. In her letter, Milder-Hauptmann asked Schubert whether he would permit the 'Suleika' song to be published also in Berlin, where it had been especially appreciated and there was already a demand for copies. And she asked for any other songs which he felt might be suitable for her coming concert tour. Shortly before his death, on 19 November 1828, Schubert fulfilled this request when he composed for her the splendid 'Der Hirt auf dem Felsen' (The Shepherd on the Rock) D965 for soprano, clarinet, and piano. After his death, Milder-Hauptmann continued to be an enthusiastic performer of his songs, frequently in high-profile concerts.

Throughout the early months of 1825 things were going rather well for Schubert. There were performances of his music in the mid-week concerts

---

[31] Ibid.   [32] *Doc.* 423–4, *Dok.* 291.

of the Gesellschaft der Musikfreunde. His songs, piano duets, and dances were appearing in print. He was enjoying new friendships, including that of Sophie Müller, and the now frequent company of Schwind and Bauernfeld. With these two, many secrets were shared. Bauernfeld was still in love with Clothilde (or Klothilde), who had supposedly been his mistress since 1821, but in January 1826 he began to tire of her company, or at least of her behaviour in public. On 28 January of that year there was a grand carnival ball at the home of one Herr Tratner in Nussdorf, to which he and Clothilde were invited (Schubert was not present). On this occasion Clothilde pleased neither Bauernfeld nor his friends. Because she was apparently suffering from exhaustion and bashfulness, Bauernfeld felt some pity for her; but he was also irritated and embarrassed. The next day, when he visited Schwind and confessed his disappointment with his girl, he received some comfort from Schwind's laughing retort: 'We're all the same!'[33] But Schwind continued to adore his Nettl Hönig, although the devoutly religious and well-brought-up young lady still held him at arm's length. 'Schubert sniggers at both of us', commented Bauernfeld; 'but [he] is not quite heart-whole himself. He has slept a few times at my place, and then it all came out.'[34] At this time, the object of Schubert's attention might have been either Sophie Müller or Caroline Esterházy.

As we have seen, there are many indications that for some while Schubert had been in love with, or to some degree infatuated with Caroline Esterházy. In February 1828 Bauernfeld wrote in his diary 'Schubert seems to be seriously in love with Countess Esterházy. I am happy for him. He is giving her tuition.'[35] On Schubert's affection for the countess, information left by Baron Schönstein is helpful. He was a close and devoted friend of the Esterházy family and a frequent visitor to their homes in Vienna and Zseliz. He also knew Schubert well. When he provided information about Schubert to the composer's would-be biographer Ferdinand Luib (in 1857), Schönstein must have been eager to represent the relationship between Caroline and Schubert in a good light, but also to clear up any earlier misrepresentations of the facts which could have been damaging to the Esterházy family's reputation. His account may well have more than a grain of truth. He referred in a passage already quoted[36] to a love affair with the maidservant in Zseliz, which began soon after he arrived at the schloss, and which in time gave way to the 'more poetic flame' of his love for Caroline. Schönstein was convinced that Schubert was, and remained for the rest of his life, in love with the young countess, but that she, perhaps with 'no idea of the degree' of his love, did not return it and retained only

[33] WL i. 37. [34] G. Eder, 'Schubert und Caroline Esterházy', *Brille*, 11 (1993), 13.
[35] WL i. 68. [36] See pp. 196–7 above.

'the greatest regard for him and his talent'. That she could tease him, twitting him with failing to dedicate any compositions to her, suggests a certain intimacy and informality in their friendship.

Bauernfeld confirmed his own belief in Schubert's love for Caroline when he wrote, in 1869:

while he was fairly realistic in regard to certain things, Schubert was not without his infatuations. Actually, he was head over ears in love with one of his pupils, a young Countess Esterházy, to whom he also dedicated one of his most beautiful piano pieces, the Fantasy in F minor for pianoforte duet. In addition to his lessons there, he also visited the Count's home, from time to time, under the aegis of his patron, the singer Vogl,[37]

and, after referring to Schubert's black depressions during his final years, he added: 'Fortunately in our friend's case an idealized love was at work, mediating, reconciling, compensating, and Countess Caroline may be looked upon as his visible, beneficent muse, as Leonore to his musical Tasso.'[38] Josef von Spaun confirmed Schubert's infatuation with the young countess, while yet deploring any assertions that the composer would have turned for satisfaction to another girl, such as the chambermaid, 'on the side'. He wrote, in an outburst of loyalty to Schubert's memory, and possibly with innocent confidence in his friend: 'I am absolutely convinced that, during the time of his affection for his pupil, the Countess, an affection which, though hopeless owing to their different circumstances, was deep and heartfelt, Schubert had no relationship . . . with any other girl . . .'.[39]

Moritz von Schwind may have been saying something of importance when in his 1868 drawing, *A Schubert Evening at Josef von Spaun's*, he placed a portrait of Caroline Esterházy, who was not one of the guests at the musical evening, on the centre of the wall behind the gathering: the Countess Caroline was the inspiration, the source of Schubert's compositions, and the one to whom, as the composer told her, everything was dedicated. Schwind saw Caroline as Schubert's Muse, even as his 'distant beloved', the 'ferne Geliebte' of Beethoven's song-cycle.[40] The countess's great-niece, Countess Coudenhove, wrote of the family's understanding of what they chose to believe was the relationship between pupil and mentor: 'It never occurred to Caroline to feel more than a warm friendship for Schubert, although in the family it was admitted that he had a slight crush on her'. The family, and friends such as Schönstein, took it for granted, probably correctly, that Caroline's feelings would be governed by propriety, the

[37] *Mem.* 233, *Erin.* 267.   [38] *Mem.* 234, *Erin.* 268.
[39] *Mem.* 362, *Erin.* 417.   [40] Eder, 'Schubert und Caroline Esterházy', 15.

'excellent education she had received, which would have made her well aware of the social divide between herself and the composer, and of her responsibility to her family in matters of the heart'.[41] The discovery in recent years of a collection of albums of Schubert's music, especially songs, which were in her possession and bore her signature does not add seriously to any argument that she was in love with him. It is easily explained by a gentle affection for, and fond memories of Schubert, and the fascination for her of his music, quite a lot of which she had come to know in his company. The argument that the annulment of her marriage, which she had contracted at the late age of 38 to a man five years her junior (Count Carl Folliot von Crenneville), supports the view that Caroline may have reciprocated Schubert's love does not hold water. But whatever their relationship, Caroline must have shared some of Schubert's intimate thoughts about his compositions. Her parents do not appear to have tried to keep her apart from Schubert, nor to have harboured fears for her heart. In any case, it is impossible to conceive that Schubert, a syphilitic of humble origins and often penniless, or Caroline could have entertained any thoughts of a formal or physical personal relationship. Schubert wrote to Kupelwieser in March 1824: 'Imagine a man, I say, whose most brilliant hopes have perished, to whom the felicity of love and friendship have nothing to offer but pain, at best . . .'.[42] In a letter to his parents of late July 1825 (written in Steyr), after asking after each of his siblings and in particular his brother's growing family, Schubert added the abrupt comment on the married state: 'I renounce it myself.'[43] For him, any object of his love was always likely to be unattainable. Yet he was a man of intense sensuality; and he obviously loved other women. That his passion was awakened by a sweet-natured, kindly young countess whom he knew to be out of his reach and could only set on a pedestal, is surely as probable as is the likelihood that she felt pity for him as a sick young man, and held nostalgically to her admiration and affection for him, especially after his death. For Schubert in his mid-twenties to have inspired the affections, and perhaps devotion, of both Sophie Müller and Caroline Esterházy, he must have possessed some charm, even if he had not retained the good looks of his late teens. Rieder's portrait of him, much admired when it was painted, points admirably to that possible charm.

The reason for Schubert's sudden departure from the Esterházy estate with Baron Schönstein in the autumn of 1824 is nowhere specified, although homesickness for Vienna and some ill health are the most likely causes, along with the strains of living at such close quarters with the admired

---

[41] Eder, 'Schubert und Caroline Esterházy', 15.
[42] *Doc.* 339, *Dok.* 234.   [43] *Doc.* 436, *Dok.* 300.

Countess Caroline and, as suggested earlier, a need to satisfy his sexual appetite. When the Esterházys left Vienna for Zseliz in the summer of 1825, Schubert may have been glad to go off in the opposite direction, to find distraction and new inspiration in unfamiliar surroundings and to be in company other than that of Zseliz. Interestingly, for a while, until August or September, he abandoned the composition of songs. His mind was now preoccupied with the creation of larger instrumental forms, and in particular a new, grand symphony.

When Schubert departed from Vienna for his summer 1825 vacation and tour with Vogl, he left Schwind in a suspicious and irritable mood on two counts. First, Schwind thought that Schubert had slighted his beloved Nettl Hönig—or 'sweet Anne Page' as she was known to the friends—by not turning up at her home, as Schwind had expected, to bid Nettl farewell. Secondly, he was jealous of Bauernfeld, who he considered had overstepped the bounds of propriety by playing piano duets with Nettl and then walking her home without first asking his permission. His anger with Bauernfeld soon passed; for some others with whom he quarrelled it did not. His strong dislike or intolerance of Ferdinand Sauter (Dinand), Eichholzer, Huber, and even Vogl was well known to his friends. So also were his equally strong positive passions, including his infatuation with Schober and love for several women. Of these, he described the warmhearted Katharina Lászny (née Buchwieser) in his familiar effusive style:

What a woman! If she were not nearly twice as old as I and unhappily ill, I should have to leave Vienna, for it would be more than I could stand. Schubert has known her a long time, but I met her only recently. She is pleased with my things and myself, more than anybody else except you . . . so now I know what a person looks like who is in ill repute all over the city, and what she does.[44]

Lászny had been a beautiful young singer of talent and vivacity who seems to have acquired a reputation for both a love of music and art and for licentious behaviour dating back to the time of the Congress of Vienna. How well Schubert knew her, and what their relationship was are not known, but he dedicated to her two songs in February 1825 (D672, D707) and the piano duet *Divertissement à l'hongroise* D818 in 1826, the latter in deference to her Hungarian husband. The respectable Anna Milder-Hauptmann sent greetings to Lászny via Schubert in March 1825, adding: 'I wish I could sing your songs to that amiable and art-loving lady.'[45] In 1827 Lászny was still alive (she died on 3 July 1828),[46] and it was at a dinner in her house early in that year that Schubert met the composers Hummel and Ferdinand Hiller.[47]

---

[44] *Doc.* 401–2, *Dok.* 275–6.   [45] *Doc.* 409, *Dok.* 280.   [46] *Doc.* 789n, *Dok.* 524n.
[47] *Doc.* 619n, *Dok.* 417n; *Mem.* 282–4, *Erin.* 324–6.

Lászny was also held in affection as a colleague and friend by Vogl and other singers, some of whom performed at her house.[48]

Schubert left Vienna in the third week of May, and was certainly in Steyr by 20 May. Vogl had been there since the beginning of April,[49] and was already delighting music-lovers both there and in Linz with performances of Schubert's songs. On these occasions before Schubert arrived, he was frequently accompanied by the composer's old friend from the Stadtkonvikt, Albert Stadler. Although the programme of Schubert's travels with Vogl is fairly clear, some of the dates are uncertain. The tour began and ended in Upper Austria with visits to Steyr and Linz, and included a return to this 'base' between two journeys, first to Gmunden on Lake Traun and then to Salzburg and Gastein and a further week in Gmunden. One might fancifully compare their itinerary to a slightly modified 'sonata rondo' (without the customary key changes):

  ⌈ 1. Steyr, Linz, Steyr   20 May–4 June (2 weeks)
  | 2. Gmunden   4 June–*c*.12 July (6 weeks)
  ⌊ 3. Linz, Steyr   15 July–*c*.10 August (2–3 weeks)
     4. Salzburg, Gastein   11 August–4 September (3½ weeks)
  ⌈ (5.)
  | 6. Gmunden   10–16 September (1 week)
  ⌊ 7. Steyr, Linz   *c*.17 September–*c*.5 October (2½–3 weeks)

Only the absence of a return to Steyr and Linz (5) after Gastein and before Gmunden breaks the basic structure of the rondo. In addition to this itinerary, there were occasional overnight stops *en route*, which brought the total length of Schubert's tour to nineteen weeks.

    A few hours before Schubert arrived in Upper Austria for the start of this 'Tour à la Sonata Rondo', Josef von Spaun had to leave Linz to take up a new appointment in Lemberg (now Lwów, in Poland). His departure was a great disappointment to Schubert, who had been looking forward to seeing his old friend, and he felt it especially keenly during the three days he was in Linz, staying with Spaun's sister Marie and her husband, Anton Ottenwalt. From Linz, Vogl and Schubert made a day excursion to the magnificent monastery of St Florian, where Vogl had friends to whom he had already introduced some of Schubert's songs. Now those friends had the opportunity to hear Vogl sing with the composer accompanying. On the way back from Linz to Steyr, on 26 or 27 May, they visited the Kremsmünster monastery, as they had earlier in 1823,[50] and here again in

---

[48] *Doc.* 667n, *Dok.* 449n.   [49] *Doc.* 411, *Dok.* 282.   [50] *Doc.* 290n, *Dok.* 200n.

the evening they performed songs by Schubert.[51] Schubert also played the variations movement of his new Sonata in A minor D845, written earlier in the year, and, with the help of a Kremsmünster resident, piano duet marches (probably D819) and the Variations in A flat D813. The sonata variations 'pleased especially', not least for the sounds the composer produced from the instrument. Several told him that 'the keys became singing voices under my hands, which, if true, pleases me greatly, since I cannot endure the accursed chopping which even distinguished pianoforte players indulge in and which delights neither the ear nor the mind.'[52] Back in Steyr, the two musicians settled for a further ten days, Vogl to enjoy his home environment, Schubert to make music with, and enjoy the company of the Schellmanns, Kollers, and Sylvester Paumgartner, with whom he was probably staying on this occasion. On 4 June they set off on the next stage of their travels, to Gmunden on the beautiful Lake Traun.

Schubert remained in Gmunden for six weeks,[53] Vogl perhaps for only part of the time. Here they lived in the comfortable home of Ferdinand Traweger, a merchant whom Schubert had met some years previously in Vienna. (In 1818, while he was in Zseliz, his brother Karl, on tour as a painter seeking suitable landscape subjects for his pictures, wrote to Schubert of the welcome he had received in Gmunden from Traweger.)[54] Traweger was very musical, had according to Schubert a 'magnificent pianoforte',[55] and was a great patron of music. Albert Stadler, comparing him with the Steyr patron, described him as 'a second Paumgartner'.[56] His house was situated close to the landing-stage in the town. Traweger and his wife Elisabeth had three children, the youngest of them a 4-year-old boy Eduard, with whom Schubert seems to have struck up a special rapport. The boy was some two years older than Schubert's own little half-brother Andreas whom, along with his slightly older half-sisters, Maria and Josefa, he held in great affection. The ability of Schubert, usually reserved and shy in personal communications, to win the confidence of small children, is an interesting trait of his personality. Schubert was rather slow to develop personal and trusting relationships, and chose his intimate friends carefully, if not always wisely. Once a friendship was established, he could be tenaciously loyal (as on the occasion of the rift in the reading-circle in 1824, when, as we have seen, Schubert with Schwind supported Schober in what he saw as his friend's betrayal by Bruchmann). He rarely opened his heart to other than closest friends. As with many creative people, his deepest feelings found expression in his art. And yet there were occasions when he desperately needed both to give and to receive affection; and in the absence of

---

[51] *Dok.* 287. [52] *Doc.* 436, *Dok.* 299. [53] *Doc.* 432–3, *Dok.* 296–7.
[54] *Doc.* 97, *Dok.* 65. [55] *Doc.* 432, *Dok.* 297. [56] *Mem.* 154, *Erin.* 179.

old friends, he seems to have found in some small children exactly the responses he longed for. He could relax with Eduard Traweger in the same way that, in the often tense atmosphere of the Rossau schoolhouse, he could enjoy playing with his little half-siblings. Many years later (in 1858), and with what degree of accuracy it is impossible to judge, Eduard Traweger recounted how at this time Schubert had taught him a song which he never forgot from his *Schöne Müllerin* cycle, 'Guten Morgen' (Good Morning).[57] His father was particularly fond of male-voice quartets, and it is probable that, during the six weeks Schubert spent with them, he composed for his host music to a sixteenth-century Latin text, the drinking song 'Edit Nonna' (The Nun Eats) D847, and 'Nachtmusik' (Night Music) D848 (also for male-voice quartet).

In Gmunden Schubert was welcomed at the home of the schoolteacher Johann Nepomuk Wolf, where he made music with the daughter of his hosts, Anna (Nanette), then 17 years old, who sang and played the piano well. The two of them, and presumably for the most part when Vogl was away from Gmunden, sometimes performed songs and piano duets to small audiences at the home of Franz Ferdinand Ritter von Schiller,[58] an important man in the area, both politically and socially. In addition, Schubert was a frequent visitor at the beautiful thirteenth-century Ebenzweier castle on the banks of Lake Traun three miles from Gmunden. The castle was owned by Florian Maxmilian Clodi, a widower whose second wife, Therese, an aunt of Josef von Spaun, had died in 1814, leaving an invalid husband who in 1825 was described as 'blind, gouty and bedridden'.[59] The eldest of their four children was also called Therese. Only 11 years old when her mother died, Therese gradually took over the running of the home and the estate, and thus earned the name in the neighbourhood of 'Schlossherrin' (châtelaine). But to Schubert's friends, this much admired young cousin of Spaun's, 23 years old when the composer first met her, was the 'Lady of the Lake', so named after the heroine of Walter Scott's epic poem, from which Schubert had already selected several passages to set to music that year. Fairly early on during their stay in Gmunden, Vogl and Schubert had been out to Ebenzweier; but in the third week of June Therese was still deliberating on how she could best, and correctly, invite them to stay for a few days at the castle. On this subject, Therese wrote to her brother Max (the second child), whom Schubert had met in the company of Fritz and Franz von Hartmann in Vienna early that year, at Schubertiads held in the shared home of Enderes and Witteczek. Her letter shows not only her interest in

---

[57] *Mem.* 168, *Erin.* 197.

[58] Aulic Councillor of the Holy Roman Empire, and chief steward of Gmunden's salt-mines.

[59] *Doc.* 422n, *Dok.* 290n.

Vogl and Schubert and in their music-making, but also her sensibility: 'That Vogl and Schubert have already come to see us I think I have told you. I should so much like to invite them, yet do not know as yet how to go about it. Twice I have heard Vogl sing and Schubert play: it is and remains a divine pleasure to hear these two.'[60] As mentioned earlier, Therese was 'worshipped' by the ever susceptible, romantic young Schwind, who was just a year or so her senior.[61] Between the families of Traweger, Wolf, Schiller, and Clodi, Schubert found plenty of opportunities to make music, both with and without Vogl. He was content in the comfortable Traweger household near the edge of the lake, where he was made to feel welcome and his compositions were valued. As Schubert expressed it, Traweger was 'a great admirer of yours truly'.[62]

In a letter to Spaun written on 21 July soon after his return to Linz, Schubert described life in Gmunden and his contentment, despite the disappointingly unsettled weather throughout their stay: 'living there was so pleasant and free-and-easy. At Councillor von Schiller's we had much music, among other things some of my new songs, from Walter Scott's "Lady of the Lake", of which especially the "Hymn to the Virgin Mary" [Ave Maria] appealed to everyone.'[63] A few days afterwards, still in Linz, Schubert wrote to his parents in similar vein:

I lived at Traweger's, very free and easy. Later, when Councillor von Schiller was there, who is the monarch of the whole Salzkammergut, we (Vogl and I) dined daily at his house and made music there, as we also often did at Traweger's house. My new songs from Walter Scott's 'Lady of the Lake' especially had much success . . . a hymn to the Holy Virgin . . . it appears, touches every soul . . .[64]

Earlier in the same letter, Schubert had described Gmunden with enthusiasm: 'the landscape is truly heavenly and deeply moved and benefited me, as did its inhabitants, particularly the excellent Traweger.'

Around 12 July, Vogl and Schubert said goodbye to their friends in Gmunden and set off on the return journey to Linz and Steyr, stopping for a day or two in Püchelberg, near Wels, where Vogl had friends. Between Friday, 15 July, when Schubert arrived in Linz, and his move on to Steyr on 25 July, he divided his time between Linz and Steyregg castle, some five miles east of Linz. The castle was the summer residence of the Count and Countess Weissenwolff, whose guest he was. The Countess Sophie was a great lover of music, an accomplished singer (contralto) and pianist, and a very good friend of Anna von Hartmann who, since her marriage to Count

---

[60] *Doc.* 422, *Dok.* 290.   [61] *Doc.* 423n, *Dok.* 290n.   [62] *Doc.* 432–3, *Dok.* 297.

[63] *Doc.* 433, *Dok.* 297.   [64] *Doc.* 434–5, *Dok.* 299.

Revertera in April 1824 had been living in Przemysl—now in Poland.
Schubert's music was a great favourite in the Weissenwolffs' home; indeed,
in his letter to his parents written on 25 July, Schubert used the same expression for the countess's admiration of his music as he had earlier to Spaun for
Traweger's: '[she] is a great admirer of yours truly', adding also that she
'has copies of all my pieces and sings many of them very prettily [*recht
hübsch*]'.[65] As in Gmunden, Schubert performed his recently composed
Walter Scott songs to the delectation of his hosts and their friends. In
Steyregg, according to Schubert:

[the Countess Sophie] even dropped a few hints that the dedication of them [the
Scott songs to her] would be anything but disagreeable. But I intend to use a
very different procedure with the publication of these songs from the usual one,
which yields so very little [financial reward], since they bear the celebrated
name of Scott at their head and may in that way arouse greater curiosity, and,
by the addition of the English words, might make me better known in England
too.[66]

The idea of publishing the Scott songs in an alternative English-language
version had been his intention for some while. Unfortunately, in setting the
songs to music with no knowledge of English, he overlooked the differences in metre and scansion between the translation he was using and
Scott's original. He never solved the problem in a manner that would have
made the musical settings acceptable in English. The seven 'Lady of the
Lake' songs were eventually published by Artaria in Vienna in two volumes on 5 April 1826 (in all except one case—'Normans Gesang'—with
added but unsingable English text.) And the dedicatee was indeed the
Countess Weissenwolf.

   In May Schubert had spent only two nights in Linz with the Ottenwalts;
when he returned on 15 July it was to be for a slightly longer period. Anton
Ottenwalt was obviously nervous about the visit, very anxious to please
their guest and perhaps concerned about his somewhat unpredictable
behaviour. They went to considerable lengths to ensure that he felt welcome and at ease. In his room, one which had formerly been occupied by
Josef von Spaun, he had a writing table at which he could work, books to
read, and all he might need for his comfort. In his turn, Schubert appeared
as a thoroughly appreciative guest, behaving impeccably and giving great
pleasure to his hosts.[67] There were, however, things about which the
Ottenwalts could do little: the absence of Spaun, the weather, and the
inanity of much of the conversation around him.

---

[65] *Doc.* 435, *Dok.* 299.   [66] Ibid.   [67] *Doc.* 429–30, 441–3, *Dok.* 295–6, 303–4.

When he reached Linz on this, his second visit that summer, the unsettled weather of the first weeks of the holiday had changed to oppressive heat. Schubert complained in a letter of 21 July to Spaun:

Here I sit at Linz, half dead with sweating in this frightful heat, with a whole book of new songs, and you are not here! Aren't you ashamed? Linz without you is like a body without a soul, like a headless horseman, or like a soup without salt . . . As you see, I'm getting positively unjust towards the rest of Linzdom, since after all I am quite happy in your mother's house and in the company of your sister, Ottenwalt [her husband] and Max [Spaun's brother], and seem to see your spirit flash from the body of many another Linzer. Only I fear that this spirit will gradually flash itself away entirely, it's enough to make you burst.[68]

He showed his familiar intolerance for the conventional conversations of social gatherings in Linz in a somewhat exaggerated description to Spaun:

Altogether, it is a real misery how everything becomes petrified into insipid prosiness everywhere, how most people look on at this quite unconcernedly, or even feel comfortable with it, and how they quite calmly glide over this slime into the abyss. To go upwards is harder, of course; and yet this rabble could be driven in pairs easily enough, if only something were done from up above.[69]

On the other hand, he was grateful to his hosts for arranging visits in the cooler evening air to the hills around the town from where he enjoyed magnificent views. Each evening, except perhaps on one evening when there was music-making, Ottenwalt and Max von Spaun took him for a walk to Jägermayr's, a popular hostelry with a fine garden on a ridge of hill (the Freinberg) to the west of Linz, overlooking the river. Here they quenched their thirst before moving down to the Castle inn, another hostelry with a pleasant garden, at the foot of the castle hill beside the river Danube, where the ladies (Marie and her mother, Frau von Spaun) joined them for supper.

The Ottenwalts' description of Schubert's visit was enthusiastic and emotional. The composer seemed to be in excellent health,[70] and he appeared to enjoy their hospitality. Ottenwalt wrote to Spaun with particular feeling of their last evening together, when the two men sat talking late into the night:

I have never seen him like this . . . serious, profound and as though inspired. How he talked of art, of poetry, of his youth, of friends and other great people, of the

---

[68] *Doc.* 431–2, *Dok.* 296.　　[69] *Doc.* 432, *Dok.* 296.　　[70] *Doc.* 429, *Dok.* 295.

relationship of ideals to the realities of life, etc! . . . I cannot tell you how wide-
ranging or consistent his convictions are—but there were glimpses of a world-
view that is not second-hand.[71]

Ottenwalt continued: 'That is why I am so glad that he seemed to like being
with me and was inclined to show us that side of himself, which one shows
only to kindred spirits; that is why I felt the need to write to you about it.'
On 25 July Vogl joined the Ottenwalts and Schubert for lunch, together
with Therese Haas, a friend of Countess Weissenwolff and a favourite of
Max von Spaun and Albert Stadler.[72] After the lunch, Vogl left with
Schubert for their next destination, Steyr. During their stay in Linz, as
Ottenwalt recorded: 'We heard Vogl three times, and Schubert himself con-
descended to sing something after breakfast [on 25 July?] among ourselves,
and also played his marches, two- and four-handed variations and an overture on the pianoforte'.[73]

Of the probable two weeks that Schubert and Vogl spent in Steyr on this
occasion little is known. On their way to Salzburg from Steyr on 10 August
they stopped at Kremsmünster, where they were warmly welcomed again,
but did not stay the night.[74] Schubert had grown fond of the monastery, not
only on account of the welcome he received and the popularity of his music
there, but also for the beauty of its seventeenth- and eighteenth-century
buildings, its famous observatory tower, and its commanding situation and
impressive surroundings, which incorporated a small river at the entrance
to the monastery complex. From Kremsmünster they travelled on towards
Salzburg, stopping one night at an inn in Vocklabrück, which Schubert
described as a 'dreary hole' (*ein trauriges Nest*).[75]

Ferdinand Schubert wrote a long letter to his composer brother on
4 August, beginning with his disappointment that Schubert had not waited
for his vacation that September so that they could have travelled together
through Upper Austria and the Salzburg region. His longing for Upper
Austria was, he wrote, indescribable, but for this year he would have to settle for Lower Austria for his own travels (on a vacation taken, as was usual,
without his wife and family). Meanwhile, he was intensely interested in all
that his brother was doing, the landscapes he saw and the people he met,
and he asked him for a nice, detailed description particularly of Salzburg,
Gastein, and the surrounding areas. Schubert duly responded and wrote a
detailed account of his travels, which he did not post but handed to
Ferdinand on his return to Vienna. Unfortunately the original descriptions

---

[71] *Doc.* 442, *Dok.* 304.
[72] Also a sister of Karl Haas, a friend of Max Clodi. (Clodi later moved in the Hartmanns' circle
of friends while studying in Vienna, and attended Schubertiads.)
[73] *Doc.* 441, *Dok.* 303.   [74] *Doc.* 456, *Dok.* 313.   [75] Ibid.

are lost, and the only version to survive is that which Ferdinand published in 1833 in his own book *Der kleine Geograph* (a school textbook, illustrated by their brother Karl) and republished six years later in Schumann's Leipzig journal, *Neue Zeitschrift für Musik*. As a result of editing by Ferdinand, quotations from the letters as they have survived are likely to be in a revised form, perhaps with some descriptive additions, and not exactly as Schubert wrote them. However, these, together with a few historical explanations added by myself, provide a fair picture of what impressed Schubert.

On the final stretch of the journey into Salzburg, they passed through 'amazingly beautiful' countryside, skirting the Wallersee, the colour of whose water and situation impressed Schubert enormously, as did the ever higher mountain ranges around them. The villages they went through were sadly neglected, the buildings, showing signs of former affluence, were now in a sorry state. The skies darkened as they came nearer to Salzburg, making the mountains appear threatening. Finally, probably on Tuesday, 11 August, they crossed the bridge over the rushing Salzach and entered the city. Salzburg had been a rich and magnificent ecclesiastical and princely capital in Mozart's time, but after the secularization of the Salzburg province and its ceding first to Bavaria in 1809, and then in 1816 to Upper Austria, it was no longer ruled by a powerful prince-archbishop. There were a large number 'of wonderful buildings, palaces and churches',[76] but many affluent employers had left the city. There were few people to be seen on the streets and many signs of poverty and neglect. Four- or five-storey houses, once teeming with communities of several families, were now empty or partially occupied. Some of the buildings looked dingy and uncared for, and in many of the town squares grass grew around the paving stones. Soon after Schubert and Vogl arrived in Salzburg it began to rain. After they had deposited luggage in their rooms at the Blackamoor inn, where they were to spend the next two or three nights, Vogl wasted no time before contacting an old acquaintance, Johann Christian Pauernfeind, a merchant and former mayor of the city, who lived near the inn. Through Pauernfeind, whom Vogl had alerted in advance to their imminent arrival, they received an introduction to Maria Hieronymus, Count von Platz, president of the Salzburg law courts. Vogl and Schubert drove through dismal, wet streets directly to the count's home where they were 'most kindly received' by the family, 'our names being already known to them', as Schubert wrote.[77] After polite exchanges:

[76] *Doc.* 458, *Dok.* 314.   [77] *Doc.* 457, *Dok.* 314.

Vogl sang some of my songs, whereupon we were invited for the following
evening and requested to perform our bits and pieces before a select circle; and
indeed they touched them all very much, especially the 'Ave Maria' [Walter Scott]
already mentioned in my first letter. The manner in which Vogl sings and the way
I accompany, as though we were one at such a moment, is something quite new
and extraordinary for these people.[78]

It was no snobbery on Schubert's part when he described to his brother
how he and Vogl, having been duly 'auditioned' on their first day in
Salzburg, were asked to perform at an important aristocratic soirée on the
second evening. Very probably the artists received some payment from the
distinguished audience, or the host, or both.

If heavy rain prevented the two men from sightseeing on their first day
and a half in Salzburg, on the morning after their performance at the salon
of Count Platz they climbed the Mönschberg, admired the imposing
fortress on its heights, and enjoyed the bird's-eye view of the fine buildings
below. They then visited the impressive domed early baroque cathedral, 'a
heavenly building'. For Schubert, accustomed to the dark of St Stephen's
gothic cathedral in Vienna, it was the brightness of the interior that now
thrilled him most. 'The light, falling through the dome, penetrates into
every corner. This extraordinary brightness has a divine effect'.[79] From the
cathedral, they moved on to the abbey church of St Peter's, where Michael
Haydn had lived and worked as organist and choirmaster. Having performed his church music as a chorister, first in the Lichtental church,[80] then
in the Imperial Court chapel, and having later sung in some of his male-
voice quartets, Schubert had great respect for Michael Haydn, and was
moved by the sight of a recently erected monument to the revered composer: 'A heavy tear fell from my eye, and we moved on', he told his
brother. After the morning's sightseeing, Vogl and Schubert lunched with
Pauernfeind, and then, the weather now having brightened, the two men
were able to climb another of the hills surrounding Salzburg, the
Nonnberg, from where they had a grand view of the 'glorious' Salzburg
valley. At this point Schubert broke off his description with 'The rest of
Salzburg's sights which I shall see only on my return journey, I shall leave
until then'.[81] The next day, one of brilliant sunshine, 'the finest day in the
world and of the world',[82] the two men left Salzburg, Schubert certainly
under the impression that they would be returning on their way back to
Gmunden in three weeks' time. The *Salzburger Zeitung* announced their
departure the day after they left in an entry under 'visiting foreigners': 'At

---

[78] *Doc.* 457–8, *Dok.* 314.   [79] *Doc.* 458, *Dok.* 314.
[80] Benedikt, 'Schubert und das Kirchenmusik-Repertoire', 110.
[81] *Doc.* 459, *Dok.* 315.   [82] *Doc.* 466, *Dok.* 319.

the Blackamoor Inn: Hr. Michael Vogl, retired [pensioned] Imperial Court Opera Singer from Steyr, and Hr. Franz Schubert, musical composer from Vienna.'[83]

Schubert was in high spirits when, nine days later and now back in Steyr, he took up again the letter to Ferdinand which he had begun on 12 September. In his description of the journey to Gastein from Salzburg there are passages in which the brand of humour suggests that they are Schubert's own. After depicting the drive through the scenery of the Salzburg valley 'as if through Elysium', he added the qualification: 'except that it has the advantage over that paradise that we sat in a delightful coach, a convenience denied to Adam and Eve'.[84] Schubert was understandably disappointed when Vogl would not stop to view the Salzberg mines, 'for his great soul, spurred on by gout, urged him on to Gastein, like a wanderer in a dark night who yearns for a ray of light'.[85] After the magnificent beauty of the first part of the journey came the terrifying grandeur, as he saw it, of the mountains further south. Here he felt imprisoned by the 'incredibly high rocky walls' around them, and a 'fearful abyss' below. He continued:

Amid this terrifying nature man has sought to commemorate his even more dreadful bestiality. For it was here that the Bavarians on one side and the Tyrolese on the other of the Salzach, which here makes its tumultuous way far, far below, indulged in that frightful massacre at which the Tyrolese, concealed in the rocky heights, fired down with hellish shouts of triumph on the Bavarians, who were endeavouring to gain the pass, but were hurled wounded into the depths without ever being able to see where the shots came from. This most infamous act, which went on for several days and weeks, was marked by a chapel on the Bavarian side and a rough cross in the rock on the Tyrolese, partly to commemorate and partly as a sacred sign of expiation. Thou glorious Christ, to how many shameful actions must Thou lend Thy image! Thyself the most awful monument to mankind's degradation, Thine image is set up by them as if to say 'Behold! we have trampled with impious feet upon Almighty God's most perfect creation; why should it cost us pains to destroy with a light heart the remaining vermin, called Man?'[86]

Although it must be remembered that the pious Ferdinand may have added to what Schubert wrote about his reaction to the massacre of Bavarian troops by Tyrolean soldiers in the Lueg pass, this passage also contains clues to Schubert's religious thinking. Schubert was nurtured in the Roman Catholic Church from an early age by his parents, through his contacts with the Lichtental church, the Imperial Court chapel, and the Stadtkonvikt run by the Piarist order. In the Austria of Schubert's day the

---

[83] *Dok.* 308.
[84] *Doc.* 466, *Dok.* 319.
[85] *Doc.* 467, *Dok.* 320.
[86] *Doc.* 467, *Dok.* 320.

Roman Catholic Church worked closely with the state in efforts to prevent, and to resist, revolutionary tendencies in the populace. At a time when sermons, along with all public speeches and lectures, were subject to censorship controls, some severe restrictions were introduced to limit the religious debate and to repress any tendency towards defection from conformity. Freethinkers, like Ignaz Schubert, were closely watched by church and state. The worldly powers and interests assumed by the church had little relevance to the spiritual needs of the people; and the Christian concept of a compassionate God did not fit easily with the politically more convenient demands for obedience. As a result of the church's rigidity and prominence in state affairs, some people of more independent mind turned away from the established church and sought their God elsewhere. In his poem 'Mein Gebet' (see p. 173 above), written after a period of serious illness, is found the strongest evidence hitherto that Schubert believed firmly in some kind of God, in immortality and an afterlife.[87] Aware of the degradation brought on him by his illness, 'lying, annihilated in the dust, racked by unknown sorrow', the speaker of the poem yearns with 'holy zeal' for life 'in a fairer world'; and he prays that his degradation may be translated into a 'purer, stronger state'. But there is a difficulty for those looking for a conventional Christian prayer; for Schubert prays that he may be washed clean in the waters not of the Christian river Jordan, for example, but of the pagan river Lethe, the river of oblivion. His anger and dismay at the 1809 massacre in the Lueg pass reveal his outrage at what he saw as conventional 'Christian' reaction to an atrocity: the church commemorating with Christian symbolism an evil crime of war. The terms in which his indignation were couched show that he had respect for basic tenets of the Christian faith, but no time for those actions of the established church which smacked of inhumanity or corrupt worldliness. For Schubert was intolerant of 'worldliness' in church, state, and society. His natural inclination was for spiritual rather than worldly values, although this did not mean that he was immune to 'worldly' practices (some perhaps well outside the bounds of the socially acceptable). His spiritual values are exemplified in his sense of the importance of suffering and of compassion, and by his belief in the divinity of beauty and the joy it can inspire. Both are evident in entries in his notebooks of 1816 and 1824, and in some of his letters to Ferdinand.

Schubert was not alone in his vision of a connection between God and beauty, especially the beauties of nature. While a student at the Stadtkonvikt, like many of his contemporaries, he had fallen under the spell of Klopstock. The teleological argument for the existence of God, which

---

[87] *Doc.* 279, *Dok.* 192–3.

Klopstock's works illustrated,[88] caught the imagination of a generation, who shared a new sensibility to nature. For Schubert, this component of his religious belief was to prove an influence not only on his thinking but also on his choice of poems to set to music, and his creative response to poetry. His senses were certainly awakened to the existence of a superhuman controlling power, and he perceived this power as a Creator—God of beauty and compassion. His God was not merely the inspiration of the church, nor was the church the exclusive source of his beliefs. Whatever was beautiful in the world was also divine or divinely inspired.

Schubert described his attitude to the composition of sacred music in his letter to his father of 25 July 1825: 'I have never forced myself to piety; and never compose hymns or prayers of that kind unless it takes me unawares; but then it is usually the right and true piety.'[89] His sacred music, all written with a view to performance during church services, was in the same musical idiom as much of what he had sung in the Lichtental church and Court chapel, and in accord with religious tastes of the day. In his case, the music was natural and without affectation, specifically without 'forced devotion', in keeping with attributes of his personality and manner of composing as stressed by several of his friends. It combined the musical character then generally associated with musical piety and spirituality with the fruits of Schubert's own unmistakable genius. In his five completed settings of the mass (*Missale Romanum*), from the first in F of 1814 to the last in E flat in the summer of 1825, he followed conventional forms and accepted dynamic conventions implied in the text, although the complexity and length of the music increased considerably in the final two masses (those in A flat and E flat). Fortunately for Schubert, current conventional piety was not so strict that the church authorities forbade the adaptation or accommodation of ecclesiastical texts by composers to fit their musical needs. Schubert made numerous such changes in the masses, mostly by repeating passages with some reordering of the words, and occasionally by omitting a phrase, although this would appear to be more by accident than design, with just one exception. In each of the masses the words 'Et unam sanctam catholicam et apostolicam Ecclesiam' do not appear. From an early age Schubert was deeply opposed to belief in 'one catholic and apostolic church', as his righteous indignation in the summer of 1825 at memorials to the Lueg pass massacre exemplifies. He never set these words to music.

Schubert's understanding of God was through His creation rather than through mystical inspiration or devotional piety. No documents have

---

[88] A further example of this argument is to be found in Gellert's famous poem 'Die Ehre Gottes aus der Natur' (The Praise of God in Nature), set by Beethoven.

[89] *Doc.* 435, *Dok.* 299.

survived which indicate whether he attended church services regularly, if at all, or willingly, in later life. On the other hand, his brother Ferdinand, with whom he retained a close relationship, and who had a growing reputation in Vienna as a church musician, was always involved with church activities. Yet it is very unlikely, if not impossible, that Schubert would have applied, with any real hope of success, for the position of Vice-Kapellmeister in the Court chapel[90] if the church had been anathema to him. And his failure in this application did not deter him from composing further sacred music, including the large-scale and often thrilling Mass in E flat D950, in 1828, whether with a view to further applications for a position as a church musician or no.

On 28 March 1824, in his lost notebook, Schubert wrote: 'It is with faith that man comes into the world . . . in order to understand anything, I must first believe in something'.[91] Perhaps his faith in an all-powerful God came first, and from this he was able to work out his own religious position and beliefs, and their meaning for his life. Such was his religion, and one which was probably not very different from that of many of his closest friends.

We return now to the journey of Schubert and Vogl from Salzburg, begun almost certainly on 14 August, a Sunday. Schubert was relieved when they escaped from the high alpine path down through a narrow gorge carved out by the raging river Salzach and into a more open stretch of land.[92] After passing through Werfen, a market town with an imposing fortress, they reached Gastein late in the evening of the same day. They took rooms in the Straubinger-Hütte for the three-week period recommended for the 'cure' that Vogl intended taking. And here they remained until their departure three weeks later to the day, on 4 September.[93] During this time, Vogl bathed and took the waters while Schubert, with time on his hands and energy from the invigorating Gastein air, had plenty of opportunity to compose and to enjoy the beauty of his surroundings. He returned to the symphony he had been forced to lay aside after leaving Gmunden; and he wrote the first draft of the vigorous Piano Sonata in D D850, which he was to dedicate to Karl Maria von Bocklet. Although the few letters of Schubert's which have survived from the period of his summer tour do not explicitly refer to his working on a new symphony, he had already mentioned it to friends. Thus Schwind in Vienna wrote to him: 'About your Symphony we may be quite hopeful. Old Hönig [Ludwig, Father of Karl and Nettl] is Dean of the Faculty of Jurisprudence, and as such is to give a concert. That will afford the best opportunity so far of having it

[90] *Doc.* 520–1, *Dok.* 354.   [91] *Doc.* 337, *Dok.* 233.   [92] *Doc.* 468, *Dok.* 320.
[93] *Doc.* 454, *Dok.* 312.

performed.' He then added, with some false hopes: 'indeed we count upon it'.[94] Spaun was convinced that Schubert had written the bulk of the symphony in Gastein,[95] as was Bauernfeld.[96] On the other hand, even before his visit to Gastein, Schubert was known by Anton Ottenwalt to have worked on a new symphony at Gmunden which he said was to be performed 'in Vienna this winter'.[97] As Ottenwalt wrote this in a letter to Spaun on 19 July while Schubert was staying with him in Linz, it must be assumed that the symphony was begun well before the composer arrived in Gastein on 14 August.

Also staying in Gastein at the same time as Vogl and Schubert were Mozart's widow Konstanze von Nissen and the Hungarian Johann Ladislaus Pyrker of Felsö-Eör, who had been appointed Patriarch (archbishop) of Venice in 1820. Pyrker was also a poet. He and Schubert had met first in Vienna, also in 1820, at the home of Matthäus von Collin, after which, in the following year, the composer dedicated his Opus 4 songs to him.[98] Schubert made quite an impression on Pyrker on both occasions, and in Gastein they spent some time together, Schubert also setting two of his poems to music: 'Das Heimweh' (Homesickness) D851 and the magnificent 'Die Allmacht' (Omnipotence) D852, both of which he dedicated to the poet. For a while Vogl had the idea of travelling to Italy with Pyrker, but he changed his mind when his friend had to leave on 3 September, the day before Vogl's cure was completed. The singer and Schubert set off, as planned, on the next day, but Vogl had changed his mind about returning to Salzburg. They were to make straight for Gmunden instead. On this occasion, they stopped just long enough in Werfen to climb up to the castle high on a hill overlooking the town, described by Schubert for his brother: 'it is d——d high, but affords a splendid view of the valley, bounded on one side by the immense Werfen mountains, which can be seen from as far as Gastein.'[99] Where they visited or lodged over the next few days and nights as they made their way back to Gmunden is not known, but when they arrived, early in the second week of September, their friends in the town were already expecting them. Schubert now relaxed into what he imagined would be another few weeks in the Lake Traun area. He made contact with friends and planned the following days with enthusiasm. When after only one week in Gmunden Vogl suddenly announced that they were leaving the very next day, Schubert reacted with considerable disappointment and perhaps some justifiable displeasure. With little time to say farewells and to write notes of apology for unfulfilled engagements, his irritation at Vogl's autocratic manner of organizing their vacation increased.

[94] *Doc.* 451, *Dok.* 310.   [95] *Mem.* 24, 356, *Erin.* 32, 410.   [96] *Mem.* 31, *Erin.* 40.
[97] *Doc.* 430, *Dok.* 295.   [98] *Doc.* 180, *Dok.* 128.   [99] *Doc.* 468, *Dok.* 320.

Throughout the tour Schubert was dependent on the planning and whims of Vogl, who almost certainly financed most, if not all, of their travels. That he did so is confirmed by a letter which has survived, written to Schubert in Gmunden on 19 May 1828 by Ferdinand Traweger. This was in answer to a request from Schubert, who was considering a return to Gmunden that summer for another holiday, for information about Traweger's usual charges for board and lodging. Traweger replied:

You really embarrass me; if I did not know you and your open, guileless way of thinking, and if I did not fear that in the end you might not come, I would make no charge. But in order to get the idea out of your head, that you would be in anybody's way, and so that there is nothing to stop you staying as long as you like, listen: for your room, which you know, including breakfast, lunch and supper, you will pay me 50 kreuzer W.W. [20 kr. KM], per day, and pay extra for what you wish to drink.[100]

From this letter it appears that Schubert had little or no idea what Vogl had paid for his accommodation in 1825. At the same time, it becomes clear that, because Schubert was indebted to Vogl for his lodgings, he was not in a position to argue when the singer refused to visit the famous Salzberg salt mines, insisting instead on driving straight through from Salzburg to Gastein, so that he could begin his cure for the painful gout from which he was suffering as quickly as possible. And it explains why, eager to shorten the time before he set off for Italy, he insisted on leaving Gmunden so abruptly on their second visit. He wanted to get back to Steyr and start making preparations for his six-month Italian journey. This sudden change of plan is recorded in a letter of Schubert's to a friend, Johann Steiger von Amstein, who had been a member of the reading-circle in Vienna from November 1823 and who was now, like Schubert, in Gmunden. The composer explained that he could not keep an appointment because of Vogl's decision 'to leave *tomorrow*!! I only learnt this early today, so you will forgive me. Do not be angry, for I much regret it. In the evening [this evening] I hope I may still see you both at your tavern.'[101]

Over the next year or two Schubert's irritation with Vogl resurfaced in the musical context of his songs, and some tension existed between them, but never approaching breaking-point (as it did in 1821). Vogl's mannered way of singing became more exaggerated with the years, and he offended Schubert by taking licence with his music in a manner offensive to the composer. He added ornamentation to the vocal line, reflecting an attitude of 'affectation and complacency',[102] to which Schubert objected. 'Vogl

---

[100] *Doc.* 775–6, *Dok.* 517.   [101] *Doc.* 463, *Dok.* 317.
[102] L. Sonnleithner: *Mem.* 112, *Erin.* 131.

often produced a passing effect by a tonelessly spoken word' reported Sonnleithner, 'by a sudden outburst, or by a falsetto note, but this could not be justified artistically'. As Schubert began to write songs with the voice and performances of Baron Schönstein in mind rather than those of Vogl, so Vogl began to look to other accompanists who were more accommodating to his way of performing than was the composer. Stadler and the young Albert Schellmann were among them.

Schubert and Vogl, having left Gmunden on 14 or 15 September, were overnight guests at Kremsmünster on 16th, continuing their journey to arrive at Steyr the next day. Schubert was still under the impression that he would not be returning to Vienna until the end of October, but within a day or two Vogl, who was surely also tiring of Schubert's company, informed him that he was thinking of moving on to Italy, now with a Count Haugwitz, at the end of September or early October.[103] As a result, Schubert realized that he was likely to return to Vienna a month earlier than he had anticipated. Again, little is known of their two-week stay in Steyr, but at the beginning of October, probably on the first day of the month, Schubert set off ahead of Vogl for Linz, where he once more stayed with the Ottenwalts and spent a night at Steyregg castle as guest of the Count and Countess Weissenwolff. He made this journey in the company of Albert Stadler, who described their visit:

We spent a very pleasant time in Count Weisenwolff's house there. Count Johann was an enthusiastic art-lover, Countess Sophie a very talented singer . . . I still think with pleasure of our stay at that time in their castle, Steyregg (a bare hour from Linz, on the Danube). I shared a bedroom there with Schubert and I still clearly remember how he sang me a motive from *Die Zauberflöte*, in bed, for me to sing the second part to, and what amusement it caused him that, for a long time, I could not find the lower part. The next morning I was on my feet very early and wanted to show him the glorious surrounding country from a near-by hill. Nothing could persuade him to join me, he preferred his bed, and I had to take the walk alone.[104]

At Steyregg there was much music-making, as there had been on Schubert's earlier visits in the previous July. There was also a musical performance in Linz at the home of Anton von Spaun on 3 October, in celebration of the birthday of Spaun's wife, when again the Walter Scott songs were especially acclaimed. By this time, Schubert's friend and duet partner, Josef Gahy, had arrived in Linz in the company of Franz von Spaun's mother-in-law, Babette Wanderer, and two of her daughters. It was soon arranged that within the next day or two Schubert would accompany Gahy,

---

[103] *Doc.* 465n, *Dok.* 319n.   [104] *Mem.* 149–50, *Erin.* 174.

who had the use of a hired carriage, on his return journey to Vienna. After all the uncertainties of arrangements during the last weeks and growing tension between Vogl and Schubert, not surprising after more than four months spent much in each other's company, Schubert was eager for home and the familiar life of Vienna. Perhaps more to the point, he knew that in his absence both Schober and Kupelwieser, neither of whom he had seen for two years, were back in the capital, and he longed for their company and renewal of the intimacy of their friendship.

9

FRIENDS, PUBLISHERS, THE GESELLSCHAFT DER MUSIKFREUNDE
(1825–1826, Part II)

As soon as Schubert arrived back in Vienna, he took up residence again in the Fruhwirthaus. He now began a series of long and convivial evenings socializing with his friends. Bauernfeld's entry in his diary for early October sums it all up:

Schubert is back. Inn and coffee-house gatherings with friends, often until two or three in the morning.

> Wirtshaus, wir schämen uns,
> Hat uns ergötzt;
> Faulheit, wir grämen uns,
> Hat uns geletzt.

[Inn, we are ashamed, has delighted us; Laziness, we grieve, has refreshed us.]

Schober is the worst in all this. True, he has nothing to do, and actually does nothing, for which he is often reproached by Moritz.[1]

From this time onwards, Bauernfeld was rather frequently in Schubert's company. The close friendship had begun in the previous February and had been interrupted after only three months by the composer's tour with Vogl. For some weeks that summer, of the inner circle of Schubert's friends only Bauernfeld and Schwind were left in Vienna. Both kept in contact with Schubert while he was away by letter. Bauernfeld was studying hard for his final law examinations during this period, and in August was delighted to learn that he had passed with flying colours.[2] He was now

---

[1] *Doc.* 469–70, *Dok.* 321.   [2] WL i. 30.

eager to find congenial lodgings where he could live not too expensively. In September he wrote to Schubert suggesting that they and Schwind should find rooms together, an idea which Schubert, then looking forward to the freedom of his own home in the Fruhwirthaus, received with little enthusiasm.[3] For the time being, Bauernfeld considered himself to be on vacation; but he was already on the look-out for a permanent appointment. Meanwhile he had some Shakespeare translations to complete. Although these brought in much-needed money, he was beginning to tire of the work, sensing that it was responsible for a certain stagnation in the development of his own dramatic writing.

Schwind was also working hard during the summer months, intent on mastering professional skills as a painter, and finding any excuse he could to visit the Hönig household, where he continued to court the favour of Nettl. Schwind had come to like and admire Schober before the latter's departure two years earlier, and kept up a frequent correspondence with him. As already mentioned, many of Schubert's earliest letters to Schober might strike post-Freudians as homoerotic in tone; but his characteristically immoderate youthful enthusiasms at this time, rather than a homosexual relationship, could account for his affectionate effusions. On Schober's return to Vienna at the very end of June, Schwind wasted no time in bringing his two friends, Schober and Bauernfeld, together. Shortly after this Bauernfeld wrote in his diary, with his usual perceptiveness:

Schober has arrived from Breslau . . . He led a somewhat adventurous life and was for a time an actor à la Wilhelm Meister. He is five or six years older than us, and a bit of a man-of-the-world, full of blarney and disputatiousness, and a favourite with women, in spite of being rather bow-legged. We at once began an agreeable relationship . . . Moritz . . . worships him like a god. I find him fairly human, but interesting.[4]

Before Schubert arrived back on the scene, Bauernfeld had already been taken by Schober and Schwind to Atzenbrugg for his first visit there, thus cementing their friendship; and shortly after this, in mid-October, Bauernfeld moved into a room in Schober's home on a temporary basis, after Kupelwieser had moved out.[5]

Kupelwieser had returned to Vienna early in August, eager to establish himself as an artist and to plan his marriage to Johanna Lutz. While he looked for suitable permanent lodgings, presumably with appropriate space for a studio, he accepted on a temporary basis Schober's offer of a room in the apartment he shared with his mother. Kupelwieser, now in his thirtieth year, was a somewhat changed man after his stay in Italy, with a keen sense

---

[3] *Doc.* 464, *Dok.* 318.   [4] *Doc.* 428, *Dok.* 294.   [5] WL i. 32.

of responsibility and strong religious convictions. It now transpired that he had little in common with Schober, and he seems quite quickly to have distanced himself from Schober's circle of friends. The nature of this circle had also changed radically in the two years he had been away, largely as the result of the rift between Bruchmann and Schober, which had never healed. The new members of Schober's wider circle were appreciably younger, without responsibilities, many of them students. The young ladies who occasionally joined in their social activities were likewise young and carefree, if not frivolous.

The central core of the more intimately bonded Schubert–Schober circle now included Schwind and Bauernfeld, the latter often with his friend Ferdinand von Mayerhofer, who was in Vienna from early November 1825 until the following April.[6] In the final months of 1825 and in the company again of Schober, Schubert seems to have reverted to some of his habits of 1821–2. As these included heavy drinking and smoking, he was following a dangerous path from which his good friend Spaun, had he been in Vienna, might well have endeavoured to divert him. In his New Year's Eve satire *The Outcasts* Bauernfeld portrayed Schubert as a disciple of Schober, though less adoringly so than Schwind (alias Harlequin), listening to Schober's outrageously self-indulgent ideas, enjoying his base pronouncements on the virtues of idleness and depravity. On 31 December Schubert was ill and unable to play the role of Pierrot created for him. Whatever the indisposition that kept him away from the celebrations, after three months back in Vienna he was to some degree unwell. During the previous summer months on vacation he had lived sensibly, enjoying the pure air of the Austrian countryside, walks, good food, and modest drinking. His friends there suggested that he was in robust health and had ample creative energy. Back in Vienna, he was easily deflected from the ordered way of life which had proved beneficial to his now fragile health. But he was content with the change, and was probably enjoying again the seedy sexual underworld of Vienna. Many of those whom formerly he could have numbered among his friends, and who were now established in respectable society in the city, distanced themselves from him. Amongst these was Leopold Sonnleithner who, while critical of Schubert's behaviour, was still helping him wherever he could with his career. Others found that Schubert was increasingly forgetful or neglectful of them, as he had been in the critical years 1821–2.

Schubert's neglect of old friends is exemplified in his behaviour towards Anton and Marie Ottenwalt when they visited Vienna in late November and stayed with her brother Franz's parents-in-law, the Wanderers, in the

---

[6] Ibid. 32, 38.

Nussdorf suburb. Herr Wanderer was a surgeon. His wife Babette, with her two unmarried daughters, had met Schubert in Linz a few months earlier, when Gahy accompanied them on their summer vacation. In a letter to Josef von Spaun describing their visit, Ottenwalt sounded less than content with Schubert's social conduct, very much aware of his 'passions of an eagerly burning sensuality'; and yet the strength of his criticisms was alleviated by Schubert's good relationship with other friends: 'he seems to have truly devoted sentiments for friends. He is cheerful and, I hope, well too . . .'. Of Kupelwieser, Ottenwalt wrote: 'He is . . . keeping more to himself, so that Schubert and Schwind mourn the loss of a good pal and more generally, the decline of the old circle.'[7] His wife added a relevant postscript for her much-loved brother:

At Schober's . . . we spent an evening too, where Schubert sang really beautifully and played [duets] with Gahy . . . About Schubert I have good reason to complain, for he did not once come to see me, which was very noticeable compared with the assiduous visits of the others [friends in Vienna], and yet he seemed so at home with us at Linz; yet when I saw him again at Schober's, and so friendly, I could not be angry with him after all: one must make allowances for such genius.[8]

When Schwind wrote to Schubert on 1 September 1825 telling him that Worzischek, who had been first Court organist since 1824, was dying, he assumed that Schubert would be interested in applying for the position. He added: 'So far as I can gather, to make a success of it will be a matter of grinding the organ on a given theme. There must surely be an organ in Gmunden where you can practise.'[9] If one of Anselm Hüttenbrenner's recently rediscovered unpublished memoirs of Schubert (written in 1860) is to be believed, then Schwind may have had good reason for this assumption. Hüttenbrenner wrote that one summer, presumably that of 1825, considerable effort on Schubert's behalf was made by the influential Court Music Count Dietrichstein, helped by recommendations from Weigl, Mosel, and Vogl, to win for Schubert the position of Imperial Court organist. In advance of Worzischek's death, and without the post being advertised, Schubert was offered it. Had this not been an internal appointment, there would have been competition for the post and, as Schwind suggested, skill in improvisation at the organ would have been an important requirement. As it was, Schubert was not interested. He declined the invitation, and with it the opportunity for a steady and reliable income. After some time Simon Sechter, the deputy organist, was appointed; the position of deputy went to Schubert's old associate of 1816, Assmayr. (In 1822

---

[7] *Doc.* 476, *Dok.* 326.   [8] Ibid.   [9] *Doc.* 452, *Dok.* 310.

Ferdinand Schubert, recognized in his day as a fine organist,[10] had competed unsuccessfully along with Sechter and others for the position of first Court organist.) Although those wishing to help Schubert may have been upset at his lack of enthusiasm for the post, he seems to have set his sights on the more prestigious and demanding position of Vice-Kapellmeister, which had been vacant since 1824, when Kapellmeister Salieri had retired and his deputy, Eybler, appointed to succeed him.[11] Meanwhile, towards the end of 1825, with this ecclesiastical appointment in mind, Schubert set to work on revising the first version of the Mass in A flat, which he had hoped to dedicate to the emperor or empress. He completed the second version early in 1826. In addition, he had managed to persuade Diabelli to publish, in the summer of 1825, several of his earlier short sacred works (which appeared as Opp. 45–8, D739, D136, and D223) and the Mass in C D452. A few weeks later, on 8 September, all except one of these (the Offertorium D136) were performed in the church of St Ulrich (or Maria Trost) on the feast of the Blessed Virgin, presumably with Ferdinand Schubert either directing or playing the organ.[12] Ferdinand had now been living in Vienna's western suburb of St Ulrich with his family for some two years, and here, as was his custom, he had soon made his not insignificant musical talents available to the church.

As already mentioned, Schubert had been forced to wait until 1821 before he was considered acceptable as a member (and performing member) of the Gesellschaft der Musikfreunde. By 1825 there were almost 1,000 members, of whom some 400 hundred were performing members. Here, in only four years, he had established for himself a considerable reputation as a composer; and the number of performances of his music, although exclusively of songs and quartets, at the Thursday-evening chamber concerts of the society was second only to those of Rossini's, and surpassed those of the music of Mozart and Beethoven.[13] These musical entertainments (*Abendunterhaltungen*), or 'club' concerts, were arranged by different members of the society. There were usually six or seven items in each programme, the first almost always by tradition a string quartet or quintet, those by Haydn, Mozart, Beethoven, and Mayseder (the violinist who had played in the 1814 performance of Schubert's Mass in F at the Lichtental church) featuring most frequently overall in the years 1821 to 1828. The final item was virtually always an operatic ensemble or the finale of an act, with piano accompaniment, and often with soloists and chorus, so as to

---

[10] E. Benedikt, 'Ferdinand und Franz Schubert zu Ostern 1820 in Altlerchenfeld', *Brille*, 13 (1994), 79–80.
[11] *Doc.* 521n, *Dok.* 355n.   [12] *Doc.* 455, *Dok.* 312.
[13] Biba, 'Schubert und die Gesellschaft der Musikfreunde', 25.

involve as many performing members of the society as possible. In between there were likely to be one or two other operatic excerpts—a solo aria, solo ensemble, or both—and one or two instrumental solos or ensembles of various kinds. On almost every occasion between 1821 and 1828 when Schubert's vocal music was performed there was just one work of his, and this either a *Lied* or a vocal ensemble. On just three evenings both a *Lied* and an ensemble were included. Schubert's *Lieder* were generally placed second in the programme, after a string quartet (or a quintet). His vocal ensemble, frequently a male-voice quartet, came towards the end. In evenings of such varied musical entertainment it is surprising that not once, during his lifetime, was an instrumental piece of Schubert's played. Despite this, by 1825, Schubert had friends in high places in the society; he was honoured for what he had already achieved, and still two years off 30, had much expected of him. His election as one of twenty deputies to the committee of the Gesellschaft early in September, which gave him the stamp of respectability, took place while he was in Gastein. That he received a total of thirty votes, only three less than Worzischek, one of the most respected members of the society, and thirteen more than the Court Kapellmeister, Josef Weigl,[14] is proof of his secure position in the musical establishment.

Schubert's growing musical reputation at the start of 1826 was reflected in his close association with the committee of the Gesellschaft der Musikfreunde and its small executive core of directors, who had considerable power and influence in the musical life of Vienna. It was attested by the circulation of engraved or lithographed copies of two portraits of himself painted in 1825, by Rieder[15] and Teltscher,[16] which were now available for purchase in Vienna. His music was fairly frequently featured in concerts, and a considerable amount of it, especially songs and piano music, was being published. Those publishers showing interest in his compositions included Sauer & Leidesdorf, Matthias Artaria,[17] Pennauer,[19] Thadäus Weigl (younger brother of Josef Weigl), and Hans Georg Nägeli (the Swiss publisher). Schubert's pleasant accommodation in the Fruhwirthaus and his way of life as it appeared to Vienna's musical world fitted with his status as an apparently successful composer in that world. They were also in keeping with a modest but regular income; unfortunately, this he did not have.

Vogl returned from Italy in April (1826), shortly afterwards to announce his engagement to Kunigunde, the daughter of an artist and former custo-

[14] Biba, 25–6.　　　　[15] *Doc.* 477–8, *Dok.* 326–7.　　　　[16] *Doc.* 503, *Dok.* 343.

[17] Artaria published the Gastein Piano Sonata in D D850 and *Divertissement à l'hongroise* D818 for piano duet, for which two works Schubert received a total fee of 300 fl. KM.

[18] Cappi & Co.'s publications included Schubert's Dances D783 in Jan. 1825.

[19] Pennauer published the Piano Sonata in A minor D845, dedicated to the Archduke Cardinal Rudolph.

dian of the Belvedere art gallery, Josef Rosa. They were married on 26 June, a few weeks before the bridegroom's fifty-eighth birthday. Little is heard of Vogl in Schubert's musical circles during most of this year. Indeed, the two men may have seen very little of each other until the end of 1826 when once again they appeared together, performing Schubert's songs. Meanwhile Schubert continued to delight friends and acquaintances with his own performances, both playing and singing, as at Schober's on 10 January, and at Sophie Müller's. At the actress's salons he also sometimes played duets with his new duet partner, Jenger, who had recently arrived in Vienna from Graz.

While some of the friends from Schober's circle were amusing themselves during the carnival season of 1826 at countless balls, Schubert was busy composing vocal works, including the Goethe 'Wilhelm Meister' settings. On 19 and 30 January he attended two rehearsals of his String Quartet in D minor ('Der Tod und das Mädchen') D810, composed two years previously, before its first performance on 1 February. This première of the second of his three last and great quartets took place at the home of a colleague and acquaintance, Josef Barth, a tenor in the Court chapel choir, and formerly a singer in concert performances of Schubert's male-voice quartets. Barth lived at this time in the inner-city winter palace of Prince Josef Schwarzenberg, in whose household he held an official position. The string quartet was repeated shortly afterwards, also at a private concert, in the home of Franz Lachner, with whom he had been acquainted for the past three or four years. Lachner, a young Bavarian (b. 1803), was now an assistant conductor at the Kärntnertor-Theater.

Another aspect of Schubert's musical life at this time is revealed in his participation in a private performance at the home of a distinguished lawyer in Vienna, Karl Josef Pratobevera, on 17 February. The occasion was the birthday of Pratobevera, in celebration of which a melodrama for speaker and piano, composed by Schubert at the request of the family, was performed. The melodrama, entitled *Abschied von der Erde* (Farewell to the Earth) D829, was the final monologue of a dramatic one-act poem, *Der Falke*, by the dedicatee's law-student son, Adolf. Members of the Pratobevera family had become enthusiasts for Schubert's music, and the composer is known to have attended their home on several occasions. Whether he was there each time in a professional (paid) capacity or as an acquaintance is not clear.[20]

During 1825 and 1826 Schubert's contacts with the well-respected four Fröhlich sisters increased. Anna was a singing-teacher at the

---

[20] It is possible that it was in this house that, some time between 1826 and his death, he arrived drunk for a party, and subsequently behaved disgracefully: see p. 152 above.

Conservatoire, for whose female students he composed his setting of the Psalm 23 in December 1820. Barbara (Betti) married the flautist Ferdinand Bogner (also a professor at the Conservatoire), for whom Schubert is thought to have composed early in 1824 the 'Trockne Blumen' Variations for flute and piano D802. Josefine, a fine contralto, sang Schubert's songs. Grillparzer was often at the house of the Fröhlich sisters, sometimes in attendance on the beautiful Katharina, with whom he had fallen in love. The Bogners also frequented the musical salons of Sophie Müller, where they sometimes met Schubert. He was still a welcome guest at Sophie Müller's, both at musical salons, at more informal musical occasions, and at her table for small luncheon or supper parties, although the intense period of their friendship and music-making together early in 1825 was never resumed.

Despite the paucity of records concerning the relationship between Schubert and Schober, and the complete absence of any information about their attending theatres or concerts together, it has been clear that the men were, for extended periods of their lives, on terms of considerable intimacy. Schubert was frequently one of those present when Schober, who enjoyed entertaining friends and acquaintances (and liked the influence this gave him over them), opened his home for a party, a Schubertiad, or dancing and, in the earlier years, for meetings of the Bildung Circle and reading-circle. Thus the composer was present at a party at Schober's given in the Upper Bäckerstrasse apartment on 10 January 1826.[21] On this occasion Bauernfeld, knowing in advance that Schubert was to perform songs of his own composition and wanting to bring the composer and the poet Johann Gabriel Seidl together again, invited Seidl to this 'feast of song'.[22] A few weeks later Schubert composed the first of his eleven settings of Seidl's poems, six of them written during this year. Schubert was again present four days later when Schober invited his friends to a sausage-dance.[23] On this occasion, Schubert was persuaded to play for the dancers. Shortly after this, Bauernfeld noted in his diary how one afternoon he went alone to Schober's home, where he became aware of Frau von Schober's distress and anger at her son's attitude and the manner in which he was squandering her inheritance. Bauernfeld wrote: 'He is unfortunately frequently quarrelling with his good mother, who disapproves of his way of life.'[24] After living in their home for several weeks towards the end of 1825, Bauernfeld had now moved to a simple but less stressful abode in the Landstrasse suburb; but he was well placed to interpret the strained relationship between mother and son.

---

[21] *Doc.* 503, *Dok.* 343.   [22] Ibid.   [23] *Doc.* 504, *Dok.* 343.   [24] WL i. 37.

Although Schober enjoyed hosting parties at which Schubert's songs featured, there must be considerable doubt as to the depth of his interest in music. Bauernfeld, on the other hand, was certainly a music-lover, and a fair pianist. On Sunday, 19 February he went with Schubert to one of the Gesellschaft der Musikfreunde's grand Sunday midday concerts held in the assembly hall, the Redoutensaal, of the Imperial Palace, the Hofburg. The programme included Beethoven's Egmont Overture and Second Symphony and the 'Hallelujah' Chorus from Handel's *Messiah*. Schubert, newly elected an official of the Gesellschaft, ate together with Bauernfeld after the concert, and they then moved on to an afternoon subscription concert given by the Schuppanzigh Quartet in the hall of the Gesellschaft. The programme included a quartet by Haydn and a Mozart string quintet. Grillparzer was also present at this concert. Bauernfeld summed up the afternoon as 'everything heavenly'.[25]

Bauernfeld and, perhaps to a lesser degree, Schubert, were beginning to show impatience with Schober. On 8 March Bauernfeld wrote of the friends in his diary:

Schober surpasses us all in mind, and much more so in speech! Yet there is much in him that is artificial, and his greatest strengths threaten to be suffocated in idleness.—Schwind's is a glorious pure nature—though always fermenting, as if he were going to burn himself out. Schubert has the right mixture of the idealist and realist. The world seems fair [*schön*] to him. Mayerhofer [his friend Ferdinand] is simple and natural, for all that Schober asserts that he is a kind of easy-going intriguer.—And I? Ah, if only one could know oneself! Until I have done something worthwhile I am no human being.[26]

And at the end of March he wrote: 'Schubert and I hold faithfully together against many a Schoberian folly. Moritz wavers. He is completely at the command of the [his] sweet Anne Page [Nettl Hönig].'[27]

In the last week of February Bauernfeld received the final, and much-needed, payment for his work on the Shakespeare translations, with which he thought he had now finished.[28] 'And now what shall I live on?', he added. His studies completed, he faced a period of several months before the autumn, when he was likely to be appointed to one of the junior government positions which were offered to young law graduates. He would start at the bottom of the ladder, probably working only four hours a day, in the mornings. This would provide him with sufficient income for the necessities of life, while still leaving him plenty of time to pursue his career

[25] *Doc.* 510, *Dok.* 347, WL i. 38.   [26] *Doc.* 516, *Dok.* 351.
[27] *Doc.* 517, *Dok.* 351, WL i. 38.   [28] WL i. 38.

as an author. But meanwhile he had no source of income. Fortunately for him, early in April his friend Ferdinand Mayerhofer von Grünbühel, formerly a sailor in the imperial navy, then professor of mathematics at the Wiener Neustadt Military Academy and a collaborator with Bauernfeld on the New Vienna Shakespeare edition, was commissioned to survey and map parts of Carinthia. To do this, he would have to travel there for a period of several months, equipped for the task by the military authorities, with an adequate allowance to cover expenses. When Mayerhofer invited Bauernfeld to join him, on the understanding that they would be sharing the allowance, his friend readily accepted.[29] For Bauernfeld, this would be a cheap holiday, a 'journey into the blue',[30] during which he would have opportunities not only to enjoy new scenery, but also to write poetry and plays. After a celebratory farewell meal with friends in Vienna, including Schubert, Schwind, and Schober, they set out early on the morning of 15 April on travels that were to keep Bauernfeld away from the city until the end of July.[31]

Bauernfeld left Vienna with a specific request from Schubert: that he should write an opera libretto on the theme of *Der Graf von Gleichen*. This was the subject for an opera on which, after some initial disagreement they had finally agreed. By the end of May the libretto was finished, and Schubert informed. Since the end of 1823, when he had composed incidental music for *Rosamunde*, Schubert had shown little interest in writing again for the theatre and had no incentive to do so. Now, with the promise of this new libretto, his interest was reawakened. Bauernfeld, after separating from Mayerhofer, stopped for a while in Gmunden and, knowing of Schubert's wish to return to the town and Lake Traun area, he suggested his friend should join him there. He would then be able to hand over the libretto of *Der Graf von Gleichen* to the composer. However, in a letter of 10 July Schubert explained that, for financial reasons, it was impossible for him to travel. But he was eager for the return of Bauernfeld to Vienna, both to enjoy again his company and to receive from him the promised libretto. There was now a reason for urgency: the Kärntnertor-Theater management had approached him anew about another opera. He needed the play; and he needed the money a completed opera might bring:

come to Vienna as soon as possible. Duport [Barbaja's administrator] wants an opera from me, but the libretti I have set so far do not please at all, so it would be splendid if your libretto were favourably received. Then at least there would be money, if not fame as well! . . .

Please do come as soon as possible!

Because of your opera.[32]

---

[29] WL i. 38.   [30] Ibid. 39.   [31] *Doc.* 523–4, *Dok.* 356.   [32] *Doc.* 539, *Dok.* 366–7.

A postscript to this letter is also of interest, as it adds to the evidence of Schubert's good reputation and the affection he inspired in friends in Linz. He told Bauernfeld that, if he stopped in Linz on his way back to Vienna, 'you need only mention my name to be well received'.

Back in Vienna, Bauernfeld proved a good friend to Schubert, his company cheerful and stimulating. It seems likely that he had been behind their applications early in the year for membership of the Ludlams Höhle club in the city. This club, named after a play by one Oehlenschläger which was performed at the Theater an der Wien in December 1817, was active in the 1820s as an informal meeting-point for men connected with the arts, notably writers, composers, actors, and singers. A fair proportion of the 100 members were foreigners, coming from Berlin, Naples, St Petersburg, Copenhagen, and Ireland. The members included Salieri, Castelli, Weber, Moscheles, Rellstab, Rückert, and Gyrowetz, and friends of Schubert such as Assmayr, Josef Götz, and Ludwig Tietze (both singers who took part in performances of Schubert's music), Karl Pachler (with whom Schubert was to stay in the next year in Graz), Josef Kupelwieser, Seidl, and, from 4 March 1826, Grillparzer.[33] The scene was one in which both Schubert and Bauernfeld could have felt very much at ease. Some of the members were obviously very distinguished in their fields, but the high jinks and buffoonery they got up to at meetings were legion. Weber, for one, in 1823 was at first totally bemused by the goings-on;[34] but he was grateful later for the kindness shown to him there at the time of performances of *Euryanthe*. All members bore pseudonyms peculiar to their achievements. Thus Weber was 'Agathus, der Zieltreffer, Edler von Samiel' (concocted from characters in *Freischütz*), and Grillparzer was 'Saphokles Istrianus' (punning on his play *Sappho*). Although there was apparently nothing subversive in the deliberations or antics of members of the club, it eventually excited the interest and concern of Prince Metternich's security officers who, stimulated into action by a disaffected unsuccessful applicant for membership, raided the premises in April 1826, three or four days after Bauernfeld left Vienna. Some members, including Grillparzer, who had only recently joined, were put under house arrest while their homes were thoroughly searched for incriminating evidence. Nothing was found, but the Ludlams Höhle never again opened its doors. For Bauernfeld and Schubert, who had by now both been accepted but not yet inducted as members, the demise of the club must have come as a disappointment. And yet Schubert was surely relieved at escaping, if only by the skin of his teeth, a second confrontation with the police.

[33] Porhansl, 'Auf Schuberts Spuren in der "Ludlamshöhle" '.
[34] J. Warrack, *Carl Maria von Weber*, 2nd edn. (Cambridge, 1976), 304.

In the early part of 1826 Schubert was having some success in getting his music published, and also with its reception. On 1 March the Leipzig *Allgemeine musikalische Zeitung* published a lengthy and complimentary review of his Piano Sonata in A minor D845, the last and by far the most impressive of his three piano sonatas in this key, which had just appeared in print. The seven Walter Scott settings which were so popular with many private audiences, particularly during the composer's 1825 tour with Vogl, were issued on 5 April (by Artaria), and other songs on the following day by Thaddäeus Weigl. But Schubert needed more income than publications alone could provide. His sights had long been set on the position of Vice-Kapellmeister of the Court chapel. In his application on 7 April 1826, Schubert underlined his suitability for the post: he was a native of Vienna, son of a schoolmaster, and aged 29; he had enjoyed the 'most gracious privilege of being for five years a pupil of the Imperial and Royal Seminary as a boy-chorister of the Court'; in composition he had received 'thorough instruction' from the recently retired Salieri, and he enclosed the reference Salieri had written for him in 1819 stating that he was 'entirely suited to any Kapellmeister's post'.[35] Schubert also claimed that his compositions, both vocal and instrumental, were known 'not only in Vienna, but throughout Germany', and he already had among his compositions in readiness for performance 'five Masses with accompaniments for larger and smaller orchestras'. Finally he added an optimistic note: 'he has not the advantage of employment and hopes by means of an assured career to attain fully to his artistic goal'.[36] The competition was intense for this position, the applicants including Ignaz von Seyfried, Adalbert Gyrowetz, Konradin Kreutzer, and Wenzel Würfel, all of whom were already established professional conductors and composers in Vienna, and also, rather surprisingly, Anselm Hüttenbrenner. In the event, and supposedly to save further expense from the Court coffers, early in January 1827 it was announced that Josef Weigl, who was already Kapellmeister at the Kärntnertor-Theater, had been appointed, and was required to fulfil the demands of the Court chapel jointly with those of the theatre, without further payment (though ultimately this was not the case). The applicants were informed at the end of that month. But throughout 1826 Schubert had cherished the hope that he might be successful.[37]

In May Schubert was clearly depressed and unable to compose, despite the presence in Vienna for at least part of the time of his old friend Anselm Hüttenbrenner.[38] However, by the end of the month he was a little brighter and able to write a longish letter to Bauernfeld and Mayerhofer, with some

---

[35] *Doc.* 126, *Dok.* 86.   [36] *Doc.* 520–1, *Dok.* 354.   [37] *Doc.* 599, *Dok.* 404.
[38] *Doc.* 527n, *Dok.* 359n.

ironic content: 'Please don't stay away so long, it is very sad and miserable here—boredom has taken the upper hand too much already. From Schober and Schwind nothing but lamentations are to be heard, far more heart-rending than those we heard during Passion Week.—I have hardly been to Grinzing once since you left, and with Schwind not at all . . .'.[39] He wrote of *Die Zauberflöte*, performed at the Theater an der Wien that it had been done 'quite well'; of *Der Freischütz* at the Kärntnertor-Theater that it had been done 'very badly'; while he had enjoyed enormously the comic farce (with songs) *Herr Josef und Frau Baberl* at the suburban popular theatre in the Leopoldstadt, describing it as 'incomparable'. He praised Bauernfeld's poems, especially one he had sent to the composer with his last letter, and then added: 'I am not working at all. The weather here is really dreadful, the Almighty seems to have foresaken us altogether, the sun simply refuses to shine. It is May, and we still cannot sit in the garden! Awful! appalling!! ghastly!!! and the most cruel thing on earth for me!'[40] That he was not working, with a depression aggravated by bad weather and absence of bright sunlight, is to some degree confirmed by the lack of any known compositions dating from this month. At the end of the letter Schubert was in more hopeful mood: 'Schwind and I intend going to Linz with Spaun in June. We can arrange a meeting there or at Gmunden, only let us know for certain—as soon as possible. Not in two months' time. Farewell both!'[41] By June the sun was shining again and Schubert, his depression having passed, was back at work. During the last ten days of that month, he completed the last of his three great string quartets, that in G D887.

During the period that Schubert was depressed, Schwind was also in low spirits, and no great company for anyone. As Schubert wrote to Bauernfeld: 'Schwind is quite in the dumps about Nettl!'[42] Schwind had already told Bauernfeld in a letter that his love affair was progressing badly after she had accused him of 'want of religion', to which he had angrily retorted: 'Go and fall in love with the Pope!'[43] Schober, on the other hand, was at present a more cheerful companion, but unfortunately for Schubert now seldom available. After recovering from some indisposition earlier in the summer, he had been driven by financial necessity to try his hand again at a profession, this time as a businessman managing a lithographic institution. Meanwhile, he and his mother had moved from their Vienna apartment into accommodation in the north-westerly suburb of Währing.

In June Schober wrote a long letter to Bauernfeld explaining his changed situation.[44] He and his mother had to vacate their pleasant apartment in

[39] *Doc.* 528, *Dok.* 360.   [40] *Doc.* 528–9, *Dok.* 360.   [41] Ibid.
[42] *Doc.* 539, *Dok.* 367.   [43] WL i. 46.   [44] Ibid. 46–8.

Vienna to make room, at short notice, for the military representative of Milanese nobility and his family (Milan being then part of the Austro-Hungarian empire), who had been posted to Vienna.[45] Schober found the move difficult, especially on account of the inconvenience caused by having to leave the apartment well equipped with domestic furnishings, some of which had to be bought in specially and in accordance with the new tenants' requirements. He was therefore grateful during this time for the assistance of the tall, gawky young conductor Franz Lachner, who called each day to see how he could help. Throughout the move, Schober's mother may have been of little assistance. She was still grieving for her younger daughter Sophie, who had died early in 1825, less than two years after her marriage to Zechentner. Schober was now the only surviving child, after the deaths of his elder brother Axel and his two sisters. There was considerable tension between mother and son, as Bauernfeld had observed early in the year. She, an unhappy and often lonely woman, despaired of his way of life; he in turn was irritated by what he considered to be her constant complaining. That money was short, largely as a result of Schober's profligate lifestyle and refusal to settle to any career, was evident to all his close friends, and there was some sympathy for his mother. The worsening of their financial situation presumably meant that, whereas in early days Schubert had lived rent-free with them, by now the Schobers were only too pleased to accept payment from first Kupelwieser and then Bauernfeld when they lodged temporarily with them late in 1825. That neither painter nor writer remained very long in their home may have been a consequence of the uncomfortable atmosphere created by the unhappy relationship between mother and son.

The tension between the Schobers eased somewhat after the move to Währing and Franz von Schober's entering upon paid employment. He described for Bauernfeld how this entailed an early-morning rise at 7 a.m., and daily travel into Vienna by coach. He found it very inconvenient that he usually missed the 1.30 p.m. public coach home, and then had to face the prospect of the drag on foot back to Währing through the summer heat of early afternoon. The business, on the other hand, was going quite well, and in Währing he enjoyed the pleasant countryside, although he complained with some irony of noisy country neighbours. He also mentioned that he was expecting Schubert to arrive that day to stay with him: 'I only hope he keeps his word.'[46] A few weeks earlier Schober had complained to Schubert that not once did he visit him while he was ill (in May), to which Schubert replied with naïvety, and no doubt unconscious ineptitude: 'But you are never to be found at home!'[47] (In fact, the most likely explanation for not visiting his friend was his own depression at this time.) If Schubert did not arrive in Währing that day in June, then this was certainly not the first occasion that he failed to keep an appointment. His unreliability was legendary. He certainly spent some time in Währing during July; for it was here in this month, as he wrote on his manuscripts, that he composed four vocal works (D888–D891), including the popular Shakespeare settings, 'Ständchen' (Serenade: Hark, hark, the lark) and 'Who is Sylvia?'.

Bauernfeld arrived back in Vienna after his three-month absence in late July, receiving a great welcome when he alighted from the Danube boat at Nussdorf. It was evening, and Schubert and Schwind had been awaiting his arrival in the nearby coffee-house. 'Where is the opera?' asked Schubert (according to Bauernfeld). 'Here!' was the author's reply. 'I solemnly handed him the *Graf von Gleichen*.'[48] The three men left at once for Währing to join Schober. Here 'according to the old custom, we all spent the night together, and how much we had to tell! Poetry is over [for Bauernfeld], the prose of life begins anew.'[49] But 'poetry', here used figuratively, was not yet over for Bauernfeld in practice; he received a further request from the editors of the New Vienna Shakespeare edition to translate the poems and sonnets of Shakespeare. At length, on 10 September, Bauernfeld, now desperately in need of permanent employment, received news of his appointment as a junior official in the Lower Austrian county government at the Landhaus: 'It is as though I were under sentence to be hanged.'[50] Like many young men about to begin unrewarding work in bureaucratic Vienna at this time, he dreaded the boredom and restrictions it would entail. There was real joy, however, in Schubert's favourable reaction to Bauernfeld's opera libretto, despite well-founded fears that it might be rejected by the government censors on account of its bigamous theme.

The exuberance of Bauernfeld's reception on his return to Vienna did not blind him to the state of his friends. As we have seen, Schubert was 'ailing . . . Schwind morose, Schober idle, as usual, and as to myself, there's still travel fever in my blood!'[51] Schubert was in some way sick. Whether because of depression, a resurgence of symptoms of syphilis, or for some other reason, his condition had deteriorated. Ill health could have dulled his initial urge to set to work immediately on the opera despite, as Bauernfeld saw it, his continuing enthusiasm, which is supposed to have survived undiminished even after they heard from the censors in October that the play was unacceptable in its present form. A few weeks before hearing that the

[47] *Doc.* 532, *Dok.* 362.   [48] *Doc.* 545, *Dok.* 370.   [49] Ibid.   [50] WL i. 51.
[51] *Doc.* 548, *Dok.* 372.

censors had rejected Bauernfeld's libretto, on Sunday, 17 September, Schubert attended the wedding of his old friend Leopold Kupelwieser to Johanna Lutz. Tradition has it that on this happy occasion Schubert very willingly took his seat at the piano for the dancing that followed, and would allow no one else to relieve him throughout the evening. As was customary, and to Schubert's sorrow, after his marriage Kupelwieser withdrew completely from meetings of the friends in inns and coffee-houses, although he and his wife continued to attend Schubertiads, as they had at Spaun's, and some concerts which included Schubert's music.

In the late summer of 1826 increasing financial problems forced Schubert to leave his pleasant lodgings in the Fruhwirthaus and move first to the Schobers' home in Währing and later, on their return to Vienna, to their apartment in the Bäckerstrasse. Financial necessity also impelled him to approach publishers again, with a view to selling more of his compositions. The Swiss publisher Nägeli, who had first made contact with Schubert the previous summer, was still interested in obtaining a piano sonata from him for a series he was producing; and Schubert responded promptly to this request (which was passed on to him by Czerny, acting as a go-between), agreeing to supply a sonata on condition that he received advance payment of 120 fl. KM.[52] Unfortunately, nothing came of this correspondence as the series petered out.[53] On 17 August Schubert wrote letters to both H. A. Probst and to Breitkopf & Härtel in Leipzig in an attempt to awaken their interest in his music, offering them a choice from songs, string quartets, piano sonatas, and the Octet. To Breitkopf he added: 'In any case I should regard it as a special honour to enter into relations with so old and famous an art establishment',[54] and to Probst a similar expression. Two weeks later Probst replied that he was: 'very gladly prepared to contribute towards the furtherance of your artistic reputation so far as lies in my power. Only I must frankly confess to you that our public does not yet sufficiently and generally understand the individual and often brilliant but perhaps now and then somewhat curious procedures of your creations.'[55] He went on to ask, in the light of this proviso and in order to attempt to break into the market slowly but successfully, that Schubert should first submit some songs and piano music, both solo and duet, suitable for amateur performers of modest accomplishment. Two weeks later Breitkopf & Härtel in their answer proposed that, as the firm was 'as yet wholly unacquainted with the commercial success' of his compositions,[56] he might be willing in the first instance to accept instead of payment a number of free copies of any works of his they published:

[52] *Doc.* 536, *Dok.* 365. [53] *Doc.* 541, *Dok.* 368. [54] *Doc.* 547–8, *Dok.* 372.
[55] *Doc.* 549–50, *Dok.* 373–4. [56] *Doc.* 551, *Dok.* 374.

we propose that you begin by sending us one or two pieces for the pianoforte, solo or duet. If our hopes of a favourable success are in any way fulfilled, so that we may be able to offer you a decent cash remuneration for the following works, we shall esteem it a pleasure to have thereby made relations with us agreeable for you.[57]

Such arrangements, more suitable for a beginner than a composer already well known in Vienna, were not what Schubert was looking for. He needed his financial rewards immediately. Despite this, he appears to have offered Probst three of his compositions, unsuccessfully as it turned out on this occasion; on what terms is not known. With Breitkopf, the negotiations went no further.

The affection and understanding that existed between Schubert and his brother Ferdinand are clearly perceptible in the letters they exchanged while Schubert was out of Vienna. When they were both in the city there are, understandably, few written references to their meetings or association. But they were most surely in touch in various ways, as was each with their father and his second family in the Rossau schoolhouse. The brothers probably visited the schoolhouse after the birth, on 3 February, of their latest (and last) half-brother. It is possible, but less likely, that they were present three weeks later when, on Thursday, 23 February, their father was honoured with citizen's rights of Vienna (*das Bürgerrecht der Stadt Wien*), and took the citizen's oath—at a cost to himself of 24 fl. KM in taxes. The decree, dated 9 February, announcing the honour, which was awarded on the recommendation of both the local church and the Rossau community, declared that it came in recognition both of Franz Theodor's forty-five years' exemplary service as a schoolteacher and of his seventeen years' charitable work with children from impoverished families.

The award of citizen's rights was certainly an honour, and one which had practical implications for the recipient; but these fell well short of the privileges and entitlements of those who received the more prestigious title of Freeman of the City, which is sometimes mistakenly claimed for Schubert's father. Franz Theodor had done well for his school and its pupils, and he was a conscientious father in his own way; but he did not grow any easier to live with as he grew older. Ignaz presented a somewhat lurid picture of his father's 1824 name-day celebrations, in which the elderly man's pomposity and self-importance, anathema to both Ignaz and Franz, came through only too clearly. He had grown increasingly, and to at least some of his family, embarrassingly deferential and obsequious in his attitude to authority, whether civil or ecclesiastical. But he had worked hard in earlier

---

[57] *Doc.* 551, *Dok.* 374–5.

years in order to be able to buy the Himmelpfortgrund schoolhouse. When this was at length sold in the autumn of 1826, Schubert's share was just 200 fl. KM, not a large sum but one which, in his present financial predicament, he could certainly use, if only to pay off accumulated debts.[58]

Whatever music Schubert may or may not have been working on during 1826, he was almost certainly adding the finishing touches to his grand Symphony in C major, begun in summer 1825, but for long mistakenly believed to date from the final year of his life. The term 'grosse' was never used by Schubert, and was introduced after his death to distinguish this lengthy work from the shorter Sixth Symphony in C D589, of 1817–18. The sheer size of the work caused Schubert considerable trouble at the revision stage. Until the late autumn, he continued to amend the manuscript of the symphony until, between 28 November and 31 December, he handed his score to the directors of the Gesellschaft der Musikfreunde.[59] This was eventually sent by the society to copyists, who prepared orchestral parts for a projected performance. Soon after these were completed, in 1827, the symphony was attempted by the orchestra of performing members of the Gesellschaft with a view to including it in one of their Redoutensaal concerts, but found to be too long and too difficult for the players. A month after his death, on 14 December 1828, the Gesellschaft performed the earlier Symphony in C major rather than this, his last completed symphony, in one of the Sunday concerts. The 'Great' Symphony only received its first performance on 21 March 1839 in Leipzig, when the conductor was Mendelssohn.

Schubert's two symphonies in C major were his last completed works in this genre. C major was also the key of his 'Reliquie' Sonata for piano, which he laid aside unfinished earlier in 1825, only a few weeks before he began the last symphony; and meanwhile he had used some of the sonata's best pianistic ideas in his Piano Sonata in A minor, which came between the two. The 'Reliquie' Sonata, in its content and textures, is in many respects symphonic rather than pianistic, and from a comparison between this and the symphony which followed it is apparent that in the sonata Schubert anticipated many features of that symphony. This applies especially to rhythms, repeated and effectively driving motifs, antiphonal writing (as for orchestral strings and woodwind section) and modulatory progressions. Common to both works are the long build-ups to climaxes achieved by repeating short, vivid passages in different keys in striking modulatory format, followed by gradual releases of tension over similar time-scales. I have already suggested in Chapter 8 that the approach and retreat from climaxes

[58] *Doc.* 555–6, *Dok.* 377–8.   [59] Biba, 'Schubert und die Gesellschaft der Musikfreunde', 30.

in the first and third movements of the 'Reliquie' Sonata are associated with an epic character, and it is this powerful epic quality that dominates in the symphony. Just as those intent on developing a new national German opera were looking for a nobler and richer romanticism by choosing subjects based on epic tales of the medieval and chivalric ages, so Schubert was attempting a grand structure for this symphony in an effort to create a serious and intense work with powerful and dramatic effects.

Schubert's presentation of the 'Great' Symphony in C major to the Gesellschaft der Musikfreunde was his only gift to the society, although he had previously made his compositions freely available for its concerts, and for those of the Conservatoire associated with the society. In the early autumn of 1826 he wrote to the directors, the inner core of the executive committee, informing them of his decision to dedicate this, his most recent symphony, to the society.[60] The secretary of the society was Josef Sonnleithner, uncle of the composer's friend and early patron, Leopold. Both Leopold and his father Ignaz were also directors. At the next meeting of the directors, on 9 October, the vice-president, Hofrath Rafael Georg von Kiesewetter, gave notice of Schubert's proposal, the timing of which proved embarrassing. It had already come to the notice of the committee, perhaps via the Sonnleithners, that their young deputy was in straitened circumstances and, in appreciation of his work for the Gesellschaft, they had decided on an earlier occasion to discuss the possibility of awarding Schubert a grant to help tide him over a difficult period. On the same 9 October the sum of 100 fl. KM was agreed, and to avoid any confusion that it might be considered a payment or reward for the now promised symphony, it was to be paid out of the 'expenses' account (*Ausgabe*). The money was to be handed over to the composer as quickly as possible, and before Schubert delivered the symphony. A proviso, which points to the urgency of the settlement of this matter, was added: should the full 100 florins not be immediately available from Gesellschaft funds, then the Secretary himself would make up the sum as a temporary measure so that the whole grant could be paid promptly to Schubert. This was done three days later, the money sent with an accompanying letter from Kiesewetter:

You have repeatedly given proof of interest in the Gesellschaft der Musikfreunde . . . and exerted your excellent talent as a composer on its behalf and particularly that of the Conservatoire.

Appreciating your indubitable excellence as a composer, the Society desires to tender you appropriate proof of its gratitude and esteem and requests you to accept the enclosed, not as a fee, but as a token of the Gesellschaft's sense of

---

[60] *Doc.* 559, *Dok.* 380.

obligation towards you, and of the thanks with which it acknowledges the interest you have shown it.

On behalf of the Governing Body of the Gesellschaft der Musikfreunde in the Austrian Imperial State.

Kiesewetter[61]

Kiesewetter was a distinguished Aulic Councillor and an influential man in the musical world of Vienna. His son Karl[62] and daughter Irene[63] were both acquainted socially with Schubert. Schubert acknowledged receipt of the award on 20 October.[64] As a result of the payment of this grant and the directors' determination to dissociate it entirely from the composer's gift of the symphonic score very shortly afterwards, there was some distortion in the Gesellschaft's records concerning the receipt of the symphony. The result of this distortion and later misunderstandings of existing information was total confusion over the identity of the C major Symphony. The autograph score has been in the possession of the Gesellschaft der Musikfreunde since 1826, but for some 150 years the date of its composition, as given by the composer on the first page of his score, was read as 1828, the last year of Schubert's life, rather than 1825, the year in which Schubert visited Gastein. Since the late 1970s, when paper studies and archival research proved without doubt that this symphony was composed in 1825, it has been accepted that the so-called 'Gastein' Symphony, written in the summer of 1825 and long considered 'lost', and the 'Great' C major Symphony are indeed one and the same. Close examination of the Gesellschaft's records has also been fruitful for the light it has thrown on the role of Schubert in the society. After his election as a deputy in 1825, in June 1827 he was to be elected one of the fifty full representatives (executive members), a position of real responsibility in the affairs of the society. That he fulfilled his responsibilities satisfactorily and conscientiously is suggested by the fact that, after his death, the Gesellschaft took over arrangements, and paid all expenses for his Requiem Mass, held on 23 December 1828 in the Court church of St Augustine in Vienna.

Works of Schubert's were included in four out of seven evening chamber concerts of the Gesellschaft between 16 November and the end of 1826. On 2 December one of his overtures, probably that originally intended for *Alfonso und Estrella* which he had then used for the two *Rosamunde* performances in December 1823, opened an orchestral concert at the Kärntnertor-Theater, a benefit performance for the two Lewy brothers, who were both horn-players in the theatre orchestra. A group of three of

---

[61] *Doc.* 560, *Dok.* 381.   [62] *Doc.* 319, *Dok.* 221.   [63] *Doc.* 473, *Dok.* 323–4.
[64] *Doc.* 562, *Dok.* 382.

his songs was published on 24 November (as Op. 65—D360, D649, D753) and one of his waltzes in a Christmas collection on 23 December. As in the summer months, in November and December he appears to have composed very little, if at all. On the other hand, with the return of Josef von Spaun to Vienna after a long absence, there were many meetings and parties of the friends which Schubert sometimes attended, making it unlikely that he was suffering from the deep depression that periodically resulted in unproductive weeks. Those whom he met with Spaun at the Anchor inn and Bogner's coffee-house at this time included most of the old friends of Spaun's circle left in Vienna who were still bachelors, and several younger ones. (Franz von Hartmann listed the names in diary entries: Schubert, Schwind, Bauernfeld, Sauter (Dinand), Schober, Enderes (then living at Spaun's), Lachner, Enk, Max von Spaun (then visiting his brother), Derffel, Gahy, Haas, Randhartinger, and the von Hartmann brothers.)

Apart from the meetings in hostelries, there were several musical evenings during this period, some of them in Spaun's comfortable apartment. Thus, one Friday evening, on 8 December, there was a party to which Spaun, whose younger brother Max was then staying with him, invited his musical friends in Vienna and some of their old family friends from Linz. Schubert, Schwind, Bauernfeld, Enderes, and Schober were present, along with the young Franz and Fritz von Hartmann. The evening took the usual form of such occasions, beginning with Schubert's music, piano solos, and songs performed by Schubert and Vogl, followed by a 'splendid supper' and lively conversation accompanied by smoking.[65] Exactly a week later Spaun gave another and much bigger party, an occasion generally considered to be the first grand Schubertiad, with some forty guests, male and female. Performances of music by Schubert and then another fine feast were this time followed by dancing. The same friends as in the previous week were there, along with Vogl and his wife and Gahy, who performed with Schubert in the musical part of the evening as singer and duettist. There were several other married couples, including the Witteczeks and Kupelwiesers, and also Babette Wanderer, Baron Schlechta, Grillparzer, Johann Mayrhofer, Huber, and Derffel. Franz von Hartmann mentioned all these by name in his diary; and there may have been more. The evening was a happy one, and afterwards the hard core of friends— Schubert and Schober, Bauernfeld and Schwind, Derffel and the Hartmann brothers—repaired to the Anchor inn, where they continued talking until nearly one o'clock. The next day there was a Schubertiad at the Hönigs'.

Two days later, on the Sunday, Schubert and his friends drove in two

---

[65] *Doc. 568, Dok. 386.*

carriages to the Nussdorf suburb for lunch with the Wanderers (the family of the surgeon, one of whose daughters was married to Franz von Spaun), an outing from Vienna which was organized and paid for by Josef von Spaun. The party consisted of Josef and Max von Spaun, the Hartmann brothers, Schubert, Derffel, Enderes, and Gahy, while Schober, Schwind, and Bauernfeld arrived, with several others, only after lunch. These last two seem to have disturbed the contentment of the gathering, by taking it upon themselves to sing and play some of Schubert's songs, 'quite lamentably' according to Franz von Hartmann;[66] but after some dancing the afternoon guests left and 'the old cosiness returned'. In the now quieter ambience, there was more music-making: 'Schubert sang splendidly, especially 'Der Einsame' [The Solitary One] by Lappe and 'Trockne Blumen' [Dried Flowers] from the *Schöne Müllerin* songs. Betty [Wanderer] too sang three of those songs charmingly. Then Schubert and Gahy again played enchantingly'. The music was followed, in more light-hearted vein, by gymnastics and conjuring tricks, after which the guests rode back to Vienna in the same carriages in which they had arrived, Josef von Spaun, Schubert, Derffel, and Fritz Hartmann in one, Enderes, Max Spaun, Gahy, and Franz Hartmann in the other. After first calling at Spaun's apartment, they set off once again for the Anchor inn, walking 'in pairs, Fritz and Max at the head, then Enderes and Gahy, then Schubert and Pepi [Josef] Spaun, and lastly Derffel and I.' Only at 11.30 did they separate and wend their different ways home. The very next evening, some of those who had so enjoyed their excursion on the previous day were at the Witteczek's home for another Schubertiad.

Spaun had arranged all these events to entertain his younger brother Max, who was the same age as Schubert, on a visit to Vienna from Linz. The programme for Max included visits to the theatre with some of his friends, as well as parties and concerts. Otherwise, almost every evening the brothers met the same core of friends at the Anchor inn or at Bogner's coffee-house. After a full couple of weeks in Vienna, Max von Spaun, known as Spax to his friends, returned home to Linz for Christmas. But the meetings of the friends did not stop. On 30 December a relaxed evening's chatting at the Anchor ended with some harmless horseplay, a snowball fight, which Franz von Hartmann described: 'Spaun is on my side, Fritz and Schober on Schwind's. . . . Spaun protects himself magnificently against the bombardment with his open umbrella. Schubert and Haas take no part in the fight. Home, where the porter [*Hausmeister*] was rude because we rang noisily.'[67] On the next evening Schober hosted a rather quiet, but appar-

---

[66] *Doc.* 574, *Dok.* 390.   [67] *Doc.* 584, *Dok.* 396.

ently convivial New Year's Eve party, attended by Enderes, Spaun, Schwind, Schubert, Bauernfeld, and the von Hartmanns. There were no women present this year. Conversation flowed merrily and they smoked. Shortly before midnight they sat down for supper and waited for midnight to strike. Schober's mother, 'looking like a ghost', joined them as they welcomed in the New Year with glasses of Hungarian Tokay. When the party broke up at two o'clock, the guests 'waded' (*wateten*) off home.[68]

For Schubert the final month of 1826 was a time of delightful, relaxed sociability with good friends centred on the amiable Spaun, and performances of his music to ever appreciative audiences of friends and acquaintances in the homes of some of those friends. By this time he had temporarily moved from the Schobers' home and was living alone, for the last time, on the south-eastern bastion near the Karoline Gate. There are no indications that his health was troubling him; and it is not known for certain what, if anything, he was composing or planning. But he was content at this time, another of the happier periods of his life. By his standards, 1826 was not a productive year. And yet the works he completed included not only the Symphony in C major but also one each of his finest string quartets (June) and piano sonatas (October), both in G major, and some exceptionally fine songs, including those to texts by Goethe (the 'Wilhelm Meister' songs in January), Seidl, Schlechta, and Schulze: no mean achievement.

[68] *Doc.* 585, *Dok.* 396.

10

GLOOM AND CREATIVITY
(1827)

FOR a few weeks from the end of 1826 Schubert lived alone, but in February he returned to the Schobers', to their new home in the smarter surroundings of the Tuchlauben. Here they occupied the second floor of the house known as the Red Hedgehog, next door to the rather grand premises of the Gesellschaft der Musikfreunde, the Blue Hedgehog, which the society had occupied since 1822. Schubert now had the use of two rooms and a 'music closet', presumably an annexe to one of the rooms, and for this comparatively spacious accommodation it is likely that he paid rent. Schober was the manager and possibly joint owner of the Lithographic Institute which was situated in the Michaelerplatz and where he had been employed since the summer of 1826.[1] Although his new apartment was more elegant and larger than that in the Bäckerstrasse, his business was struggling, and he would have been grateful for the little extra income that Schubert's rent provided. For his part, Schubert now had both a pianoforte always to hand and the opportunity to entertain his own guests in the privacy of his rooms.

All in all, 1827 began well for the composer. He was apparently in rather good health; his professional prospects were encouraging; his personal life was enriched both by pleasant lodgings and by the presence in Vienna and favourable influence of Josef von Spaun. Except for a disappointing letter at the end of January intimating that his application for the position of deputy musical director at the Court chapel had been unsuccessful, his career progressed satisfactorily through the year. There were many performances of his music, especially in the weekly subscription series of 'little concerts' of the Gesellschaft der Musikfreunde; and there were some fourteen new publications of his compositions (with opus numbers) in the first five months of the year alone, with more in the pipeline. Thus, finan-

[1] WL i. 48, *Doc.* 828, *Dok.* 554.

cially, his situation was promising. The works that were published (by Diabelli, Haslinger, and Artaria) included not only the customary songs and dances, but also two larger works: the Sonata for Piano in G D894 and the *Rondeau brillant in B minor* for violin and piano D895. His fame as a composer was spreading as performances and new publications of his music were mentioned or reviewed in journals at home and abroad, including Berlin, Leipzig, Frankfurt, Mainz, and London. In June he was elected a full representative (committee) member of the Gesellschaft der Musikfreunde.

In the course of the year Schubert was frequently to be found in the evening among friends at their latest favourite haunt, the Castle of Eisenstadt, a tavern near the Graben in the central area of the city. Towards the end of May, like many of his Viennese friends and their families, he moved out of the city. Until late July he stayed in Dornbach, a village north-west of Vienna famed for its new wine, in the guest-house The Empress of Austria.[2] However, this did not isolate him from the city, and he continued to visit it for both work and pleasure. While in Dornbach, in the middle of June, Schubert began work at last on the opera *Der Graf von Gleichen* D918. Also and for the fourth year in succession in the month of June, after an unproductive period of several weeks he embarked on a new composition of some magnitude. In June 1824 he had begun the piano duets, the Sonata in C ('Grand Duo') and the Eight Variations in A flat; in 1825, the 'Great' C major Symphony; in 1826, the String Quartet in G. In June 1828 he was to start the Mass in E flat. This cyclic pattern had begun after his illness of 1823; it also seems to have run in conjunction with his depressions each spring, which had latterly been accompanied by heavy drinking.

In September Schubert enjoyed a three-week holiday in Graz with his friend Jenger, both of them staying as guests of the Pachler family; and in these surroundings Schubert's music was enthusiastically received. He was already troubled to some degree by recurring headaches, and by the end of the year these were worse, sufficiently so for him to refer to them in a letter to his hostess in Graz.[3] He must have known by this time that these headaches were symptoms of advancing syphilis; and yet neither he nor his friends were unduly worried. Nor did uncertain health deter him from planning a return visit to Graz the next autumn. Even more importantly, headaches and fears of illness did not get in the way of his advancing plans for an important private concert entirely of his own music for the early part of 1828. This was to take place in the concert hall of the Gesellschaft der

---

[2] WL ii. 94.   [3] *Doc.* 679, *Dok.* 457.

Musikfreunde, where many of his vocal works had already received performances in the society's own chamber concerts.

As is normal in human relationships, the personality of each of Schubert's friends or, collectively, of groups of his friends, overlapped with and stimulated different parts of his personality. Yet, as is almost essential for all creative artists, he retained an intensely private dimension, nurtured in solitude; and it was out of this that his greatest music was born. Once he had thrown off the restrictions imposed by classical expression and rejected the ideals which dictated the artist should suppress, in the cause of artistic purity, any overt indulgence of personal feelings in his art, he took on board the Romantic concepts which encouraged the artist to express his own experiences and emotions. Much of Schubert's music now reflected his own intimate world, and this sometimes, as in the gloomy Piano Sonata in A minor D784 written during his illness of early 1823, resulted in highly personal and idiosyncratic statements. After he contracted syphilis, Schubert was often in pain and distress and lost the capacity for uninhibited joy. His music was frequently born out of suffering: the 'sorrows' to which he referred in his notebook of 1824, which, when combined with his 'musical understanding', gave to the world the greatest 'pleasure'. The products of his solitude were not the same as before; the ebullience of some of his earlier music was replaced by determined, even hypomanic energy. His emotional experience had widened, or deepened to include sublime beauty and grandeur, serenity and might, melancholy and mania, grief and eloquence, other-worldliness; but the gentler, more sympathetic parts of his musical universe were now often disturbed by outbursts of violence, anger, and despair, often shocking in their impact. It is of course dangerous to attempt to understand or analyse a composer's motivation through his musical statements, although creations of the Romantic era lend themselves better to this exercise than those of other periods. Another approach is through observation of his relationships, in Schubert's case his marginalization in much of the company he kept, his need for the stimulating company of other creative artists, and the importance to him of solitude.

Schubert was probably never the central character in any social gathering outside musical performances. This is certainly true of the meetings in inns and coffee-houses described in their diaries by the von Hartmann brothers, where Schubert's presence is referred to in very offhand manner. True, as young men from the provinces studying at Vienna University, they (like most others) were unaware of his greatness, even although they were often impressed by his talent for song composition. On the other hand, they were apparently singularly unimpressed by his personality, as is evident by default in the diaries, which were written not for posterity but as records of their own subjective responses to events and occasions at that time. Spaun was for them the centre of the circle of friends; and clearly he was fond of the student brothers. Members of their family in Linz, and particularly their elder sister Anna von Revertera (who had been generously hospitable to Spaun when he was posted to Lemberg in 1825) were also friends of Spaun, who was also very attached to Josef von Gahy, a rather shy but likeable man, slightly younger than himself. Gahy also had a good relationship with Schubert based on his passionate love of music.[4] He was a fine pianist, a much appreciated exponent of Schubert's music for dancing, and one with whom Schubert greatly enjoyed playing piano duets. His description, written some thirty years after Schubert's death, of the composer as duet partner is charming, and unique in its depiction of what good company Schubert could be:

The hours I spent making music with Schubert are among the richest enjoyments of my life and I cannot recall those days without being deeply moved. It was not only that, on such occasions, I learnt much that was new; but the clear, fluent playing, the freedom of conception, the manner of performance, sometimes delicate and sometimes full of fire and energy, of my small, plump partner afforded me great pleasure; this was still further enhanced because it was just on these occasions that Schubert's genial nature was displayed in its full radiance and he used to characterize the various compositions with humorous interpolations, which sometimes included sarcastic, though always pertinent, remarks. My friendly relationship with Schubert (with whom I was on terms of the intimate 'Du') remained unclouded until his death.[5]

Another of Spaun's friends, Karl von Enderes, was a few months older than Spaun; he was an especially gentle and kindly man, and a great admirer of Schubert.[6] Spaun and his friends, like the Hartmanns, Gahy, and Enderes, had much in common in their comfortable, educated, professional backgrounds, and they were socially totally at ease in each others' company. The older men of the group in particular were fond of Schubert and enjoyed a close relationship with him (implied by the familiar 'Du' referred to by Gahy). Their affection was genuine, as was their appreciation of his company and intelligence. When he was in a sociable frame of mind, they valued his fellowship; when he was not, they were tolerant of his moods and social failings. Their primary interest in him, however, was on account of his musical gifts, the joy and pleasure he gave them, the talents that amazed them, and their desire to help him in his career as far as they were able. Probably most of their meetings with him were either in public places of refreshment or entertainment, on excursions they made together, or else

---

[4] *Mem.* 358, *Erin.* 412–13. [5] *Mem.* 176–7, *Erin.* 203. [6] *Mem.* 358–9, *Erin.* 413.

on occasions to which Schubert was invited in order to perform his music for their delectation, and that of their friends. For Spaun, Witteczek, and, in earlier years, Leopold Sonnleithner, such occasions were also intended to advance his reputation and to encourage sales of his songs. It is very unlikely that any of them, even Spaun, viewed Schubert as socially unreservedly acceptable in their own domestic or professional surroundings; and it is doubtful whether the composer received invitations from them to non-musical domestic gatherings. But this would not have upset Schubert; indeed, he would not have wanted it otherwise, and they knew this.

If Schubert was a little short on social graces and unable to enter fully into the social and family lives of some of his middle- and upper-middle-class friends in Vienna, with musicians there were no such restraints. He was increasingly seen in the company of musical colleagues, in particular Lachner, Randhartinger, Slawjk, and Bocklet. In April 1827 Slawjk and Bocklet played, in Schubert's presence, his *Rondeau brillant* for violin and piano at the home of Domenico Artaria. This was a promotional occasion, to celebrate Artaria's publication of the piece.

In the early months of 1827 Schubert attended several Schubertiads and musical evenings with friends. Thus on 12 January Spaun hosted a comparatively small Schubertiad, which took its now customary form. It began with performances of Schubert's songs and piano duets, performed by Vogl, Gahy, and the composer, and ended with the gymnastics (without Schubert taking part) which were now all the rage amongst young men in Vienna, ever since physical education had been popularized by the nationalist and liberal publicist 'Turnvater' Ludwig Jahn in the 1810s. On 15 February Schubert, Schober, and Vogl and his wife were invited to a carnival 'celebratory evening of music, recitation and dancing' given by the wife, Mina (Wilhelmine), of their friend Witteczek.[7] Witteczek, another good friend of Spaun's, for years regularly hosted Schubertiads and was an avid collector of Schubert's music, of which he himself made many copies. During the carnival period there were weekly Saturday-night sausage-dances at Schober's, at some of which Schubert (and Gahy) played. In addition to much musical activity, Schubert was fairly frequently to be found late at night with his friends in either the Anchor or Castle of Eisenstadt inns. Bauernfeld and Schwind were now frequently in Schubert's company.

Schubert had recently, probably towards the end of 1826, discovered Wilhelm Müller's first twelve *Wander-lieder* poems, published as a set in 1823, and to which Müller later added another twelve poems, at the same

---

[7] R. Steblin, 'The Peacock's Tale: Schubert's Sexuality Re-considered', *NCM* 17/1 (1993), 23.

time reordering some of the original twelve. Together these twenty-four poems were published in 1824 as the *Winterreise* (Winter's Journey). Schubert discovered the full cycle later in 1827; but meanwhile throughout February and the early days of March most of his creative energy was expended upon the composition of this, the first part of his *Winterreise* song-cycle.[8] Much speculation about these songs is based on the false premiss that they were the creation of Schubert alone when in a depressed state of mind, already perhaps suffering from premonitions of early death. The first supposition, which overlooks the role of Müller, is of course false. Müller was a young German poet, a little over two years older than Schubert, who wrote the first twelve poems of the cycle in 1821 at a time not of abject despair or unhappiness but of particularly fruitful creativity and contentment. Despite an inherent restlessness (as reflected in his frequent choice of Romantic *Wanderlust* as the theme of his writings), he had recently (in 1821) settled into a happy marriage with a charming young wife of good family and considerable musical accomplishment.[9] His preoccupation with rejection and despair in *Winterreise* had no obvious parallel in his own life; and presumably he had no cause for thoughts or premonitions of his own death. Müller in fact died suddenly in Dessau, his hometown, in his own bed on the night of 30 September 1827 in circumstances usually described as mysterious. In the traditions of nineteenth-century Romanticism, explanations for his death included suggestions that he was assassinated—poisoned on account of spying activities; but there is no evidence to support this theory. His wife affirmed that he died in his sleep of a heart attack.[10] Although Müller's completed *Winterreise* cycle was published in 1824, Schubert only began composing the second half after Müller's death, and the possibility cannot be excluded that he had heard very recently of the poet's demise, or did so just after he began composing the later songs.

Müller had spent two months in Vienna from the end of August 1817 (when he was 22), while *en route* for Italy and Greece; and it was here that he became an ardent philhellenist[11] and supporter of the cause for Greek independence. Vienna at this time was the centre of the Philikí Etairía, an organization founded to promote the independence of Greece from Turkey. Müller came into contact with members of the organization and,

[8] Although the fair copy is dated Feb. 1827, it is possible that he began sketches for the songs a few months earlier, in late autumn or winter of 1826. See S. Youens, *Retracing a Winter's Journey; Schubert's 'Winterreise'* (Ithaca, NY, 1991), 26.

[9] Ibid. 8. [10] Ibid. 9.

[11] S. Youens, *Schubert: Die schöne Müllerin* (Cambridge, 1992), 3.

through this and his interests in Viennese popular theatre and in literature in general, he quickly made friends among the city's artist colony.[12]

If his social activities are anything to go by, Schubert was in no way depressed or sombre when he composed the first twelve *Winterreise* songs. Indeed these twelve songs, and the initial song of the second part, 'Die Post' (The Post), are not radically different in their impact from others of his finest songs written in the last years of his life. These are great songs, of intense and wide-ranging emotions, the music inspired by Müller's straightforward themes and picturesque winter imagery. The traveller, the poet, the rejected lover, the singer of the songs, walks away from the girl he has lost (to a socially more acceptable suitor) and the district where she lives and he has courted her. He is a victim of despair, overcome by self-pity, misery, loneliness, and pain in an empty, hostile, and frozen landscape. Such is the mood of the first twelve songs of *Winterreise*. But the pain and despair of the traveller had not yet unremittingly entered Schubert's soul.

A few days after completing the songs, or most of them, Schubert was with friends (Spaun, Schober, Bauernfeld, and the Hartmann brothers) at the Castle of Eisenstadt inn, where a lively discussion developed on 'the Greeks, the Hungarians and Grillparzer',[13] and on the 'Turks and Lord Cochrane' (who was given command of the Greek navy in March 1827).[14] The interest of Schubert and his friends in the poet of his latest songs, the 'Greek Müller' as he was known, may well have triggered this discussion, which was a topical subject in 1827 at the time of the alliance between Britain, France, and Russia to protect Greece against Turkish attacks. Probably in the course of this meeting, Schubert invited his friends to visit him the next evening at Schober's 'to hear some of the new compositions',[15] about which he had just been telling them. By the time they were all as-sembled that Sunday evening—Spaun, Schwind, Bauernfeld, and the Hartmann brothers, along with Josef Kriehuber (a gifted painter and litho-grapher), his wife of less than five weeks, and her pretty sister Louise Forstner, nicknamed by her admirers 'the flower of the land',[16] Schubert had still not put in an appearance. At length, after Schwind had entertained them by singing several of Schubert's earlier songs, at 9.30 they (presum-ably without the ladies) made their way to the Castle of Eisenstadt, where Schubert also soon arrived and 'won all hearts by his amiable simplicity, despite having disappointed us by his artist's negligence'.[17] Schubert had much on his mind at this time, but the ultimate cause of his ill manners is

---

[12.] C. C. Baumann, *Wilhelm Müller* (Pennsylvania, 1981), 11.

[13] Franz von Hartmann: *Doc. 612, Dok. 412.*

[15] Fritz von Hartmann: *Doc. 613, Dok. 413.*

[17] *Doc. 613, Dok. 413.*

[14] Fritz von Hartmann: ibid.

[16] *Doc. 609, Dok. 410.*

likely to have been an imminent performance of his String Quartet in G major. The very next day (5 March) he wrote a note to Lachner requesting him to hand over to the carrier of the note the score and instrumental parts of this quartet because, as he explained, the violinist Slawjk was arranging a run-through of the work two days later.[18] On that day, the quartet was duly played for the first time, by Slawjk, Lachner, Schubert, and an unnamed fourth musician. On the following day, not only were two vocal works of Schubert's performed, rather than the usual one, in a chamber music concert of the Gesellschaft der Musikfreunde, but the composer himself made one of his rare appearances as accompanist, on this occasion of his friend the tenor Tietze in a performance of his setting of Walter Scott's 'Normans Gesang'.

Anton Schindler, Beethoven's friend and first biographer, was well acquainted with some of Schubert's friends, including Anton and Josef Hüttenbrenner. As a result of these contacts, some time in February 1827 Schindler took copies of sixty of Schubert's songs to Beethoven for his perusal.[19] Beethoven had certainly known of Schubert, who in 1822 had asked for and received his permission to dedicate to him a set of variations for piano duet (Eight Variations on a French Song D624, written in Zseliz in 1818). When Beethoven received the songs he was already a very sick man, a few weeks short of death. Schindler reported that the older composer's attitude to Schubert's music, as at the time of the dedication of the piano duet, may have been tarnished by what Schindler described as the excessive enthusiasm for Schubert's music amongst some of his friends and supporters.[20] Beethoven's later compositions were finding few admirers in Vienna and his popularity had declined over recent years in a manner that made him even more sensitive to current popular tastes and enthusiasms. He may have marked the frequency with which Schubert's name appeared as composer in the programmes of the Gesellschaft der Musikfreunde chamber concerts (for Schubert in 1827 ten times in total, while not once for Beethoven, although the story at the society's grand Sunday concerts was different[21]). If a hard core of the organizers of these concerts was using its influence on Schubert's behalf, Beethoven may have resented it. Be that as it may, according to Schindler (writing in 1831) Beethoven was enormously impressed with the songs he examined early in 1827, exclaiming: 'Truly, in Schubert there dwells a divine spark! . . . If I had had this poem, I would have set it to music too!'.[22] Schindler continued, if with some of his customary unreliable colouring:

---

[18] Ibid.   [19] Schindler: *Mem.* 307, *Erin.* 353.   [20] Ibid.
[21] Biba, 'Schubert und die Gesellschaft der Musikfreunde', 25.   [22] *Mem.* 307, *Erin.* 354.

the respect which Beethoven acquired for Schubert's talent was so great that he now also wanted to see his operas and pianoforte works; but his illness had already developed to such an extent that he could no longer satisfy this wish. Nevertheless he still often spoke of Schubert and prophesied 'that he will still make a great stir in the world' and, at the same time, expressed regret at not having got to know him earlier.[23]

Whether or not Schubert visited Beethoven on his deathbed, as claimed by Schindler[24] and the Hüttenbrenner brothers[25] but denied by Spaun,[26] cannot be determined on the evidence available. However, an account by Friedrich Rochlitz of a visit he made to Vienna in the summer of 1822, the year of publication of Schubert's duet variations dedicated to Beethoven, suggests that the two composers were to some degree personally acquainted at that time. Through the good offices of the violinist Karl Holz, also a friend of Schubert's, Rochlitz, was invited to meet Beethoven in his apartment. Schubert also met Rochlitz, who claimed that Beethoven had spoken to Schubert about him.[27] It has been suggested that the mere presence in Vienna of Beethoven inhibited Schubert's self-confidence and his musical development. This, in my opinion, cannot be true. Schubert certainly did not lack self-confidence in the value of the best of his own music; and he had already shown that he was in no way inhibited in his development of musical genres, not just the *Lied*. He was forward-looking. He was also a compulsive composer and, unlike Beethoven, who was supported by a wealthy patron, from 1825 onwards he was largely dependent for survival on the publication and performance of his music. To some degree he was an opportunist, composing music for people with whom he was in close contact and whose talents he valued and understood; and there were nothing unusual in this. He was also prepared to listen to their comments and advice. Just as he had written the *Rondeau brillant* for his friends Slawjk and Bocklet in October 1826, so in December 1827 and for the same players he composed the Fantasia in C D934 to suit their virtuosic talents. (They gave the first public performance of the Fantasia in the following January.) It is likely that his colleagues Schuppanzigh (violin), Linke (cello), and Bocklet (piano), all of whom he had in mind when he wrote the Piano Trio in E flat D929, had something to do with the cuts he authorized in the last movement of the Trio in 1828,[28] and Bocklet perhaps influenced the cuts to the

[23] Schindler: *Mem.* 308, *Erin.* 354.　　　　　　[24] *Mem.* 325, *Erin.* 373.

[25] *Mem.* 66, 192, *Erin.* 77, 221.　　　　　　[26] *Mem.* 366, *Erin.* 422.

[27] Kreissle, *Schubert*, i. 264; *Allgemeine musikalische Zeitung* (Leipzig), 2 Jan. 1828. (I am indebted to T. G. Waidelich for drawing my attention to this article.)

[28] E. Badura-Skoda, 'The Chronology of Schubert's Piano Trios', in E. Badura-Skoda and P. Branscombe (eds.), *Schubert Studies: Problems of Style and Chronology* (Cambridge, 1982), 294.

first of the *Drei Klavierstücke*, D946, also written in 1828. It is also interesting to note which, and how few, of his early compositions Schubert later
considered worthy of publication. Again, one must wonder whether, had he
lived longer, he might have made efforts to prevent some of his music from
ever coming to light. He would not have been the first or last composer to
conceal, suppress, or even destroy immature works or those that fell short
of his own standards.

When Beethoven died on 26 March 1827, at the age of 56, much of
Vienna was in mourning. The funeral service, which Schubert attended
in the company of Bauernfeld, was held in the afternoon of 29 March
at Holy Trinity church in the Alsergrund parish (not far from the city
orphanage where Ferdinand Schubert had taught from 1810 to 1820, and
opposite the general hospital, where Schubert had been a patient in 1823).
The service was a long one, and afterwards a large crowd followed the
bier to the Währing district cemetery, a distance of about a mile. The
Berlin *Allgemeine musikalische Zeitung* of 23 May (*sic*) described the
scene:

the magnificently decorated bier followed the priests. On the right walked the
Kapellmeisters Eybler, Hummel, Seyfried and Kreutzer, on the left, Weigl,
Gyrowetz, Gänsbacher and Würfel—all holding white crêpe ribbons attached to
the bier. They were accompanied on both sides by a long line of torch-bearers,
including Castelli, Grillparzer . . . Anschütz, Böhm, Czerny . . . Mayseder . . .
Lannoy, Linke . . . Schubart [*sic*] . . . Schuppanzigh and many others. At the back
of the solemn procession came pupils of the Conservatoire and the St Anna music
students, the distinguished dignatories such as the art-loving Count Moritz von
Dietrichstein, Privy Councillors Mosel and Breuning . . .[29]

The torch-bearers, musicians, and writers, thirty-six in all, wore black but
had white lilies pinned to their coats, while the torches were draped with
black crape ribbons.[30] When they reached the cemetery, the cortège
stopped outside and, as only priests were permitted to speak at the grave-
side, the actor Heinrich Anschütz, a friend of Schubert, delivered here the
funeral oration which Grillparzer had written for the occasion. The funeral
was a major event in Vienna, attended by an estimated 10,000 people, the
occasion impressive and moving. Afterwards Schubert left the cemetery
with Bauernfeld, Enderes, Schober, and the Hartmann brothers. In the
evening he was among those who, in the Castle of Eisenstadt talked into the
early hours of the morning 'of nothing but Beethoven, his works and the
well-merited honours paid to his memory to-day.'[31]

[29] *ND* 501.   [30] *ND* 475; Kobald, *Alt-Wiener Musikstätten*, 319–20.
[31] Fritz von Hartmann: *Doc.* 623, *Dok.* 419.

The inclusion of Hummel as torch-bearer amongst the leading musicians in Vienna is interesting. In March 1827 Hummel travelled from his home in Weimar for the express purpose of visiting Beethoven before he died. In Hummel's company was the youthful Ferdinand Hiller, his pupil and a future piano virtuoso. While in Vienna they often dined with the sociable Katharina von Lászny, an old friend of Hummel's, as she was of Vogl, Anna Milder-Hauptmann, Schubert, and Schwind among many others. On one such occasion, Vogl and Schubert were also invited. Hummel, who knew little of Schubert or his music before this, was then 49; Hiller was an impressionable 16-year-old. Many years later, in 1879, Hiller wrote of this occasion and the effect it had on himself and his revered teacher:

after . . . dinner Schubert sat down at the piano with Vogl at his side—the rest of us settled down comfortably in the large drawing-room, wherever we felt inclined, and then began a unique concert. Song after song ensued—the performers inexhaustibly generous, the audience inexhaustibly receptive. Schubert had but little technique, Vogl had not much of a voice, but they both had such life and feeling, and were so completely absorbed in their performances, that the wonderful compositions could not have been interpreted with greater clarity and, at the same time, with greater vision. You did not notice the piano playing nor the singing, it was as though the music needed no material sound, as though the melodies, like visions, revealed themselves to spiritualized ears. Of my emotions, of my enthusiasm I dare not speak—but my master, who already had almost half a century of music behind him, was so deeply moved that tears trickled down his cheeks.[32]

Schubert never forgot his meeting with Hummel, nor Hummel's warm response to his music, and in the following year, when he composed his last three piano sonatas, he planned to dedicate them to the great pianist–composer. (As they did not appear in print until 1839, two years after the death of Hummel, the publisher Diabelli elected to dedicate them instead to Robert Schumann.)

Schubert admired and revered Beethoven, and his death shocked him deeply.[33] However, his spirit soon revived. During the weeks following the funeral there were several successful performances of his music. Those of two of his vocal quartets in a gala concert in Graz and at a concert in the smaller Redoutensaal of the Imperial Palace on 6 April were followed by the first public performance of his Octet on 16 April (Easter Monday) in Schuppanzigh's last subscription concert of the season.[34] A newly com-

---

[32] *Mem.* 283–4, *Erin.* 325–6.   [33] Spaun: *Mem.* 137, *Erin.* 160.
[34] Also performed was an arrangement for two pianos and string quartet of Beethoven's Piano Concerto No. 5, the 'Emperor', with Czerny as 'solo' pianist: *ND* 476.

Oſtermontag den 16. April 1827

wird

das letzte

Abonnement = Quartett

des

Ignaz Schuppanzigh,

unter den Tuchlauben, zum rothen Igel (im kleinen Ver=
ein=Saale) Nachmittags von halb 5 bis halb 7 Uhr,
Statt haben.

Vorkommende Stücke:

1. Neues großes Octett für 5 Saiten= und 3 Blas=Inſtrumente,
   von Herrn Schubert.

2. An die ferne Geliebte. Ein Liederkreis für eine Singſtimme
   und Clavier=Begleituug, von Beethoven.

3. Großes Clavier=Concert (aus Es dur), von Louis van
   Beethoven, arrangirt für zwey Pianoforte und Quartett=Beglei=
   tung, gefälligſt vorgetragen von Herrn Carl Czerni und Herrn
   von Pfaller.

Eintrittskarten ſind auf dem Graben, in der Kunſthandlung des Herrn
T. Haslinger (vormahls Steiner & Comp.) zu haben.

FIG. 5. Programme of a recital given by the Schuppanzigh String Quartet on Easter Monday 1827, in the concert hall of the Gesellschaft der Musikfreunde, which included a performance of Schubert's Octet. Reproduced by kind permission of the Gesellschaft der Musikfreunde.

posed male-voice quartet accompanied by four horns, a setting of Seidl's 'Nachtgesang im Walde', played at a midday Sunday concert on 22 April, coincided with another in the Lower Austrian County Hall where Schubert appeared, as on 8 March, as Tietze's accompanist in Walter Scott's 'Normans Gesang'. Apart from these public concerts, there were several musical soirées and Schubertiads in which Schubert took part. The first, on 10 April, was a rather grand affair, 'a great evening party',[35] at which Schubert accompanied Tietze in some of his songs, and perhaps in deference to the recently deceased Beethoven, the latter's 'Adelaide'. (This was another occasion on which it seems very unlikely that Tietze and Schubert would have performed without payment.) Thereafter, there was a large Schubertiad at Spaun's (on Saturday 21 April), a grand send-off for Anton

[35] *Doc.* 625, *Dok.* 421.

and Marie Ottenwalt before their return to Linz three days later, after a visit to Vienna, and another at the Witteczeks' two days later. At both of these concerts Schubert accompanied Vogl, who was now back in circulation after his marriage. Immediately before this, on 19 April, Schubert attended the final *Concert spirituel* of the season to hear a further performance of Beethoven's Ninth Symphony, on this occasion just the first movement, and the Coronation Mass by Cherubini. Thus Schubert was musically and socially well occupied. There are no known completed major compositions which date from this period, nor were there any from the following month, May, suggesting that Schubert may have been entering upon another seasonal depressive phase. As we have seen, in May he moved out for a few weeks to Dornbach. Meanwhile Jenger continued to communicate with Frau Pachler in Graz, promising a visit from Schubert and himself in September.

In Dornbach Schubert enjoyed the fresher air, fine weather, and country walks in the charming neighbourhood. It was a beautiful summer, and as Spaun described it, the fruit ripened quickly and the harvest was both plenteous and early.[36] Schubert still paid occasional visits to Vienna, meeting friends at the Castle of Eisenstadt inn. He was now drinking heavily again, as is confirmed by comments in Bauernfeld's letters to his friend Ferdinand von Mayerhofer. Thus, on 5 June he wrote: 'Schubert is living in Dornbach and drinks there, instead of here . . . he is feeling the inadequacy of our lives'[37] On the other hand, on 27 August, some weeks after Schubert's return to Vienna, Bauernfeld was able to write that Schubert 'is drinking less'.[38] The young dramatist had good reason, apart from consideration for his friend's well-being, for concern over his drinking. Almost a year earlier he had handed over to Schubert the completed libretto of *Der Graf von Gleichen*, after the composer had put him under considerable pressure to complete it quickly. Schubert received it with thanks, but then, while according to Bauernfeld still voicing enthusiasm for the opera, surprisingly laid it aside. Even after the censors' not unexpected total rejection of the play in October 1826, Schubert continued to express his determination to compose the music, and yet he did nothing about it until the following summer when on 19 June, in another mood of reawakened creativity, he began it at last.

The summer months for Schubert were marked by musical success and a promising outlook. Of special importance was his election early in June by

---

[36] Letter of 22 July to Anna von Revertera: WL ii. 90.   [37] WL i. 61.
[38] Ibid. 67.

members of the Gesellschaft der Musikfreunde (some thousand of them, if all had voted) to full membership of the committee of that establishment. The promotion from deputy to full representative member was prestigious, carrying with it practical responsibilities for the smooth running of the society. (What these were in Schubert's case is not known.)[39] On the same day that he wrote a letter to the committee accepting this honour, he wrote to Frau Pachler in Graz accepting her invitation to stay with her in the autumn. He continued to encourage Viennese publishers to take an interest in his music, and succeeded in persuading Thaddäus Weigl to issue his latest piano duet.

As the summer progressed Schubert was increasingly hopeful that his Symphony in C, much of it composed in the summer of 1825, would be performed during the following season at one of the major Sunday concerts of the Gesellschaft der Musikfreunde. For some while now the score, his gift to the Gesellschaft, had been with copyists who were preparing the orchestral parts.[40] Early in August these were completed, and an entry was made to this effect in the society's account book for September. It had taken two copyists to complete the mammoth task. According to Leopold Sonnleithner:

Soon after it was composed, the great C major Symphony was rehearsed by the Gesellschaft der Musikfreunde in practices at the Gesellschaft's Conservatoire; but it was provisionally put on one side because of its length and difficulty. It was not until 15 December 1839 that a performance of this symphony, and in its entirety, was planned for one of the Gesellschaft's concerts; but at the very first rehearsal the paid 'artists' refused to carry out the necessary number of rehearsals, as a result of which the Concert committee had to confine themselves, for this occasion, to the first two movements.[41]

But Schubert had not lost heart.

Things were changing with the circle of friends which had flourished at the end of 1826 with Spaun at its centre, as the various professions of the members tended to encourage them along different paths. But relationships were also changing. Already back in March the once close relationship between Schober and Schwind had run into trouble when the painter lost patience with Schober not only on account of his indolence, but also, and more pressingly, over his courting of yet another young woman of their acquaintance with whom he had supposedly fallen in love.[42] Schwind strongly disapproved of his conduct in this courtship. Of Schober virtually nothing is known from July onwards for most of the rest of the year, except

[39] Biba, 'Schubert und die Gesellschaft der Musikfreunde', 26. [40] Ibid. 31.
[41] *Mem.* 431, *Erin.* 498. [42] WL i. 60.

that he was working at the Lithographic Institute. Since the time when he was an attractive and lively youth in the Bildung Circle, he had grown somewhat pugnacious, short-tempered, and generally less agreeable in the company of his old friends. Although his mother's family seems to have been respectable, his own behaviour and attitudes increasingly distanced him from much of conventional Viennese middle-class society. Yet with him Schubert was totally relaxed and at ease. They may have had their disagreements, but they understood and accepted each other.

During September 1827, the vacation period, Schubert, Spaun, and Schwind were all out of Vienna. Schubert was with Jenger in Graz. Spaun was on holiday in Linz with his family. Schwind was at first in Munich, and then on a leisurely journey home which included, at the very end of the month, a visit, also to Linz. Of those closest to Schubert during the year, we know most, through letters and diaries, about Schwind, Spaun, and Bauernfeld. Of these, Schwind was still much in love with Nettl Hönig, and in June, in order to establish his career prospects so that he could offer her marriage, he began to plan a period of study in Munich.[43] He left Vienna early in August with a recommendation from Grillparzer to the German fresco painter Peter von Cornelius, director of the Munich Academy of Fine Arts since 1824.[44] He did not return until late October. Bauernfeld told Mayerhofer in a letter of 27 August that after the departure of Schwind there had been a 'hole' in the circle, as the result of which Bauernfeld had spent a lot of time on his own, although he did sometimes visit Grillparzer, who had become something of a mentor to him. Meanwhile he read much and learned languages, particularly English and Greek, and 'regarding poetry, I have this summer written 5 acts of three different plays'.[45] He was now employed in the district council offices,[46] and to his agreeable surprise was finding his duties as a bureaucrat enjoyable, his working hours (mornings only) congenial, and his colleagues pleasant.[47] His relationship with Clothilde now well over, he was determined 'not to fall in love again so easily, perhaps even never again'.[48] Spaun's attendances at the Castle of Eisenstadt had also been less frequent of late, in part because he had recently discovered a passion for swimming and horse-riding, but also because in August (as in April) his sister and her husband, Marie and Anton Ottenwalt, were staying with him in his large apartment, which he was delighted to share with visitors. It is also possible that by this time he was becoming aware of the charms of Franziska Roner von Ehrenwerth, who was quite soon to become his wife.

[43] WL i. 61.   [44] *Doc.* 662–3, *Dok.* 446.   [45] WL i. 66.
[46] *Mem.* 236, *Erin.* 270.   [47] WL i. 66.   [48] Ibid.

When Spaun had first arrived back in Vienna, in the autumn of 1826, to take up residence after an absence of some five years, he found himself much in demand in society (to which Schubert never belonged) because of his reputation, as he put it, as an amiable bachelor. A highly eligible bachelor was nearer the mark. He soon discovered that the social whirl of larger gatherings was giving him no pleasure and so, during the winter of 1826/7, he began to establish a circle of men and women of his own choosing, his personal friends, whom he invited to his home for music and pleasant conviviality.[49] In the establishment of this new circle of friends, which had nothing to do with the conventional bachelor circles, Schubert and Vogl, as he readily admitted, played an important role through their readiness to provide the musical entertainment which began the proceedings. This was followed by supper, conversation and, if ladies were present, dancing; if they were not, perhaps gymnastics. Spaun wrote of this period to Anna von Revertera, who already in 1826 had been encouraging him to marry, especially after he had shown strong domestic instincts when visiting her and her husband in Lemberg.[50] In response to their tactful suggestion, Spaun had declared (in July 1826) that he dearly wished to marry: 'I have never before felt so strongly what I lack in my life to fill the emptiness in my heart. Sadly I have not been fortunate enough to meet a young woman from whom I might hope for sincere love. For years I have lived apart from girls and been to some degree frightened off by them.'[51] If only he could meet a girl who shared his interests and concerns, whom he loved and who returned his love, he would 'marry her without a moment's hesitation; but sadly I have little hope of this'. Now, a year later, he wrote of Vogl's very happy (though late) marriage to a good wife, and of how, 'loving and loved', the singer had blossomed: his health and humour greatly improved, and his voice much restored.[52] For himself, in Vienna he had recently come to know many young ladies 'with lovely faces', but he despaired of finding a bride amongst them. They all wanted to be entertained, and they were frivolous-minded. If he was ever to marry, then he reckoned he would have to seek a wife not in Vienna but in Linz.[53] A different attitude to women was expressed many years later by Schwind who, born and bred in the capital, might have been expected to hold views if not conventional, not too different from those of many other Viennese men. The remark was made to his pupils; 'We men represent the serious side of life, women the delightfully

---

[49] WL ii. 90.

[50] He had also impressed the parents with his devotion to their baby daughter, Spaun's godchild.

[51] WL ii. 78.   [52] Ibid. 92–3.   [53] Ibid. 94.

cheerful side. Both belong together, forming, as the shells of a nut, a complete whole.'[54]

The diaries and letters of the Hartmann brothers paint an interesting picture of the lives of socially minded young men of middle-class background in Vienna. When they arrived in the capital as students, they found the social life and attitudes rather different in the Imperial capital from those to which they were accustomed in Linz, where the atmosphere was more relaxed and friendly. They now moved almost entirely in male society, the exceptions being when they visited their relatives in the city (the von Schallhammers) and those of Spaun (the Wanderers), and during carnival. Fritz von Hartmann wrote to his elder sister Anna von Revertera: 'Contact with young women was rare, except at Carnival time, partly on account of our position as young bachelors, partly as a result of our experience of the possibly time-consuming effects of such contact when taken seriously. My time was badly needed for my law studies and for learning French.'[55] During carnival, most of their spare time was enthusiastically given over to dancing.

As in many parts of Europe, in middle-class Vienna young men and women lived very much apart. For the men it was normal to belong to a circle of like-minded male friends, many of whom became close. After marriage they deserted the bachelor circle for domesticity; but even before this many went their separate ways, diverted by professional interests, as was happening in 1827 to Schubert and his friends. Although Schubert's home background was very different from that of Spaun, the Hartmanns, and their circle, and he never took on board the social attitudes of his middle-class friends, he had shared the same kind of early education, and was most at ease when in their all-male company. They respected and admired him both as a composer and for the sharpness of his intellect, enjoying his company and enthusiasms despite his sometimes coarse Viennese sense of humour. With the women it was a different story. He was rarely if ever at ease with the female society enjoyed by his friends; the modest background of his own family had left him ill prepared for this. To them he seemed awkward and shy, unpractised in, or unwilling to acquire, the requisite art of conversational pleasantry and mild flirtation, unable to relate to them unless they shared his musical enthusiasms. It is probable that in Upper Austria and in Styria, which he was soon to visit, he was more relaxed in the company of less sophisticated women.

---

[54] A. W. Müller, *Mortiz v. Schwind* (Eisenach, 1871), 58; quoted by Steblin in 'The Peacock's Tale', 19.
[55] WL ii. 86.

On Monday 3 September, at 9.30 in the evening, Schubert set off in the company of Jenger for Graz, a journey which, by express coach, took approximately twenty-four hours. Their host, Dr Karl Pachler, was a brewer and barrister of some popularity and influence in the town. His wife, Maria Leopoldine, who had lived all her life in Graz, was an able pianist, and in her youth had been a rather beautiful young lady. Beethoven had first heard of her in 1811, before her marriage, when she was 17 years old. They eventually met in 1817 and made music together. On his return to Vienna, he wrote to her: 'I have not yet found anyone who performed my compositions as well as you do; and I am not excluding the great pianists, who often have merely mechanical ability or affectation. You are the true fosterer of my spiritual children'.[56] Schubert was eager to meet his hostess, of whose talents and kindness he had heard much, and of whom Beethoven had thought so highly.

Schubert's stay in Graz was packed with musical events, excursions, and picnics. It started a little unfortunately, however, when on his first full day there he failed to enjoy the performance of Meyerbeer's opera *Il crociato in Egitto* at the Landständisches-Theater.[57] The original Italian libretto was adapted and translated into German for this performance by his old associate Josef Kupelwieser, the author in 1823 of the text for his own opera *Fierrabras*. (Kupelwieser was now secretary jointly to the theatres in Graz and Pressburg, the position he had held formerly at the Kärntnertor-Theater in Vienna.) Three days later, on the Saturday evening, there was a grand charity concert in Schubert's honour at the Landständisches-Theater organized by the Styrian Musical Society, of which he had been elected an honorary member in 1823. All proceeds from the concert: 'without any deduction of costs, which an anonymous person has declared himself willing to defray, will be devoted in equal parts to the inhabitants rendered necessitous by the floods that have lately occurred in the plains, and the needy widows and orphans of country schoolmasters whose annual support is incumbent on the Musical Society by statute.'[58] The success of the occasion was ensured, according to the announcement of the concert in the official *Grazer Zeitung*, not only by the full co-operation of the Styrian capital's musicians and music-lovers, but also by 'the kind collaboration on the part of an artistic and greatly celebrated composer from the metropolis'. The music composed by this celebrity, Schubert, consisted of three items: Walter Scott's 'Normans Gesang', the female chorus 'Gott in der Natur', and the male-voice quartet 'Geist der Liebe'. Here the composer made

[56] *The Letters of Beethoven*, ed. and trans. E. Anderson, 3 vols. (London, 1961), 708.
[57] *Doc.* 664n, *Dok.* 447n.   [58] *Doc.* 664–5, *Dok.* 448.

another of his rare public appearances as performer when he accompanied the song and quartet.

After the weekend Schubert and Jenger, in the company of Anselm Hüttenbrenner and the Pachlers, made a three-day visit to the castle of Wildbach some twenty miles south-west of Graz, which was managed by an aunt of Dr Pachler, Anna Massegg. Again they made music, assisted by Massegg's eldest daughter, in a beautiful 'blue room' with fine views across the garden; and they were refreshed by generous supplies of the excellent local wine, the Schilcher, a light rosé which proved a particular favourite with Schubert.[59] Other visits included several to the beautiful Haller castle just outside Graz (which in other years the Pachlers were in the habit of renting for the summer). They received other invitations, including one to visit his old friend Anselm Hüttenbrenner in his own home, and to meet his wife and children.

In Graz there were several very successful Schubertiads at the Pachlers, who invited from amongst their many friends some of the keenest music-lovers in the town. On these occasions Schubert had to accompany himself in his songs, there being no other singer available. He also played duets with Jenger, and perhaps tried out one or two of the first set of Impromptus, on which he was working at the time. On a particularly important occasion for Schubert, both Dr Pachler and Anselm Hüttenbrenner were present to hear the composer play through parts of his opera *Alfonso und Estrella* to the musical director of the Landständisches-Theater, Josef Kinsky, in an effort to excite his interest in the work. Schubert had not given up hope of performances of his two grand operas, *Alfonso* and *Fierrabras*, the first of these especially, after their rejection by the Kärntnertor-Theater in 1822 and 1823. In 1825 he was seeking interest in the first opera, his favourite, in Berlin[60] and Dresden.[61] In the summer of 1826 he told Bauernfeld that the management of the Kärntnertor-Theater was pressing him for libretti of his operas,[62] and he again sent them that of *Alfonso*. After his return from Graz in 1827 he wrote to Frau Pachler that he was still awaiting the return of this libretto from the theatre's producer, Josef Gottdank, who had now had it 'for months'. Again, on 18 January of the next year, he wrote to Frau Pachler: 'How are things with the opera? Are there good singers in Graz? I am still unable to get back my copy of the libretto from the beastly Gottdank, but I will now make a big effort, as it seems to me the delay is due to nothing but ill-nature.'[63] In his memoirs, written in 1854, Hüttenbrenner wrote: 'Kinsky remarked that Schubert imposed too heavy

[59] *Doc.* 666n, *Dok.* 449n.   [60] *Doc.* 408, *Dok.* 280.   [61] *Doc.* 444, *Dok.* 308.
[62] *Doc.* 528, 539, *Dok.* 360, 366–7.
[63] Letter quoted in Waidelich, *Schubert: 'Alfonso und Estrella'*, 34.

a burden on the orchestra and chorus and asked him if he would agree to some of the numbers, which were written in C sharp major and F sharp major, being transposed down a semitone by the copyist; to which Schubert admittedly agreed but, as it seemed to me, reluctantly.'[64] Schubert's letter and Hüttenbrenner's information suggest that the Graz theatre may have tried out part of the opera in rehearsal, but then rejected it. Had it been accepted, then a copy of the libretto would have been required in a hurry for the Styrian censors. During the time that the theatre was showing this interest in *Alfonso*, Schubert must have been greatly heartened.

On 20 September, after a little over two weeks in Graz, Schubert and Jenger set out on the return journey to Vienna, promising to visit their friends in Graz again as soon as possible. They took a different route to the one they had come by, taking four days in all. The first night they stayed in the sixteenth-century town hall of Fürstenfeld with the Bürgermeister and his wife, who were friends of Jenger. After exploring this handsome fortified town on the Austro-Hungarian border, they moved on to Hartberg, stopping for their second night in a comfortable inn where the host, also a vintner and wine-merchant, and until the year before the town magistrate, was also known to Jenger. On the following morning they left at 5 a.m., only breakfasting on arrival at Friedberg, from where they climbed to the summit of the Eselberg. From here, on a fine, clear day, they enjoyed magnificent views for miles around in all directions. Leaving Styria behind them, they stopped for the last two nights at the pretty Schloss Schleinz, an eighteenth-century classical building situated in a fine park. Their host, a merchant, was another acquaintance of Jenger's, and with him and his family and two other guests they spent the last days of their holiday very pleasantly.[65] Both Schubert and Jenger arrived back in Vienna in excellent spirits and with many fine memories. Two days later they sent Frau Pachler letters of deep gratitude for the exceptional kindness she had shown them. Jenger wrote that they would never forget the time they had spent with the Pachlers, 'the more particularly because both Schubert and I have very seldom spent such glorious days as we did recently at dear Graz and its environs, among which Wildbach and its cherished inhabitants take the first place.'[66] Schubert wrote:

Madam,
Already it became clear to me that I was only too happy at Graz, and I cannot as yet get accustomed to Vienna . . . At Graz I soon recognised an artless and sincere way of being together, and a longer stay would have allowed me to take to it even

---

[64] *Mem.* 180, *Erin.* 207.
[65] L. Porhansl, 'Schuberts Heimreise von Graz', *Brille*, 12 (1994), 113–21.
[66] *Doc.* 671, *Dok.* 452.

more readily. Above all, I shall never forget the kindly shelter, where, with its dear hostess and the sturdy 'Pachleros' [Dr Karl], as well as little Faust [b. 1819], I spent the happiest days I have had for a long time. Hoping to be yet able to prove my gratitude in an adequate manner, I remain, with profound respect,

> Most devotedly yours,
> Franz Schubert

P.S. The opera libretto I hope to be able to send in a few days.[67]

Schubert came away from Graz with two tasks to accomplish. One was to obtain and send to Pachler, for the use of the theatre, the libretto of *Alfonso*. The second was to compose a little duet suitable for young Faust Pachler to play with his mother on his father's name-day, on 4 November. Jenger received a letter from Frau Pachler at the end of September requesting him to be sure to remind Schubert of his promise to her son, and asking that he make sure Schubert finished and posted it in time for him to practise it before the name-day celebration.[68] Schubert composed the duet Marsch in G, or 'Kindermarsch', D928 on 12 October and sent it with a letter to Frau Pachler on the same day.[69] In this letter he mentioned that he was not really happy with the piece, and he was afraid that Faust would not be very pleased with it either, for: 'I do not feel that I am the right person for this kind of composition.' He also referred to a return of his 'usual headaches', about which Frau Pachler was clearly informed already. Finally, he brought up the matter of the libretto he was supposed to have sent: 'Pray give Dr Karl my heartiest good wishes for his name-day and tell him that the book [libretto] of my opera, which that sloth Gottdank has had for months to read through, has still not been returned to me.'

Schubert had enjoyed a particularly happy, successful, and promising visit to Graz; happy in the friendships and warmth of the welcome he received, successful in the appreciative reception of his music, and promising particularly in the theatre's interest in his opera. The journey home had been a break from music and a time of contented relaxation. Schubert, refreshed and full of ideas for new projects, was now very ready to return to a period of concentrated activity. He soon completed his first set of Impromptus; and he returned to the last twelve of the *Winterreise* songs, on some of which he had apparently been working during the summer.[70] Sketches for his latest opera, *Der Graf von Gleichen*, seem to date from his holiday in Graz. He wrote these, some of them in pencil, on small pieces of manuscript

---

[67] *Doc.* 670–1, *Dok.* 451–2.   [68] *Doc.* 670, *Dok.* 451.   [69] *Doc.* 679, *Dok.* 457.
[70] Youens, *Retracing a Winter's Journey*, 28.

paper, cut from larger sheets, which he probably carried around with him. These also awaited further attention. Work on the opera, however, was gradually pushed to one side as he began serious preparations for the concert of his own music which he was now planning for early in the following year. With this in mind, it is possible that he completed in October the first of his mature piano trios, that in B flat D898.[71]

In a letter to Anselm Hüttenbrenner of 18 January 1828, after first seeking Anselm's help for his brother Karl, who had applied for an art-teacher's post in Graz, Schubert referred enthusiastically to a performance by Bocklet, Schuppanzigh, and Linke of his 'new trio', probably that in B flat, in the hall of the Gesellschaft der Musikfreunde on 26 December. Schubert must have been glad of the opportunity to hear this trio, which he was considering for inclusion in the programme of the coming concert of his music. Also on that evening, there was a performance of another of his works, the 96-bar-long Cantata for Irene Kiesewetter D936, for solo male-voice quartet and full chorus with piano accompaniment, written to celebrate the recovery after an illness of the young lady pianist to whom it was dedicated (the daughter of the president of the Gesellschaft der Musikfreunde).

Apart from these concerts, virtually nothing is recorded of the whereabouts or activities of Schubert during the last three months of 1827. He was present sometimes, or even frequently, at the Castle of Eisenstadt where, according to Franz von Hartmann, after Hartmann's return to Vienna for the new university year in late October or early November, the friends 'Enk, Schober, Schubert and Spaun' were to be found 'every Wednesday and Saturday'.[72] This was after the return at the end of October of Spaun, who had been in Linz for a month on vacation, and of Schwind from Munich. Thus, for much of October, both Bauernfeld and Schubert were probably living rather quietly, immersed in their work, the dramatist on *Der Brautwerber* (The Wooer) which occupied him from July until December, Schubert on the many compositions written in this highly creative period, and in particular the second part of *Winterreise*.

On the day before he left Graz, Schubert had felt it incumbent on him to write to one Franz Selliers de Moranville (Jenger's successor in Graz as Chancellor at the Court War Council and formerly an enthusiastic member of the Gesellschaft der Musikfreunde in Vienna), apologizing for his failure to keep a promise, probably an appointment. He did not give a detailed reason, merely stating: 'If you knew how impossible it had been for me to do so, I am sure you would forgive me.'[73] From the letter to Frau Pachler of

[71] Badura-Skoda, 'The Chronology of Schubert's Piano Trios', 277–95.
[72] *Doc.* 685, *Dok.* 462. [73] *Doc.* 669, *Dok.* 451.

12 October mentioned above, it is evident that she was fully aware of Schubert's headaches, and may have witnessed his suffering while he was her guest, perhaps even at the time when he should have met Selliers. Three days after writing to Frau Pachler he wrote another letter, to Anna Hönig, excusing himself from her party that evening as he was 'ill', and in such a way that made him 'totally unfit for society'.[74] The tone is similar in his excuses to both Selliers and Nettl Hönig. Schubert's health was beginning to break down, whether aggravated by bouts of heavy drinking or no. His doctor had undoubtedly warned him of the danger signs, so Schubert must have realized that his long-term prognosis was bad. The headaches, together with other unpleasant syphilitic symptoms from which Schubert may have been suffering, and uncertainty as to when they might strike, were a constant reminder of his illness, although at this stage he may not have imagined that he had barely a year of life left to him. Declining health is likely to have been a contributory factor in the development of a dark mood which descended on him during October and November while he was composing the last twelve songs of the *Winterreise* cycle. But ill health was not the main cause. 'Gloom' was the term used by Spaun to describe Schubert's state of mind; and he was sure that it was induced by the composition of these songs. He also believed the composer was of the same opinion:

For a time Schubert's mood became gloomy and he seemed upset. When I asked him what was the matter he merely said to me 'Well, you will soon hear it and understand'. One day he said to me 'Come to Schober's today, and I will sing you a cycle of grisly songs. I am anxious to know what you will say about them. They have affected me more than has been the case with any other songs.' So in a voice wrought with emotion, he sang the whole of the *Winterreise* through to us. We were quite dumbfounded by the gloomy mood of these songs . . .[75]

A different explanation for Schubert's black despondency is that he was suffering again from depression. However, Spaun would without doubt have distinguished between the symptoms of his friend's customary attacks of 'melancholia' and the gloom of this period. Also, in the past his depressions had been more likely to inhibit creativity rather than stimulate it. Mayrhofer wrote of the *Winterreise* songs: 'the poet's irony, rooted in despair, appealed to him', and Schubert expressed this despair 'in cutting tones' (*in schneidenden Tönen*).[76] The despair of the poems had temporarily cut deep into Schubert's mind.

---

[74] *Dok.* 458.   [75] *Mem.* 137–8, *Erin.* 160.   [76] *Mem.* 15, *Erin.* 20.

Early in the year, when he composed the first twelve songs of *Winterreise*, Schubert was in good spirits and in sociable mood. He was not then affected by despair in the same way as he was later, when working on the second set. Many performers of the complete cycle are very conscious of a new dimension to the second half of the cycle, an increased intensity and sense of threat. Although this may be recognized by the listener as part of the dramatic economy of the cycle, this explanation is not the only one. The self-absorbed wanderer is now less closely bound up with his surroundings; correspondingly in Schubert's music, the singer is aware of an increasing isolation from his pianist, a vulnerability and loss of support. There is indeed a new relationship between the vocal line and the piano accompaniment. This is particularly evident in 'Der greise Kopf' (The Hoary Head; no. 14), 'Letzte Hoffnung' (Last Hope; no. 16), and the final song of the cycle 'Der Leiermann' (The Hurdy-gurdy Man), in each of which there are passages where the singer is minimally supported by the piano, for example (in nos. 14 and 16) by single bar-long sustained chords in the bass register. In 'Die Krähe' (The Crow; no. 15), on the other hand, much of the accompaniment is pitched in the treble register. Schubert achieved gripping intensity in all these songs with an economy, even a frugality of notes in all registers. The very starkness and evocative power of the songs represent a new dimension in song-writing.

Neither Müller nor Schubert was working in complete isolation from influence when they wrote the *Winterreise* cycle of poems and of songs. Müller, who knew Uhland personally, was familiar with that poet's *Wander-Lieder*, a set of nine poems from which he borrowed poetic images and themes. Schubert thought highly of the settings of these poems by Konradin Kreutzer, Kapellmeister at the Kärntnertor-Theater from 1822 to 1827, settings which were published in Augsburg in 1818 as *Neun Wander-Lieder*.[77] According to Spaun, Schubert, while still living at the Stadtkonvikt, was a great admirer of Kreutzer's *Wander-Lieder* settings.[78] Now, some fifteen years later in his *Winterreise* songs, Schubert had transformed the earlier *Lied* into a supremely expressive and concentrated song form.

When Schubert in the home of Schober, where he was then living, introduced his closest friends to the complete *Winterreise* song-cycle, they were stunned by the persistent gloom and stark power of the songs. In an age when variety of mood in musical performances was considered a necessary virtue, they were at a loss for words. Only Schober, whose musicality and musical judgement I have already called into question, was brave, or frank, enough to admit to disliking all except one song: 'Der Lindenbaum' (The

---

[77] Youens, *Retracing a Winter's Journey*, 29–30.   [78] *Mem.* 27, *Erin.* 35.

Linden Tree, no. 5). But Schubert was right when, after claiming that he preferred these songs to all others he had written, he assured his friends that they too would come to like them in time.[79] According to Spaun: 'From then on he was a sick man, although his condition gave no cause for anxiety.'[80] Spaun stated at the start of his account that 'for a time' Schubert was upset by these songs. As Spaun had not returned from his vacation until the end of October, it is probable that Schubert did not complete the cycle to his own satisfaction until some time in November. But the gloom they elicited did not persist for too long. By December he was busy composing chamber and piano music of a very different kind.

From December date also the second set of Impromptus D935, a much stronger, more extrovert set than those he wrote in August and September. It would seem that in these pieces, as in the Fantasia in C for violin and piano D934 and the Piano Trio in E flat D929, all of which Schubert was composing in December 1827, he had in mind the pianism of the Czech virtuoso Karl Maria von Bocklet. A new virtuosity is indeed demanded of all the performers, although the technical brilliance required of the pianist is outstanding, and of a kind that Schubert himself did not begin to have. There is also a very positive quality of power and determination in some of this music of December which again is leagues away from the introversion of *Winterreise*, completed only a few weeks earlier. Schubert had travelled far from, even if he had not forgotten, the gloom of the song-cycle, and was now planning for his future concert. It is to these plans that we now turn.

---

[79] *Mem.* 138, *Erin.* 161.   [80] Ibid.

11

SUCCESS AND SICKNESS

(1828)

IF Schubert's health was causing concern during 1828, there are no recorded references to illness or indisposition until he moved to his brother's new apartment early in September. To what extent his family and friends were aware of his sickness before this must remain conjectural. To all intents and purposes, and apart from the persistent headaches and later giddiness, which a few of his friends do seem to have known about, he appeared to be reasonably fit and leading a normal life. Further retrospective comments, however, suggest that he was to some degree neglecting himself, spending a lot of time on his own (apparently distancing himself from old friends), sometimes negligent or unreliable (or both) in relationships, drinking heavily, and perhaps indulging in unsavoury sexual activities.

Outstanding and influential events of the year included his benefit concert of his own music on 26 March and the betrothal and marriage of Josef von Spaun. If Schubert was spending less time with the usual old friends of the Spaun and Schober circle, he was obviously with musician colleagues and friends more than ever before. Because the usual commentators saw less of him, they left little information about Schubert's life in this, his final year; but it is evident that his dreams of success through publication of his music did not materialize, nor did the projected holidays in Gmunden and Graz. On the other hand, during the year he created a remarkable quantity and quality of music of all kinds, including many of his greatest and most loved works. Meanwhile, the number of public or semi-public performances of his music remained much the same as in the previous year.

The year began with a New Year's Eve party at Schober's, just as it had in the previous two years and in 1823 (that is, in each year that Schober was in Vienna from 1822 onwards). Franz von Hartmann, who was at the party as usual with his brother Fritz, described the occasion:

On the stroke of 12 we (Spaun, Enk, Schober, Schubert, Gahy, Eduard Rössler—
a young medical student from Pest[1]—Bauernfeld, Schwind and we two) drank to
each other and to the New Year with Malaga. Bauernfeld then read a poem suitable to the occasion. At 2 o'clock we left for home, and on St. Stephen's Square we
congratulated Enk on his birthday.[2]

This celebration was another private evening party of older and younger
members of the circle of friends. Again, there were no women present.
Although the Hartmann brothers referred to many meetings of the friends
early in the year at the 'ale-house', Bogner's coffee-house, or, on
16 January, 'ins Beisel' (in the pub, in Viennese dialect), they mentioned
Schubert only rarely. Many of the meetings were in the Partridge or Snail
inns and, on Saturday evenings, after the weekly meetings of the reading-
circle, at Schober's home.

　　　Early in January, and soon after Spaun announced his engagement,
Schober restarted the reading-circle, which had been in abeyance for
almost four years. A dozen or so members met on Saturday evenings in his
apartment in the Tuchlauben where Schober, perhaps on the strength of his
earlier experiences as an actor, was usually the reader to the assembled
company from books largely of his own choosing. These included works of
Kleist, Tieck, Heine, and Aeschylus (*Prometheus*), as well as his own writings. After the 'serious' part of the evening, the members retired to one of
their favourite hostelries nearby where drink, smoking, and conversation
were the rule. Here they frequently met other friends, and on one such
occasion, in July, Schubert was specifically mentioned as having joined
them late in the evening by Franz von Hartmann, whose diary is a useful
source of information on the circle's activities. The names of all those who
attended the reading sessions, apart from Schober and the Hartmann brothers, are not known. Only once, on 2 August, was Schubert certainly present. Schwind, Ferdinand Sauter, and Karl Enk are sometimes mentioned
by Hartmann, along with a few less familiar names of mostly younger men,
students at the university or at the Academy of Fine Arts. The absence of
Schubert's name from the incomplete lists does not exclude the possibility
that he was present at more meetings. He lived on the premises, so his presence could have been taken for granted. However, in the light of Schubert's
preoccupation with, amongst other compositions, his new opera, the piano
duet Fantasia and *Auf dem Strom* (On the River) D943 for tenor, horn, and
piano, the composer may well have had little inclination for regular literary
evenings led by Schober and attended by enthusiasts, many of whom were

<hr>

[1] Rössler, like Schubert, was then lodging at Schober's: *Doc.* 704n, *Dok.* 473n.
[2] *Doc.* 703–4, *Dok.* 473.

strangers to him. Quite frequently Spaun, sometimes with Enderes and Sauter, was already at the inn when the readers arrived. However, the remaining members of the old circle of friends were showing signs of drift-ing apart, just as they had in the previous summer. Inner tensions and intol-erances, now associated particularly with Schober, tended to lead to unpleasant disagreements which disrupted and weakened the former har-mony. Thus on 2 January, perhaps without Schubert being present, there was a disagreement between Spaun and Schober over the issue of whether duels should be fought or no. Schober grew increasingly heated and bel-ligerent in his arguments, until for all present the situation became dis-tinctly unpleasant. When Spaun, an ever-calming influence, suggested that the argument had gone quite far enough and they should stop, Schober exploded with anger, so putting himself in a very unsavoury light with such as the Hartmanns. Once again it was Spaun who poured oil on troubled waters. On the next evening, when the two men met again, this time in Bogner's coffee-house, Spaun with admirable grace shook Schober by the hand and restored equanimity in the group. Three weeks later, on 23 January, there was another dispute. The Hartmanns and a few others were visiting Schwind in his home in the Mondscheinhaus when, as the younger brother, Franz, reported, there was some 'ugly bawling', without pointing the finger of blame at any one in particular. It was not quite such a serious quarrel on this occasion; when afterwards they moved on to the inn on the ground floor of the same building, tempers were soon calmed. Yet these two quarrels in the space of three weeks suggest that the atmosphere was not as happy as it had been.

In the mean time, on 16 January, Spaun, who until then had told only a few of his friends, announced to them all that some ten days earlier he had become engaged to be married to Franziska von Roner. The announcement came shortly before the arrival from Linz of his sister Marie and her hus-band Anton Ottenwalt, who had come to complete his final examination for a doctor's degree in law. On 19 January more than a dozen of their friends, of whom Schubert was almost certainly one, gathered in the inn (some coming straight from a meeting of the reading-circle) to welcome the Ottenwalts.[3] The presence of Spaun and now Ottenwalt, both older men with impeccable manners, had a civilizing and calming effect on the friends. For Spaun this was a time not only to enjoy again the visit of his family, but also to share with them and his fiancée the joy and celebrations of their betrothal, and to plan their marriage. For Ottenwalt it also had an impor-tant professional dimension, and one week after his arrival, on Saturday

---

[3] *Doc.* 715, *Dok.* 479.

26 January, he successfully gave the obligatory legal lecture on which his doctoral award and his future career depended.

No doubt while Ottenwalt was in the city he and his wife took the opportunity to attend concerts, and especially those which featured the music of their friend Schubert. Thus on 20 January they could have heard Slawjk and Bocklet perform the recently completed Fantasia in C for violin and piano at a midday concert organized by Slawjk in the County Hall, a performance which received a mixed reception. It came at the end of a long programme and a fair number of the audience walked out before the end.[4] On 24 January the Ottenwalts may or may not have been able, as non-members, to attend the ninth in the series of evening chamber concerts of the Gesellschaft der Musikfreunde at which Schubert's *Ständchen* (Serenade) D920, with text by Grillparzer, received its first, and very successful, semi-public performance.[5] At the previous (and first) performance of the Serenade, a private birthday celebration the previous August, Schubert had been invited to attend, but in the event 'forgot all about it'.[6] At this Gesellschaft concert his presence was again encouraged, but once more he failed to appear until, that is, his friend Walcher rooted him out from the nearby Oak Tree ale-house. Schubert, as before, had totally forgotten the occasion. His response on hearing his composition for the first time, as remembered by one observer, was appreciative: 'Do you know, I had no idea it was so beautiful.'[7] Before the Ottenwalt's departure from Vienna on 5 February, they may have attended on 31 January (Schubert's birthday) the tenth evening concert of the Gesellschaft when one of Schubert's three songs (D837, D838, D839) for Ellen from Walter Scott's *Lady of the Lake* was sung. It is most likely that on 2 February they were in the audience when the composer himself again accompanied the tenor Ludwig Tietze singing his 'Romanze des Richard Löwenherz' (Romance of Richard the Lionheart) D907 from Scott's *Ivanhoe* in another midday concert in the County Hall. This concert was generally acclaimed, although one critic, while praising the work, felt that the composer had set too fast a tempo for the singer's comfort.[8]

Surely the happiest occasion of all for the Ottenwalts during their stay in Vienna was the grand party given by Spaun on 28 January to celebrate his betrothal. When Spaun first spoke of his plans for a party to Schubert, the composer at once responded (as remembered by Spaun): 'While it makes me sad that we are going to lose you, you are doing the right thing and have chosen well; and although I ought to be angry with your fiancée, I should

[4] *Doc.* 715–16, *Dok.* 480; *ND* 578, 586.   [5] *Doc.* 723, *Dok.* 484; *ND* 605.
[6] Breuning: *Mem.* 252–3, *Erin.* 289.   [7] *Mem.* 253, *Erin.* 289.
[8] *Doc.* 730, *Dok.* 489; *ND* 589.

like to do something to please her. Invite her, and I will bring Bocklet, Schuppanzigh and Linke and we will have some music as well.'[9] The evening began not with the usual songs associated with Schubertiads, but with instrumental music played by some of the finest artists in Vienna. According to Spaun: 'Bocklet played a trio with Schuppanzigh and Linke and afterwards, with Schubert, his variations on an original theme [in A flat?] for piano duet, the latter with such fire that everyone was delighted; and immediately afterwards Bocklet embraced his friend with joy. We remained together until after midnight. It was the last evening of its kind [in Spaun's home].'[10]

As was normally the case, the musical part of the evening was followed by dining, dancing, and general conviviality. Franz von Hartmann wrote that there were in all some fifty people present: 'We nearly all got tipsy. We danced—I a great deal with Frau von Ottenwalt. Then most of us went to Bogner's [coffee-house], where we stayed till 2.30.'[11] Two days after the betrothal celebrations there was a more traditional Schubertiad at the home of the Witteczeks at which Vogl and Schubert performed songs. Josef Witteczek, who was now a Court secretary, had over the years hosted many such musical evenings featuring Schubert's music, often with Vogl present to sing his songs. His wife Wilhelmine (née Watteroth) was apparently a spirited and capable young lady with many social talents. Their party on 30 January began with a Schubertiad and was followed by 'supper, then dancing, then a drinking bout, all very jolly . . . It was 2 o'clock before we left in high spirits', according to Franz von Hartmann.[12] As so often, the musical performance began the evening's entertainment, but was only a part of it. Indeed, on this occasion a few of the guests arrived after the music. Food and drink thereafter was the rule at Schubertiads, and almost inevitably when ladies were present this was followed by dancing.

The piano trio played at Spaun's betrothal party was almost certainly that in E flat D929,[13] the performance proving to be something of a rehearsal for Schubert's own concert two months later. That he was able to bring with him to Spaun's home leading professional musicians indicates the respect and friendship that had developed between the musicians and Schubert. Since his election to the committee of the ostensibly amateur but professionally influential Gesellschaft der Musikfreunde, he was spending his time and sharing his life more than ever before with professional musicians, in addition, that is, to singers such as Vogl, with whom he had long been associated. Schubert was now often to be found in the Oak Tree, their

---

[9] *Mem.* 138, *Erin.* 161.   [10] Ibid.

[11] *Doc.* 725, *Dok.* 485.   [12] *Doc.* 729, *Dok.* 488.

[13] Badura-Skoda, 'The Chronology of Schubert's Piano Trios', 277–95.

favourite haunt, with the violinists Schuppanzigh, Slawjk, Böhm, and Holz, the cellist Linke, the horn-player Josef Lewy,[14] pianists, composers, and conductors such as Horzalka,[15] Josef Lanz (with whom in November Schubert attended a lesson in counterpoint with Sechter[16]), Lachner, and probably the singers Tietze and Walcher. All of these were connected with Schubert as associates and colleagues during this last year of his life. At the Oak Tree inn Schubert and his musician friends had plenty to talk about, and he also received through them occasional invitations to perform (for money) as pianist and composer in homes of the aristocratic or wealthy. On one such occasion, there was a Twelfth Night musical evening at the home of a Viennese barrister, Dr Kaspar Wagner (related by marriage to the lawyer Karl Josef von Pratobevera for whom, in February 1826, Schubert had composed the melodrama *Abschied von der Erde*). Schubert failed to appear, as was now becoming only too customary. Sometimes illness may have been the reason, but according to the loyal Spaun, there was often no excuse; he merely forgot. Spaun wrote that during the summer months: 'In summer he had to be out of doors and then it sometimes happened that, because it was a fine evening or congenial company, he forgot an invitation, often one even in aristocratic society. This caused annoyance, but that hardly bothered him at all!'[17] Spaun might have added that Schubert was now just as likely to forget appointments in the winter months when enjoying the company of friends in the taverns of central Vienna. His reputation for unreliability was spreading and became another cause of his increasing marginalization. Personal friends might put up with his thoughtlessness; but others, especially those relying on him to entertain their guests on a professional basis, were understandably less tolerant, and their employment of him soon began to fall away.[18]

Further proof that men such as Spaun and the Hartmann brothers enjoyed a life apart from the one they shared with Schubert, just as he had his own with his family and musician friends, comes in an account of Shrove Tuesday celebrations (on 19 February) which Spaun once again arranged, at the home in Nussdorf of his relatives, the Wanderers.[19] A well-orchestrated and happy surprise visit of Spaun and seven male friends, complete with a prepared supper which they carried with them, ended with dancing. This was the last evening of carnival, and in the Lent which followed there would be no more dancing. Schubert was not in the party on this occasion, and there being no musical dimension other than dancing

---

[14] *Doc.* 567n, *Dok.* 385n.   [15] *Doc.* 263n, *Dok.* 181n.   [16] *Doc.* 350–1n, *Dok.* 242n.
[17] *Mem.* 136–7, *Erin.* 159.
[18] No information on the scale of fees or remuneration for such work is available.
[19] WL ii. 101–2.

makes it unlikely that he was invited, although he was in circulation at this time. Not long after this, on the night of 24 or 25 February, Schober, Enk, and Franz von Hartmann met Schubert by chance in the company of the composer Horzalka and violinist Slawjk.[20] The six men repaired to Anton Schneider's coffee-house, next door to the Partridge inn, where some of them played skittles and they stayed drinking grog until 2.30. A few days before this he had been with the Hartmanns and a few other friends, including Bocklet, in the Leibenfrost coffee-house; and Hartmann recorded meeting Schubert some days later when he (Hartmann) and two friends were enjoying a walk in the Hernals district, not far from Dornbach, an area which Schubert knew well.

In February Schubert was planning his private concert, the arrangements for which were now pressing. For this reason he was seen rather more than usual with friends who were helping him with the programme and practicalities of such a venture. On 5 March Schubert was at a rather smart soirée in the company of Vogl and Grillparzer,[21] both of whom he hoped would feature in the programme: Vogl as singer, Grillparzer as poet. Schubert was hoping to finish in time for the concert the cantata *Miriams Siegesgesang* (Miriam's Song of Victory) D942, with text by Grillparzer, for soprano, mixed choir, and piano. Arrangements for the concert were presumably discussed on this evening, and the next day he sent a letter through Jenger, asking permission of the committee of representatives of the Gesellschaft der Musikfreunde (of which he himself was one) to hold his private concert on 21 March at 7 p.m. in the society's hall in the Red Hedgehog. Before submitting his application which, in the light of his standing with the Gesellschaft, was presumably a formality, he had already sought the obligatory permission of the two court theatres to hold the concert on this day. The original day he asked for, a Friday, was soon afterwards changed to the following Wednesday, the 26 March. This concert was to include a large number of performers, and Schubert must have been at pains, while drawing up the best and most varied programme he could, to accommodate the colleagues, both professional and amateur, who were willing, or had offered, to take part. Before final arrangements were decided, he agreed the new date for the concert which, fortuitously or intentionally on Schubert's part, coincided with the first anniversary of the death of Beethoven. In his setting of Rellstab's *Auf dem Strom* for tenor, horn, and piano, to be performed by Tietze, Lewy, and himself, and

[20] In Slawjk's benefit concert the month before, on 20 Jan., the programme had begun with the first movement of 'a new symphony' by Horzalka. In the same programme Slawjk played the first movement of a violin concerto and a set of solo variations for violin of his own composition, before the final item in the programme: Schubert's Fantasia in C for violin and piano D934: *ND* 568.

[21] *Doc.* 746–7, *Dok.* 499.

written especially for this occasion, he paid homage to Beethoven's memory in an almost exact quotation of the opening four bars of the Funeral March from the 'Eroica' Symphony at the start of his setting of the second of the poem's five stanzas.[22]

Schubert completed *Auf dem Strom* two or three weeks before the day of the concert. He was not able to finish either the piano duet Fantasia in F minor or Grillparzer's cantata. In place of the cantata, he decided at short notice to include another of his settings of Grillparzer's poems, *Ständchen*, which fortunately Josefine and Anna Fröhlich had performed, with a female chorus of Anna's Conservatoire pupils, a few weeks before in the same hall. The day before Schubert's concert informative announcements, including details of the programme, appeared in the principal journals of Vienna, as was then customary: the *Wiener Allgemeine Theaterzeitung*, *Wiener Zeitschrift für Kunst, Literatur, Theater und Mode*, and *Der Sammler*. Although the *Theaterzeitung* referred to the works to be performed as a series of his most recent compositions, only *Auf dem Strom* was brand new; but all except one other item, a single song, had been completed during the last three years. The complete programme was:

1. *First movement of a new string quartet* performed by Böhm, Holz, Weiss, and Linke.
    (Previously unperformed rather than 'new', this was presumably his last quartet, that in G D887 of 1826.)
2. *Four songs with piano accompaniment* performed by Vogl and the composer:
    (*a*) 'Der Kreuzzug' (The Crusade) D932 (by Leitner)
    (*b*) 'Die Sterne' (The Stars) D939 (by Leitner)
    (*c*) 'Fischerweise' (Fisherman's Air) D881 (by Schlechta)
    (*d*) 'Fragment aus dem Aeschylus' (from Aeschylus' *Eumenides*) D450
    (The Leitner songs dated from November 1827 and January 1828, that by Schlechta from March 1826, and that taken from Aeschylus from June 1816.)
3. *Ständchen* by Grillparzer, performed by Josefine Fröhlich and female pupils of the Conservatoire, and conducted by Anna Fröhlich.
4. *New trio for pianoforte, violin, and violoncello*, performed by Bocklet, Böhm, and Linke.
    (The trio was that in E flat D929.)
5. *Auf dem Strom* by Rellstab, song with horn and pianoforte accompaniment, performed by Tietze and Lewy jun.

[22] R. Hallmark, 'Schubert's "Auf dem Strom" ', in E. Badura-Skoda and P. Branscombe (eds.), *Schubert Studies: Problems of Style and Chronology* (Cambridge, 1982), 40–6.

6. *Die Allmacht* D852 by Ladislaus Pyrker, song with pianoforte accompaniment, performed by Vogl.
(The song was composed in August 1825.)
7. *Schlachtgesang* (Battle Hymn) D912 by Klopstock, double chorus for male voices.
(Dating from February 1827, this was probably accompanied.)

Schubert took part as a performer in the concert, accompanying all the vocal works, both solo and (presumably) concerted. Until the previous year he had refused to perform as a pianist in public or semi-public concerts, restricting his appearances to the salon scene. In 1827, however, on several occasions he had accompanied Tietze in performances of his songs, and a local singer in concerts of the Styrian Musical Society in the Landständisches-Theater in Graz. Bocklet, on the other hand, was the pianist in the piano trio, as he had been in all performances of Schubert's piano chamber music over the last year. When the same trio was played at Spaun's betrothal party, Schuppanzigh had been the violinist; but at the end of March he was ill and his place in the trio and string quartet was taken by Josef Michael Böhm.

The programme of Schubert's benefit concert followed the pattern of mixed fare set by the chamber concerts of the Gesellschaft der Musikfreunde, beginning with (part of) a string quartet and ending with a rousing vocal ensemble. The quartet movement was the only item which did not include the piano. The choice of the E flat Piano Trio, the other instrumental work played, rather than that in B flat or another of his chamber works with or without piano, suggests that Schubert was satisfied with this trio as the centrepiece of the concert. He had heard it performed at least once before by almost the same players. The first movement is both challenging and sublime, clearly constructed, full of contrast and variety, alternately bold and confident, restless, sympathetic, and delicate. In the second movement the main theme is given first to the cello, an instrument for which Schubert had a special understanding (a subject to which we shall return in the context of the String Quintet in C). The melody here was not one of his original lyrical themes, but an adaptation of the melody of a Swedish song, 'Se solen sjunker' (The Sun is Sinking). He had heard the composer–tenor, Isak Berg, sing this song at the home of the four Fröhlich sisters (in the Spiegelgasse) on a visit he made to Vienna shortly before Schubert composed the trio. According to Leopold Sonnleithner, Schubert had taken great pleasure in Berg's performances,[23] while Gerhard von Breuning spoke of him being 'captivated by his [Berg's] music'.[24] Berg was

[23] *Mem.* 115, *Erin.* 134.   [24] *Mem.* 251, *Erin.* 287.

a singing pupil of Schober's brother-in-law, Siboni, then director of the Conservatoire in Copenhagen, who had previously lived and worked in the Kärntnertor-Theater in Vienna.[25] The third movement, Scherzo and Trio, is one of Schubert's finest movements in this form, with lively canonic imitation, and full of charm and surprises. The final movement is the least satisfactory, and several who heard the work in its original form felt that it was also far too long. Neither Schubert nor Bocklet, the pianist in this performance and earlier in Schubert's Fantasia in C for violin and piano, would have wanted to experience again a large proportion of the audience walking out before the end of the last movement, as had happened on 20 January. At some stage between the first performance of the Trio and its publication towards the end of the year, and most probably before his important March concert, Schubert was persuaded to cut the last movement. He removed 99 bars from the original 846 bars, a subject to which we shall return in connection with his negotiations with the publisher, Probst.

The concert was well attended by an enthusiastic audience which included many of Schubert's friends, acquaintances, and admirers. Viennese journals rather surprisingly failed to report the event, the explanation given for this usually being that interest in the newly arrived Paganini and his thrilling violin-playing at his first concert in Vienna three days later had diverted attention from the efforts of the local-born composer and his compositions. Be that as it may, the Vienna correspondent of the Leipzig *Allgemeine musikalische Zeitung* mentioned Schubert's concert in conjunction with another privately organized concert of Linke's (in memory of Beethoven) a few days earlier: 'If all these works [by Beethoven], performed to perfection [at Linke's entertainment on 23 March], afforded an indescribable aural treat, the same must be said with hardly less emphasis in praise of that *soirée musicale* which the excellent Schubert held in the very same place on the 26th.'[26] (The date of Linke's concert, 23 March, and problems of rehearsing for both concerts may have caused the cellist to request that Schubert change the date of his from the projected 21st.) The Vienna correspondent of the Berlin *Allgemeine musikalische Zeitung* also reported the event, clearly irritated by partisan applause at Schubert's concert: 'The numerous gathering of friends and patrons did not stint resounding applause after each number and saw to it that several of them were repeated.'[27] (This comment calls to mind an earlier remark of the critic of a Leipzig journal after the première of *Die Zwillingsbrüder* in 1820: 'That Herr Schubert has many friends active on his

---

[25] M. Willfort, 'Das Urbild des Andante aus Schuberts Klavier Trio in Es-dur, D 929', *ÖMZ* 33 (1978), 277–83.

[26] *Doc.* 756, *Dok.* 504; *ND* 613.   [27] *Doc.* 757, *Dok.* 505; *ND* 624.

behalf was shown at the first performance.'[28]) Schubert's friends were indeed delighted by the concert, and saw it as a great personal success for the composer: 'I shall never forget how glorious that was' (Franz von Hartmann);[29] 'Enormous applause, good receipts' (Bauernfeld).[30] In his obituary notice written almost exactly one year later, Spaun wrote:

It was only the urging of his friends and the inadequacy of his income that finally induced him . . . to give a concert for his own benefit . . . which Vogl, Tietze and Fraülein Fröhlich enriched by the beauty of their excellent singing and Bocklet by his excellent pianoforte playing. The exceptional responsiveness of the packed audience matched the rare enjoyment of his evening, which will certainly remain unforgettable (to those present).[31]

Almost thirty years later Sonnleithner wrote:

His friends advised him to give a concert and this he decided to do; but since he was not at all the man to initiate anything of this kind himself, it was once more his friends who, gladly and with affection arranged and managed the concert. The result was success in every way, and provided Schubert with a considerable sum of money.[32]

Bauernfeld provides the information that the concert made a profit for Schubert of almost 800 fl. WW (320 fl. KM). The young Marie von Pratobevera (who later became sister-in-law to Heinrich Kreissle von Hellborn, Schubert's first biographer), writing to her fiancé, then in Styria, told of her pilgrimage with members of her family earlier in the day to the cemetery in Währing where Beethoven was buried, to see his tombstone. In the evening she attended Schubert's concert: 'Everybody was lost in a frenzy of admiration and rapture. There was clapping and stamping . . . .'.[33]

There were good reasons why Schubert failed to complete both the piano duet fantasia and the cantata *Miriams Siegesgesang* in time for this benefit concert. The duet, whether he had hoped to include it in his concert or no, was of great personal significance for him: it was written for, and dedicated to, the Countess Caroline Esterházy. He could not on any account compromise his highest standards or hurry the amendments to this work, and it was not completed in its final form until a few weeks after the concert. In a totally different way, the cantata was a challenge for Schubert. He was writing it while under the influence of Handel's choral music. On its first performance, after Schubert's death, on 30 January 1829, one critic wrote, somewhat effusively: 'in this piece . . . Schubert fused the strength

[28] *Doc.* 139, *Dok.* 96; *ND* 38.   [29] *Doc.* 754, *Dok.* 504.   [30] Ibid.
[31] *Mem.* 28, *Erin.* 36.   [32] *Mem.* 115, *Erin.* 134.   [33] *Doc.* 760, *Dok.* 507.

and seriousness of Handel with the passion of Beethoven.'[34] Schubert had long been an admirer of Handel's oratorios, excerpts of which were frequently performed in the series of *Concerts spirituels* and in the Sunday midday concerts of the Gesellschaft der Musikfreunde.[35] Anselm Hütten-brenner claimed that the Messiah was one of Schubert's (and his) favourite works,[36] that the composer admired 'Handel's mighty spirit' as much as that of Beethoven, and that 'in his leisure hours he used to play through operas and oratorios from score with great avidity. . . . Sometimes when playing through Handel's works, he sprang up as though electrified and cried: "Oh, the daring of these modulations!" '[37] (The quotation from the first aria, 'Comfort Ye' from Messiah in bars 17–28 of the *Drei Klavierstücke*, composed in May 1828, is evidence of his knowledge, if not of the influence, of Handel's oratorio.[38] Leopold Sonnleithner, usually a very reliable witness, told how: 'a few months before his death Schubert visited the Fröhlich family and told them that he had acquired the scores of Handel's oratorios. He added: "Now for the first time I see what I lack; but I will study hard with Sechter so that I can make good the omission." '[39] Breuning claimed that the Handel scores were presented to Schubert as a gift.[40] Another witness (Josef Hauer, a serious music-lover who as a young medical student had played second violin in the first, private, performance in 1826 of Schubert's String Quartet in D minor)[41] told how 'In the last years of his life Schubert also wanted to get on closer terms with Handel.'[42] Schubert had but one lesson (jointly with Lanz) with Sechter, on 4 November, a week before he took to the bed from which he never rose. The influence of Handel on his music of 1828, in works including *Miriams Siegesgesang*, the *Klavierstücke*, and the Mass in E flat, therefore resulted entirely from his own private study of Handel's scores.

The reception of Paganini and his violin-playing in the spring and summer of 1828 gives further indication of the state of music in Vienna and Viennese attitudes to musical performance. At his first appearance on 29 March the audience was not large; but his remarkable skill, magical performances, and mysterious, charismatic personality quickly attracted the crowds. The Viennese correspondent of the Dresden *Abendzeitung* summed up the impact he made:

The most wonderful, most extraordinary musical phenomenon, a comet on the musical horizon, of a kind which returns perhaps only once in a thousand years, is

---

[34] *ND* 698.   [35] *Doc.* 510n, 610; *Dok.* 347n, 411.   [36] *Mem.* 70, *Erin.* 81.
[37] *Mem.* 180, *Erin.* 206–7.
[38] I am indebted to Donald Burrows for drawing my attention to this quotation.
[39] *Mem.* 114, *Erin.* 133.   [40] *Mem.* 255, *Erin.* 292–3.
[41] *Doc.* 500n, 508n, *Dok.* 345n, 346n.   [42] *Mem.* 177, *Erin.* 204.

at this time within our walls. It is Paganini! . . . Only one voice is to be heard in the city and this cried out 'Harken to Paganini!' The man has now given five concerts, and netted at least 70,000 Gulden, W.W. [28,000 fl. KM] . . . It is not surprising that, in comparison to him, all other musical performers are put in the shade.[43]

The wizardry of Paganini was the talk of the town, the audiences revelling in his virtuosity and marvelling at the electrifying power of the 45-year-old violinist to hold them spellbound. Each repeat performance was sold out, so that his originally passing visit was prolonged to a four-month season of fourteen concerts. Some six years earlier the Viennese had been moved to feverish excitement by Rossini and his operas, and the English musician Edward Holmes, after visiting the city, described the obsessive reaction of opera audiences: 'there is scarcely a corner of Europe in which the tastes of the operatic community can be worse. It has been said that the people of Vienna are Rossini mad'.[44] Holmes continued with an account of the frivolous fashion in the city for everything Italian, or connected with Rossini, not only for the music but for language, dress, and behaviour. The enthusiasm six years later for Paganini followed a similar pattern: 'The public became absolutely intoxicated . . . Hats, dresses, shawls, boots, perfumes, gloves etc. appeared in the shop windows "à la Paganini". His portrait was displayed everywhere; his bust adorned the sticks of the Viennese dandies, and even dainty dishes were named after him. The Emperor conferred upon him the title of "Virtuoso of the Court." '[45]

Schubert bore no grudge against Paganini when adulation of the violinist caused the critics to overlook his own benefit concert. In fact, Schubert may have been present at his opening concert in the Redoutensaal of the Imperial Palace on the following Saturday. In any case, when he persuaded Bauernfeld to accept as a gift a five-florin ticket for a stalls seat for Paganini's fourth concert on 4 May, this was for Schubert his second attendance at the Italian's concerts. Schubert told Bauernfeld: 'I have already heard him once . . . I tell you, we shall never see the fellow's like again! And I have stacks of money now [after the benefit concert]—so come on!' Bauernfeld described the concert: 'So we heard this diabolically heavenly violinist . . . utter amazement at his diabolical arts . . . According to custom I was treated at the inn, after the concert, and a bottle more than usual was charged to enthusiasm.'[46] In a letter to Frau Pachler, Jenger praised

[43] (*Doc.* 756–7); *ND* 620.
[44] E. Holmes, *A Ramble among the Musicians of Germany. By a Musical Professor* (London, 1828), 116.
[45] *Grove Dictionary of Music and Musicians*, 3rd edn. (1927), s.v. Paganini.
[46] *Mem.* 228, *Erin.* 261.

Paganini, whom he had also heard twice, as: 'the greatest violin virtuoso who has ever existed and will ever be born . . . One can only hear, admire and marvel at him.'[47] In a lost letter to Anselm Hüttenbrenner of this period Schubert wrote simply; 'In the *Adagio* I heard an angel sing.'[48]

The 320 fl. KM which Schubert received as the profits from his private concert was small money in comparison with Paganini's receipts for his concerts in much larger venues (some 28,000 fl. KM in total); but to Schubert the money was welcome indeed. After he had paid outstanding debts, and with some prospect of money to come from publications, he thought he could now look forward without financial anxieties to another holiday that summer.

In addition to preparing for his concert in March, Schubert had also been conducting a correspondence with publishers. In the current unfavourable musical scene in Vienna where, with just two exceptions (the String Quartet in A minor and *Rondeau brillant*), publishers were showing little interest in his chamber and orchestral music, Schubert felt it necessary to approach publishers abroad, and particularly in Germany. Apart from his concern that he might have almost glutted the Austrian market with his songs, he was eager to get away from the potential situation that he would be regarded as one of the general run of composers of the day of popular trifles rather than as a serious composer of instrumental musical as well as songs. By February 1828 he already had an appreciable number of completed or almost completed works he considered ready for publication, and on this basis he began a serious correspondence with Probst and Schott, both in Leipzig, which was to continue right up to the time of his death nine months later. Unfortunately in Germany, as in Austria, the situation was far from easy. Unless a composer was already well regarded and his music sought after, a publisher was unlikely to accept items other than small pieces for amateurs, i.e. for the domestic market, such as simple vocal and keyboard compositions neither too long nor demanding of technical abilities.

Schubert had met Probst, who was also the German agent for the Viennese publisher Artaria, during a visit the latter made to Vienna in the spring of 1827. (It is possible that this was the occasion of the private concert at the premises of Artaria when Schubert's *Rondeau brillant* was performed by Slawjk and Bocklet, at the time of its publication.)[49] In February 1828 Schubert received a friendly and encouraging letter from Probst. After first referring to his pleasure at meeting the composer and making

[47] *Doc.* 770, *Dok.* 513.   [48] *Mem.* 67, *Erin.* 78.
[49] *Doc.* 599n, 629, *Dok.* 404n, 423; *ND* 478.

some positive remarks about his latest songs and piano duets, he said he was convinced 'more and more that it would be easy to promote your name throughout the rest of Germany and the North, in which I will gladly lend a hand'.[50] He asked for any songs or vocal pieces and piano duets that were not too demanding of performers, and promised fair and prompt payment for works accepted and published. Concerning the larger works, Probst asked Schubert to select the works he sent carefully, not to offer them to other publishers, and to keep their negotiations confidential. Perhaps by coincidence, on the same day as Probst, Bernhard Schott wrote to Schubert in encouraging terms but a less personal manner. He asked for 'pianoforte works or vocal pieces for one or several voices, with or without pianoforte accompaniment. . . . If you have a number of things in stock and would like to send us a list of them, this would also be most agreeable to us.'[51] He added: 'we also have an establishment in Paris where we will likewise promote your compositions'; but there was no firm offer to publish. Unfortunately for Schubert, neither Probst nor Schott showed in their letters any inkling of interest in his instrumental music, apart, that is, from piano works.

Despite the German publishers' preference for trifles, probably encouraged by professional musician colleagues in Vienna, Schubert persisted. On 21 February he replied to Schott, offering a varied collection of vocal works, but only after he had listed various instrumental compositions: a piano trio (whether that in B flat or in E flat is not stipulated), two string quartets (those in D minor and G major), the duet Fantasia in F minor, the Fantasia in C for violin and piano, and the second set of impromptus. All of these works except the string quartets and first piano trio he had completed within the last eight weeks or so. (The duet Fantasia was virtually completed by this time, but not to his final satisfaction.) He then referred in general terms to 'three operas,[52] a Mass [in A flat] and a Symphony [in C]'. These he mentioned 'only in order to make you acquainted with my striving after the highest art'.[53]

Probst's letter to Schubert reached him somewhat later than that of Schott, after it was delivered first to his namesake Josef Schubert in the Wieden suburb. He replied to both only on 10 April. Referring to the E flat Piano Trio, he wrote to Schott: 'I have . . . had copies made of the Trio you wanted (which was received at my concert by a packed audience with such extraordinary applause that I am being pressed to repeat the concert).'[54] He also had copies to hand of the impromptus and a five-part male-voice

[50] *Doc.* 735, *Dok.* 492–3.   [51] *Doc.* 736–7, *Dok.* 493.
[52] *Alfonso und Estrella, Die Verschworenen*, and *Fierrabras*.
[53] *Doc.* 739–40, *Dok.* 495.   [54] *Doc.* 764, *Dok.* 509–10.

chorus, and: 'if you would care to have the Trio for 100 fl. KM, and the other two works together for 60 fl. coinage, I can send them off at once. All I should request is publication as soon as possible.' To Probst he made similar suggestions:

I should be delighted to let you have some works, if you are inclined to agree to the reasonable fee of 60 fl. K.M. per sizeable book. I need hardly assure you that I shall not send you anything which I do not regard as good work, at least in the opinion of its composer and some select circles, and, when all is said and done, it must be above all in my own interest to send good works abroad.[55]

Probst replied to this quickly, asking for the trio on trust, though offering, perhaps in error, a much lower fee than Schubert intended—only 60 fl. KM rather than the 100 fl. he had asked Schott for. Schubert seems to have decided reluctantly to accept the lower fee, both because of his need for immediate money and in the interests of beginning a working relationship with Probst that might prove more productive in the future. His stipulations, however, included 'the speediest possible production' and the 'despatch of 6 copies' to himself. He insisted that 'the cuts indicated in the last movement [of the trio] are to be most scrupulously observed'. He also requested that it be performed for the first time (presumably at a publisher's promotion concert) 'by capable people' and, most particularly, that Probst ensure 'a continual uniformity of tempo at changes of the time-signature in the last movement. The minuet at a moderate pace and *piano* throughout; the trio, on the other hand, vigorous except where *P* and *PP* are marked.'[56]

The speedy publication did not follow and in a letter to Probst on 1 August Schubert, clearing up the matter of the opus number for the trio, showed concern for its progress: 'I beg that the edition should be free of errors and look eagerly forward to it. This work is to be dedicated to nobody, save those who find pleasure in it. That is the most profitable dedication.'[57] Delays continued until on 2 October he again approached Probst, in some desperation:

I beg to enquire when the Trio is finally to appear. Can it be that you do not know the opus number yet? It is 100. I await its appearance with eager anticipation. I have composed, among other things, 3 sonatas for piano solo, which I should like to dedicate to Hummel. Moreover, I have set several songs by Heine of Hamburg, which were extraordinarily well received here, and lastly turned out a Quintet for 2 violins, 1 viola and 2 violoncellos.[58]

To this, Schubert's last letter to the publisher, Probst replied promptly: the E flat Trio was now ready and his copies should arrive shortly. (In fact,

---

[55] *Doc.* 765, *Dok.* 510.   [56] *Doc.* 774, *Dok.* 516.   [57] *Doc.* 796, *Dok.* 529.
[58] *Doc.* 810–11, *Dok.* 540.

Schubert died before they did.) And of his new compositions, including the last three piano sonatas and the String Quintet in C D956, Probst was interested only in the songs.[59] The trio appeared that October without, as requested, the 99 bars of the last movement. To the quintet and piano sonatas we return later.

Schott's last letter to Schubert was written on 30 October, three weeks before the composer's death. He rejected the second set of impromptus, which their Paris branch had decided were too difficult for their customers. For the male-voice quintet, 'Mondenschein' (Moonlight) D875, which he was happy to publish, the composer was offered a half (30 fl. KM) of the joint fee Schubert had requested for these and the impromptus. So the negotiations with Schott and Probst, which had begun so promisingly early in the year, ended with little progress having been made, apart from the tardy publication of the piano trio. Schubert had been sorely vexed by the experience, his irritation exacerbated by ill health, though the affair was probably no worse than he had already experienced with Viennese publishers. Had he lived longer, he might have persisted, and, now that the two doors had been opened in Leipzig, with more success. A further minor incident reveals again the kind of difficulties he faced in gaining credibility as a composer. In July 1828 he received a letter from another German publisher, Karl Brüggemann in Halberstadt, who asked whether Schubert was willing to contribute short pieces for solo piano for an album he was producing for amateur pianists of only moderate accomplishment. Schubert responded positively, but was deterred eventually by the restrictions on length of each piece to a maximum of 'two sheets'. The correspondence ended before any transaction was entered into.[60] While Brüggemann's initial letter, addressed to 'Franz Schubert, Esq., Composer, Vienna' (Herrn Franz Schubert, Wohlgeboren) was once again first delivered to Josef Schubert, indicating that in his home city his fame was not universal, Brüggemann's approach indicates that Schubert's reputation as a successful young composer in musical circles in north Germany was sufficient for a music publisher there to seek him out, as had the Swiss Nägeli in 1826.

When Spaun announced his engagement to Franziska von Roner early in January, Schubert was delighted for him, but sad that his marriage would inevitably lead to less frequent meetings with his former friends. The composer was present at the wedding on 14 April, along with Spaun's closest friends, the Witteczeks, Enderes, and Gahy.[61] It may not have been a

---

[59] *Doc.* 814, *Dok.* 542.   [60] *Doc.* 783–5, 792, 797, *Dok.* 522–3, 527, 530–1.

[61] He is unlikely to have received an invitation to the wedding, three weeks later, of L. Sonnleithner (ennobled, with his father Ignaz, to von Sonnleithner in the following month) who, though much interested in Schubert as a musician, moved in different social circles.

coincidence that Schubert's increasing association with other musicians coincided with the gradual withdrawal of Spaun from his circle of friends during his courtship, ending in a total break after his marriage. Spaun had been something of a father figure in the group; but now the not-so-young bridegroom (he was 39, his bride seven years younger) was preoccupied with married life, to Franziska's gain and the circle's loss.

Early in March, shortly before Schubert's benefit concert, Moritz von Schwind, perhaps with the thought of Spaun's approaching marriage spurring him on, dressed for the occasion in a festive frock coat, went to the home of his beloved Nettl Hönig to ask for her hand in marriage.[62] His reception was not quite what he expected: no doubt on account of both his agnosticism and his lack of money or sure prospects, he was firmly told by Nettl's father that, although he would reluctantly agree to their betrothal, Schwind must now seriously begin to prepare himself for marriage, not least by working to establish his position as a responsible and successful artist. The marriage was likely to be a distant goal. Schwind had not enjoyed the interview, was shocked by its severity, and returned in very low spirits, almost in despair, to describe what had happened to Bauernfeld and Schubert. They were in an agreed coffee-house, waiting to congratulate the happy suitor and celebrate his betrothal. Instead they had to try to cheer him, Schubert by some good-natured teasing.[63] From now on Schwind was determined to study in Munich, hoping that this would advance his career and hasten the time when he and Nettl could marry. He was not to know then that in some eighteen months, in October 1829, the engagement would be broken off, ostensibly on account of her deep religiosity and his inability to tolerate her beliefs. (In 1832 she married Bauernfeld's good friend, Ferdinand von Mayerhofer.)

During this year, as in the previous few years, in April and May Schubert entered into a period of unproductivity associated with depression and heavy drinking. Bauernfeld commented on the consumption of 'one bottle [of wine] more than usual' after Paganini's concert on 4 May. Yet he may have been totally unaware that Schubert did not go directly home after they parted that night, but moved on to the Snail inn, where he and Franz von Hartmann sat on 'quite merrily until 12.30', presumably still drinking. At the end of the same month von Hartmann wrote that he and his youngest brother Louis (on a visit to Vienna), together with Enk and Schubert, went out to Grinzing to drink the new wine. When they returned late in the evening they were all somewhat tipsy, 'but Schubert especially'.[64] This may

---

[62] *Doc.* 754, *Dok.* 504. [63] *Mem.* 239, *Erin.* 274.

[64] *Doc.* 787, *Dok.* 524. In the Hartmann family chronicle for this year, presumably written some time after the event, Hartmann suggested that Enk was the most affected by alcohol on this occasion: WL ii. 103.

not have been serious drinking, but the effect on Schubert's health would not have been for the better.

Amongst the professional musicians with whom Schubert was now frequently keeping company was the Bavarian Franz Lachner, who later (c.1835) described a two-day excursion they made together early in June 1828, on the invitation of one Herr J. Schickh, to Baden and Heiligenkreuz. This was presumably Josef Kilian Schickh, a playwright and former contemporary of Schubert's at the Academic Grammar-School, and not his uncle, the almost 60-year-old Johann Schickh, editor of the *Wiener Zeitschrift für Kunst, Literatur, Theater und Mode*, who had already included twelve of Schubert's songs as supplements to his journal. They travelled by coach to Baden, the spa town south of Vienna, spending the night there. During that evening Schickh announced that at six the next morning they would drive to nearby Heiligenkreuz, where the beautiful Cistercian monastery had a fine and famous organ. The two composers agreed that in the course of the evening each would compose a fugue to perform on the instrument. Lachner told how 'towards midnight we had both finished . . . [at] Heiligenkreuz . . . both fugues were performed in the presence of several monks from the monastery. Schubert's fugue (for four hands), in E minor, has been published . . . My fugue remains unpublished.'[65]

In the spring and summer of 1828 two groups of four songs by Schubert were published by the Lithographic Institute in Vienna, of which Schober was then director. The first group (Op. 106: D922, D926, D927, D891) was dedicated to Frau Pachler, the second (as Op. 96: D939, D909, D768, D881) to Charlotte (Maria Karoline), Princess von Kinsky. The princess, to whom Beethoven had dedicated three groups of his songs, was the widow of that composer's patron, and also a good singer herself. She held musical soirées in her home, and at one of these, probably in the autumn of 1827, Baron Schönstein was invited to sing and took Schubert with him as his accompanist. After this, the princess granted Schubert permission to dedicate the Op. 96 songs to her, and he sent her a copy on their publication. A letter of appreciation which she wrote to him in early July has survived.[66] She thanked him for the copy, looked forward to hearing them performed by Schönstein and himself in the coming winter season (presumably at another musical evening), and enclosed a monetary 'modest token of my gratitude'. Spaun (in 1858) described just such an evening at Princess Kinsky's when Schönstein had been invited specifically 'to perform his [Schubert's] songs before a very aristocratic audience'.[67] The listeners were 'enraptured', and 'surrounded Baron Schönstein with the most ardent

---

[65] *Mem.* 195–6, *Erin.* 224–5.   [66] *Doc.* 790, *Dok.* 526.   [67] *Mem.* 135, *Erin.* 157–8.

appreciation . . . and congratulations on his performance'. No one took any notice of the insignificant-looking composer–accompanist except Princess Kinsky, who was embarrassed by, and tried to apologize for, this neglect. He thanked her for her concern, but assured her that he was not the slightest bothered or offended; he was accustomed to being ignored on such occasions, and was happier so, as attention embarrassed him. Had it not been for his illness and then death in the following November, he would no doubt have returned with Schönstein that winter to perform the songs at the home of the illustrious dedicatee.

After Spaun's marriage, the group of friends which had centred around him seemed to lack motivation and again, as in the summer of 1827, it began to fall apart. Schober continued to conduct the now weekly meetings of the reading-circle during the summer months, now in his summer residence outside Vienna,[68] but few of those who attended had belonged to the old circle of friends. Schwind was going his own way, intent on his studies and spending as much time as he could with Nettl Hönig. From early in 1828 Bauernfeld appeared rather infrequently at former meeting-places, keeping company instead with his friend Ferdinand von Mayerhofer, who again shared his lodgings in the Landstrasse until he left to rejoin his regiment in mid-July. Bauernfeld had been informed in March that his comedy *Der Brautwerber* (The Suitor) had been accepted for performance at the Burg-Theater in Vienna,[69] but was disappointed by many delays and difficulties over its production. In June he took a short holiday with Mayerhofer, for part of which they were joined by Schober, who again proved quarrelsome, getting into an unpleasant disagreement with Mayerhofer.[70] When in August Bauernfeld's play at last went into rehearsal, he was nervous and uneasy. At the première on 5 September, his début in the theatre, Grillparzer, Schubert, Schwind, and Schober were among his friends there to support him; and they had arranged to meet him afterwards for a celebration at 'the inn' (the Partridge perhaps). But Bauernfeld did not turn up. He had decided that his play was a disaster. Although there had been applause, he recognized this as representing no more than a *succèss d'estime*, an honourable failure. He could face no one, and walked the streets of Vienna in despair until, shortly before midnight and quite by chance, he met his friend and mentor Grillparzer on his way home from the inn where Bauernfeld's friends had arranged to meet him. Grillparzer was 'most amiable',[71] but this could not prevent Bauernfeld the next morning from registering feelings of utter dismay. Schubert and Schwind visited him and endeavoured to cheer him, and the composer, who had himself suffered his

[68] *Doc.* 796, *Dok.* 529.   [69] WL i. 68.   [70] Ibid. 69.   [71] *Doc.* 805, *Dok.* 536.

own deep disappointments in the theatre, insisted that he had enjoyed the play enormously: 'We all did! And we aren't fools you know!' Bauernfeld replied, half angry and half laughing: 'What use is that if I'm one?'[72] The reviews were poor, and the play was taken off after just four performances. Bauernfeld left Vienna for another holiday, once more totally disheartened.

The improvement in Schubert's financial situation after his March concert led him to plan a return visit to Gmunden during the following summer. He and Jenger were also discussing a return to the Pachlers' in Graz, but their plans for a summer trip were thwarted by problems for Jenger at work: proposed military manœuvres at this time made it impossible for him to take a vacation.[73] Meanwhile Schubert was again in financial difficulties, for which reason he had to decline the invitations to Upper Austria; but he hoped his situation would improve sufficiently by September for him to be able to travel to Graz. By that time, as Jenger told Frau Pachler, the composer would be carrying with him 'a new operetta',[74] *Der Graf von Gleichen*, on which he was now again working.[75] (This suggests that the composer, who returned to the opera that autumn after a gap of some months, was now intending to finish it.) Unfortunately, by the end of August Schubert's health was causing him considerable concern, and on 25 September he wrote, from his brother Ferdinand's home to Jenger, and one might hope also to Frau Pachler, explaining that 'Nothing will come of our visit to Graz this year, as money and weather are wholly unfavourable.'[76] He did not mention here that the move from his home with Schober in the inner city to his brother's new apartment in the Wieden suburb was on account of his health and on the advice of his doctor.

Schubert dated the beginning of his last large-scale sacred work, the Mass in E flat D950, 'June 1828', although he began sketching parts of it earlier in the year.[77] He never heard it performed or rehearsed. Like the Mass in A flat, it requires a proficient and well-rehearsed chorus; and the long contrapuntal choral sections, in the writing of which Schubert was clearly influenced by Handel's oratorios, make considerable demands on the vocal stamina of the singers. The circumstances for which he wrote this impressive mass are uncertain; but a reviewer of its first performance on 4 October 1829[78] wrote that, by special request of the composer, this took place in the Holy Trinity church in the Alsergrund. The director was Ferdinand Schubert. (The church's own choirmaster Michael Leitermayer

---

[72] *Mem.* 238, *Erin.* 272.   [73] *Doc.* 789, *Dok.* 525.   [74] *Doc.* 806, *Dok.* 537.
[75] E. Hilmar (ed.), *F. Schubert: Der Graf von Gleichen*, facs. edn. (Tutzing, 1988), 11; *Catalogus*, 29.
[76] *Doc.* 807, *Dok.* 537–8.   [77] *Catalogus*, 8.
[78] In the *Wiener Allgemeine Theaterzeitung*: ND 748.

was an acquaintance of Schubert, and like him, a former pupil of Michael Holzer in the Himmelpfortgrund.) Six weeks later Ferdinand conducted a second, but somewhat inadequate performance in his own church of St Ulrich (Maria Trost).[79] The occasions for which two other sacred works were written, both minor compositions dating from the summer and autumn of 1828, are clearer. In July Schubert produced an 89-bar setting of Psalm 92 D953, to a Hebrew text. It was written on the request of the musically gifted Salomon Sulzer (1804–90), born in Hohenems, cantor of the new Jewish synagogue in Vienna which had been inaugurated in 1826. According to the custom of the time, the psalm was set for unaccompanied mixed chorus and solo quartet (from the choir) with a central solo section for baritone, sung by the cantor (in this case Sulzer). Psalm 92, a song of thanksgiving and praise, was of special importance in the Jewish liturgy, a 'Song for the Sabbath' which was sung in the Friday evening service and twice during the Sabbath morning service. Although stylistically Schubert's setting resembled the Christian church music with which he was familiar rather than music for the synagogue, and the melody has no Hebrew characteristics, Schubert followed closely, and with some skill, the meaning of the text and the prescribed Hebrew accentuations. To do this, he must have had considerable assistance and guidance from Sulzer, of whose relationship with Schubert unfortunately nothing else is known.[80] The work was performed soon after its composition in 1828.

Schubert composed a very different sacred piece on the dedication of new bells at the church of the Holy Trinity in the Alsergrund on 2 September (the church at which Beethoven's funeral had taken place in 1827). This was a short, 21-bar, slow piece for male-voice quartet and mixed chorus with wind accompaniment, 'Glaube, Hoffnung und Liebe' (Faith, Hope and Love) D954, to a text by an actor at the Burg-Theater and occasional poet, Johann Reil.

The impressive collection of fourteen songs published less than a year after Schubert's death as his swansong, the *Schwanengesang* D957, were written between August and October 1828 although there is evidence to suggest that some of the songs may have occupied him before this.[81] This collection—seven by Rellstab, six by Heine, and one by Seidl ('Die Taubenpost'—Pigeon Post D965A), which has nothing in common with the other songs, especially the Heine settings, and does not fit easily in the collection—in no way constitutes a song-cycle as do *Die schöne Müllerin*

[79] *Doc.* 804, *Dok.* 535, *ND* 756, 767.

[80] E. Brody, 'Schubert and Sulzer Revisited', in Badura-Skoda and Branscombe (eds.), *Schubert Studies* (Cambridge, 1982), 47–60.

[81] *ND* 689; R. Hilmar-Voit, 'Zu Schuberts "Letzten Lieder" ', *Brille*, 6 (1991), 48–55.

and *Winterreise*. While there is a strong case against the notion that Schubert used for the first group of songs copies of the poems made by Rellstab himself and formerly owned by Beethoven, it is known that Schober introduced him to the Heine songs, which had been the subject of two meetings of the reading-circle early in the year, on 12 and 19 January. That Schubert in no way considered the songs as a cycle is confirmed by his letter to Probst of 2 October (already quoted) mentioning that he had recently written 'several songs by Heine'. These are fine poems, vivid yet concise, and Schubert's settings show him to be at the summit of his powers as a composer of songs. In this context, it is expedient to remind ourselves briefly of the enormous influence that Schubert had through his songs on future generations of composers in the manner they set German texts to music. The magnificent 'Der Atlas', for example, the first of his Heine settings, is both a thrilling song and an admirable example of the way in which Schubert anticipated, or influenced at a distance, Wagner's dramatic, expressive vocal writing. Both 'Der Atlas', bearing the sorrows of the world on his shoulders, and 'Am Meer' (By the Sea) are also particularly striking examples of the expressive intensity of Schubert's piano accompaniments in these last songs. In 'Am Meer', where the piano paints a sad scene of rising mist and swelling sea, associated with the mysterious weeping of the girl, the music is dramatic, affecting, and concentrative. It is a sound-painting comparable with an atmospheric landscape by Turner, or by his exact contemporary, the German artist Caspar David Friedrich (1774–1840). Thus, over a period of some fifteen years Schubert, while yet a young man, had developed the *Lied*, both vocally and pianistically, into a sophisticated and compelling art-form which was to have an enormous influence on composers who came after him.

Although I have generally avoided detailed discussion of Schubert's music, here, at the end of his life, a brief look at some characteristics of his last works seems appropriate, if not essential to an understanding of the composer in this period. According to the dates given by Schubert on some of the autograph manuscripts, and to a comment he made in a letter to Probst, he composed in September 1828 a wealth of music of such high quality that it is difficult to comprehend how one man could have achieved so much so quickly. The last three piano sonatas, in C minor, in A, and in B flat, D958–D960, several of the *Schwanengesang* collection, and the supremely beautiful String Quintet in C D956 were all completed in the space of a few weeks that autumn. In the case of the piano sonatas, the existence of earlier sketches proves that, while September was the month of completion and of writing out the scores, the creative process began several months earlier. Undated sketches of the C minor Sonata seem to date from the late spring of 1828,[82] at which time Schubert worked on all four movements. Similarly, his sketches, or incomplete first versions, of all the movements of the other two sonatas were written down between June and August.[83] Only for the String Quintet is there no documentary evidence pointing to its possible roots in an earlier period. Schubert's autograph manuscript of the quintet, along with any sketches that may have existed, have long been lost. Nothing is known about its composition except that Schubert, in his letter to Probst of 2 October, implied that it was newly completed.[84] It is indeed possible that this unique and highly concentrated composition was from beginning to end the product of only a week or two of intense creativity. At the same time, musical evidence seems to confirm that parts of it at least must have been conceived after he had completed the Piano Sonata in B flat.

Of the three last piano sonatas, only that in B flat is written in Schubert's characteristic inward, brooding style. It is presumably for this reason that this final sonata remains the most loved and admired, although all three are now part of the standard piano-recital repertoire. A comparison of the slow movement of this sonata with that of the quintet reveals interesting similarities and certain distinctive differences in Schubert's conception of the two works. They share the same key signature of four sharps, the one indicating C sharp minor and the other E major, both unusual choices for compositions in B flat and C major. In both works the long, sustained, and intense opening melody, entering with no introduction, lies in the middle register. This is played by the pianist's right hand in the sonata, and by the second violin, supported by viola and first cello, in the quintet. The melodic line of both themes in the first four bars is almost identical, although there are considerable harmonic and tonal differences which soon cause the melodies to diverge.

The sonata's slow movement was conceived (as the summer sketches show) before the quintet, although Schubert must have been composing the chamber work at almost, if not exactly, the same time as he was completing the fair copy of the sonata, which he did on 26 September. To a considerable degree, therefore, the two works are contemporaneous. Performances of the slow movement of the sonata on Viennese fortepianos of the 1820s have strengthened my feeling that Schubert, intentionally or unintentionally, was thinking in terms of a string quartet when he wrote it. Indeed, the outer sections might almost have been a first version of, or more likely, his first thoughts for, the quintet's slow movement. The emotional content, however, is not the same. The sonata is darker, with restrained unease,

---

[82] *Catalogus*, 98.   [83] Ibid. 98–9.   [84] *Doc.* 811, *Dok.* 540.

(a) Piano Sonata in B flat D960, bars 1–9; (b) String Quintet in C D956, bars 1–9;
(c) Basic melodic structure

sometimes attempting to break out but soon pulled back again, while there is more light in the outer sections of the quintet, and greater calm. In the central section, however, the two movements could scarcely be more different. For the piano, Schubert wrote a song-like passage typical of his intense, self-absorbed writing in solo piano works. (There are also strong echoes here, in texture and harmony, of the second movement, scherzo in A flat, of Beethoven's Piano Sonata Op. 31 No. 3.) For the quintet his mood is in complete contrast: angry and disturbing, uncomfortable, with complex rhythms and sophisticated structures. Here is a violent outbreak, not of passing anger, but of sustained fury and despair, fraught throughout until the music finally slowly sinks, as if exhausted, to an anguished *PPP*, and then resolves simply in a calming, or resigned sustained cadence which brings it back to E major and a return of the opening section. Whereas in the sonata movement the first section returns with only comparatively small changes in the presentation of the material, in the quintet, while second violin, viola, and first cello sustain the melody and its accompaniment as before, the first violin and second cello decorate with a filigree of varied ornamental dialogue, a miracle of expressive invention.

Schubert's use of a second cello rather than a second viola, as in Mozart's string quintets,[85] may have had something to do with the piano trios of 1827 and 1828, in particular the last in E flat. Here the piano frequently plays the ensemble bass line, leaving the cello free for a more lyrical role. Indeed, in the *andante con moto* (slow) movement of this trio, the pianist's left hand has passages of markedly cello-like character. There are other examples of this cello-like writing for the left hand in Schubert's piano music. The tone of the cello in its warmest register clearly had a special expressive appeal for the composer, as did the tenor-baritone or high-baritone voice, of similar range to this cello register, for which many of his songs were originally written. An early example of his preference for the cello in an orchestral composition comes in the surprising opening unison cello statement of the 'Unfinished' Symphony of 1822. In his last string quartet, that in G, composed in June 1826, Schubert's use of the cello as solo instrument was daring, and he may then have felt that a supplementary cello would open up more opportunities in his string chamber music in the future.

Schubert attended what may have been his very last musical party on 27 September at the home of Ignaz Menz, a medical doctor from Graz (where he was a friend of the Pachlers) and now Jenger's new landlord. In replying to Jenger, through whom the invitation had come, Schubert wrote: 'I accept with pleasure, for I always very much like to hear Baron Schönstein sing.'[86] From this letter it would appear that Jenger was already accompanying Schönstein, as he is known to have done, presumably now in place of Schubert, as the result of the composer's declining health and increasing unreliability over the previous months. On the other hand, Schubert was so intensely involved with his compositions that withdrawal from salon performances, as well as the belated passing on to the publisher Haslinger of the second part of *Winterreise*, may have been indications as to where his priorities lay. Of course he had no idea at this stage that he had barely seven weeks left to him for composition before, in early November, he became first seriously, and then fatally ill. During this time he was work-

---

[85] Schubert knew well, and greaatly admired, Mozart's five string quintets. He had heard one of them in June 1816: *Doc.* 60, *Dok.* 45. More recently, in 1824, he had borrowed the scores of all five quintets from Josef Hugelmann: *Doc.* 363, 365n, *Dok.* 250, 251n.

[86] *Doc.* 807, *Dok.* 537–8.

ing, except for the three days he spent, for reasons of his health, on a walking excursion with his brother Ferdinand. He completed his last solo song, 'Die Taubenpost', and, for Anna Milder-Hauptmann, the song he had long promised to write for her, the delightful 'Der Hirt auf dem Felsen' (The Shepherd on the Rock) D965 for soprano, clarinet, and piano (to text by Wilhelm Müller and Helmina von Chézy), and also two short sacred pieces.

Schubert's single setting late in 1828 of Seidl's 'Die Taubenpost', given his habit of setting to music a series of poems, often unconnected, by a single poet, might suggest that he had in mind further songs to texts by this poet who, though seven years younger than himself, was already making his name. Four of Schubert's Seidl songs composed in 1828 had already, on 13 August, been published by Thaddäus Weigl as 'Vier Refrainlieder' (Four Refrain Songs) D866, dedicated 'in friendship' to the poet. In an announcement of this publication in the *Wiener Zeitung*, Weigl wrote that the public's long-cherished wish for songs by Schubert of a merry or comic nature was gratified with these charming songs.[87] Nine days earlier, on 4 August, when returning poems to Seidl—probably those of the Refrainlieder—Schubert had enclosed a letter, almost certainly ironical, saying that he was unable to find 'anything practical or musically usable in them'.[88] At the same time, he asked for the return of two of his 1826 settings of Seidl's poems which he now wanted to publish. These songs with two others, published by Josef Czerny, appeared on the day of Schubert's funeral.[89]

In the short time left to him, Schubert worked on a new symphony, in D, D936A, of which he left fairly extensive sketches of three movements, all in short (piano) score, with some indications of orchestration. An early sketch of the first movement probably dates from the summer of 1828, but a later version and sketches of the second and third movements, which he composed in reverse order, were written that autumn, mostly in October. Schubert was very probably working on the second, a slow *andate* movement, at the moment at which he became too ill to write any more.[90] It is a haunting piece in B minor, the key of his 'Unfinished' Symphony written only a few weeks before he developed the syphilis which may have caused him to abandon that work. Six years later, the unfinished Symphony in D was probably his true swan song.

---

[87] *Doc.* 798, *Dok.* 531–2; *ND* 629.

[88] *Dok.* 529–30.   [89] *ND* 644.

[90] The same manuscript of this *andante* contains exercises in counterpoint which he had done for Simon Sechter, presumably immediately after his lesson with him on 4 Nov., only two weeks before he died.

Schubert was well aware that syphilis was likely to shorten his life, but in 1828 he was totally unaware of how close he was to death. In an effort to understand why this was, and what caused this, by all accounts, sudden and unexpected demise, we turn now to a recapitulation on his well- or ill-being in the last two years of his life, and a close look at his final illness.

12

THE FINAL ILLNESS

UP to the age of 25 Schubert, by all accounts, enjoyed better than average health. The situation changed radically at the end of 1822 when he contracted venereal disease. Thereafter, such positive descriptions of him as 'enjoying sound health',[1] 'so healthy and vigorous',[2] 'robust physique',[3] appear only in contrast to accounts of his bouts of illness. During the last six years of his life, with the possible exception of a year or so from 1825, he suffered some ill health, and latterly he was to varying degrees a sick man. Although the disease was never named as such by his contemporaries in their memoirs and reports on his life, their allusions to it and the symptoms point indubitably to syphilis. There was no complete cure for syphilis, and the best he could hope for was that the illness, after its secondary stage, would remain latent. If this were the case then, despite the long-term sentence, he could for a while lead an almost normal life; and he could compose music. Although at the start of 1823 he followed his doctor's advice carefully, Schubert was unfortunate indeed when later that year he succumbed to a recurrence of symptoms. Thereafter, periods of ordered living for a while resulted in comparative well-being, while periods of carelessness, whether brought on by illness-related despair or by cyclothymic moods which weakened his resistance to temptation, were frequently followed by outbreaks of ill health. Throughout this time his doctors would have advised him that under no circumstances should he consider marriage. For the remainder of his life the fear of a sudden relapse in the disease should have precluded all sexual relationships. But for a young man of powerful sensuality and strong passions, such a sentence was appalling, and he rebelled. There is sufficient evidence to suggest that, while of necessity he rejected marriage, he was not averse to the sexual favours for sale in brothels or meeting-places for prostitutes, where syphilis was endemic.

[1] Spaun: *Mem.* 28, *Erin.* 36.   [2] Bauernfeld: *Mem.* 33, *Erin.* 43.
[3] Blahetka: *Mem.* 10, *Erin.* 14.

Schubert died at three o'clock in the afternoon of 19 November 1828. We shall now follow the course of his illness during his last weeks, and endeavour to determine the immediate cause, or causes, of his death just two months before his thirty-second birthday.

Already in the autumn of 1827 Schubert was seriously troubled by recurring headaches (a symptom of both secondary and tertiary syphilis); and his final illness dated, according to Spaun, from the time of completion of the *Winterreise* song-cycle in November of that year. Yet for the first seven or eight months of 1828 he seemed to be leading a normal life. On the advice of his doctor (Rinna), he left his lodgings with Schober in the inner city on 1 September and, unwell and suffering now from 'constant giddiness and rush of blood to the head',[4] he moved to the new home of his brother Ferdinand situated outside the city, in the Wieden suburb, and close to the beautiful Theater an der Wien. It was hoped that the fresher air would suit him better than that in the overcrowded city. During September, while living in Ferdinand's apartment in what is now the Kettenbrückengasse, and already in indifferent health, Schubert composed with feverish industry some of his greatest music. But this prolific activity was taking its toll, and early in October, probably again on his doctor's advice, he undertook with Ferdinand and one or two of his brother's friends, a three-day walk into Lower Austria and the Burgenland (then in Hungary), including a stop at Eisenstadt to visit the tomb of Josef Haydn. Before this he may have been showing unhealthy lack of interest in food; and indeed Bauernfeld wrote that for some while Schubert had been complaining of loss of appetite and of feeling unwell. Whether this was over the last week or two or over a longer period of time is not clear.[5] Ferdinand made a special point in a mini-biography of the composer (published in the Leipzig *Neue Zeitschrift für Musik* in the spring of 1839) that during the three days of their walking holiday Schubert 'ate and drank most moderately'.[6] When they got back to Vienna, somewhat refreshed, he returned to his work; but his condition again began to deteriorate. When, in 1839, Ferdinand described his brother's final illness, he suggested that there was a critical beginning to terminal sickness on 31 October, just nineteen days before Schubert died; he tasted 'fish, but threw down his knife and fork on the plate, claiming that it made him feel sick, as though he had been poisoned; after this he ate and drank hardly anything but medicines'.[7]

The official cause of Schubert's death was given in documents and contemporary accounts as *Nervenfieber* (nervous fever); thus *Nervenfieber*

---

[4] Kreissle, *Schubert*, ii. 136.   [5] *Mem.* 238, *Erin.* 272.   [6] *Mem.* 37, *Erin.* 47.
[7] Ibid.

appeared in the Viennese register of death,[8] the church registers of his funeral service and burial, Schubert's father's family chronicle, and in the obituaries and announcements of his death, and was used by his family and friends both at the time and for some decades after. Later in the nineteenth century several of Schubert's friends, including Bauernfeld in 1869 and Lachner in 1881, referred to *Typhus* rather than *Nervenfieber*. In the eighteenth and early nineteenth centuries, in German-speaking countries *Nervenfieber* was synonymous with typhus, as the entry for *Nervenfieber* in the great thirty-two-volume Grimms' *Deutsches Wörterbuch* makes perfectly clear. However, the relationship between *Nervenfieber*, the German *Typhus*, and typhoid fever needs clarification.

In the decades after Schubert's death great advances were made in the understanding and diagnosis of typhus and its distinction from typhoid (originally meaning 'like, but not the same as typhus') fever.[9] *Nervenfieber* was used for a range of illnesses, including the typhus kind, such as gaol-fever, military fever, and puerperal (childbed) fever, as well as for typhoid fever. The corresponding English term was either 'continued fever' (continuous high fever), 'intermittent fever' (periods of high and low fever alternating) or 'remittent fever' (periods of high fever and normality alternating). Only later in the century, and after considerable advances in knowledge as a result of morbid anatomy (post-mortem examination), was the louse-borne typhus infection distinguished from the disease which became known as 'typhoid fever', a bacteriological (usually food- or water-carried) infection.[10] The term *Nervenfieber* in Austria during the first decades of the nineteenth century can now be understood. It covered a group of prevalent illnesses, today recognized as synonymous with both typhus and typhoid infections, of a serious and often fatal kind, associated with continuous fever and various but not always strongly definable symptoms, such as skin rashes as yet difficult to distinguish from each other. In all likelihood, *Nervenfieber* should be translated into English as continuous fever.

At the end of his life Schubert was very probably suffering from continuous fever, most likely from bacterial typhoid fever. However, when Josef Kenner claimed that the disease Schubert had contracted in 1822 came, as he put it with tactful ambiguity, from 'an episode in Schubert's life . . . [which] only too probably caused his premature death and certainly

---

[8] *Dok.* 549.

[9] I am indebted to the medical historian, Dr Irvine Loudon, for this information on 19th-c. understandings of 'continued fever' and the distinctions betwen typhus and typhoid fevers.

[10] The breakthrough came in 1880 with the discovery of Edwin Klebs, German pathologist and bacteriologist, of the typhoid bacillus. The principal characteristic of typhoid fever was ulceration (lesions) in the small intestine; but in Schubert's day nothing was known of this.

hastened it',[11] he was voicing the opinion shared by many of Schubert's closest friends, including Spaun, that syphilis played a part in his death, even if it was not the ultimate cause. He contracted the fever after his move to the Wieden suburb. Here, with his resistance to, and ability to fight, infection lowered by his syphilitic illness and the treatment he had received for it, his condition worsened. It is likely that at first his doctor failed to recognize his new infection, because, with a few exceptions discussed below, all related to the abdomen, the symptoms in the first two weeks or so would have been little different from those from which he was already suffering as a result of his syphilis: headache, malaise, generalized aches and pains, and lethargy. After this, his doctor may have been alerted by sudden and rapid deterioration in his condition to possible causes other than syphilis. Kreissle, in his biography dating from 1865, for which he collected material, both verbal and written, from those who knew Schubert, tells how, on 16 November, three days before the composer died, the doctors attending him, Vering and Wisgrill, decided that his symptoms 'showed the likelihood of an imminent attack of nervous fever'.[12] After this, according to Ferdinand, they changed Schubert's treatment. The two doctors who visited him during his last days were no ordinary doctors; but then Schubert was no ordinary man. He was by now a well-respected composer in Vienna and an elected member of the committee of the prestigious Gesellschaft der Musikfreunde, and he numbered many in powerful positions amongst his acquaintances. His own doctor, Ernst Rinna von Sarenbach, who advised Schubert in early September 1828 to move to his brother's home, continued to attend him for some while after this. Rinna was well acquainted with Schober's family, and his daughter Cäcilia (though then a young teenager) attended at least one of the carnival balls at their home in 1827.[13] He was a Court physician, personal medical adviser to the emperor, and later the author of a medical book.[14] Rinna himself fell sick temporarily after visiting Schubert on 11 or 12 November[15] and arranged for a friend and colleague, Dr Josef von Vering, to take over care of his patient. From 1813 Vering had been an army doctor in military hospitals, and after this he specialized in the treatment of syphilis. He had written two books on syphilis before 1828: the first *On the Treatment of Syphilis by Embrocation with Quicksilver*,[16] published in Vienna in 1821, and *Syphilido-Therapy*,[17] also

---

[11] *Mem.* 86, *Erin.* 100.   [12] Kreissle, *Schubert*, ii. 139.   [13] *Doc.* 603, *Dok.* 407.

[14] *Repertorium der vorzüglichsten Kurarten, Heilmittel, Operationsmethoden, u.s.w. aus den letzten vier Jahrzehenden* (A Repertory of the Principal Spas, Remedies, Operating Methods, etc., of the Last Four Decades) (Vienna, 1833–6).

[15] Breuning: *Mem.* 256, *Erin.* 293–4.

[16] *Über die Heilart der Lustseuche durch Quecksilber-Einreibungen.*

[17] *Syphilido-Therapie.*

published in Vienna, in 1826.[18] On 16 November, when he was called again to visit Schubert, he brought with him for a second opinion Dr Johann Baptist Wisgrill, who had sung in the Court chapel choir with Schubert from 1808 to 1811. He was also star scholar of his class in the Academic Grammar-School they both attended. Wisgrill was another young doctor of considerable brilliance, and the author of many books. (His fee for the consultation, paid on 20 November, was 5 fl. WW, while Rinna, who was paid a total of 105 fl. WW on 21 January next, probably passed on the appropriate share to Vering.[19])

At this point in any investigation of Schubert's illness, a problem arises: contemporary accounts and comments and remembered details, though they are helpful, cannot be used as reliable evidence of what actually happened or was said. In addition, they may have been affected, even engineered, to fit perceived or desired conclusions. More reliable evidence is found in the one letter the composer wrote (on 12 November), in a list of his medical expenses, and from a few events that took place during the last weeks of his life. But before I turn to these, I will look first at the probable progress of his illness in those last weeks.

If Schubert contracted typhoid fever, it is likely that in the early stages he would have experienced marked loss of appetite. This is also recognized as a side-effect of mercury, with which Schubert was being treated for his syphilis. In these circumstances, the main pointers to typhoid fever in the first week or so of the disease would have been abdominal discomfort with distended stomach, and later the outbreak of a rash of small rose-coloured spots on his trunk, in no way to be confused with the skin eruptions of the late stage of syphilis. There is no evidence that Schubert had, or did not have, this rash, although the ointments prescribed in the last week of his illness might have some relevance here. On the other hand, although the rash is a well-recognized manifestation of typhoid fever, it does not occur in every case. Once again, for Schubert there is no clear evidence either way. If there were recognizable manifestations of typhoid or any other form of continued fever, these became apparent only from 16 November, after which the severity of his condition caused increasing alarm.

In the light of our understanding of syphilis in the nineteenth and twentieth centuries, of its treatment in the 1820s and of Schubert's condition during the last months of his life, it is likely that he was in the tertiary stage of syphilis at the time of his death, whether or not he had typhoid. In this stage of the disease neurosyphilis, particularly meningeal, and cardiovascular manifestations can occur; and it is known that Schubert suffered from

---

[18] *Dok.* 547.   [19] *Dok.* 837, 898, *Dok.* 563, 579.

both headaches and rushes of blood to the head and back to the heart (*Blutwallungen*). Today the progress of the disease is far slower; but in the early nineteenth century it was more virulent and more likely to be fatal, and death came much more quickly. Schubert also suffered from anaemia, probably both syphilitic and a result of the usual vigorous treatment with mercury, a toxic poison, that he was receiving. Whether he drifted away from life in those last days from profound inanition, or he developed a stroke (the result of neurosyphilis), or suffered heart failure will never be known. Undoubtedly, weakness from malnutrition would have compounded all these problems. If he contracted typhoid fever in this weakened state, then any possible recovery from typhoid would have been compromised by malnutrition, syphilis, and toxicity from mercurials and from alcohol.

If Schubert's final illness began on 31 October with a feeling of being poisoned, after which he consumed almost nothing except medicines, his condition was not so serious that he was immediately confined to bed, or to the house. Three days later, on Monday, 3 November, he attended a Latin requiem mass composed by Ferdinand, presumably sung at a weekday memorial service, in the parish church of the Hernals district north-west of Vienna. The brothers, who had arisen early to walk the four or five miles to Hernals,[20] followed the church service with a three-hour walk, in the company of the choirmaster, who was a good friend of Ferdinand and already also well known to Schubert. No wonder that on the return journey Schubert 'complained greatly', as Ferdinand told, of lassitude![21] Yet on the following day he felt able, or forced himself, to walk again purposefully to and from the home of Simon Sechter, the Court chapel organist. The distance was little over a mile in each direction, but the purpose, to attend with his friend Josef Lanz their first lesson in counterpoint and fugue with Sechter, required mental energy and alertness. On the prearranged day of their second lesson in the following week Schubert was already very sick and in bed. In the mean time, if Baron Schönstein is to be believed, on either the Saturday or Sunday evening, 8 or 9 November, Schubert attended a supper party given by the baron. His host described the composer as being in excellent form, 'absolutely well . . . unusually merry', indeed 'almost unrestrained in his gaiety, a mood which might well have been induced by the large amount of wine he drank that evening'.[22] He took to his bed, probably on 11 November, whether or not he had been affected by excess alcohol. He never left the house again. Soon after this he was visited by

---

[20] Kreissle, *Schubert*, ii. 137.   [21] *Mem.* 38, *Erin.* 48.   [22] *Mem.* 101, *Erin.* 118.

Spaun who brought his copy of the Psalm 23 setting for Schubert's correction. Spaun wrote that 'his condition did not seem to me at all serious. He corrected my copy in bed, and was glad to see me, saying "There is really nothing the matter with me [no pain], only I am so exhausted I feel as though I were going to fall through the bed" . . . I left him without any anxiety'.[23] Schubert was feeling weak, but there was no diminution in his mental capacity; nor was there when two or three days later he sat up in bed, albeit with difficulty, in order to finish correcting the proofs of the second part of the *Winterreise* song-cycle, sent to him by the publisher Haslinger.[24]

Schubert wrote a note to Schober, his very last letter, probably on 12 November (the day Schober received it). In it he described himself as 'ill', adding that he had eaten and drunk nothing for eleven days.[25] (This again contradicts Schönstein's claim, written in 1857, that Schubert attended his supper party only a few days before.) He was still just able 'to totter feebly and shakily' between his bed and a chair, but if he attempted to take nourishment, he vomited immediately. Meanwhile, he was lovingly cared for by his 13-year-old half-sister, Josefa.[26] (Ferdinand, now a professor at the teachers' training college, was presumably out at work by day. His wife, Anna, had a family of young children to care for, the eldest now 12 years old.) Schubert ended his letter to Schober with a request for the loan from his library of any books by the American novelist James Fenimore Cooper which the composer had not yet read; and he gave the names of four that he had.[27] Schober was asked to leave the books at Bogner's coffee-house, which was situated not far from the teachers' training college, whence Ferdinand would collect them. Schubert wanted light reading, and for this he chose these translations of adventure stories, which were now very popular in German-speaking countries. Two days later, on 14 November, he was too ill to leave his bed. As he could no longer be left solely in the charge of Josefa, a female nurse was engaged to look after him. On the previous day, and as was only too customary, he had been bled, thus worsening the already devastating effects of his severe anaemia, which can be associated with typhoid fever, syphilis, and mercury treatment.

A story concerning Schubert's last days, supposedly originating from Karl Holz, was passed through an intermediary to the nineteenth-century music historian Ludwig Nohl (who in 1858 referred to Schubert's disease as Typhus).[28] This told of a visit of Holz's string quartet to play to Schubert just five days before he died. Although it is difficult to believe, especially on

---

[23] *Mem.* 139, *Erin.* 162.   [24] *Mem.* 28, 38; *ND* 717.   [25] *Doc.* 819, *Dok.* 546.
[26] Spaun: *Mem.* 139, *Erin.* 162.
[27] *The Last of the Mohicans, The Spy, The Pilot, The Pioneers*: *Doc.* 820, *Dok.* 546.
[28] *Erin.* 344.

so little evidence, that this visit could have been as late as 14 November, it transpires that it may just have been possible. Holz, who Schubert knew well, had played second violin in the rehearsal orchestra which met regularly at the home of Ignaz Sonnleithner between 1815 and 1824.[29] A good amateur violinist himself, he also played occasionally in the string quartets of Schuppanzigh and Josef Michael Böhm.[30] Holz had also taken part in early performances of Schubert's string quartets in A minor and in G, and in the Octet. Holz recounted how, in response to Schubert's desire to hear Beethoven's String Quartet in C sharp minor Op. 131 (1826), he brought three other players with him to the composer's apartment, where he was at the time suffering from 'a slight indisposition . . . from which he had not completely recovered, [and afterwards] grew enormously worse . . .'.[31] After they had performed the quartet Schubert was so moved, overcome as they thought by 'such transports of delight and enthusiasm', that they feared for his well-being. Holz's description leaves the impression that Schubert was in a state of collapse at the end of the performance. As there is no suggestion that he heard the music from his bed, it is possible that the day was indeed Friday 14 November, the time either the morning or early afternoon, and that his total exhaustion after hearing the music marked the moment of his permanent retirement to bed. This would then have been the last time he sat in a chair, and Beethoven's Quartet the last music that he heard, as Holz claimed. (Ferdinand also made this claim for his own Latin requiem at Hernals; but in matters concerning his own compositions, which were clearly of great importance to him, he was unreliable. In any case, he would not have been present during the day when the quartet was played and could therefore easily have overlooked the musical occasion when, on his return home from work, he found his brother's condition so much worse.)

In the last days of Schubert's life some of his friends, including Schober, may have been frightened to visit him for fear of infection, not of syphilis, but of whatever was causing the fever. Schober was well aware of the seriousness of Schubert's syphilitic condition (and Dr Rinna was giving him frequent, if not daily, reports on the state of his patient). He would have been aware of the risks he would have incurred at the end of 1822 (when Schubert returned to the Rossau schoolhouse), had he continued to share his home with his friend during the highly infectious secondary stages of the disease, but must also have been aware that in the tertiary stage visitors

---

[29] *Mem.* 342–4, *Erin.* 394–7.

[30] From summer 1825 Holz was for a while a close attendant on Beethoven; but in Dec. 1826 Schindler, who had deeply resented Holz's intrusion and himself kept away from Beethoven for over a year, returned to the master's side during his final illness. *Beethoven's Letters*, 1230.

[31] *Mem.* 299, *Erin.* 344.

were not in any danger. Thus Ferdinand, when he took his brother into his family home in the autumn of 1828, saw no cause for concern, whether for themselves or for Josefa. Of those friends who did visit Schubert in his last days—and certainly of Spaun, Lachner, and Bauernfeld (Schwind was now away in Munich)—none referred in any way to infection or to visible signs of the disease, such as skin lesions on Schubert's head, neck, or hands. (Lesions on his head would certainly have precluded any barber from attending the sick man, but one did on 16 November, according to the surviving statement of his medical expenses during the period of his acute illness.) Spaun, indeed, came close to implying that his friend's appearance was almost normal,[32] and he also said that on death Schubert's countenance was unchanged.[33] However, the reality may have been rather different. In the statement of Schubert's financial affairs, from 12 to 19 November and a few days afterwards, prepared by Ferdinand for his father, who was Schubert's legal executor, there are entries which provide evidence of another scenario.[34] These are for medicines, ointments, and powders which were paid for on 12, 13, 15, 16 (two separate entries for medicines on this day), 17, and 19 November. (The fee for blood-letting on 13 November also appears in the account.) Ointments are entered for 15 and 18 November, mustard powder on the 16th and 'powder' on the 18th. On the 15th, the ointment entry was accompanied by one for vesicatory-plaster (*Viskatur-Pflaster*), which would have contained the blistering agent cantharidin. This was then frequently used in attempts to cauterize syphilitic skin lesions, although cantharidin has also been applied in cases of pericarditis (inflammation of the membranous sac which encloses the heart), one of the symptomatic manifestations of cardiovascular syphilis in an advanced stage.[35] Assuming that after less than a week in bed Schubert was not troubled by bedsores or the rash of typhoid fever (which does not in fact require specific treatment), then the ointments, plasters, mustard powder, and unidentified powder (possibly talcum) point to a strong likelihood that he was suffering from syphilitic skin eruptions (*gummata*), probably on his trunk, legs, and buttocks, and therefore invisible to visitors. The female nurse, engaged from 14 November, would have been responsible in the first instance for the treatment of the skin eruptions, of which the young Josefa probably knew nothing. Additional purchases of 'Haarlinsen' and 'Limonen' are mentioned. The former is something of a mystery. The latter could have applied to whole fresh lemons or limes, providing refreshing

---

[32] *Mem.* 139, *Erin.* 162.   [33] *Mem.* 28; *ND* 717.   [34] *Doc.* 836–7, *Dok.* 652–4.
[35] A. E. W. McLachlan, E. Livingstone, and S. Livingstone (eds.), *Handbook of Diagnosis and Treatment of Venereal Disease*, 4th edn. (Edinburgh, 1951), 141; Martindale, *The Extra Pharmacopaeia*, i (London, 1952), 322–3.

citrus drinks which would also have given Schubert some protection against scurvy; or they might have been lemon-scented infusions needed for refreshing the air of the sick-room.

When Dr Vering, deputizing for Dr Rinna, visited Schubert in the second week of November, he saw little hope of saving his life. According to Gerhard von Breuning, the doctor's nephew, his pessimism was aroused on account of 'advanced disintegration of the blood' (*wegen vorgeschrittener Blutenmischung*) in his patient.[36] This diagnosis of what today would be recognized as profound (severe) anaemia, may appear surprising in the light of the then limited knowledge of structure of the blood. However, extreme pallor would be enough to make a diagnosis. It is also very probable that at this stage Schubert had suffered severe intestinal bleeding caused by the typhoid. Such an alarming development of Schubert's illness would have alerted Dr Vering, if he had not already realized it, to the probability that Schubert was suffering from *Nervenfieber* in addition to syphilis. On 16 November he brought Dr Wisgrill with him for a second opinion on the treatment of his patient; together they decided on a new treatment, in a last desperate attempt to avert Schubert's imminent death. Unfortunately, no details or records of this treatment have been preserved, except that as a matter of urgency a second, male, nurse was engaged to share the task of looking after Schubert. The nurse arrived the next day. This same day, the Monday, Schubert received probably his last two visitors: first the amiable young conductor Franz Lachner (one of his duet partners), and after this his good friend Bauernfeld. Lachner called in the morning, when he found Schubert very weak but fully conscious and ready to communicate. He complained of feeling 'a dead weight lying here . . . as though I was going to fall through the bed', a remark similar to that made to Spaun a few days earlier. But he was clearly not without hope of recovery and talked with some enthusiasm of his plans for the future.[37] Lachner's visit had obviously tired Schubert, for in the afternoon, when Bauernfeld arrived, he was weaker and complained of burning in his head as well as of sleeplessness and lassitude.[38] Otherwise, he felt no pain and remained 'not without hope of recovery'. He was lucid, seemed pleased to talk of their opera *Der Graf von Gleichen*, and even began making plans, according to Bauernfeld, for their second operatic collaboration in the future. But he was fast losing strength, and although he did not then sink into the delirium which was intermittently afflicting him during his last days—delirium 'during which he sang ceaselessly', according to Spaun[39]—Bauernfeld must have been very relieved when Ferdinand arrived with the two doctors, and he could

[36] *Mem.* 256, *Erin.* 193–4.   [37] *Mem.* 290, *Erin.* 334.
[38] *Mem.* 33, *Erin.* 43.   [39] *Mem.* 28; *ND* 717.

leave his friend in their care.[40] By the evening the composer was violently delirious and had to be restrained, and from now on his condition worsened rapidly. On the following day (the 18th) while hallucinating he struggled to get out of bed, imagining that he was in a strange room or place, and desperate to escape. But he had quiet moments. Ferdinand, writing in 1839 of his brother's last days, told how on the evening before he died Schubert called him to his bedside and weakly spoke to him: 'Ferdinand! put your ear to my mouth. What is the matter with me?' Ferdinand tried to comfort him, assuring him that they were all 'very anxious to make [him] well again' and that the doctors had declared he would recover soon, provided that he followed their advice. Some hours later, when Dr Vering arrived, Schubert looked directly at him, grasped the wall with one feeble hand and said slowly and earnestly: 'Here, here is my end!'.[41] But shortly before this, as Ferdinand wrote in a letter to his father two days after his death, Schubert hallucinated again. To quote from this letter:

on the very evening before his death, though only half conscious, he [Schubert] said to me: 'I implore you to take me to my room, not to leave me here, in this corner under the ground; do I not deserve a place above ground?' I answered him: 'Dear Franz, rest assured, believe your brother Ferdinand in whom you have always trusted, and who loves you so much. You are in the same room as you have always been in so far, and lying on your bed!'—And Franz said: 'No that's not true: Beethoven is not lying here.'—Could this be anything but an indication of his inmost wish to repose by the side of Beethoven, whom he so greatly revered?!'[42]

Strangely, and perhaps suspiciously, Ferdinand never again referred to these words of Schubert's in any later description of the composer's death, nor do any of his intimate friends with whom Ferdinand would have been in contact and to whom he was likely to have repeated this conversation. As it was reported in a private letter to a rather difficult father when they were both mourning Schubert's death, and knowing Ferdinand's tendency to fabricate information when to do so seemed expedient, it is surely conceivable that Ferdinand invented the scene in the interests of his much-loved brother, in order to persuade their father to agree to Schubert's burial in a manner which Ferdinand felt appropriate: in a grave as close as possible to that of Beethoven.

To summarize: At the time of his death Schubert had a continuous high fever. He may have had a typhoid rash, and he was probably affected by *gummata* associated with tertiary syphilis. He was anaemic and probably

---

[40] *Mem.* 238, *Erin.* 272.　　[41] *Mem.* 38, *Erin.* 48.　　[42] *Doc.* 825, *Dok.* 550.

suffering from mercurial poisoning. Rushes of blood to his head indicate probable cardiovascular disease; and he was probably neurosyphilitic, with symptoms including meningeal headaches, insomnia, dizziness, and general lassitude. By other more specific symptoms of neurosyphilis, such as impaired memory, loss of concentration, visual problems, and nervous irritability, he may or may not have been affected. However, there is considerable overlap between the symptoms of neurosyphilis and of mercurial poisoning, and he probably suffered a combination of the effects of the disease and the toxicity of the treatment. At the same time, none of the effects of tertiary syphilis was specific enough in these early stages for them to have been identifiable with certainty, even if they were by this time understood by the specialist doctors who examined him. Only the ugly skin *gummata*, if he had them, would have pointed with certainty to tertiary syphilis. But his burst of prolific activity on his compositions of September and October proves without doubt that he could not have been suffering from an ineluctable syphilitic decline in his mental powers.

If virtually all reports of his death at the time gave the cause as nervous (continued) fever, there could be two explanations. The first is that it was true. In that case, Schubert probably contracted typhoid fever during the last two or three weeks of his life when he was already sick, but not yet mortally so, in the third stage of syphilis. The second is that family and close friends alike did not want it to be generally known that Schubert suffered from, or died of, syphilis, an ugly disease which, despite the frequency of its occurrence, still carried a stigma. Nervous fever needed no further explanation in the official register of deaths or in the church register. For those closest to the composer, and particularly for his family, such an illness would have been preferable to a socially unacceptable disease associated with sexual profligacy. Schubert's father, who had only recently been honoured with the title of Citizen of Vienna, had spent his working-life tirelessly seeking respectability and status in the city of his adoption. He had married the second time into a family somewhat superior to his own socially, including among its members a silk manufacturer and a rather successful Roman Catholic priest. In his turn Ferdinand, though totally devoted to Schubert and a great admirer of his genius, was an ambitious educationist who had made an excellent start in his chosen career. Their sister Maria Theresia had married well; her husband, Matthias Schneider, was a grammar-school teacher. The family was going up in the world. Schubert was now well known and respected in Vienna as a composer, and his reputation was spreading; but he had sometimes let the family down by his unpredictable behaviour, and rumours may have been rife concerning the cause of his death. In an effort to quell such rumours, Ferdinand may have stressed the occasion when Schubert rejected his fish supper as marking the beginning of the illness that killed him, and also that the rapid course of the disease was normal in one dying of nervous fever. In the same context, the strange silence of members of his family supports the long-held suspicion of a cover-up of Schubert's personal life and suppression of some details about his final illness. The refusal of Therese Grob (now Bergmann) after his death to give any information about the composer or of their relationship could also have had something to do with a family conspiracy of silence; for from 1825, when Ignaz Schubert married her aunt, as Ignaz' step-niece she was part of that family. Putting up a smokescreen like this was a common procedure in nineteenth-century Europe, especially by the families of young men who died of syphilis. In covering up a very important part of Schubert's life, his sexual propensities and activities, maybe also destroying some of the evidence, his family and friends have certainly made the biographer's task a difficult one. Whatever the wishes of his family or decision of his doctors at the time of his death, all available evidence seems to point to the ultimate cause of Schubert's death being typhoid fever in a man afflicted with active tertiary syphilis and compounded by the toxic effects of treatment and self-neglect.

13

BURIAL AND MEMORIALS

W HEN Schubert fell into a coma on the evening of 18 November, Ferdinand wrote a note to his father informing him that his son was dying. On the next day his father replied, bidding Ferdinand to seek comfort in God and trust in His wisdom and goodness; He would give him strength and courage. And, Franz Theodor continued: 'See to it, to the best of your ability, that our dear Franz is forthwith provided with the Holy Sacraments for the dying, and I shall live in the comforting hope that God will fortify and keep him.'[1] But Schubert never regained consciousness and, unable to take the sacraments from the priest summoned by Ferdinand, received only 'extreme unction'. That afternoon he died.

The day after his son's death, as the next of kin, his father ordered the printing of 150 copies of the customary announcement of death, including information on arrangements for the funeral which was to take place the next day:

Yesterday, Wednesday, at 3 o'clock in the afternoon, fell asleep, to wake to a better life, my most dearly beloved son Franz Schubert, musical artist and composer, after a short illness and having received the Holy Sacraments, in the 32nd year of his age.

At the same time, I and my family have to announce to our honoured friends and acquaintances that the body of our dear departed son will be carried to the Parish Church of St Joseph at Margareten, on Friday, 21st inst., at 2.30 pm, from the house No. 694 on the Neu-Wieden, in the newly-built street next to the so-called Bischof-Stadel, there to be consecrated.

Franz Schubert
Schoolmaster in the Rossau

Vienna, 20th November 1828[2]

Early on the next morning, at 6 a.m., before his father had time to complete arrangements for the interment, Ferdinand wrote to his father with consid-

---

[1] *Doc.* 822–3, *Dok.* 548.   [2] *Doc.* 824, *Dok.* 549.

erable urgency conveying his own wish, and that of friends, that Schubert should be buried not, as would be expected, in the nearest cemetery, at Matzleinsdorf (where Gluck's grave was), but in the Währinger Ortsfriedhof, the Währing district cemetery, where Beethoven had been laid to rest in March 1827:

Very many are expressing the wish that the body of our dear Franz should be buried in the Währing churchyard . . . I have therefore spoken to Rieder about it and enquired what outlay this transfer funeral would involve, and it comes to about 70 florins, KM—Much! Very Much!—Yet surely very little for Franz!—I for my part could spare 40 fl. at the moment, having cashed 50 yesterday.— Besides, I think we may confidently expect that all the expenses caused by his illness and his burial, &c., will soon be defrayed by his estate.

So, dear Father, if you agree with me another great load would be removed from my mind. But you would have to decide at once and to inform me by bearer of this, so that I may arrange for the arrival of the hearse. Also, you would have to see to it that the priest at Währing is informed before this morning is out.

21st November 1828, 6 a.m.   Your sorrowing son
                                              Ferdinand[3]

In the first part of this letter, quoted above, Ferdinand had described Schubert's semi-conscious distress; very near to death, he had said 'Beethoven is not lying here'.[4] As I have said, it is probable that Ferdinand exaggerated, if not made up, this story in a ploy to win their father's agreement to Schubert's burial in Währing despite the added expense. Ferdinand had found out the cost of interment there from his schoolteacher friend Johann Rieder, who was now a district official in the Währing suburb. Whether Ferdinand's story of his brother's fears on his deathbed was true or not, his father at this point agreed to his request, and arrangements for the burial in Währing went ahead. According to the undertaker's account of expenses for Schubert's funeral, apart from the charge for the printed announcements, there was a small charge for bringing a personal verbal invitation to the neighbours who did not require written notification.[5] This account also gives such information as that, for this 'second-class' funeral (out of a possible three classes) the coffin was painted; the corpse was dressed in a fine-quality shroud; a handsome pall and a cross to be carried in the cortège were hired for the occasion; and, as at Beethoven's funeral, there were black crape ribbons, twenty-two of them, attached to the bier. Also hired were two red cloaks for the professional bearers of the coffin.[6]

---

[3] *Doc.* 825, *Dok.* 550.   [4] *Doc.* 825, *Dok.* 550.   [5] *Dok.* 552.   [6] *Dok.* 552–3.

Schubert's first biographer, Kreissle, gave a description of the funeral
which, in the absence of written evidence, was presumably based on
descriptions given to him verbally. Schubert had lain since his death on a
bier, dressed in the then usual simple hermit's tunic and wearing a laurel
wreath round his temples. His appearance was remarkably unchanged in
death, so that he 'looked more like a sleeping than a dead man'.[7] On the day
of the funeral the coffin was carried down the steps of the house by the two
professional bearers in their red cloaks, and presumably they also carried it
into the church. The weather was bad, however, and so the places of the
bearers were taken in the street below by a group of young men ('officials
and students') who bore it, apparently not entirely with good grace, to the
nearby church of St Joseph (the Margareten district parish church).[8] Here
the funeral took place, attended by family and close friends. By special
request of the family, Franz von Schober was the chief mourner, he who of
all Schubert's close friends left least evidence in writing of his friendship
with the composer, but may have known him and his secrets better than
any other. For this sombre occasion Schober wrote, obviously in a very
short space of time, a new poem, 'An Franz Schuberts Sarge' (By Franz
Schubert's Bier), which fitted the melody Schubert had composed in April
1817 for another of Schober's poems, 'Pax vobiscum' (Peace be with you).[9]
This was sung by a small choir at St Joseph's, accompanied, in the tradition
of *Trauermusik* (which was still extant), by wind instruments. The musicians were directed by the highly respected director of music of
St Stephen's cathedral, Johann Baptist Gänsbacher,[10] who also directed
them in a funeral motet of his own composition. After funeral prayers, the
coffin was carried out of the church and placed on a hearse, on which the
body was then borne almost three miles to the Währing cemetery.[11] This
was a long distance for mourners to walk in cold, wet weather, and one
must wonder how many dropped out of the procession before they reached
Währing. The cortège stopped first at the Währing church of St Lorenz and
St Gertrud for a second commendation by the parish priest, at which were
sung the standard Miserere, a funeral song (*Todtenlied*), and the Libera me
by a choir of children from the local school, directed by their schoolmaster.
(The costs for the choir were included in the undertaker's account.) The
cortège then moved on again to the nearby cemetery, and here Schubert's
body was laid in a grave separated from that of Beethoven by just three
others. By the time the burial service was over on that late November

---

[7] Kreissle, *Schubert*, ii. 142.   [8] *Doc.* 827n, *Dok.* 552n.   [9] *Doc.* 826–7, *Dok.* 551–2.
[10] Gänsbacher was a good friend of Weber, whom he had met when they were both pupils of the
Abbé Vogler.
[11] The Währing Cemetery was later deconsecrated and renamed the Schubert Park.

evening, it was growing dark, and those who had attended the coffin on the entire journey from Ferdinand's home to its place of rest must have been in very low spirits, the rain and darkness aggravating their grief.

After Schubert's death and burial, the customary requiem masses were said or sung in his memory in several towns in Austria, including Linz on Christmas Day 1828.[12] In Vienna the first requiem mass to be held, on 27 November, less than a week after the funeral, was a special occasion for his family, and no doubt for some of his closest friends. Invitations were again printed and sent out:

The friends and admirers of Franz Schubert, Musician and Composer, dead before his time, are herewith informed that on Thursday, 27 November 1828 at 10.30 a Requiem Mass will take place, organised by the Musical Society of St Ulrich Church. The Musical Society will perform Mozart's *Requiem*.[13]

It can surely be assumed that Ferdinand, who until very recently had lived with his family in the St Ulrich parish, and his sister Theresia (Resi) and her husband Matthias Schneider, whose home was still in the parish, were instrumental in instituting this event. Both Ferdinand and Schneider were active in the Musical Society, which had a good reputation; and the choice of Mozart's Requiem, said to be one of Schubert's favourite works,[14] suggests their participation in the choice of music. Unfortunately, there are no surviving reports or descriptions of this service. After the St Ulrich church requiem mass, all other recorded events and activities in Vienna pertaining to the death of Schubert are associated with the Gesellschaft der Musikfreunde.

After his death, Schubert's influential friends in the Gesellschaft wanted to pay their official respects, and those of all members of the society, to their fellow member in a manner they considered appropriate. It was decided that the Gesellschaft would organize and pay for a special requiem mass in the Court church of St Augustine. The announcement of this second memorial service, described variously as a 'Todtenfeyer' and 'die feyerlichen Exequien', appeared on 20 December in principal newspapers and journals in Vienna,[15] along with an invitation to friends and admirers of the composer to subscribe to a fund for the erection of a suitable memorial monument above his grave. (Those wishing to subscribe were asked to add their names to lists of subscribers available in the offices of the Gesellschaft, and in leading musical establishments in Vienna and provincial capitals.)

---

[12] Kreissle, *Schubert*, ii. 146.
[14] Schönstein: *Mem.* 102, *Erin.* 117–18.
[13] *Dok.* 556; *ND* 647.
[15] *ND* 666–8.

The proposal to erect this monument again came from Schubert's friends, working in collaboration with the Gesellschaft.[16]

Whereas the announcements of the December requiem mass in the newspapers referred only to Schubert's friends and admirers as the organizers (in collaboration with the Gesellschaft), private invitations were sent out jointly by the family of 'Herrn von [*sic*] Schubert, School Director' and 'Josef Hüttenbrenner, member of the Gesellschaft der Musikfreunde, Imperial Civil Servant [*Hofbeamter*]':

You are invited to attend a Memorial Service for Franz Schubert which will be held on 23 December at 11 o'clock in the Court and Parish Church of St Augustine, in the course of which a Requiem for double-chorus by his friend Anselm Hüttenbrenner, Musical Director of the Styrian Musical Society will be performed.

A rehearsal of the Requiem will be held on the evening of 22 December 1828 at 7 o'clock in the concert hall of the Gesellschaft der Musikfreunde des Osterr. Kaiserstaates.[17]

This was also sent to all who might wish to sing in the eight-part chorus. After the event the occasion was referred to in several journals, the general feeling being that Anselm Hüttenbrenner's composition was rather a merry piece for a memorial service. As the Viennese correspondent for the *Harmonicon* of London wrote in the issue of June 1829: 'the music [of Hüttenbrenner's mass] is full of very striking effects, and excellent in its way, but any thing else than a *Missa pro Defunctis*; the mournful import of the words and liveliness of the sounds are at such open war with each other.'[18] A clue to the choice of the mass by Hüttenbrenner may lie in the signature of his brother Josef, representing the organizers of the occasion, at the foot of the invitation quoted above. True, Anselm was a good friend of Schubert; but Josef was also an indefatigable champion of his brother's music. If he were instrumental in the choice of Anselm's mass for Schubert's memorial service, it could have been a case of nepotism.

Before he died, Schubert must have heard of the decision of 24 October of a meeting of the Gesellschaft's programme-planning committee to perform his Symphony in C of 1817–18 (D589) at their next concert on 14 December.[19] His standing in the Gesellschaft had been growing steadily over the last three years; and the inclusion of one of his vocal works in its chamber music concerts had now become almost *de rigueur*.[20] At the time

[16] *ND* 666–8.   [17] *Doc.* 845–6, *Dok.* 569.
[18] *ND* 730.   [19] Biba, 'Schubert und die Gesellschaft der Musikfreunde', 31–2.
[20] *ND* 729.

he died, the omission of his large-scale compositions from all the society's grand Sunday concerts in the large Redoutensaal of the Imperial Palace since that of 1821, when for the first and last time one of his orchestral works (an overture) had been performed, was at last about to be redressed. Leopold Sonnleithner acted as go-between for the composer in the arrangements for this performance, handing over to the Gesellschaft the score of the symphony, from which orchestral parts were duly prepared by professional copyists.[21] (As far as the Gesellschaft was concerned, because they knew nothing of the two movements of the Symphony in B minor of 1822, this earlier Symphony in C was the last symphony Schubert had composed before the epic Symphony in C of 1825–6.) The symphony, as planned, opened the programme[22] and was acclaimed as a youthful work which 'bore unmistakable traces of the budding genius in its wealth of melody'.[23] The concert in the Redoutensaal represented a breakthrough for Schubert, and should have been an important occasion for him. That he did not live to hear it was a sad irony of fate.

One of the movers behind the appeal for funds for a monument at Schubert's grave was Anna Fröhlich who on 20 December, the same day as advance notice of the Gesellschaft's requiem mass for the composer and the opening of the fund appeared in newspapers, wrote to officers of the Gesellschaft with a special request: for permission to use the society's concert hall the following month for a concert to raise money for Schubert's monument.[24] Half of the proceeds were to go towards the monument, the other half to be used for the benefit of poor students of the Conservatoire, some of whom were to participate in the concert.[25] The request was readily granted in a letter drafted by Schubert's friend Jenger, as assistant to the secretary of the Gesellschaft, and signed by the vice-president, Kiesewetter,[26] the same people who signed the acceptance of Schubert's own request for the use of the same hall for his concert in March 1828. In both cases, free use of the hall was granted. After Schubert's concert of his own music, he had written (on 10 April) to the publisher Schott that he was being encouraged to repeat the concert. This may be why there are some close parallels between the concert arranged for his fundraising memorial appeal and Schubert's own concert ten months before. The programme of the memorial concert, given on 30 January 1829, included three works performed on the earlier occasion: the Piano Trio in E flat, 'Die Allmacht', and

---

[21] Payment for this work was entered in the Society's list of expenses for Dec. 1828.

[22] *ND* 660.

[23] *ND* 742. The same symphony was performed again in one of the *Concerts spirituels* on 12 Mar. 1829, and then described as a 'precious legacy' of the composer: *ND* 729.

[24] Biba, 'Schubert und die Gesellschaft der Musikfreunde', 33.

[25] Ibid.   [26] Ibid.

Auf dem Strom. The trio was again played by Bocklet, Böhm, and Linke.
Vogl was replaced in the song by J. K. Schoberlechner. In place of the horn
solo in *Auf dem Strom*, Linke played an alternative cello part, which may
have been written by Schubert. The name of the pianist for the vocal numbers was not given in the programme. In addition to these three numbers
(out of a total of seven), the programme included the last song Schubert
wrote, 'Die Taubenpost' (Seidl) and, to start the concert, his cantata
to Grillparzer's poem, *Miriams Siegesgesang*, which he had been unable to
finish in time for his own concert. The final item was the complete finale to
Act I of Mozart's opera *Don Giovanni* (sung in German), the final sextet of
which was a great favourite at Gesellschaft concerts. By coincidence, the
sextet had also brought to a close the grand Gesellschaft concert in
November 1821, at which the overture by Schubert was performed. This
concert was so successful that it was repeated in its entirety in the same
venue on 5 March, and more money was thus raised for the memorial
fund.[27] In the meantime, Schober had been appointed to mastermind the
artistic and practical side of the commissioning and design of the memorial,
in collaboration with the chosen craftsmen who were to build it. In 1829 a
young artist Josef Alois Dialer was commissioned and sculpted a bronze
bust of the composer, which was mounted in a simply styled gravestone
carved by a stonemason, Anton Wasserburger. Those who knew Schubert
well claimed the bust was an excellent likeness. The highly respected
Grillparzer was invited to compose a suitable inscription for the epitaph.

The completed monument was set up at the grave in Währing in the
summer of 1830,[28] complete with Grillparzer's epitaph, then considered
entirely appropriate, later much criticized, now generally understood in the
light of Schubert's known achievements at the time of his death:

> The art of music here entombed a rich possession,
> but far fairer hopes.[29]

Schubert must now have seemed to be finally at rest in the grave at
Währing. In fact, both his grave and that of Beethoven underwent repair in
1863, and the remains were exhumed before reburial. They were disturbed
again a quarter of a century later, in 1888, when they were transferred to
the Musicians' Grove of Honour in Vienna's new central cemetery in
Simmering, where they remain to this day.[30]

Mozart's music—his Requiem—was chosen for Schubert's first
requiem mass at St Ulrich's church and again—the Act I finale from *Don
Giovanni*—as the final item in the two 1829 memorial concerts. Both,

---

[27] *ND* 705.   [28] *Dok.* 582.   [29] *Doc.* 899, *Dok.* 580.   [30] Eckel: *Doc.* 926–7.

according to Anselm Hüttenbrenner, were among Schubert's favourite works,[31] and they reflect his particular affinity for Mozart's music, notably the chamber music, symphonies, and operas. There are affinities, too, in the manner in which they both composed, sometimes conceiving a composition in its entirety before writing it down, and then preparing a manuscript of the bare outline, as a reminder for the time when the work was to be completed in manuscript. And both men composed an abundance of masterpieces in the last months, even weeks, of their short lives. One must wonder what Schubert might have produced had he lived three or four more years to attain the same age as Mozart when he died.

The year 1828 was one in which Schubert's reputation was slowly spreading, not only in German lands but to more remote parts of the Austro-Hungarian empire, to France, and to England. Had he lived longer, he might have looked back on this year as a turning-point in his fortunes, with the promise of publication of more of his instrumental works as well as a wider appreciation of his greatest songs. As it was, immediately after his death there was no one amongst his family or friends who fully appreciated the wealth and quality of his instrumental music, or who was willing or able to persuade publishers to make more of it readily available to the public. Ferdinand did his best, but was unable to overcome the natural cautiousness of the publishing profession, and many of his brother's greatest works remained in obscurity for many years.[32] Schubert apparently accepted his fate, whether good or bad, with true Biedermeier resignation. He neither expected nor asked for sympathy, and might have brushed it aside if it had been offered. Pain and suffering were for him part of life. He probably never sought opportunities to travel, but when they arose he took them gratefully, enjoying new relationships, fresh surroundings, and beautiful countryside. When the time came to return Vienna, he did so with pleasure, looking forward to seeing old friends and family and enjoying again his customary way of life in the city. Shortage of money rather often restricted him, but he felt no deep sense of grievance as a result. When he had money, he spent it freely on himself and on others, generous to a fault, as some friends described him, and certainly financially incompetent. He suffered both physical and mental distress. He enjoyed social intercourse with good companions, and also the isolation in which he was most productive.

[31] *Mem.* 70, *Erin.* 81.

[32] The following list shows some of these, with the date of first publication in parenthesis: string quartets in D minor (1831) and G major (1851), String Quintet (1853), the 'Unfinished' Symphony (1867) and 'Great' Symphony in C (1840), three late sonatas for piano in C minor, A major, and B flat and B flat Piano Trio (1839), Piano Duet Allegro in A minor ('Lebensstürme') (1840), Mass in E flat (1865).

Helped by his lively sensitivities, he was rightly stimulated by his surroundings, but also strongly activated by a vibrant private life. And, thus inspired, he lived intensely. As Sonnleithner wrote: 'Thus lived Schubert, and so he was. His earthly pilgrimage was brief; but the spirit that comes from his music lives on.'[33]

For Sonnleithner, the spirit of Schubert's music would live on. For Grillparzer, the music he left was 'a rich possession', but his life had been too short for him to fulfil his potential. A few of Schubert's closest friends and colleagues acknowledged his extraordinary talent, and some even his genius; but they failed to recognize his outstanding achievements largely because they knew nothing, or little, of what these achievements were. Schubert talked little about his compositions; and in the latter part of his life, after he had grown away from essentially amateur performances of his early music by orchestral players and church choirs, there were few performances of anything but his vocal compositions, music for the piano, and some church music. Thus, apart from songs, most of his mature works recognized today as the finest fruits of his genius, were unknown and never performed in his lifetime; or if they were once or twice, then these were usually chamber works performed in private salon concerts to audiences of at most a hundred or so people. For the works which were the fruits of his final months, the Mass in E flat, the late piano sonatas, the String Quintet, and the final songs, there was no time for performances in Vienna before he died. His benefit concert in the previous March had been a considerable success, and, had he lived longer, more such concerts would have followed. This year could without doubt have been a turning-point in his life and seen his recognition as a major composer of instrumental music, both in Austria and in Germany.

Schubert died, as he had lived, with many secrets. Of the musical secrets, a large number of compositions, unknown to any save a very few during his life, have fortunately come to light. His personal secrets will remain hidden unless written evidence ever turns up. Meanwhile, whatever is to be learned of Schubert from his own words and from descriptions of him by those who knew him, and whatever understanding of the man and his music can be gleaned from this, most particularly of his varying moods and strongest passions, it is to the spirit of his music, as Sonnleithner expressed it, that we return. And it is this spirit, the result of a life 'dedicated to Art' towards which he had been encouraged in 1813 by Theodor Körner, that touches the heart and enriches the soul of those who listen now to Schubert's music.

---

[33] *Doc.* 857, *ND* 692.

SELECT BIBLIOGRAPHY

SOURCE MATERIAL, COLLECTED WORKS, CATALOGUES

F. Schuberts Werke: Kritisch durchgeschene Gesamtausgabe, ed. E. Mandyczewski, J. Brahms, *et al.* (Leipzig, 1884–97).

F. Schubert: Neue Ausgabe sämtlicher Werke (Neue Schubert Ausgabe), ed. W. Dürr, A. Feil, C. Landon, *et al.* (Kassel, 1964–   ).

Deutsch, O. E., *Schubert: A Documentary Biography*, trans. E. Blom (London, 1946).

—— *Schubert: Die Dokumente seines Lebens* (Kassel, 1964).

—— *Schubert: Die Erinnerungen seiner Freunde* (1st pub. Leipzig, 1957; reissued Wiesbaden, 1983).

—— *Schubert: Memoirs by his Friends*, trans. R. Ley and J. Nowell (London, 1958).

—— *Franz Schubert: Thematisches Verzeichnis seiner Werke in chronologischer Folge* (Kassel, 1978).

Franz Schubert: Dokumente 1817–1830, i: *Texte*, ed. T. G. Waidelich (Tutzing, 1993).

Hilmar, E., *Verzeichnis der Schubert-Handschriften in der Musiksammlung der Wiener Stadt- und Landesbibliothek (Catalogus Musicus VIII)* (Kassel, 1978).

BOOKS

Abraham, G. (ed.), *Schubert: A Symposium* (London 1947; reissued 1952).

Badura-Sokda, E., and Branscombe, P. (eds.), *Schubert Studies: Problems of Style and Chronology* (Cambridge, 1982).

Bauernfeld, E. von, *Erinnerungen aus Alt-Wien*, ed. J. Bindtner (Vienna, 1923).

Baumann, C. C., *Wilhelm Müller* (Pennsylvania, 1981).

The Letters of Beethoven, ed. and trans. E. Anderson, 3 vols. (London, 1961).

Brown, M. J. E. B., *Schubert: A Critical Biography* (London, 1958).

—— *Essays on Schubert* (London, 1966).

—— *Schubert* (New Grove; London, 1980; pbk. edn. 1982).

Brusatti, O. (ed.), *Schubert-Kongress Wien 1978* (Vienna, 1979).

—— and Hilmar, E. (eds.), *Katalog: Franz Schubert, Ausstellung der Wiener Stadt- und Landesbibliothek zum 150 Todestag des Komponisten* (Vienna, 1978).

Chusid, M. (ed.), *Schubert: Symphony in B minor ('Unfinished')* (1st pub. New York, 1968; 2nd edn. 1971).

De Quincey, T,. *Confessions of an English Opium Eater and Other Writings*, ed. G. Lindop (Oxford, 1985 edn.).

Feuchtmüller, R., *Leopold Kupelwieser und die Kunst der Österreichischen Spätromantik* (Vienna, 1970).

Frisch, W. (ed.), *Schubert: Critical and Analytical Studies* (Lincoln, Nebr. 1986).

Glossy, C., *Aus Bauernfelds Tagebüchern* (Vienna, 1895).

Gramit, D., *The Intellectual and Aesthetic Tenets of Franz Schubert's Circle* (UMI, Mich., 1989).

Gülke, P., *Franz Schubert und seine Zeit* (Laaber, 1991).

Hayter, A., *Opium and the Romantic Imagination* (London, 1968).

Hilmar, E., *Franz Schubert in seiner Zeit* (Vienna, 1985) trans. R. G. Pauly, *Franz Schubert in his Time* (Amadeus, Portland, Oregon 1988).

—— (ed.), *F. Schubert: Der Graf von Gleichen*, facs. edn. (Tutzing, 1988).

—— *Schubert* (Graz, 1989).

Hinrichsen, H.-J. (ed.), *Franz Schubert: Fantasie in F-moll D 940*, facs. edn. (Tutzing, 1991).

—— (ed.), *Franz Schubert: Reliquie sonata, mit Beitragen*, facs. edn. (Tutzing, 1992).

Hirsch, M. W., *Schubert's Dramatic Lieder* (Cambridge, 1993).

Holland, H., *Moritz von Schwind: Sein Leben und seine Werke* (Stuttgart, 1873).

Holmes, E., *A Ramble among the Musicians of Germany. By a Musical Professor* (London, 1828).

Jamison, K. Redfield, *Touched with Fire* (New York, 1993).

Kobald, K., *Alt-Wiener Musikstätten* (Zurich, 1919).

—— *Franz Schubert und seine Zeit* (Zurich, 1928).

Kramer, R., *Distant Cycles: Schubert and the Conceiving of Song* (Chicago, 1994).

Kreissle von Hellborn, H., *Franz Schubert* (Vienna, 1865); ET: A. D. Coleridge, 2 vols. (London, 1869).

Langevin, P.-G. (ed.), *Franz Schubert et la symphonie: Éléments d'une nouvelle perspective* (Paris, 1982).

Litschauer, W. (ed.), *Neue Dokumente zum Schubert-Kreis*, 2 vols. (Vienna, 1986 and 1993).

McKay, E. Norman, *The Impact of the New Pianofortes on Classical Keyboard Style: Mozart, Beethoven and Schubert* (West Hagley, 1987).

—— *Schubert's Music for the Theatre* (Tutzing, 1991).

McLachlan, A. E. W., Livingstone, E., and Livingstone, S., *Handbook of Diagnosis and Treatment of Venereal Disease*, 4th edn. (Edinburgh, 1951).

Martindale, *The Extra Pharmacopoeia*, i, 23rd edn. (London, 1952).

Mosel, I. von, *Versuch einer Aesthetik des dramatischen Tonsatzes* (Vienna, 1813).

Neumayr, A., *Musik und Medezin: Am Beispiel der Wiener Klassik* (Vienna, 1987).

Newbould, B., *Schubert and the Symphony: A New Perspective* (London, 1992).

O'Shea, J., *Music and Medicine* (London, 1990).

Pasley, M. (ed.), *Germany: A Companion to German Studies* (London, 1972).

Reed, J., *The Schubert Song Companion*, 2nd edn. (Mancheser, 1986).

—— *Schubert* (The Master Musicians; London, 1987).

Storr, A., *The Dynamics of Creation* (1st pub. London, 1972; 2nd edn. 1976).

—— *Solitude* (1st pub. London, 1988; 2nd edn. 1989).

Waidelich, T. G., *Franz Schubert: 'Alfonso und Estrella'* (Tutzing, 1991).

Warrack, J., *Carl Maria von Weber* (1st pub. Cambridge, 1968; 2nd edn. 1976).

Weatherall, D. J., Ledingham, J. G. G., and Warrell, D. A., *Oxford Textbook of Medicine* (Oxford, 1983–4); see esp. articles by G. W. Csonka, E. B. Adams, R. Nicol Thin.

Wigmore, R., *Schubert: The Complete Song Texts* (London, 1988; repr. 1992).

Youens, S., *Retracing a Winter's Journey: Schubert's 'Winterreise'* (Ithaca, NY, 1991).

—— *Schubert: Die schöne Müllerin* (Cambridge, 1992).

ARTICLES IN EDITED VOLUMES

Badura-Skoda, E., 'The Chronology of Schubert's Piano Trios', in Badura-Skoda and Branscombe (eds.), *Schubert Studies* (Cambridge, 1982), 227–95.

Biba, O., 'Franz Schubert und die Gesellschaft der Musikfreunde', in Brusatti (ed.), *Schubert Kongess Wien 1978* (Vienna, 1979), 23–36.

Branscombe, P., 'Schubert and the Melodrama', in Badura-Skoda and Branscombe (eds.), *Schubert Studies* (Cambridge, 1982), 105–41.

Brody, E., 'Schubert and Sulzer Revisited', in Badura-Skoda and Branscombe (eds.), *Schubert Studies* (Cambridge, 1982), 47–60.

Gardiner, P., 'The German Idealists and their Successors', in M. Pasley (ed.), *Germany: A Companion to German Studies* (London, 1972), 369–426,

Hallmark, R., 'Schubert's "Auf dem Strom" ', in Badura-Skoda and Branscombe (eds.), *Schubert Studies* (Cambridge, 1982), 25–46.

Hilmar, E. 'Ferdinand Schuberts Skizze zu einer Autobiographie (In memoriam Ignaz Weinmann)' in *Schubert Studien: Festgabe der Österreichischen Akademie der Wissenschaften zum Schubert—Jahr 1978*, ed. F. Grasberger and O. Wessely, Wien 1978, pp. 85–117.

McKay, E. Norman, 'Schuberts Klaviersonaten von 1815 bis 1825: Dem Jahr der "Reliquie" ', in H.-J. Hinrichsen (ed.), *Franz Schubert: Reliquie Sonata, mit Beitragen*, facs. edn. (Tutzing, 1992), 43–63.

Weinmann, I., 'Ferdinand Schubert', *MGG* (Kassel, 1965).

Winter, R., 'Paper Studies and the Future of Schubert Research', in Badura-Skoda and Branscombe (eds.), *Schubert Studies* (Cambridge, 1982), 209–75.

ARTICLES IN JOURNALS

Benedikt, E., 'Die "Meldzettel" von Schuberts Eltern', *Brille*, 10 (1993), 42–4.

—— 'Schubert und das Kirchenmusik-Repertoire in Lichtental', *Brille*, 12 (1994), 107–11.

—— 'Ferdinand und Franz Schubert zu Ostern 1820 in Altlerchenfeld', *Brille*, 13 (1994), 79–84.

Biba, O., 'Schubert's Position in Viennese Life', *NCM* 3 (1979), 106–13.

Brown, M. J. E. B., 'Schubert's "Wandererfantasie" ', *MT* 92 (1951), 540–2.

Chézy, W., 'Erinnerungen aus Wien: Aus den Jahren 1824 bis 1829', *Deutsche Pandora* (Stuttgart, 1841), 167–90.

Dürhammer, I., 'Zu Schubert Literaturästhetik', *Brille*, 14 (1995), 5–99.

Eder, G., 'Schubert und Caroline Esterházy', *Brille*, 11 (1993), 6–20.

Gramit, D., 'Schuberts "bildender Umgang": Denken und Ästhetik bei Schuberts Jugendfreunden', *Brille*, 8 (1992), 5–21.

—— 'Constructing a Victorian Schubert: Music, Biography, and Cultural Values', *NCM* 17/1 (1993), 65–78.

—— 'Schubert and the Biedermeier: The Aesthetics of Johann Mayrhofer's "Heliopolis" ', *ML* 74/3 (1993), 355–82.

Hilmar-Voit, R., 'Zu Schuberts "Letzten Lieder" ', *Brille*, 6 (1991), 48–55.

Hoorickx, R. von, 'Schubert's Reminiscences of his Own Works', *MQ* 60/3 (1974), 373–88.

—— 'Ferdinand Schuberts "Entlehnungen" aus Werken seines Bruders Franz', *Brille*, 3 (1989), 13–16.

—— 'Wieder einmal: Entlehnungen Ferdinand Schuberts', *Brille*, 8 (1992), 30–1.

Jacobson, D., and Glendening, A., 'Schuberts D 936A: Eine sinfonische Hommage an Beethoven', *Brille*, 15 (1995), 113–26.

Litschauer, W., 'Unbekanntes zur Schubert-Ikonographie', *Brille*, 6 (1991), 57–65.

—— 'Schubert und die Klaviere seiner Zeit', *Brille*, 8 (1992), 114–16.

—— 'Unbekannte Dokumente über Schubert und die Klaviere seiner Zeit', *Brille*, 11 (1993), 133–6.

McClary, S., 'Music and Sexuality: On the Steblin/Solomon Debate', *NCM* 17/1 (1993), 83–8.

Macdonald, H., 'Schubert's Volcanic Temper', *MT* 99 (1978), 949–52.

McKay, E. Norman, 'Schubert's "Winterreise" Reconsidered', *MR* 38/2 (1977), 94–100.

Mayer, A., 'Der Psychoanalytische Schubert', *Brille*, 9 (1992), 7–31.

Porhansl, L., 'Auf Schuberts Spuren in der "Ludlamshöhle" ', *Brille*, 7 (1991), 52–78.

—— 'Schuberts Heimreise von Graz', *Brille*, 12 (1994), 113–21.

Rakowitz, D., 'Schubert und die Freimaurer', *Brille*, 11 (1993), 137–42.

Sams, E., 'Schubert's Illness Re-examined', *MT* 121 (1980), 15–22.

Solomon, M., 'Franz Schubert's "My Dream" ', *American Imago*, 38 (1981), 137–54.

—— 'Franz Schubert and the Peacocks of Benvenuto Cellini', *NCM* 12/3 (1989), 193–206.

—— 'Schubert: Some Consequences of Nostalgia', *NCM* 17/1 (1993), 34–46.

Steblin, R., 'Franz Schubert und das Ehe-Consens Gesetz von 1815', *Brille*, 9 (1992), 32–42.

—— 'Die Atzenbrugger Gäste-Listen', *Brille*, 9 (1992), 65–80.

—— 'Nochmals die Atzenbrugger Gäste-Listen', *Brille*, 10 (1993), 35–41.

—— 'The Peacock's Tale: Schubert's Sexuality Reconsidered', *NCM* 17/1 (1993), 5–33.

Vitálová, Z., 'Schubert in Zseliz', *Brille*, 8 (1992), 93–102.

—— 'F. Schubert und Zeliezovce', *Občasnik*, 1 (1994), 3–8.

Waidelich, T. G., 'Addenda zur neuen Ausgabe der Dokumente', *Brille*, 12 (1994), 20–32.

—— 'Weitere Addenda zur neuen Ausgabe der Dokumente', *Brille*, 15 (1995), 5–45.

Webster, J., 'Music, Pathology, Sexuality, Beethoven, Schubert', *NCM* 17/1 (1993), 89–93.

West, E., 'The Musenalmanach and Viennese Song 1770–1830', *ML* 67 (1986), 37–49.

—— 'Schuberts Lieder im Kontext: Einige Bemerkungen zur Liedkomposition in Wien nach 1820', *Brille*, 12 (1994), 5–19.

Winter, R., 'Whose Schubert?', *NCM* 17/1 (1993), 94–101.

Willfort, M., 'Das Urbild des Andante aus Schuberts Klavier Trio in Es-dur, D 929', *ÖMZ* 33 (1978), 277–83.

MUSIC INDEX

Index of Schubert's Compositions mentioned in this book

GENERAL INDEX